TRAVELER

vietnam

TRAVELER

vietnam

by James Sullivan
photography by Kris LeBoutillier

National Geographic
Washington, D.C.

福

CONTENTS

Pages 2–3: Ha Long Bay's limestone karst landscape
Opposite: Paper lanterns for sale in Hoi An

TRAVELING WITH EYES OPEN

Alert travelers go with a purpose and leave with a benefit. If you travel responsibly, you can help support wildlife conservation, historic preservation, and cultural enrichment in the places you visit. You can enrich your own travel experience as well.

To be a geo-savvy traveler:

- Recognize that your presence has an impact on the places you visit.
- Spend your time and money in ways that sustain local character. (Besides, it's more interesting that way.)
- Value the destination's natural and cultural heritage.
- Respect the local customs and traditions.
- Express appreciation to local people about things you find interesting and unique to the place: its nature and scenery, music and food, historic villages and buildings.
- Vote with your wallet: Support the people who support the place, patronizing businesses that make an effort to celebrate and protect what's special there. Seek out local shops, restaurants, and inns. Use tour operators who love their home—who love taking care of it and showing it off. Avoid businesses that detract from the character of the place.
- Enrich yourself, taking home memories and stories to tell, knowing that you have contributed to the preservation and enhancement of the destination.

That is the type of travel now called geotourism, defined as "tourism that sustains or enhances the geographical character of a place—its environment, culture, aesthetics, heritage, and the well-being of its residents." To learn more, visit National Geographic's Center for Sustainable Destinations at *nationalgeographic.com/travel/sustainable.*

vietnam

ABOUT THE AUTHOR & PHOTOGRAPHER

After graduating from the Iowa Writer's Workshop in 1992, **James Sullivan** bicycled solo from Saigon to Hanoi up Vietnam's Highway 1. This trip led to the publication of *Over the Moat,* a memoir of courtship in Vietnam. He has written travel features for *National Geographic Traveler, The New York Times,* and other leading publications. He lives with his wife and two children in Hue, where he is working on a novel about Vietnam.

Kris LeBoutillier has photographed assignments for *National Geographic Traveler,* including stories about Tasmania, Singapore, Rajasthan, and Vietnam. He is the author and photographer of *Journey Through Phnom Penh* and *Journey Through Ho Chi Minh City,* both published by Marshall Cavendish. Represented by Getty Images, LeBoutillier has worked for such diverse clients as *Forbes Asia, Smithsonian, Spa Magazine,* and the Discovery Channel.

British-born **Ron Emmons** updated and wrote new features for the 2010 and 2014 editions of this guide. Now living in Chiang Mai, North Thailand, Emmons is the author and photographer of several books, including *Portrait of Thailand* and *Walks along the Thames Path.* His features appear regularly in various publications. Samples of his work can be seen at *ronemmons.com.*

Charting Your Trip

Snaking like a serpent along Southeast Asia's Pacific Rim, Vietnam encompasses a rich variety of landscape, climate, and culture from the mountains of the north to the Mekong Delta's wetlands, a distance of more than 1,250 miles (2,000 km). It is a land as rewarding for adventurers seeking natural wonders as for culture-vultures eager to understand the nation's traditions.

Given the wealth of options worth seeing and activities worth doing, the real challenge for travelers is deciding on an itinerary. Wandering the streets of Hanoi's Old Quarter, in the north of the country, features high on lists, as does a cruise on nearby Ha Long Bay and a trip to hill-tribe markets around Sa Pa near the Chinese border. Then again, in southern Vietnam, the colonial architecture and buzzing nightlife of Ho Chi Minh City (formerly Saigon) exerts a strong attraction, as do the pine-scented hills around Dalat, the relaxing coastal beaches of Nha Trang and Mui Ne, and the floating markets of the Mekong Delta.

Public transportation in Vietnam is reasonably accessible, but distances can be deceptive. Vietnam Airlines *(vietnamairlines.com)* offers relatively cheap service to the country's major cities, including the popular Ho Chi Minh City/Hanoi route. Alternative choices for travel include the long-distance tourist buses or the 30-hour train ride between these cities operated by Vietnam Railway *(vietnam-railway.com)*. While it is not recommended that foreigners rent cars, ask at your hotel about hiring a car and driver;

Water puppets dramatize the traditional stories of rural Vietnam.

be sure to negotiate a price before leaving. Tourists do, however, rent motorcycles to explore the countryside.

NOT TO BE MISSED:

A Weeklong Visit

It's impossible to see all of Vietnam in a week, so tough choices have to be made. Though most international flights arrive in Ho Chi Minh City, Vietnam's biggest city, it is only a two-hour flight to Hanoi, the country's administrative capital, a place more quintessentially Vietnamese.

If you start in **Hanoi,** you'll need a few days to explore the narrow streets of the Old Quarter, wander around refreshing Hoan Kiem Lake, and visit its well-organized museums and temples. Top of your list should be the Temple of Literature, the monuments in Ba Dinh Square, and the History Museum. An evening treat not to be missed is a performance of water puppets, a theatrical form unique to the country.

For variety, extend your stay in the north, by spending a day and a night cruising around **Ha Long Bay** (90 miles/145 km east of Hanoi), marveling at the jagged skyline created by the limestone outcrops. After that, take a train from Hanoi 217 miles (350 km) northwest and pass a couple of days in the hills around **Sa Pa,** trekking to hill-tribe villages or visiting colorful markets on an arranged tour or by rented motorbike.

Or, if you wish, fly back to **Ho Chi Minh City** from Hanoi for a few days to discover the curious mix of venerable temples, colonial architecture, and towering skyscrapers. Apart from the French stones of empire such as the Notre Dame Cathedral and former Hôtel de Ville, the city's main attractions are its museums (especially the War Remnants Museum) and its markets. As the gastronomic capital of the country, this is also the place to get better acquainted with the subtle tastes and textures of Vietnamese cuisine. It takes a couple of days to see the city's sights, but allow another day for a combined trip to the **Cu Chi Tunnels** and the **Cao Dai Great Temple,** the first a reminder of war and the second a hope of peace.

Visitor Information

The Vietnam National Administration of Tourism website *(vietnam tourism.com)* offers a wealth of information about destinations and culture, including upcoming festivals countrywide. The Word *(wordhanoi.com* and *wordhcmc.com)* and AsiaLife *(asialifemagazine.com/vietnam)* are slick publications that publish news, features, and reviews of the constantly changing scene in Vietnam's two major cities; they are distributed free in locations frequented by tourists. Hanoi Grapevine *(hanoigrapevine.com)* also publishes a calendar of art and music events in Hanoi and Saigon.

Biking along the Perfume River past Thien Mu Pagoda in Hue

What to Pack

Light, casual clothes are sufficient for most locations in Vietnam, though if you're planning to visit the central or northern highlands between November and February, you'll need a sweater and jacket. When visiting temples, avoid wearing shorts and sleeveless tops. Indispensable items are a hat to protect you from the sun and an umbrella for rain, which can fall out of season, as well as sunscreen if you are heading for the beach. If you plan to do a lot of reading, take books or your e-book reader with you, as the choice of English-language titles in bookstores is very limited.

Another appealing option is to spend part of the week in central Vietnam, taking in the ancient monuments and houses in **Hue** and **Hoi An,** both designated as UNESCO World Heritage sites. Many visitors cite Hoi An as their favorite place in Vietnam for its combination of car-free streets, historic buildings, and silk tailors. Located midway between Hanoi and Ho Chi Minh City, Hue and Hoi An's neighbor, **Danang,** are accessible by plane or train.

If You Have More Time

A second week would allow exploration of the country's south and central regions, though again be selective as there are so many varied attractions. If you didn't visit Hue and Hoi An in the first week, it's worth stopping off for a few days, though if lounging on a beach sounds more appealing, you'd be better off going to **Nha Trang** or **Mui Ne** halfway along the south-central coast. Nha Trang is a mecca for party animals, while Mui Ne attracts the sporty with its breezes that are ideal for kite- and windsurfing.

When to Visit

Due to its varied climate, different parts of the country are better visited at different times of year. Vietnam's high season runs from November to February, when the weather is at its best in the south and is usually fine in the north (although it can still get chilly in the hills).

However, the weather is more conducive to beach activities at Nha Trang on the coast, from June through October. Be aware that from July through November, typhoons can tear across the central and northern provinces, causing floods and destruction.

Other Possibilities

If you're in Ho Chi Minh City, it's an easy two-hour hop by bus down to the **Mekong Delta.** Most people limit this to a day trip, which tends to be a touristy and unsatisfying experience. The delta can be an absorbing region, with friendly folks and lush landscapes, but it is best appreciated beyond the tourist enclaves. In small towns like **Tra Vinh, Soc Trang,** and **Ha Tien,** you can feel that you're more in touch with the real Vietnam. A short 40-minute flight or express boat ride from **Rach Gia** is **Phu Quoc Island,** a real tropical getaway, and a few days spent lazing on its beaches is becoming an increasingly popular way to round off a Vietnamese adventure.

Perhaps the country's least visited region, the **Central Highlands** is especially attractive to adventurous travelers, as it borders Laos and Cambodia. Characterized by rubber, tea, and coffee plantations, it is home to ethnic minorities such as the E De, Giarai, and Bahnar. While they do not dress as flamboyantly as their northern counterparts, their culture is distinctive, particularly the towering *rong* or communal houses that anchor their settlements. The gateway to the highlands is **Dalat,** a hill station established by the French to escape the heat. It can be reached on a $70, 50-minute flight from Ho Chi Minh City.

No matter whether you decide to travel by bicycle or plane, take a guided tour or journey solo, visit sites of the Cham people or the DMZ, Vietnam is a country of diversity and beauty, so take the time to explore, learn, and enjoy.

Dollars or Dong?

If you've ever dreamed of being a millionaire, here's your chance. Change $50 and you'll instantly become a dong millionaire, which sounds great but soon becomes a headache when you try to convert one currency to the other. You'll need dong for small purchases; for larger expenses such as hotel bills it's easier to pay in dollars. Keep an eye on exchange rates, as they can fluctuate significantly even during the course of a two-week holiday.

ATMs—found in the major tourist hubs, and in secondary cities and towns—are the best way to withdraw money. If you prefer, most banks in cities and towns are set up to exchange Western currency for Vietnamese dong. Remember that most banks close between 11:30 a.m. and 1:30 p.m. Many hotels will also exchange currency at less favorable rates.

Beware of touts in Ho Chi Minh City and Hanoi who promise better exchange rates; those black market days are over.

History & Culture

Soldiers at drill in Hanoi. Opposite: Hanoi youth indulge in the sweet treats of life.

Vietnam Today

Vietnam. The name conjures so many passions that, in a random lineup of nations, Vietnam is the one that always draws the eye. But the exclamation point that has dogged the country since the turmoil of the 1950s is withering, thanks largely to the passage of time, to a reorientation of economic policies, and to the normalization of relations with the United States.

Today, Vietnam is a nation on the rise. The capital, Hanoi, was born under the name Thang Long, which means "dragon ascending," an image now befitting the country as a whole. The ascent began in 1986 when the government abandoned command economics and launched *doi moi,* a market-driven policy of fiscal reform. Doi moi rescued Vietnam from a decade of postwar privation and groomed it for emergence as one of Southeast Asia's so-called Little Tiger economies.

Now the economy is growing at 6 percent annually, one of the fastest rates worldwide. Vietnam is the second largest coffee exporter in the world, after Brazil, and the largest exporter of pepper. Trade with the United States has jumped tenfold since 2000, and the private sector continues to grow rapidly.

Following a severe hiccup during the Asian economic flu of the 1990s, investment dollars poured in by the billions. On his visit to the United States in 2005—the first by a leader of communist Vietnam—Prime Minister Phan Van Khai rang the opening bell of the New York Stock Exchange, as symbolic a break from command economics as you're likely to get.

A Rising Star

The statistics say it all: In the first twelve years of this millennium, tourist arrivals to Vietnam increased from just over two million visitors a year to almost seven million. Such an achievement is particularly impressive considering the downturn in tourism in many other countries. What's more, with no connections to any global terrorist movements, Vietnam is currently believed to be one of the safest destinations in the world for tourists.

Call it capitalist communism, or communist capitalism. That bugaboo is hardly relevant anymore and seems almost quaint in the age of al Qaeda. While terrorism has tarnished other places in Southeast Asia, like Bali and even Thailand, Vietnam's star is rising as a peaceful haven. In 2005, the world's second largest insurance broker dubbed Vietnam one of the six safest travel destinations in the world.

Good Morning No More

Headlines started blaring GOOD MORNING, VIETNAM in the early 1990s, and though breakfast may be over, brunch has only just begun. Traveling through Vietnam now, you'll feel like you've been made privy to a secret the rest of the world has yet to hear. Backpackers blazed many of the popular routes and still represent a huge contingent of foreign travelers. But the days of encountering rats in the country's best lodgings are over. Luxury hotels command the highest occupancy rates in Ho Chi Minh City and Hanoi. And Vietnam Airlines flies one of the world's newest fleets.

Word is getting out—about Ha Long Bay's incomparable seascape, the cloud-wreathed highland peaks, Mekong Delta vistas, and world-class limestone grottoes. UNESCO has chosen seven locations in Vietnam for inscription on its World Heritage List, positioning the country ahead of Thailand and second only to Indonesia as a cultural destination in Southeast Asia.

The vista from the Van Don Canal shows Ho Chi Minh City's evolution into an economic powerhouse. The Bitexco Financial Tower is center stage, with its distinctive helipad.

Its imperial vestiges evoke the dreamy world of the Orient. Sublime pagodas and venerable temples form eddies in the rushing currents of modern life, inspiring slowness and contemplation. Its cuisine is winning raves for its lightness, commingled textures, and presentational panache. Vietnam, at last, is ready for prime time. It's not quite high noon yet, but morning has indeed broken.

Open Arms

Although Vietnam suffered an estimated five million dead in its war with the United States (more than one million combatants and four million civilians), there's no visible animosity toward Americans. The Vietnamese tend not to hold grudges.

This "let bygones be bygones" attitude can puzzle Americans especially, many of whom show up with hat in hand. But no act of contrition is called for or expected. *We're glad you're here* is the gist of the reception. *We're glad you're back* is how it feels in the south.

As a population, the 92 million inhabitants of Vietnam are young, with a median age of 28. (In the U.S., the median age is 38; in Thailand, it's 34). The 93 percent literacy rate is far higher than the rate in neighboring Cambodia and Laos, and on a par with China and Thailand, where personal incomes are much higher.

They're studiously book smart as a people, but street smart, too. "They know how to do things. They know how things work," said one American lawyer who's been practicing in Ho Chi Minh City for more than a decade.

Horse sense is an unwitting perk in a relatively undeveloped economy. That will change as the economy demands specialists. Much will change, from the colorfully exotic costumes of the northern highlanders to the dearth of Western chains (though McDonald's sold its first Big Mac in Vietnam in 2014). As a traveler, you're likely to rue what you know is coming as Vietnam steps up its engagement with the rest of the world.

In the meantime, revel in what already feel like anachronisms: the teenage schoolgirls pedaling to school three and four abreast, in their immaculate silk *ao dai* dresses, like a mobile tableau on its way to yet another exhibit, or the bubbly grade-school pupils, heeding the summons from a drum, not a bell, in their blue slacks, white shirts, and red kerchiefs. Stop among them, and they'll mob you like a rock star, lobbing the same suite

How to Greet the Vietnamese

The Vietnamese are very friendly and approachable, but not all of them are comfortable shaking hands, so the safest greeting is a smile and a small bow of the head. The word for "hello" *(chao)* can be followed by any one of eight qualifiers, depending on the person you are talking to, but everyone will be happy if you can manage the general *xin chao* (pronounced sin chao).

Following are some additional phrases that should help endear you to the Vietnamese:

Ten toi la ...	My name is ...
Toi khong hieu	I don't understand
Cam on	Thank you
Khong co chi	You're welcome/ Don't mention it
Bao nhieu?	How much?
Do an nay ngon qua	This food is delicious
Xin loi	Sorry
O day co ai biet noi tieng Anh khong?	Does anyone here speak English?
Tam biet	Goodbye

Terraced rice fields corrugate the flanks of big-shouldered mountains around Sa Pa.

of questions in just-learned, imperfect English: "What your name?" "Where you from?" "What the time?" They don't care much about the answers; the chance to elicit a response from a *tay* (Westerner) is enough.

Many will ask whether you're married, how old you are, and even how much money you earn in a month. The point is not mere nosiness, but a matter of relativism. In Vietnam, getting a fix on a new acquaintance is necessary to determine the proper form of address.

Sublime pagodas and venerable temples form eddies in the rushing currents of modern life, inspiring slowness and contemplation.

The Vietnamese make scant use of the personal pronoun "I" *(toi)*. Instead, they defer to the pronoun that defines their relation to another person. For example, "I" wouldn't tell an older person about my recent trip to Nha Trang; instead, "younger brother" would tell the story. Likewise, the generic form of "you" is much less common than the relational pronoun. A young woman in need of directions to a nearby pagoda would not address an older man on the street as "you"; she would refer to him as "uncle." Everybody is related to everybody else in Vietnam. That's the way the language works.

Flower Hmong highlanders, distinguished by especially colorful costumes, are among four Hmong clans in Vietnam.

Understanding this dynamic is crucial to understanding the Vietnamese. They do not extol individualism. The laconic loner is not one of their heroes. Nguyen is by far the dominant surname, with as much as 60 percent of the population bearing the name. That's not a problem. The Vietnamese don't value distance between each other the way Westerners do. They don't need "space." They truly believe it takes a village.

In fact, this social cohesion was forged in the village, where the cultivation of wet rice historically required a collective effort. The bonds to the village and the home are more like cables than ties. Every year during the Tet lunar new year, Vietnamese migrate from all over the country, and increasingly from all over the world, for the beacon of home (see p. 35).

Precedents & Descendants

Today, Vietnam remains communist, though the hallmarks of communism—collectivization of agriculture, a planned central economy—have been dismantled in favor of a free market. Other old laws are falling by the wayside as Vietnam steps in line with the modern world.

Hanoi still won't broach political opposition. The ruling clique controls the courts, the state-run press is a dutiful mouthpiece for government leaders, and contrary letters to the editor rarely see the light of day. But those issues aren't ideological flaws. They're the prerogatives of fearful rulers who can't quite fathom the benefits of a participatory democracy and who have the mandates of Confucianism hardwired into their genes. The reforms of doi moi, like the former Soviet Union's perestroika, have not been complemented by an equivalent of glasnost (openness). The door is open here, but not all the way.

Today, Vietnam remains communist, though the hallmarks of communism—collectivization of agriculture, a planned central economy—have been dismantled in favor of a free market.

Historically, Vietnamese scholars aspired to know what had already been discovered and avoided exploration of the unknown. Similarly, as the Vietnamese chart their way both individually and socially, they often look over their shoulders to precedents set by their fathers and ancestors in general. The dead never really die in Vietnam and only fade away, traditionally, after nine generations have passed. The Vietnamese believe their ancestors return annually at Tet (see p. 35), for communion with and sustenance from their living descendants.

Ask a Vietnamese his religion, and he's likely to say Buddhism. That may be true, but it's probably just as true that he's devoted to the cult of his ancestors, as well as to the hierarchies of Confucianism, and to the mystical world view of Taoism. Names, dogma, and ideologies only go so far with the Vietnamese. During the war, that was a problem for the U.S. military, which was culturally at odds with a people whose politics were marked more by expedience than principle.

Regional Distinctions

Together with China, Japan, and Korea, Vietnam belongs to the classical world of East Asia. These countries, bound by Confucianism, Buddhism, and Taoism, are more like each other than any are like the world of the Khmer, the Thai, or the Malays. The Vietnamese, like their East Asian neighbors, adhere to social hierarchies of deference—the son to the father, the student to the teacher, the young to the old. Education has long been king: In Vietnam, a teacher was traditionally more highly esteemed than a medical doctor. However, that pecking order is now changing as prosperity and higher salaries impel admiration for the trappings of wealth.

Education has long been king: In Vietnam, a teacher was traditionally more highly esteemed than a medical doctor.

Domestically, the Vietnamese recognize three distinct regions of their country—four if you allow for the rugged highlands and the four million members of ethnic minority groups that inhabit them. The south, with Ho Chi Minh City as its hub, is aggressively commercial and socially progressive. The lion's share of foreign investment orbits Saigon, as the heart of the onetime capital of South Vietnam is still known. The north holds the keys to Vietnam's ancient past. Vietnamese civilization emerged along the Red River Delta, and northerners tend to cling more tightly to precedent and protocol. Similarly, Hue, the third region, seat of the last imperial dynasty in the central part of the country, is culturally conservative, the people more genteel and poetically inclined.

Iced coffee for sale at Cai Rang floating market on the Mekong Delta

Of course, similarities abound. Throughout Vietnam, the men drink high-test coffee and smoke cigarettes. Women do neither. The ao dai silk dress hangs in the regular wardrobe, not the closet where traditional costumes await special occasions. Women also seem to do more than their fair share of physical labor, from farming the rice paddies to roadwork. Most Vietnamese love the moon and treacly sentimental pop songs. Kitsch is not derided but exalted–in sculpted topiary, candy-colored lights that illuminate sober French railroad trestles, and the coronas of disco lights that halo Buddhist statuary in otherwise venerable pagodas.

After years of having virtually nothing, tens of thousands of Vietnamese are suddenly nouveau riche. They're building rococo villas that don't really reflect any one architectural aesthetic but as many as possible–from Slavic Europe to classical Greece and Rome and the Middle East and Disneyland, sometimes all in the same building.

In short, they're having fun, and the humor–all across Vietnam–is infectious. Thailand is known as the "Land of Smiles," but that sentiment is as relevant from the Red River to the Mekong Delta. The Vietnamese laugh at everything, from bawdy jokes to misfortune to questions they'd rather not answer, and themselves as well.

Return of the Boat People

It's a sign of the country's changing fortunes that many people who fled their homeland in the 1970s are now returning, bringing with them useful skills and vital funds that have helped to boost the economy. Nowhere is this more evident than in Ca Mau and Bac Lieu, two small Mekong Delta towns that have been transformed in recent years into smart settlements with the help of funds provided by returnees.

The Vietnam War

There's no escaping the war in Vietnam. The cyclo driver who ferries you across a southern city may launch his taxi banter with a reference to "before 1975" and his work as a soldier in the army of South Vietnam. In Saigon, the old American Embassy was demolished in the 1990s, and most other reminders of U.S. involvement in the country have now disappeared. Though you might see Zippo lighters and dog tags for sale in street markets, they are unlikely to be authentic war memorabilia.

However, casualties of that painful conflict are still visible in the form of disabled beggars on the streets, and the countryside remains littered with ordnance that failed to detonate during the conflict but blows up all too often today. Since the end of the war in 1975, more than 100,000 people have been killed by land mines and bombs. Agent Orange, an herbicide manufactured in large quantities in the United States and used to defoliate the Vietnamese countryside during the war, has been linked to myriad health problems, including cancer and genetic deformities, in untold numbers of civilians and former soldiers.

Nevertheless, the war is now far from center stage, and there are more compelling reasons to visit Vietnam. After more than a century of instability, the Vietnamese are starting to make the kind of hay the country always believed it might have, if not for all that fighting. ■

Food & Drink

Long overshadowed by the cuisines of China and Thailand, Vietnamese food is rapidly developing a following all its own. Foodies worldwide are bellying up to the country's tables in droves and filing scrumptious reports to the West, praising the lightness of the typical Vietnamese dish, the simplicity of technique, the freshness of ingredients, the deftness of presentation, and the artful mingling of flavors, textures, and temperatures.

As with many aspects of Vietnam, foreign tastes have done much to elaborate on the native palate and board. The ever influential Chinese stimulated the use of chopsticks and desire for noodles. The Cham added spice and curry. The Mongols spurred an appetite for beef. Or maybe it was the French, harbingers of bread, coffee, yogurt, and cheese, who truly turned on the taste buds to beef. No matter—it's all by now been absorbed and made new as Vietnamese.

A typical meal—a selection of different dishes—is delivered as it's prepared. Expect a multitude of tastes in a single dish and, often, in a single bite. Yin and yang are necessary companions in many dishes. If there's hot, there's got to be cold. If sweet, then sour. If soft, then crunchy.

You'll find very little butter in Vietnamese cuisine, little salt, no reduction sauces, no salad oil, no gooey red bastings—hence the Vietnamese reputation for lightness. A lot happens at the table itself. Wrapping, rolling, dipping, simmering, grilling—they're all part of a typical Vietnamese meal. Not to say there's not a lot of prep work. The chopping, slicing, and dicing of meats, seafood, and vegetables, the concoction of dipping sauces, and the intricacies of presentation are labor intensive and time consuming.

Eating Etiquette

Eating Vietnamese food is intended to be a tactile as well as gastronomic experience, so be prepared to get involved with the food on your plate. Diners are often provided with the ingredients to make delicious spring rolls, which you wrap and roll yourself. When it comes to eating rice or noodles, don't be afraid to lift your bowl to your mouth and shovel rice in, or to slurp your noodles, which is taken as a sign of enjoyment.

The Staples

The ingredient that is most indispensable to Vietnamese cuisine is *nuoc mam* (fish sauce), a pungent condiment that takes some getting used to. To make a batch, the fishermen of Phu Quoc, Phan Thiet, and other fishing villages fill vats with alternating layers of *ca com* (anchovies) and salt, wait some months, drain off the liquid, pour it back over the fermenting catch, and wait some more. Each batch is drained for a premium and lesser grades of sauce, as the Vietnamese are as finicky about nuoc mam as the Italians are about olive oil.

Rice, of course, is the preeminent staple. So fundamental is this grain to the Vietnamese diet that the term for it is virtually synonymous with consumption. When you sit down to a meal in Vietnam, you *an com* (eat cooked rice), whether

Hanoi's popular Green Tangerine offers a fusion of Occidental and Asian tastes.

your meal includes rice or not. It usually does. Most noodles are rice based, the wraps in which you roll up finger food are rice based, the ubiquitous hard liquor drunk nationwide is distilled from rice. No wonder the grain is known as white gold.

Unlike anywhere else in Southeast Asia, people here consume aromatic herbs like vegetables. A bounty of herbs accompanies many dishes, usually uncooked to retain flavor and each on a dish of its own. Asian basil, coriander, and mint top the list of favorites, joined by spring onion, chives, and watercress. Warranting special mention is lemongrass, which seems to sprout everywhere in the Vietnamese kitchen.

Where to Eat

Vietnamese eateries break down into four broad categories—restaurants, bistros, rice-and-noodle shops, and street stalls. Except at high-end venues, the ambience at most places includes fluorescent lighting, pink tablecloths, and too many chairs around smallish tables.

Typically found in hotels and larger cities, the *nha hang* (restaurant) is especially popular with foreigners. But while the best restaurants in Hanoi and Ho Chi Minh City certainly serve exquisite meals, the nha hang in general doesn't necessarily offer the best food. The kitchens are fixed, and menus typically include English translations.

Tea is the de facto national drink, served whenever people sit down together.

The *quan* (bistro) stirs up traditional Vietnamese fare, often in a garage-like setting on the ground floor of a building or in an outdoor food court shaded by a metal roof. Stools and folding chairs are the norm. Menus are occasionally in English.

The ubiquitous *com/pho* (rice-and-noodle shop) doesn't bother with a menu; you simply pick what you want from a glass case near the front of the shop. Expect simple rice and noodle dishes. However sterile the setting, these meals can be fabulous. If the sign reads COM, they only do rice; if just PHO, only noodle soup.

At street stalls, marked by a canopy to ward off the elements, you'll sit down on a tiny stool to a bowl of something—perhaps fish noodle soup, *banh xeo* (Vietnamese crepes), or *bun cha* (noodles with barbecue pork).

In the Vietnamese home, meals are traditionally served at a straw mat unfurled on the floor or on a multipurpose platform bed. Each diner eats from his or her own rice bowl, solicitously filled and refilled by mother. Otherwise, diners serve themselves and others from communal bowls.

What to Eat

Given Vietnam's 2,135-mile (3,444 km) coastline and countless rivers, lagoons, canals, and waterways, seafood is plentiful, fresh, and wonderfully prepared. The Vietnamese have a particular yen for squid and cuttlefish. Shrimp are cultivated up and down the seaboard. The coastal fishing villages net tuna, sea bass, and an array of succulent white fish. Crabs, clams, and oysters are perched on the high end of menus.

Unless you're dining at a fine place with the resources to import, the lamb and beef are likely to be inferior—in fact, the beef is as likely to be water buffalo as cow. Pork is a safe bet everywhere. Chicken is tougher and leaner than its plump Western counterpart, while duck is almost as popular as chicken. Thanks to Buddhist influences, vegetarian food is widely available and a beneficiary of long culinary cultivation.

Traditionally, fruit in Vietnam is served at dessert. Options will include the usual tropical suspects such as bananas and papayas and a variety of lesser known succulents. The fibrous white pulp of the dragon fruit is peppered with edible black seeds and grows in bulbs from a Medusa-like coif of fronds. The pomelo is a sweet grapefruit. Egg-shaped sapodilla has a sweet brown pulp. Stay alert, too, for ripe longans, star fruit, and milk fruit.

What to Drink

Tea is the de facto national drink, served whenever people sit down together. Families keep a thermos of boiling water at the ready and fill tiny ceramic teapots with green tea leaves as visitors arrive. The Vietnamese are not as refined about their consumption as the Japanese, nor do they cultivate as many varieties as China, but green tea, jasmine, artichoke, and other varieties are popular.

Coffee has been booming here for years, and Vietnam now ranks as the world's second largest exporter. Most common is the lesser grade Robusta bean, though Arabica is gaining popularity as growers tune into the world's bean of choice. Men throng the cafés each morning, patiently waiting for brews to drip from tin filters into small glasses. Most Vietnamese drink potent, espresso-size portions black or on ice, or perhaps mixed with sweetened condensed milk.

According to a popular Vietnamese proverb, "A man who does not drink alcohol is like a flag without wind." Rice wine is the traditional festive beverage, often consumed at holidays and ceremonies. No ethnic minority celebration is complete unless the men swarm a communal jar of rice wine with a bouquet of bamboo straws.

Over the last several years, beer has eclipsed wine as the most widely consumed alcoholic beverage. Vietnam brews several decent lagers, including Saigon Lager, Halida, and 333. Beer lovers often gather at streetside *bia hoi* (fresh beer) joints for cheap draft. ■

EXPERIENCE: Tasting Vietnamese Specialties

Given Vietnam's size, there are marked regional differences to the cuisines. Southern cuisine is longer on herbs, sweet-and-sour dishes, and curries. In the north, where the Chinese influence has been heavier, congees are popular, as are stir-fry and charcoal-grilled meats and fish. In the central region, chili spices much of the seafood. Hue has long been a culinary hub, thanks to persnickety emperors who demanded a wide variety of small, visually enticing dishes. But that was then. You'll eat better in Hanoi and Ho Chi Minh City these days.

While each region boasts its own specialties, the following dishes are typically available in urban centers nationwide. Be sure to try:

Banh chung. This square cake of sticky rice, bean curd, and pork meat is wrapped in banana leaves and cooked all night. It is as integral to Tet celebrations as turkey is to Thanksgiving in the United States.

Banh xeo. A Saigon sidewalk specialty, known in Hue as *banh khoai,* this crispy crepe is folded over thin strips of pork, shelled shrimp, mushrooms, and various other vegetables.

Bun bo hue. This spicy rice-noodle stew combines spaghetti-thick rice noodles, pork, beef, lots of chili, and lemongrass. A Hue specialty, bun bo hue is usually eaten at breakfast.

Bun cha. This snack of skewered, grilled pork and noodles is eaten with fish sauce, vinegar, and the *lang* herb, grown near Hanoi. It's a Hanoi specialty, as is *cha ca,* a grilled white fish.

Pho. Steeped in aromatic herbs, including coriander and mint, this rice-noodle broth features thin-sliced morsels of parboiled beef and as many as two dozen other ingredients. It's the most widely known Vietnamese dish in the West and a great source of national pride. Hanoi is the traditional home of pho and the reputed source of the best bowls.

Spring rolls. The most popular spring roll (aka imperial roll) is *cha gio,* or *nem Saigon.* These fried rice-paper wraps are filled with minced pork, bean sprouts, mushrooms, glass noodles, mint, and egg yolk. The *banh uot cuon,* often referred to as a fresh spring roll, is a spongy, pork-based rice wrap dipped in a thick peanut sauce.

The Land

A map of Vietnam describes an elongated S, swerving symmetrically along its southern sweep, tapering in the midsection, but foreshortened and bulging in the north. Mountains form the spine of this 1,025-mile-long (1,650 km) country, roughly paralleling its borders with Cambodia and Laos. But rivers and the sea provide greater definition, both visually and culturally, along the 2,135-mile (3,444 km) seaboard and the two great waterways of the Mekong and Red Rivers.

Though Vietnam is slightly larger than New Mexico, it has more than 50 times as many inhabitants. Its 92 million people inhabit just 20 percent of its land area, on the two deltas of the Red and Mekong Rivers, in the valleys, and along the littoral. It is the world's 13th most populous country, with three-quarters of its people living in rural areas. Its ethnic minority population of four million, grouped in 50 distinct tribes, dwells amid the less fertile mountains.

During the Vietnam War, U.S. planes bombed and defoliated enemy strongholds in the North and South, as well as throughout the highlands, where the Ho Chi Minh Trail carried supplies and ammunition. The bombing campaigns transformed the lush jungle and verdant farmland into denuded moonscapes. But after 1975, the fecundity of this tropical country renewed the land with vigor. Around Khe Sanh, one of the most heavily bombed areas, the landscape today is as picturesque as a nature reserve.

The Red River's nutrient-rich alluvium buoyed Vietnamese civilization more than 2,000 years ago.

The Deltas

Historically, Vietnam's defining topographical feature has been the Red River. Originating in China's Yunnan Province, the river flows southeast for 730 miles (1,170 km), exhausting itself in a delta east of Hanoi. The Red River's nutrient-rich alluvium buoyed Vietnamese civilization more than 2,000 years ago, though its floodwaters remain a grave threat. Despite a 1,864-mile (3,000 km) network of dikes, an engineering feat one historian likened to the Great Wall of China, the river still on occasion rises 30 to 45 feet (10–14 m), washing away houses, people, and livestock.

Thanks to a link with Cambodia's Tonle Sap Lake and its stabilizing influence as an absorbent reservoir, the Mekong presents a lesser threat to people of the southern delta. The Mekong's waters annually flood the region's paddies with an additional 3 to 6 feet (1–2 m) of water, spreading alluvial deposits that support three rice crops annually and sowing far less destruction. The 2,700-mile (4,320 km) river drains through nine mouths in the country's southeasternmost provinces. These branches are interlaced by a web of interconnecting channels and canals, which explains why the Vietnamese term for "country" is *dat nuoc* (land water).

The Highlands

North of the Mekong Delta, the Truong Son ("long mountains") rear up in the provinces just north of Ho Chi Minh City. In a bygone era, these highlands were a big-game paradise, harboring Indochinese tigers, Asian elephants, and Javan rhinos, though these have since been driven to near extinction by poaching and

Once the realm of fishermen, beaches along the south-central coast are fast becoming popular international tourist destinations.

habitat destruction. The southern and central highlands now offer less lethal attractions, including a burgeoning suite of nature reserves and national parks, as well as several ethnic minority villages. In Kon Tum and Dak Lak, soaring thatched communal halls and longhouses are anachronistic marvels. To meet growing worldwide demand, coffee plantations have sprung up across the region in recent years.

In Kon Tum and Dak Lak, soaring thatched communal halls and longhouses are anachronistic marvels.

From Danang to Vinh, the country's slender waist cinches to a width of 25 to 50 miles (40–80 km) between the sea and the Laotian border. The mountains here march to the sea, plunging into the waters from great promontories at the Ngang and Hai Van Passes. Remarkably, a spate of new, large mammals, including the saola and giant muntjac (see pp. 186–187), has been discovered in the hinterlands of these highlands since the 1990s.

North of Nghe An and Thanh Hoa, home territory to Vietnam's greatest leaders, the country bulges again and the mountains run northwest, paralleling the Red River to the east. Vietnam's tallest peak, Fan Si Pan, summits at 10,312 feet (3,143 m) near Sa Pa, whose vibrantly costumed denizens are one of the country's chief tourists attractions. To the north and northeast, the mountains aren't as lofty, but wind and water have sculpted their karst flanks into the country's most fantastic mountainscapes.

Seaboard

On the northern coast, similar geological forces have carved one of the wonders of the world at Ha Long Bay, a 580-square-mile (1,500 sq km) seascape of karst towers and clustered conical peaks. Undercut by the rise and fall of the tides, many towers seem to hover magically over the jade green waters.

South of the Red River Delta, the South China Sea breaks against a long, fairly regular coastline. Few beaches north of Hue attract much attention from foreign visitors, but south of Hue, the sandy spit of Lang Co heralds a tantalizing string of sandy crescents that bight the coast as far south as the Mekong Delta. The Bay of Danang has lately come into its own as one of the most beautiful bays of the world. The bays and island waters of Khanh Hoa Province (Nha Trang) host marvelous beds of coral.

Farther south, from Danang to Vung Tau, the South China Sea breaks on the coconut- and casuarina-fringed beaches of the central and south-central coast. As seafarers, the Vietnamese seldom ventured far from their shores. But the clogged harbors in places like Nha Trang and Phan Thiet speak to the nation's age-old ties to the ocean and affinity for seafood. Vietnam's best known island, Phu Quoc, hangs like a pendant off the southern coast of Cambodia, featuring placid waters and gleaming white sand.

Climate

Vietnam lies in the tropics and subtropics, but its varied latitudes and altitudes, and the fact that it lies in the East Asian monsoon zone, means that the country experiences diverse conditions.

Hanoi and the north in January and February can feel downright cold. Snow can fall in Sa Pa. The region experiences its greatest rainfall during the May-to-October monsoon season. Average daily highs range from 66°F (19°C) in January to 91°F (33°C) in June.

Nearly 2,000 karst islands rise from the waters of Ha Long Bay. Myths credit the thrashing tail of a dragon for this seascape, while geologists point to 300 million years of erosion and subduction.

The south and central regions are dependably tropical. From May to October, southwesterly monsoon winds blow through Ho Chi Minh City and the south, dumping 90 percent of the region's rain during this six-month stretch. Temperatures remain fairly stable year-round. November is the "coolest" month, with average daily highs of 88°F (31°C), while the temperature peaks at 94°F (34°C) in March and April.

In central Vietnam, the rains begin in September and continue through January, with the greatest concentration in October and November. Daily highs in Hue range from 74°F (23°C) in December to 94°F (34°C) in June, July, and August. ■

The Smaller Dragon

In Vietnam today, you're apt to see locals dancing to American pop idols and munching on baguettes, but make no mistake: Twenty years of American sway and one hundred years of the French are nothing next to the influence spawned by a thousand years of Chinese rule and cultural osmosis.

Hue's Imperial City was modeled, in part, on Beijing's imperial capital.

Just as the United States and modern Europe have mined the glories of ancient Greece and Rome to enrich their own cultures, so the Vietnamese have absorbed the politics, religion, sociology, and arts of China to refine their own. The impact is no mere accident of proximity. From 111 B.C. to A.D. 939, China controlled Vietnam as a vassal state, setting the stage for a cultural reorientation that goes right to the marrow of what it means to be Vietnamese.

The most obvious inheritance was Confucianism, a system of ethics so thoroughly woven into the fabric of Chinese and Vietnamese society that other political overlays (e.g., Marxism) are, by comparison, mere window dressing. Confucianism was especially dominant as a state religion in the imperial courts. In the 19th century, the Nguyen kings, like their counterparts in Beijing, anointed themselves as Sons of Heaven, a term that combines the mandate of a king with that of a pope.

Shortly after Vietnam cast off its Chinese overlords in the tenth century, the fledgling nation found the wherewithal to run the state in a bureaucracy staffed by mandarins. Like China, which founded its mandarinate in the first century B.C., the Ly kings established nine ranks of mandarins. They borrowed the

Chinese exam system and held literary competitions to distinguish between lesser and greater officials.

Though the Vietnamese retained their language throughout the thousand-year occupation, a third of its lexicon derives from Chinese. The native ideographic script evolved as a vernacular alternative to the Chinese Han script. Still, even after popularization of the *chu nom* script in the 14th century, Chinese persisted as the script of preference for scholars and official business until the dawn of the 20th.

The greatest of all Vietnamese poems, "The Tale of Kieu," stems from a novel penned in the 16th century by a Ming dynasty writer. Though the story is set in China, its essence is Vietnamese. Similarly, stories at the heart of Vietnamese theater, be it folk opera or classical theater, often hark back to age-old tales with origins along the Yangtze and Yellow Rivers.

The Vietnamese holiday of Tet is better known in the West as Chinese New Year (see p. 35). Tet begins with a tale that revolves around three star-crossed lovers, which is a reinterpretation of a Chinese story.

China has also influenced Vietnamese architecture, which can be seen most notably in Hue. The Nguyen kings built their imperial capital with one eye fixed on the local

Burning joss sticks, mandarin orange trees, and blossoms decorate temples and pagodas.

landscape and the other on Beijing, modeling walls, gates, moats, bridges, and audience halls after landmarks in the Chinese capital. This cultural mimicry even extends to the realm of nomenclature; both Beijing and Hue boast a Zenith Gate, a Forbidden City, and a Hall of Supreme Harmony. As the Nguyen kings prepared for death, they ordered construction of vast temple complexes anchored by mausoleums, modeled after the tombs of China's Ming dynasty.

There are, of course, cultural differences. But after more than 2,000 years of shared history, the similarities, especially to the traveler, remain obvious.

EXPERIENCE: Discover the "Indo" in Indochine

The French coined the term "Indochine" to refer to their colonial possessions in Vietnam, Laos, and Cambodia, and it was an accurate reflection of the mixed cultural influences on these countries from India and China. Since Vietnam is the easternmost of these countries, the Indian influence is predictably weaker here. It is still noticeable, however, especially in Cham culture, which flourished as a Hindu kingdom (see p. 172) throughout central and south Vietnam from the 7th to 15th centuries and has enjoyed a revival in recent years. In fact, when wandering around the overgrown ruins of My Son (see pp. 157–159), a 1,500-year-old temple complex and the premier Cham site in Vietnam, it is easy to imagine you are on the Indian subcontinent, with images of Siva and Krishna peeking out from the lush vegetation.

Beliefs

Vietnamese beliefs are a complex tangle of Confucianism, Buddhism, and Taoism, coiled about an ancient core of native dependency on spirits and goddesses. Ancestor altars anchor most homes to a spiritual realm where the dead are not inert but vital and prone to interaction with the living. Each year, the living and the dead commune in a celebratory feast during Tet.

Though most Vietnamese identify themselves as Buddhist, the term is shorthand for a range of beliefs. This often seems to include anything and everything. There's a great tradition of syncretism in Vietnam. The Chinese brought Confucianism south in the second century B.C., Buddhism arrived from India and China in the second and third centuries A.D., and Taoism seeped in as both a preoccupation of the elite and a receptacle for all those indigenous genii.

These traditions aren't mutually exclusive but pliable and absorbent. In fact, it's often said in Vietnam that you need all three—Confucianism, Buddhism, and Taoism, a trinity known collectively as Tam Giao. The Cao Dai, a homegrown sect founded in the 1920s, formally synthesized the Tam Giao as the foundation of their religion, then grafted on shoots of Catholicism and other Western religions to boot (see sidebar p. 34).

Though most Vietnamese identify themselves as Buddhist, the term is shorthand for a range of beliefs.

There's no dogma in these faiths, no overarching scripture, no clerical hierarchy. No one "attends pagoda" on a set schedule. You're likely to see only monks meditating. "Religion," a term fraught with Western doctrine and distinctions, has little relevance in the ethos of most Vietnamese.

The cult of Confucius keeps house at temples of literature *(van mieu)* and smaller temples in villages *(van tu* and *van chi)*. Tutelary spirits are worshipped in communal houses *(dinh)*. Various genii and deities are worshipped at temples *(den* and *mieu)*. Taoist gods are commonly met in temples *(quan)*. But no place of worship is as ubiquitous as the Buddhist pagoda *(chua)*.

Confucianism

As China consolidated its hold on Vietnam in the second century B.C., it insisted vassals renounce their liberal matriarchal ways and adhere to the more rigid cult of Confucius. Seeking societal harmony, Confucian ethics prescribe a hierarchy of obeisance: The son obeys the father, the subject obeys the king, the wife the husband, and the disciple the master. Such patriarchal arrangements served the prerogatives of the ruling Chinese. After Vietnam liberated itself in the tenth century, Buddhism flourished under the Ly and Tran dynasties. The country's oldest extant pagodas date from this period. Later, the Le and Nguyen dynasties hewed strongly to Confucianism, though they also built and repaired Buddhist pagodas.

The trappings of Confucianism persist today. Men dominate women. A son trumps a daughter. Education is more important than wealth. The cult of the ancestors is a form of filial piety and jibes neatly with indigenous beliefs in the omnipresence of spirits.

Costumed devotees of the Cao Dai worship at their cathedral near Tay Ninh.

In nearly every home, the family altar occupies the most hallowed place in the living room. Continually refreshed with flowers, fruit, wine, and, on anniversaries, prepared foods, this altar tethers one's departed ancestors to the living family. It's the responsibility of the family to nourish the dead with rituals and oblations.

Buddhism

As Confucianism governs societal relations, Buddhism serves the Vietnamese desire for personal salvation. If Confucianism plays to the head, Buddhism plays to heart.

Most Vietnamese Buddhists subscribe to the Mahayana branch of Buddhism, also known as the greater vehicle, and its three branches of Zen, Pure Land, and Tantra.

The Pure Land school especially is preoccupied with bodhisattvas—those who've already achieved enlightenment and could go on to Nirvana but prefer instead to help devotees.

In its purest form, there's no divinity in Buddhism. But you wouldn't know that from visiting a Vietnamese pagoda, where a pantheon of deities—warriors, kings, guardians, and other bodhisattvas—reigns from altars throughout the main sanctuary. A trinity of three Buddhas *(tam the)*, representing the Buddha of the past, present, and future, perches on the uppermost tier. The terrace below is occupied by the Amitabha Buddha, while other manifestations of Buddha and bodhisattvas occupy still lower terraces.

Taoism

Taoism is the least visible and most mystical element of Tam Giao. With the jade emperor as supreme divinity, this philosophy dwells on nothingness, on the absence of personal ambition, desire, and sensual pleasure, on simplicity, and on a belief in the world as an illusion. The yin and the yang symbolize the harmony of contradictions.

Outside the temples, Taoism is subtle and rarified. It's in the laughter you get after asking someone a question he'd rather not answer and in a pervasive lack of conviction. The populist part of Taoism trades on magic and melds nicely with native Vietnamese beliefs.

Spirits & Genii

In the supernatural world, the celestial sovereign Ong Troi (Mister Sky) lords over the universe. The Vietnamese invoke this deity—*Troi oi!*—as often as Westerners exclaim, "Oh, my God." Closer to home, spirits dwell in stones and the bowers of trees. If a boat wrecks on a stone, the spirit within is malevolent. If a tree is lush with fruit, the spirit is good.

These genii can be cajoled. The faithful, hoping for better days or a reprieve from misfortune, will burn paper oblations depicting money, motorbikes, and other proxies for the spirit's sustenance. Fortune-tellers, known as *thay*, often direct such rituals, which are held in the home, at temples, or at the site of a particular misfortune.

The Vietnamese have grafted a number of Chinese gods and bodhisattvas into their native tradition. Quan Am, the goddess of mercy, springs as much from the ancient cult of the mother saints (Tho Mau) as from the pantheon of bodhisattvas. The Taoist jade emperor reigns over the immortals and plays a crucial role at Tet.

Cao Daiism

The Cao Dai creed originated in the 1920s and is a fusion of Western and Eastern religious beliefs, incorporating elements of Buddhism, Christianity, Islam, Confucianism, and Taoism. Its strongholds are at Tay Ninh near Ho Chi Minh City and in the Mekong Delta, where its temples with dragons writhing on pillars and the religion's symbol, the Divine Eye, peering out from window frames make for eye-catching images. Among its saints, the religion counts William Shakespeare, Joan of Arc, Winston Churchill, and Victor Hugo.

Christianity

Catholic missionaries were very successful in Vietnam, partly because Vietnamese spiritual beliefs were scattered among so many traditions. Though the 19th-century Nguyen emperors executed a small number of missionaries, the reasons had more to do with a foreign threat to their reign than with ideological opposition. Today, Vietnam harbors some six million Catholics (8 percent of the population). ■

Tet

This weeklong celebration of the lunar new year, falling at the end of January or the beginning of February, dwarfs all other holidays in Vietnam. For an apt Western comparison, you'd have to combine Christmas, for the way the year revolves around it; Easter, for its spirit of renewal; and Thanksgiving, for the feast. It's also a nationwide birthday party: The Vietnamese don't mark their ages by the day they were born; instead, a baby turns one at Tet no matter when he or she was born that year.

Unicorn dances, symbolizing wealth and prosperity, take place during Tet.

Tet comes from the word *tiet,* which is the belted knot between segments of a bamboo stalk and describes the notion of transition. In preparation, Vietnamese stream home to clean the graves of ancestors, scrub the family altar, settle old debts, and cook. Pink and peach blossoms are brought into the house and temples to ward off evil spirits. And *banh chung,* a sticky rice cake, is available everywhere.

At midnight on New Year's Eve, the family marks the transition with prayers in the Gia Thua ceremony. They invite deceased ancestors home through the ritual of Gia Tien. The kitchen god that dwells in each house reports to the jade emperor, the supreme lord of Taoism, and the family prays that the report is favorable.

On the first morning, the first visitor to any house—the so-called first footer—heralds the family's luck for the coming year. Older relatives present children with *ly sy* (money) stuffed in small red envelopes. Immediate family members spend the day visiting each other. On the second day, they widen the circle to include more distant relatives, and on the third day, friends come together.

Tet rarely ends precisely after the third day, when the ancestors return to their spiritual realm sated with burnt offerings. The festivities often drift into a fourth, fifth, or sixth day, eventually petering out as people return to work.

History of Vietnam

The Vietnamese trace their origins to a legendary union between a dragon, Lac Long Quan, who came from the sea, and a fairy, Au Co, who dwelled in the mountains. Their union spawned a hundred sons, including one who became the first of the country's Hung kings. The 18 kings of this dynasty ruled over an era grounded in fact but largely embellished by myths.

The Vietnamese still celebrate the Trung sisters, who led the first great rebellion against Chinese occupation in A.D. 40.

The actual rise of the Hung kings was probably coincidental with the unification of different cultures in the Red River Valley in the seventh century B.C. These people were a commingling of the Austro-Indonesians who'd claimed the land and the Thai and Viets who came later, migrating south from China's Lower Yangtze River Valley. Their Dong Son culture persevered from the seventh century B.C. to the first century A.D. and forged abiding fame with bronze drums that have been unearthed by archaeologists throughout the region.

Archaeology aside, the Vietnamese as a people did not register their first appearance in the annals of history until the emergence of King An Duong late in the third century B.C. An Duong yanked the crown away from the last of the Hung kings and established the Au Lac Kingdom at Co Loa ("snail city"). An Duong lost his throne in a supernatural power play by his son-in-law's father, a Chinese general named Trieu Da, who first identified the fledgling country as a nation of the Viets.

The Viets didn't enjoy autonomy for long. China, even in antiquity, had too many people and too little fertile land. Thus, in 111 B.C. Han dynasty soldiers surged south and wrested control of the Red River Delta from the Viets, expanding an empire that would ultimately stretch as far as Turkistan and Korea. Experts in dikebuilding and irrigation, the Chinese taught the Vietnamese how to keep rivers at bay, brought the plow to farmers, and opened schools to teach the art of writing.

Over the next millennium, Vietnam gradually absorbed the trappings of Chinese culture. Although the people continued to cultivate their own language, they adopted Chinese characters for written communication and replaced the more liberal tenets of their own social structure with the stricter hierarchies of Confucianism, a philosophy of social organization that persists in Vietnam to this day.

Still, the Vietnamese never stopped trying to oust their foreign masters. The first great rebellion under Chinese rule was led by Trung Trac, a fearless woman who drove the Chinese from power in A.D. 40 and took to the throne as queen with her sister as a constant companion. For two years, these two Trung heroines ruled a flimsy union that collapsed shortly after the Chinese dispatched an able general to pacify the south. But Chinese dominion could not expunge the glories of Au Lac and the Hung kings, whose legendary reigns would help sustain the Vietnamese struggle for independence for the next 900 years.

Mandarin Exams

Between 1076 and 1919, Vietnam conducted a series of 185 examinations to identify its best minds. To earn a *cu nhan* (bachelor's degree) or become a *tien si* (doctor laureate), candidates had to master the Chinese language and its 5,000 characters. The exams covered philosophy, ethics, poetry, history, and political science; knowledge of exact sciences was unnecessary. Though some scholars retired to their villages as esteemed sages, most joined the country's mandarinate. In fact, this largely democratic system was the only road to public office in Vietnam.

In the tenth century, China's Tang dynasty deteriorated, and a Vietnamese leader seized the day. In a decisive battle at the Bach Dang River, Gen. Ngo Quyen (898–944) implanted iron-tipped wooden stakes into a riverbed and lured the Chinese fleet upriver at high tide. When the tide turned, the stakes impaled and sank the fleet, clinching the Vietnamese victory. The victorious general founded the Ngo dynasty at Co Loa, the ancient capital of the Au Lac Kingdom, strategically affirming Vietnam's sense of itself as an independent nation.

In 1010, the first of the great Vietnamese imperial dynasties, the Ly, came to power. Ly Thai To moved his seat of power from Hoa Lu, where Ngo Quyen's successor had established his dynasty, to Dai La, the site of present-day Hanoi. According to legend, he renamed the city Thang Long ("dragon ascending") after sighting a soaring dragon en route along the Red River.

The Ly founded a bureaucracy run by mandarins and, in 1070, dedicated the renowned Temple of Literature to the cult of Confucius. The Ly and the succeeding dynasty, the Tran, also ushered Vietnam into prosperity, building roads, a postal system, fleets, pagodas, and parks. But the warring continued unabated.

The Khmer (modern-day Cambodians) launched a series of attacks against the new Vietnamese state. The Vietnamese also battled the kingdom of Champa to the south and tangled with the Mongols in a series of 13th-century invasions. Unlike the Koreans, however, who were subdued by the Mongols, 200,000 Vietnamese soldiers under the command of Tran Hung Dao repelled the great imperialists of the 13th century.

After the Mongol repulsion, the Vietnamese resumed their wars with the Cham, impoverishing and weakening the Tran until the Chinese seized a chance and swept back to power in Vietnam.

The Le

The Vietnamese paid a harsh price under the new Chinese regime. The Ming invaders forced the peasantry to labor in the mines for gold and ores, the forests for elephant tusks and rhinoceros horns, and the fields for the cultivation of spices—all for export to China. Now the Vietnamese were riled, and to the hour came a man who ranks with Ho Chi Minh as the greatest of all Vietnamese heroes. Le Loi (1385–1433), a wealthy landowner from Thanh Hoa, resorted to the guerrilla tactics that worked so well for Tran Hung Dao, badgering the Chinese in ambush after ambush and finally winning a decisive victory at the Chi Lang defile in 1427.

Although Le Loi is remembered as the greatest Le hero, one of his successors, Le Thanh Tong (1442–1497), ushered in Vietnam's golden age during his reign from 1460 to 1497. Le Thanh Tong was a progressive and a scholar. He drew up a remarkably liberal legal code, granting rights to women and civil rights for citizens. He promoted journals for the advancement of math and science. He dispatched troops to help rebuild flood-damaged dikes. With the population burgeoning, Le Thanh Tong set his sights on the Cham lands to the south. In 1471, his troops razed the capital of their southern Cham neighbors at Indrapura, killing 40,000 inhabitants and opening the door to land-hungry pioneers, a movement known as the March to the South.

In Hanoi's Temple of Literature, the Constellation of Literature typifies the elegance of Vietnam's architecture.

Though the Le persevered through 1788, their golden age was short-lived. In the early 16th century, a Vietnamese general usurped power from the reigning Le king, and the country divided into two camps of rival lords, each of which continued to recognize the Le as overlords. But these Le kings were feckless rulers. The Trinh held true sway in the north, while the Nguyens consolidated their power below the 17th parallel.

Arrival of the Europeans

The fractious relationship between the Trinh and the Nguyens opened the door to a series of interventions by European powers. In 1545, the seafaring Portuguese established the first European settlement in Vietnam, a land they dubbed Cochinchina after an approximation of a Chinese name. The Dutch bested the Portuguese as masters of the Asia trade in the 17th century, opening factories in the north and south. Not to be left out, the English showed up in 1672, and the French opened shop in Hanoi in 1680. By 1700, both the English and the Dutch had decamped, frustrated by an inability to turn a profit.

The fractious relationship between the Trinh and the Nguyens opened the door to a series of interventions by European powers.

As profits declined, the missionaries took center stage. Alexandre de Rhodes (1591–1660), a French Jesuit, reinvigorated the linguistic work of earlier missionaries and created a Romanized alphabet as an alternative to the unwieldy native *chu nom* script and Chinese ideographs favored by the educated elite. At the same time, he baptized thousands of new Christians every year, unsettling the royalty in Vietnam. As long as the Trinh and Nguyens needed the upper hand of European technology, the missionaries were allowed a fairly liberal hand in the north and south. But once the rival camps achieved a rapprochement, the opponents of Christianity won the day: Rhodes and his Catholic colleagues were thrown out of the country.

Rhodes lobbied the governments of France and the Vatican to help reopen the door to missionary work in Vietnam, touting it as a land of incalculable riches, but he died before either got serious about the country again. While others picked up the cause Rhodes had championed, none would advance the mission as hard or as far as the French bishop Pigneau de Behaine (1741–1799).

French Colonization

In the latter half of the 18th century, the discontent that had rendered Vietnam into fertile ground for missionaries gave rise to an insurrection that united northern and southern Vietnam. In 1765, three brothers from a merchant family in Tay Son, a village on the south-central coast, rebelled against accusations of fraud. Their movement swelled with peasants bristling under a harsh mandarin system. The Tay Son wiped out most of the Nguyen lords in the south and by 1786 had wrested control of the capital in Hanoi. Mandarins from the old regime called for help from China, but the youngest Tay Son brother was able to repel the most significant Chinese incursion in several hundred years.

Meanwhile, de Behaine threw his support behind Nguyen Anh, a surviving member of the vanquished southern lords. He lobbied the cause of his protégé in the salons of Paris, persuading most of the government that Vietnam was the future of France in Asia. Though de Behaine would die of dysentery in 1799, his efforts bore fruit. In 1802, Nguyen Anh assumed the throne as Gia Long, the first king in the last imperial dynasty of Vietnam. He moved the capital from Hanoi to Hue, the centuries-old seat of the Nguyen lords, and began construction of an imperial city, using the Chinese capital as a model.

Gia Long was a Confucian king, somewhat conservative and unenlightened. His successor, Minh Mang (1791–1841), was bold and dogmatic, but, unlike his father, he would come to power during a resurgence of interest in Vietnam by European powers. Once the Napoleonic Wars ended in 1815, missionaries and merchants resumed their drumbeat for Vietnam. Minh Mang lashed out against the proselytizing, ordering the executions of seven Christian missionaries between 1833 and 1838. He and his successor, Thieu Tri, failed to read the winds of change. Their intransigence and unwillingness to compromise agitated the Gallic temper.

After the British took Hong Kong in the 1840s, the French tired of playing second fiddle to the British, Spanish, and Portuguese, each of whom had won significant concessions in Asia. Oddly enough, though, it was the Americans, not the French, who first wielded Western military might in Vietnam. In 1845, after learning that the Vietnamese had imprisoned a French missionary in Hue, the captain of the U.S.S. *Constitution* seized three mandarins as bargaining chips in a negotiation for the European's release. The ploy failed, and the United States later apologized for meddling.

Several years later, King Tu Duc executed another missionary, raising a hue and cry for armed intervention from the 40 or so missionaries then at work in Vietnam. In 1858, the French attacked Tourane (now called Danang) with purpose, landing soldiers as the vanguard of a people who meant to stay. The French evacuated the city in 1860, but by then the French back in Paris had rallied around the notion of *mission civilisatrice*, justifying their actions against the Vietnamese as a means toward enlightenment of the "yellow race."

The Vietnamese kept hoping the French, worn down by heat and disease, would simply give up and go home. The old kings of Vietnam had rallied hundreds of thousands of troops to repel invaders, but Tu Duc was not cut from the same cloth. Instead, he legalized the import of opium and put mandarin degrees up for sale. In 1863, the impotent king agreed to give up the lower third of Vietnam to France as the colony of Cochinchina. After the deaths of notable French adventurers in the 1870s and 1880s, France established protectorates in the central and northern provinces of Vietnam, known respectively as Annam and Tonkin.

Uncle Ho

Though Ho Chi Minh is the founding father of modern Vietnam and the preeminent member of the Vietnamese pantheon, the Vietnamese call him Bac Ho (Uncle Ho), not Father Ho. Kindly, avuncular portraits of the man are plastered everywhere in Vietnam, and it is true that Ho never had children of his own. But that's not the principal reason he's known as uncle. In Vietnamese families, children refer to a father's younger brothers as *chu* (uncle) and to the eldest brother as *bac*, which also means "uncle." A father's eldest brother is the most prestigious member of the clan; thus Uncle Ho is a more esteemed form of address than Father Ho.

The Resistance

The loss of sovereignty spawned a resistance movement among the disenfranchised elite. Phan Dinh Phung (1847–1895) mustered a guerrilla force that would later serve as a model for resistance in the 1940s. Renowned poet Phan Boi Chau (1867–1940) first tried to restore the monarchy, then later, in exile, favored democracy as an antidote to colonialism. Others, like Phan Chu Trinh, favored a moderate approach. Meanwhile, France propped up a series of handpicked kings and used its military might to douse the brushfire revolts in the provinces.

Enter Ho Chi Minh (1890–1969). Ho was born Nguyen Sinh Cung in a village of Nghe An Province in central Vietnam. His father was a distinguished scholar who, for mildly revolutionary behavior, fell out of favor with the imperial court in Hue. In 1911,

Ho Chi Minh was a nationalist, a socialist by temperament, and a Marxist out of expedience.

Ho shipped out of Vietnam on a French freighter and over the next several years called at ports in the Middle East, Africa, and America. In 1919, under the alias Nguyen Ai Quoc (Nguyen the Patriot), he dispatched an appeal to Allied leaders, then meeting at Versailles to hammer out the terms of the armistice. Ho's petition called for political autonomy, versus outright independence, for the Vietnamese people. His eight-point plan called for freedom of the press, association, and religion and reductions in taxes on salt, opium, and alcohol. It would not be the last time Ho's aims coincided with the precedent of America's Founding Fathers.

Although a member of Woodrow Wilson's delegation acknowledged Ho's plan, no action was taken. Wilson's 14-point plan addressed colonialism by calling for self-determination for all peoples. But it was a limp-wristed gesture compared to Vladimir Lenin's iron grip in 1920, when he declared that communist countries in the West should actively participate in the struggle for freedom by colonial peoples.

Attracted by Lenin's support, Ho traveled to Moscow in 1924 and cast his lot with the communists. The tenets of Marxism were not anathema to him or a people steeped in Confucian values. Private property was not a commodity in Vietnam but was held in trust by the state. Vietnamese entrepreneurs and capitalists garnered far less esteem than did their Western counterparts. The colonial revolutionaries loathed capitalism not so much from a philosophical standpoint, as did Marx, but because capitalism had exploited their people.

By way of China, Ho surreptitiously returned to Vietnam in February 1941 and linked up with Vo Nguyen Giap (1911–2013) and Pham Van Dong (1906–2000). Dong was the son of a mandarin who served as Emperor Duy Tan's chief of staff. Giap was also the son of a mandarin, and his maternal grandfather fought the French in the 1880s. The trio would soon become leading figures in modern Vietnam.

"You can kill ten of my men for every one I kill of yours," Ho told a French visitor during the war. "But even at those odds, you will lose, and I will win."

During World War II, the French Vichy government allowed Japanese forces to occupy Vietnam, a loss of face that broached the possibility of liberation from a European power. But the Japanese won few friends among the Vietnamese, whose food they hoarded, leading to a famine that killed two million people. As he charted his country's fate through the closing months of the war, Ho courted the sympathies of U.S. military operatives, who supplied his movement with arms in the summer of 1945.

Following the Japanese surrender, Ho, as leader of the Viet Minh resistance movement, charged into the sudden vacuum of power with the presumption of control. A delegation accepted the abdication of King Bao Dai and the imperial seal at the Noon Gate in Hue, and the Viet Minh assumed provisional power in Tonkin, Annam, and Cochinchina.

Despite the politics he'd groomed in the Soviet Union, Ho continued to pursue the sympathies of the Americans. On September 2, 1945, before a crowd of 400,000 people in Hanoi's Ba Dinh Square, he declared independence for Vietnam, beginning his speech with these words: "All men are created equal. They are endowed by their Creator with certain inalienable rights, among these are Life, Liberty, and the pursuit of Happiness."

Ho's deference to the U.S. Declaration of Independence fell on deaf ears in the West. Though the Viet Minh had seized power, the Allies had interim plans for Vietnam. At the Potsdam Conference in 1945, they'd agreed to partition the country at the 16th parallel. The British would disarm the Japanese in the South and transition the country from wartime to peacetime footing; the Chinese would do so in the North.

Ho's bold declaration notwithstanding, the Viet Minh leader capitulated to the resumption of French power in 1946, if only as a means to rid Vietnam of the Chinese. For the promised withdrawal of French troops in five years, Ho chose the lesser of two evils. "I prefer to sniff French s– for five years than eat Chinese s– for the rest of my life," he said.

But the political winds in France again shifted, and overtures toward Vietnamese independence bowed to renewed interest in Cochinchina as a republic tied to the apron strings of Mother France. At negotiations in Paris, Ho quietly deferred to the French on Cochinchina, knowing his initials on a partial agreement would not deter war at home. The French and Viet Minh soon clashed in Haiphong. Hanoi erupted in December, and the First Indochinese (French) War was on.

The End of French Rule

Until 1949, the United States pursued a hands-off policy with regard to the war in Indochina. After communist Mao Zedong took over in China and, like the Soviets, recognized Ho Chi Minh's regime, however, the Americans threw their support behind a government led by the on-again, off-again king of Vietnam, Bao Dai. As justification for underwriting the French War, the United States invoked the "domino theory": If Indochina were to fall, so would the other countries of Southeast Asia.

By 1953, the United States was funding 80 percent of the French war effort. It was a losing proposition. While the United States was game for total victory, the French had resigned themselves to a political solution. Between 1945 and 1954, some 100,000

The Vietnamese won their greatest set-piece battle of the 20th century at Dien Bien Phu. The French defeat set the stage for the 1954 Geneva Accords and a push toward autonomy.

French soldiers died in Indochina, mostly in Vietnam. The French public had lost interest in its dirty war; the Vietnamese resistance had not. "You can kill ten of my men for every one I kill of yours," Ho told a French visitor during the war. "But even at those odds, you will lose, and I will win."

General Giap made good on Ho's promise in a far-flung valley near the Laotian border, where he launched a series of human-wave assaults against the French garrison at Dien Bien Phu. The French repulsed these early advances but could not persevere against Giap's stranglehold. On May 7, 1954, the beleaguered French troops surrendered. The next day, peace talks got under way in Geneva.

With victory at Dien Bien Phu, the Vietnamese were in a strong bargaining position, but not so strong that they could demand immediate unification of the country. Negotiations bogged down on two points: where to draw the line of partition and when to hold unification elections. Eventually, the parties agreed on the 17th parallel as the

The U.S. Air Cavalry's signature UH-1 (Huey) helicopter ferried troops in and out of battle.

dividing line between North and South and on a two-year run-up to a nationwide election that would unite the country. That election would never come.

Eye of the Storm

The United States did not sign the Geneva Accords, a gesture that would have limited its options in the region. The government led by former King Bao Dai also declined to sign. Instead, with wholehearted support from the Americans, Bao Dai appointed Ngo Dinh Diem (1901–1963) prime minister of the Republic of South Vietnam. Ardently Catholic, monkish, and undiplomatic, Diem transformed the southern "regroupment" zone into a fledgling state. He won a loyal following among people who shared his faith, including some 600,000 Catholic refugees who fled south after Ho Chi Minh and other Viet Minh leaders assumed power in Hanoi.

Diem turned out to be a disastrous choice. He ruled South Vietnam without any pretense of democracy, despite the lip service paid to his U.S. benefactors. He canceled the 1956 elections, an election that Ho, who was popular throughout the country, would likely have won. With his brother Ngo Dinh Nhu as his right-hand man, Diem embarked on a campaign to purge the South of communist agents. To deny the enemy easy access to the population, Nhu displaced farmers from their ancestral homes and herded them into *agrovilles,* or strategic hamlets. The Diem regime alienated the villagers and non-Catholic religious sects, denied freedom of the press and freedom of assembly, and outlawed all political opposition. Yet Lyndon Johnson, as John F. Kennedy's vice president, would liken Diem to Winston Churchill.

Meanwhile, in the North, Hanoi was trying to get its own house in order. The government sanctioned a land reform campaign that ran amok. Roving people's tribunals harassed and humiliated countless thousands of people and executed several thousand landlords as more than 2,000,000 acres were redistributed to two million farm families.

In 1959, Le Duan, a southerner who ascended to power in Hanoi, decided the time was ripe for revolution in the South. Northerners blazed the Ho Chi Minh Trail through the highlands of Vietnam, Laos, and Cambodia to ferry troops and matériel to their southern compatriots. In 1960, a coalition of anti-Diem forces formed the National Liberation Front (NLF), or Viet Cong.

In the spring of 1963, Buddhists rallied against Diem in a movement that commanded worldwide attention after a monk from Hue doused himself with gasoline and set himself ablaze in Saigon. That November, fed-up generals of his own regime, with tacit American consent, launched a coup against Diem and executed the prime minister and his brother.

America Weighs In

Diem was gone, but the United States was no less committed to South Vietnam and the domino theory. After a skirmish with a North Vietnamese patrol boat in the Gulf of Tonkin, the United States retaliated with a congressional resolution that gave Lyndon Johnson, now U.S. President, a free hand to conduct military operations in Vietnam. Gen. William Westmoreland called for troops to protect U.S. airfields, and the first contingent of U.S. combat Marines waded ashore at Danang in March 1965, the vanguard of 72,000 troops that would arrive in the country that spring.

Fueled by the resources of a vast military-industrial complex and an overconfidence in the supremacy of airpower, the United States prosecuted the war with a hammer, ignoring the opinions of seasoned strategists who called for scalpels. In 1965, an American provincial adviser told journalist and historian Bernard Fall that the U.S. military was shooting a half million dollars worth of artillery onto unobserved targets in his region every month but spending a mere 300 dollars on intelligence gathering.

As the Marines settled in at Danang, the United States launched a bombing campaign to stop the flow of supplies down the mountainous Ho Chi Minh Trail, but it never did. The bombing intensified and moved south, or "in country," as American servicemen referred to South Vietnam. By the end of that spring, B-52 bombers were obliterating suspect targets across the south; in April 1966, the B-52s went to work on targets in the North.

Naming Wars

While the conflict between Vietnam and the United States (1965–1973) is known to most Westerners as the Vietnam War, it's known to Vietnamese as the American War. This is to distinguish it from other invasions of the country by the French, Chinese, Mongols, and Khmers. Some also call it the Second Indochina War, with the First Indochina War referring to the struggle to expel the French (1946–1954).

Westmoreland believed he could win through attrition. If he could simply kill enough Vietnamese, they'd cry uncle and give up. But he faced a tenacious enemy of unwavering resolve. The more bombs dropped by the U.S. military, the deeper soldiers from North Vietnam and the National Liberation Front dug in.

By contrast, the South Vietnamese allies of the United States, their leaders rickety and corrupt, seemed more attuned to skimming shares of American largesse than fighting. In 1966, Buddhists and other dissidents raged against the corrupt southern regime of Prime Minister Nguyen Cao Ky, as they had against Diem three years earlier. They seized power in Danang and Hue. While the larger war played on, Ky skirmished against his own army. In protest, ten more monks and nuns set themselves ablaze.

During the Tet lunar new year in 1968, the North Vietnamese and NLF coordinated a series of attacks on 31 of the 44 southern provincial capitals. The offensive surprised the Americans, who'd been expecting a pivotal battle in the central highlands at Khe Sanh, where the North Vietnamese had been building up forces for weeks. But Khe Sanh was a ruse that enabled the communists to sneak through back doors all over the country. In Saigon, communist infiltrators breached the U.S. Embassy. In Hue, they wrested control of the city and held on for 25 days as the U.S. Marines battled back. At Khe Sanh, the ruse turned into a two-month siege, despite relentless bombings by B-52 bombers.

In the end, the communists lost 50,000 combatants at Tet and failed to spark the desired uprising. The ranks of the Viet Cong were shattered, never to recover, and North Vietnamese Army soldiers migrated south in greater numbers to pick up the batons dropped by their southern comrades.

In the United States, Tet was a turning point in the war. Extensive media coverage confirmed mounting doubts and accelerated the antiwar movement in a nation already souring on a dirty war that had grown too big, with more than half a million U.S. troops on the ground in 1968. After newsman Walter Cronkite declared that the war was locked in a hopeless stalemate, Lyndon Johnson saw the writing on the wall and withdrew from the 1968 presidential race.

Richard Nixon, who as a candidate claimed to have a secret plan to end the war, took office and then prolonged the fighting another three and a half years. In 1970, he widened the war with an invasion of Cambodia that sparked broad antiwar protests. The governor of Ohio aggravated unrest at Kent State University by calling in National Guard troops, who ultimately shot and killed four student protesters.

With the revelations of a 1969 massacre of some 500 Vietnamese villagers at My Lai, many Americans had had enough. The United States turned over increasingly more military responsibilities to the South Vietnamese, who were less willing than their northern brethren to sacrifice themselves.

Embassy Memories

On Ho Chi Min City's Le Duan, the U.S. Consulate occupies the site of the wartime American Embassy. That building, with its distinctive waffled sunshade and looming white walls, was a haunting reminder of U.S. involvement in Vietnam and was razed in 1998. Today, a granite sidewalk marker memorializes an attack on the embassy during the 1968 Tet Offensive.

In Paris, U.S. National Security Council adviser Henry Kissinger matched wits with Vietnamese negotiator Le Duc Tho, trying to achieve a so-called peace with honor. When talks stalled at the end of 1972, Nixon ordered a renewal of bombing along the 60-mile (96 km) corridor between Hanoi and Haiphong, the North's main port. The United States dropped 40,000 tons (36,000 metric tons) of bombs between December 18 and December 30, excluding Christmas Day, in the most intensive bombing campaign of the war. The action forced the North Vietnamese hand, and on January 27, 1973, the enemies formally signed a cease-fire agreement in Paris.

Reunification

In the spring of 1975, Hanoi launched its final offensive against the Saigon regime. The towns and cities of South Vietnam toppled as readily as dominoes, surprising even the North Vietnamese. Hundreds of thousands of refugees—fearful of reprisals

Enduring War Images

The Evacuation Helicopter. The Burning Monk. The Crying Girl in the Picture. The Viet Cong Execution. These four potent images seared the front pages of newspapers worldwide between 1963 and 1975. Decades have passed since their initial publication, but such is the indelibility of their content that they need little introduction today.

Vietnamese evacuees board a chopper atop a CIA apartment building in downtown Saigon.

The evacuation helicopter was not perched atop the roof of the U.S. Embassy in Saigon, as captions have repeatedly stated since 1975, but on the penthouse of an apartment building at 22 Ly Tu Trong that was home to a number of CIA employees. The refugees climbing the ladder were Vietnamese, not Americans. The precariously perched Huey would not be the last to ferry refugees from the city. That flight would take off 12 hours later. On this 11th-hour run, the chopper pilot shuttled 14 or 15 passengers to Tan Son Nhat Airport.

Three years earlier, a South Vietnamese pilot had inadvertently dropped napalm near the Cao Dai temple in the town of Trang Bang, about 25 miles (40 km) northwest of Saigon. Gobs of the burning jelly splashed across the back of Phan Thi Kim Phuc, who tore off her flaming clothes and rushed into the road.

There's less certainty about the story behind the Viet Cong execution. Lt. Col. Nguyen Ngoc Loan pulled the trigger in front of Saigon's An Quang Pagoda in 1968. The executed man was a Viet Cong named Nguyen Van Lam. Loan justified the execution to Pulitzer Prize–winning photojournalist Eddie Adams by saying that Lam had killed Americans and Vietnamese. Others defend Lam as a low-level fighter who didn't deserve the brutal punishment.

Did Thich Quang Duc commit suicide on June 11, 1963, or was it immolation? Duc submitted to a dousing by gasoline and struck the fatal match himself—certainly a desperate act. But the monk lacked neither courage nor hope, two hallmarks of suicide. He was protesting repressive anti-Buddhist measures enacted by South Vietnam's Catholic leader, Ngo Dinh Diem.

like the massacres of 1968, when communist troops killed thousands during their occupation of Hue—fled south ahead of the advancing forces. They converged at ports, on airfields, and on beaches, desperately seeking evacuation. In the waning weeks of the war, nearly 60,000 Vietnamese and Americans bolted from the country, including some 7,000 people during a panic-stricken airlift out of Saigon in the last 48 hours. On April 30, North Vietnamese tanks crashed through the gates of the presidential palace in Saigon, and South Vietnam was history.

In 1994, President Bill Clinton lifted the embargo, and the following year the United States normalized relations and opened an embassy in Hanoi.

But while the communists and NLF won the war, they promptly set about losing the peace. The victors indulged in vengefulness, jailing hundreds of thousands of the South's best and brightest in gulags euphemistically called "reeducation camps." They nationalized businesses and usurped property. The vaunted "liberation" was tantamount to deprivation for the vanquished southerners.

By 1978, Vietnam was deep in a quagmire of poverty and hunger. The Khmer Rouge, embarked on a genocide of its own people in neighboring Cambodia, swerved into Vietnam and massacred thousands. The Vietnamese retaliated with invasion and occupation.

Already angered by Vietnam's postwar alliance with the Soviet Union, China invaded Vietnam in 1979. The Vietnamese drove China back, but chronic poverty and hopelessness caused an exodus of as many as two million disenfranchised people, many of them ethnic Chinese.

The boat people, as the refugees came to be known, took to the seas in rickety vessels, steering toward neighboring Southeast Asian nations and, ultimately, the promise of a better life in the West. Thousands died in the open ocean. Meanwhile, Hanoi struggled to make good on the promise of its victory, a promise ultimately fulfilled by the inauguration of a market economy and fiscal reform policy *(doi moi)* in 1986.

Renovation

After 1975, as preconditions for the normalization of relations, Vietnam insisted the United States make good on Nixon's secret promise to pay war reparations, and the U.S. insisted on a full accounting of its 2,400 soldiers still listed as missing in action (MIA). Vietnam eventually backed off its demand for reparations and economic aid, but by then the United States was busy trying to normalize relations with China.

Throughout the 1980s, the United States justified its trade embargo and the ongoing enmity by pointing to Vietnam's occupation of Cambodia and its failure to provide the "fullest possible accounting" of America's MIAs. By the early 1990s, Vietnam had decamped from Cambodia, and U.S. senators John McCain and John Kerry, both decorated veterans of the Vietnam War, were calling for an end to the trade embargo and a resumption of relations. In 1994, President Bill Clinton lifted the embargo, and the following year the United States normalized relations and opened an embassy in Hanoi. In the same year, Vietnam became a full member of the Association of Southeast Asian Nations (ASEAN).

Those landmarks released a flood of interest in this time-warped nation where labor costs were low, the market potential was enormous, and the sky was the limit. But an Asian financial crisis, coupled with governmental corruption and bureaucracy, stifled initial enthusiasm, and Vietnam watched its foreign investments plunge from eight billion dollars in 1996 to one billion in 1999.

Near the end of his presidency, Clinton visited Vietnam to lay the groundwork for a bilateral trade agreement that was signed in 2001. Membership in the World Trade Organization was granted to Vietnam in January 2007. Land redistribution combined with investment in poor, rural areas have helped eliminate much poverty and boost agriculture. But despite economic reforms in 2012, GDP has slowed in recent years. ■

Vietnamese soccer fans celebrate a goal during a Tiger Cup tournament.

The Arts

In Vietnam, some say half of the country is populated by painters and the other half by poets. That may be true, though the actors, musicians, woodcarvers, and artisans of ceramics and lacquerware might protest.

Literature

Poetry enjoys a currency in Vietnam that's been largely lost in the West. Friends write each other poems to celebrate homecomings and holidays. A waiter may serve up a few lines of verse as he dishes up your entrée. Because Vietnamese is a tonal language, a single word can have six different meanings, depending on the pitch of one's voice. Thus, the chance of lighting upon a rhyme increases by a factor of six, which may explain why poetry comes so readily to the Vietnamese.

Although the country's literary roots stretch back two millennia, Chinese invaders in the 15th century destroyed most of the early texts in an attempt to extinguish Vietnam's concept of itself as a nation apart from China. After occupation by soldiers of the Ming dynasty, Buddhist and Confucian scribes resumed work, using two scripts—Han, or classical Chinese, and *chu nom,* a homegrown ideographic script in widespread use by the end of the 14th century.

Because Vietnamese is a tonal language, a single word can have six different meanings, depending on the pitch of one's voice.

The dominant poet of Vietnam's golden age, Nguyen Trai (1380–1442), was a Confucian and profound humanist who withdrew from court life and its dispiriting intrigues to write nom poetry about society and nature. Many of Vietnam's kings also fancied themselves poets. While Nguyen Trai embraced the colloquial script for his verse, the greatest of all of Vietnam's kings, Le Thanh Tong, composed his annals in Han.

In the 18th century, Vietnamese poet Nguyen Du (1765–1820) penned *The Tale of Kieu,* an epic narrative in six-eight verse that Vietnamese quote often and reverently. In Du's interpretation of a Chinese novel, he chronicles the story of a girl sold into slavery and prostitution in order to save her family. The tale is steeped in allusions to the Confucian classics, as well as Buddhist and Taoist scriptures.

In the early 20th century, as the educated elite rebelled against colonial oppression, publishers of verse, essays, novels, and journalism initiated widespread use of the *quoc ngu* script. Developed by missionaries in the 17th century, quoc ngu is a transliteration of Vietnamese speech into the Roman alphabet. Compared to the ideographic scripts, which included thousands of characters, quoc ngu was far easier to master and so a much better vehicle of communication as revolutionaries sought to rally the populace.

In the early 1930s, literature entered a golden age as writers rebelled against Confucian strictures and explored the role of the individual. Writers shifted their focus from the stilted prerogatives of duty and responsibility to love and other emotions in novels like *South Wind,* by Hoang Ngoc Phach, and *Old Love,* by 21-year-old Luu Trong Lu.

Today, after decades of war and demands for writers to toe the party line, contemporary novelists Bao Ninh *(The Sorrows of War)* and Duong Thu Huong *(Paradise of the Blind)*

The landmark Turtle Tower rises from the midst of Hanoi's Hoan Kiem Lake.

have broken new ground in stories that resurrect the horror, not glories, of war and the harsh realities of life in postwar Vietnam.

Architecture

The Vietnamese celebrate architecture as the most illustrious achievement of their arts. With geomancy, or feng shui, as one of its principal determinants, Vietnamese architecture takes in the physical and metaphysical, the terrestrial and the celestial.

The buildings themselves, whether used for religious or civil purposes, share fundamental characteristics: massive roofs of terra-cotta tiles lofted by pillars of jackfruit and hardwood; low sheltering rooflines; and an elevated brick foundation. The country's military architecture manifests itself in citadels—some as old as 2,000 years—peppered throughout the country. Since stone was scarce, most buildings were constructed of wood. Thus, due to regional heat and humidity, the oldest extant examples of Vietnamese buildings—except for the brick citadels—date back only a couple of hundred years.

EXPERIENCE: Discovering Sericulture

While its annual silk output of 2,000 tons (1,800 metric tons) makes Vietnam a relative lightweight in an industry where China spins out 132,000 tons (120,000 metric tons) per year, its gorgeous silks are highly coveted. The village of Van Phuc, one of the highland craft villages, is the cradle of sericulture, though Lam Dong Province in the central highlands now produces the bulk of the industry's cocoons.

After fattening up larvae on mulberry leaves, silkworm farmers turn over the cocoons to the factories. These are plunked in hot water to loosen a natural glue that binds the wrap. Weavers can tease 2,000 to 3,000 feet (600–900 m) of filament from each cocoon, twisting a half dozen filaments together for a single fiber. These fibers are wound onto spools, dyed in rich colors, and applied to looms, where they are fed through templates to create a variety of motifs.

Contact **Queen Travel** (see Travelwise p. 239) to arrange a tour of Van Phuc, just 6 miles (10 km) north of Hanoi, or **Dalat Tourist** *(10 Quang Trung, Dalat, tel 063/382-3829, dalattourist.com.vn)* for suggestions on visiting the silk-producing villages in Lam Dong Province.

Military & Imperial: The most imposing structures in historical Vietnam were the citadels, with high walls, ramparts, and moats (Co Loa, Hanoi Citadel). Later, the Nguyens, with help from French advisers and European models, built citadels throughout their dominion, including the magnificent walled fortress city of Hue.

Hue is also home to the country's most marvelous collection of imperial structures. In the 19th century, the Nguyen kings used the Forbidden City in Beijing as a model for their own imperial capital, though the Nguyen versions of the Zenith Gate and Palace of Supreme Harmony are smaller, more sublime versions of the Chinese archetypes.

Civil: The epitome of vernacular architecture is the traditional *dinh,* a village's most important structure. It is a forum, courtroom, banquet hall, sports venue, theater, and temple for local tutelary gods. Most were built 300 to 400 years ago and have been renovated once or twice a century since. Elaborate carvings often adorn the interior woodwork of the dinh's truss—along the beams, purlins, and panels. The Vietnamese have identified more than 700 dinh, mostly in the Red River Delta, as cultural and historical landmarks.

Unlike the dinh, the *den* is a dynastic temple reserved for Taoist deities or national heroes like Tran Hung Dao. While the dinh serves both civilian and religious functions, the den is a religious house. A dien is a den reserved for Taoist spirits. The *van tu* is another form of religious architecture, reserved for the cult of Confucius.

Religious: The country's most religious body of architecture is the Buddhist pagoda. Pagodas *(chua)* can be as small as a single structure, like Hanoi's One-Pillar Pagoda, or comprise temple compounds that include stupas, towers, galleries, bell towers, and stela houses, like the complex at Hue's Thien Mu. From the 13th to 17th centuries, one popular form of pagoda design positioned the sanctuaries and shrines along a single axis, connected by galleries, courtyards, bridges, and gardens. Another popular arrangement positions the sanctuaries around an interior garden filled with bonsai and other flowering plants.

Inside the main sanctuary, a succession of altars bears statues that conform to a set arrangement. The Buddhas of the past, present, and future reside on the highest altar. On the tier below is Amitabha, the Buddha of the pure land, flanked by bodhisattvas. Sakyamuni sits below this tier, represented in one of several forms—as a baby, as an ascetic, or as a recumbent Buddha on his way to Nirvana. Various other bodhisattvas and Taoist deities occupy the lowest tiers.

Modern Foreign: With the arrival of French colonists in the mid-19th century came grandiose new edifices, in the neoclassical and art deco styles, with decidedly

Most of Vietnam's vaunted silk cocoons are processed in small factories near Dalat.

European flourishes such as pediments, quoins, and fluted Corinthian columns. Good examples are sprinkled throughout the country, but especially in Hanoi, Ho Chi Minh City, Dalat, and Haiphong. In the 1920s, French architect Ernest Hebrard popularized a fusion of French and Vietnamese architectural styles as the Indochinese style.

After the French War, the Soviets influenced Vietnamese architecture with functional rectangular buildings. Some interesting examples include the People's Committee building and Ho Chi Minh's Mausoleum, both in Hanoi.

Modern architectural influences can be seen in styles varying from Trang Tien Plaza shopping center's pseudoclassical facade in Hanoi to the futuristic Sofitel Plaza Hotel in Saigon. Glass-and-concrete high-rises in Ho Chi Minh City represent mainstream international traditions.

Victor Tardieu's "Portrait de Femme Assise," painted in the early 20th century

Cham Art & Architecture: From the 600s to the 1400s, Vietnam's south-central coast was dominated by Champa, a kingdom best known for its brick temple towers that dot the region and its Hindu-influenced sculpture. In recent years, many of these eye-catching structures have been restored to their former glory, showing a shift in government policy away from assimilation of minority cultures toward an emphasis on the diversity of Vietnamese culture.

The Cham tower is the most distinctive representation of that culture's architecture. The brick-built towers, known as *kalan,* rise in three stages—a base that represents the material realm, a square central section that evokes the realm of premonition, and a pyramidal top that symbolizes the spiritual realm. Inside the temple, worshippers pay homage to the chief divinity at a pedestal altar surrounded by corridors used by priests. The kalan was the centerpiece of a walled complex that included other towers and cult houses.

Brahma, Vishnu, and Siva reigned as the trinity of Cham gods and are liberally represented in statues and bas-relief on Cham temples and towers.

Painting

Despite a relatively late jump on the fine arts, the modern art scene in Vietnam is conspicuous and as vibrant as any other community in Southeast Asia. Where the Chinese accorded equivalent artistic status to painting and literature, the Vietnamese always ranked literature as the higher art form. Until the founding of the Indochina School of Fine Arts in 1925, painting fell under the folk art category in Vietnam and was most obviously practiced as an extension of wood carving.

In Red River Delta towns like Dong Ho, recognized by UNESCO as a traditional crafts village, artisans carve drawings into woodblocks and use these as printmaking templates, especially at holidays such as Tet. Motifs range from flowers to the Trung sisters to boys riding water buffalo or harvesting coconuts. Families pass down these woodcuts for generations.

Victor Tardieu (1870–1937) is widely regarded as the father of modern art in Vietnam. A Frenchman who provided more than lip service to the condescending notion of *mission civilisatrice,* Tardieu culled the most promising talent from throughout the country and nurtured the first generation of serious fine artists. Students painted with oil and lacquer and to a lesser extent on silk. After the country was partitioned in 1954, the northern school continued to draw most of its inspiration from the village and traditional crafts, while the southern school ventured West for additional themes.

In the mid-1950s, the communist government ordained social realism as the preferred style for its painters. Those who found inspiration in politics and propaganda, like Ran Van Ca, depicted a muscular, well-fed peasantry at work in bountiful fields using tractors that never rust. The illustrations did not ask questions of its audience but provided examples of strength, tenacity, and optimism. Other painters responded by publicly dabbling in sanctioned art, but going underground to follow their own muse. Artists like Bui Xuan Phai painted on whatever they could, including cardboard, matchboxes, newspapers, and old schoolbooks.

In the mid-1980s, the government loosened its grip on the content of Vietnamese imagery, and by the mid-1990s the country was awash with painters. Today, artists such as Le Hong Thai, Le Quang Ha, and Dinh Y Nhi are respected for their honest depictions of the human condition.

Art galleries command the tourist hubs of major cities, offering stunning reproductions of European masterworks and prime examples of homegrown art. Because their work is often plagued by copycat piracy, the best Vietnamese painters often keep their most affecting work out of the galleries and instead offer private showings.

In the 1300s, the country adopted the cobalt blue motif from China that remains prevalent on regional pottery.

Ceramics

Vietnam's stoneware traditions are rooted in Neolithic times, but it wasn't until independence from China in the tenth century that ceramic arts and crafts really took off. In the 1300s, the country adopted the cobalt blue motif from China that remains prevalent on regional pottery. In the 1400s, after a Chinese emperor imposed a ban on certain "blue-and-white" motifs, the demand for Vietnam's work grew throughout Southeast Asia and as far away as the Middle East.

Where the Chinese applied a rigid hand to the ornamentation of vases and plates, Vietnamese potters cultivated a more spontaneous touch. They rejected the school that adhered to "one color, one decor" and mixed motifs, combining chrysanthemums and dragons, for example, on the same piece.

In handicraft villages throughout the Red River Delta, especially at Bat Trang and Chu Dau, artisans turned out everyday objects, as well as such ceremonial objects as fluted vases, incense burners, and altar pieces. Active since the 15th century, Bat Trang is renowned for its lightness and the blurred intensity of its interpretations.

Historically, Vietnamese potters did not limit themselves to blue and white or to artistry dyed into the clay before firing. After an initial firing, a potter might add a colorful enamel overlay, elaborate on the design, and fire the piece again before glazing.

After Bat Trang's heyday in the 18th and 19th centuries, Bien Hoa, near Ho Chi Minh City, emerged as an important ceramics center. In 1903, the French opened the Bien Hoa College of Applied Arts. Artisans fused Asian and Occidental techniques in pieces that won awards at international exhibitions throughout the mid–20th century. Unlike Bat Trang potters, who painted their works, Bien Hoa artisans incised motifs into their wares.

Both Bat Trang and Bien Hoa continue to produce ceramics for the domestic and export markets. The market is glutted with ceramics from all over Vietnam, so much so that it's become difficult to distinguish quality ceramics from cheap imitations.

After Bat Trang's heyday in the 18th and 19th centuries, Bien Hoa, near Ho Chi Minh City, emerged as an important ceramics center.

Lacquerware

Travelers to Vietnam see so much lacquerware in tourist haunts that a bias inevitably arises against mother-of-pearl on lacquered backdrops. Although lacquerware has been exploited for mass consumption and all too often indulges images of archetypes such as boys on water buffalo, the medium is a specialty of East Asia and, in the right hands, a highly evocative means of expression.

Not surprisingly, the tradition derives from earlier Chinese developments and first came to prominence during the Ly dynasty (1010–1225) when an ambassador returned from a trip north with lacquering skills. Lacquer is made from the sap of the *cay son* tree. The white sap is collected at night, as sunlight darkens it.

In the 1400s, the art matured in temples and communal halls *(dinh),* where jackfruit pillars were coated in vermilion lacquer and polished to a high sheen with pumice stone. Because lacquer is an excellent defense against rot, the strategy was employed for the preservation of everything from bowls to teeth.

In the 1930s, under the tutelage of French painter Joseph Inguimberty, the medium rose from folk art status to the fine arts and achieved remarkably abstract intensity in the hands of such modern masters as Nguyen Gia Tri and Nguyen Lam.

The art form requires months to prepare wood surfaces and months more to execute the painting. The techniques involve engraving, inlaying, polishing, and coloration. Usually, the palate is limited to earth tones—black, red, and "cockroach brown"—and to inlays of mother-of-pearl and crushed eggshells.

Theater

For the traveler, water puppetry is by far the most commonly encountered of Vietnam's performance arts (see pp. 64–65). In this thousand-year-old spectacle, carved and painted wooden puppets parade, splash, plunge, and whisk over a watery stage, manipulated by puppeteers concealed behind a gauzy scrim and accompanied by an orchestra of traditional musicians.

As distinctively Vietnamese as water puppetry, *cheo* is a form of folk opera that originated in the Red River Delta in the 11th century. Traditionally, the stage was no more complicated than a straw mat unfurled before the village communal hall in an open-air setting. A drum or a gong anchors an orchestra of traditional instruments, including a moon-faced lute and flute. Characters sing and speak in a declamatory style, interpreting familiar stories that often have roots in China, like *The Tale of Kieu.* Actors accent the gist of their songs and speech with exaggerated foot and hand gestures that clue the audience into the character's intention. Songs tend to praise women and deride men through sarcasm. The audience often banters with the actors, who are free to improvise and swerve the skit in a direction that feels right for the moment.

Folk opera eventually found its way to the courts, but the aristocracy and scholars denounced the form as vulgar and rejected it, instead favoring a 700-year-old classical form of theater known as *tuong*. This theatrical style peaked during the Nguyen dynasty and, not surprisingly, reveled in epic tales of war, heroism, and court life in which virtue would inevitably prevail.

Tuong, like cheo, makes no feint toward realism. Red-faced actors are virtuous heroes, white-faced characters evil villains. Costumes are colorful, and actors' movements are stylized. To embellish emotions, actors peal off lines in distinctive diaphragm-guttural and mouth-resonating timbres.

In the 1920s, the burgeoning middle class popularized a new form of classical theater known as *cai luong*. Founded in Saigon, cai luong drifted from the Confucian ethos that infused tuong theater and focused on modern stories from pop novels, Chinese swashbucklers, and such Western literature as Molière's *The Miser*.

Only in Vietnam

Although Vietnam shares some cultural elements with its neighbors, several items are unique, instantly recognizable as Vietnamese: water puppets; *non la*, a distinctive conical hat; *ao dai*, the elegant national dress of flowing top worn over close-fitting pants; and *dan bau*, a single-stringed instrument with a sound that mimics vocal inflections.

Music

Pop music, blaring in karaoke bars and cafés, inundates Vietnam's contemporary soundscape with synthesized, melancholy love songs, yet deeper musical traditions quietly endure. The country celebrates various genres, including court music *(nha nhac)*, ritual gong music of the central highlands, folk songs *(quan ho)*, and chamber music *(ca tru)*. In 2003, 2005, and 2009 respectively, UNESCO recognized these musical forms as Masterpieces of the Oral and Intangible Heritage of Humanity.

Nha nhac means "elegant music," though "elegance" is hardly the right word for this ritual music that accompanied court ceremonies from the 15th to 20th centuries. It's more brash than sublime, freewheeling and sometimes chaotic. As in jazz, each musician orbits a commonly understood core, improvising within limits imposed by a commanding drum until called in by the cadence.

More instrumental than lyrical, the richly textured music evokes the landscape of an Asian ink brush painting. In the imperial era, the Nguyens retained both a light orchestra and a grand orchestra whose instruments consisted of lutes and flutes, clappers, and a broad array of percussion instruments such as a lithophone, cymbals, and hide drums. Today, nha nhac is performed daily in the Royal Theater of Hue's Imperial City.

In the central highlands, villagers bang gongs to commune with the supernatural world when celebrating births, weddings, housewarmings, buffalo sacrifices, and harvests. Groups of 3 to 21 musicians pound the flat or dish-shaped gongs in rhythm or in dialogues. The primitive music is not so much a masterpiece as a curious relic from human prehistory. In the villages of the Bahnar (Ba Na), E De, and Giarai, the highlanders often perform gong music to welcome guests to the communal house.

The "ho" in quan ho is rooted in the Vietnamese word for "raise the voice." These folk songs originated on the rice paddies of the Red River, where farmers used music to stimulate labor. Ho evolved into songs sung at rest and songs sung at festivals in call-and-response competitions.

The high-collared *ao dai* silk dress is both an homage to tradition and an everyday garment.

Monochords and bamboo flutes cushion lyrics that skirt melancholy tones and celebrate love in a more cheerful manner. Quan ho is as rooted to Bac Ninh Province as *pho* is rooted to Hanoi. Bac Ninh remains one of the premier venues, especially during the Quan Ho Festival, held every year after Tet.

Like quan ho, ca tru chamber music no longer appeals to young people, who complain that it doesn't play well in the modern era. It was born of the Vietnamese aristocracy that matured in the 11th century.

Ca tru singers, mostly female, performed in the royal courts, in aristocrats' homes, and for male audiences at special inns. The singer's voice is high-pitched and nasal. Her songs make music of the country's poetry. While she strikes a bamboo clapper to keep time, a musician on a long-necked lute provides the only instrumentation, though a judge in the seats does beat a small drum to express his appreciation for the performance. The audience dispenses bamboo sticks, known as *tru,* to the singer as tokens of their approval. Since being granted recognition by UNESCO in 2009, ca tru has enjoyed a revival, and visitors to Hanoi can experience its haunting sound in the Old Quarter (see Travelwise p. 264).

Fashion

The *ao dai* (long shirt) is a high-collared silk dress that Vietnamese women wear over blousy trousers. The long-sleeved garment flatters the feminine physique, molding to the arms, bosom, and waist, divulging every curve yet exposing nothing. The dress splits at the hips and flows as far as the ankles in front and rear panels. The ao dai debuted in Hanoi in 1934 as women rebelled against stodgy Confucian mores. In this modern age, women indulged in makeup, fancy hairdos, high heels, and–thanks to a reinterpretation of an older style dress by a graduate of the Fine Arts College–the ao dai.

Even more distinctively Vietnamese than the ao dai, the *non la* (conical hat) shelters farmers from tropical sun and monsoon rains like a mobile parasol. The hat is made from latania palm leaves woven about a bamboo lath. ■

Replete with a bustling Old Quarter, colonial architecture, and age-old traditions, the capital of Vietnam since A.D. 1010

Hanoi

Hoa Lo Prison relief of colonial jailer

Hanoi

While much of the world boomed in the wake of World War II, Hanoi hunkered down for another half century of hot war, cold war, and privation. This sacrifice of the city's residents is our boon, for today Hanoi is one of Southeast Asia's most captivating cities. Its Old Quarter, colonial French districts, thousand-year-old temples, and spate of lakes can feel more conjured than real.

Pedestrians beware: The streets of downtown Hanoi buzz with mopeds and motorcycles.

The city lies on the Red River in the midst of Vietnam's second most fertile region and at the heart of the country's ancient culture. In the sixth century, during Vietnam's tenure as a vassal state, the Chinese founded a settlement here known as Tong Binh, then Dai La. Ly Thai To, the founder of Vietnam's first great dynasty, moved his capital here in 1010 and renamed the settlement Thang Long ("ascending dragon") after apparently spotting a golden dragon in flight over the river. The Nguyen kings moved the capital to Hue in 1804 and renamed the city Hanoi, but Ho Chi Minh and modern Vietnam's founding fathers anointed the northern city as the nation's capital once again in 1945.

The bulldozer of the 20th century made few incursions here. In the bustling Old Quarter, life spills from the maws of 19th-century tube houses onto splendidly crowded

NOT TO BE MISSED:

A stroll beside tranquil Hoan Kiem Lake **62–63**

The marvelous antics of Vietnam's unique water puppets **64–65**

Attractive colonial architecture in the French Quarter **66–69**

Discovering the country's rich past at the History Museum **67 & 69**

Remembering the conflicts of the past at Hoa Lo Prison **69**

A walk through the colorful streets of the Old Quarter **70–72**

Visiting Vietnam's first university at the Temple of Literature **76–79**

Paying Uncle Ho a visit at the Ho Chi Minh Mausoleum **80–81** sidewalks and streets. The French districts, with their Indochinese architectural marvels and art moderne villas, do evoke a pinch of nostalgia for colonial days, no matter how you feel about colonialism.

Since the late 1980s and the advent of the *doi moi* (fiscal renovation policy), Hanoi's infrastructure has upgraded from the deplorable to the grandiose. Local chefs are whipping up some of the most creative East-meets-West concoctions, yet at reasonable prices. Museums showcase the country's most precious artifacts, covering anthropology, dynastic relics, ethnography, revolutionary history, and the fine arts. You could easily spend a week in this metropolis of nearly seven million people and never eat a drab meal or lapse into a dull moment.

A number of sites in the north (see pp. 85–110) are most conveniently experienced in day trips from the capital. ■

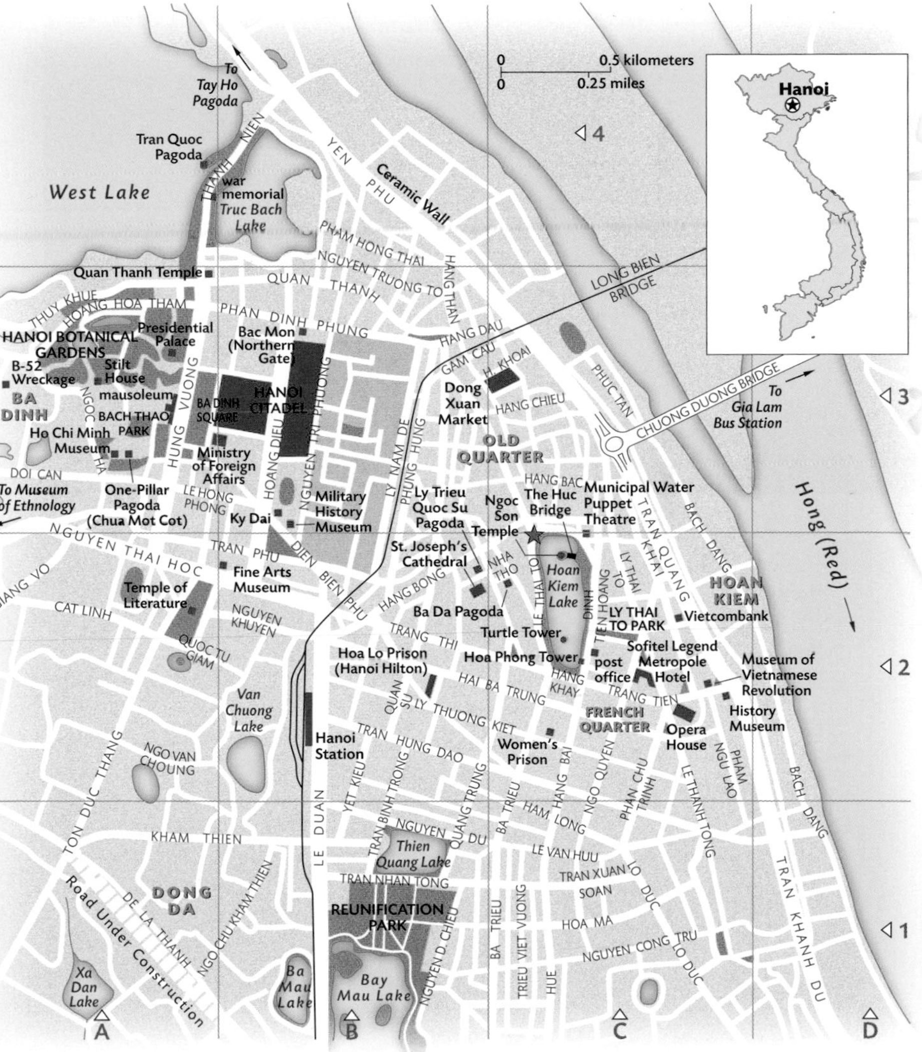

Hoan Kiem Lake & Surrounds

Hoan Kiem Lake is a medallion of avocado green water in the city. The southern fringe borders the colonial French Quarter (see pp. 66–69) while the northern section brushes the storied Old Quarter (see pp. 70–72). This 25-acre (10 ha) oasis is rimmed by a shady promenade abuzz with peddlers, hustlers, lovers, chess players, and tourists. A stroll around this soulful space, celebrated in poems, songs, and legend, is the best introduction to Hanoi.

After the Red River shifted course, this lake remained as a "souvenir" for the people of Thang Long.

Hanoi
Map 61
Visitor Information
Address: Hanoi Toserco, 8 To Hien Thanh
Phone: 04/3976-0066

Hoan Kiem Lake
Map 61 C2
Address: Entrance to Ngoc Son Temple near Dinh Tien Hoang at Lo Su
Admission: $

Locals say you can't know Hanoi unless you know Hoan Kiem.

Hoan Kiem was once part of the Red River, but sometime after 1490, the river shifted, leaving this stretch. The lake achieved legendary status during the 15th-century reign of Le Loi when a giant tortoise seized a sword the emperor had used to oust Chinese occupation forces. Formerly known as Luc Thuy ("green water"), the lake was thereafter dubbed Hoan Kiem ("lake of the restored sword").

The main attraction here is **Ngoc Son** ("jade mountain") **Temple,** on a tiny island at the lake's northern end. Rising from a mound between its two entrance pillars is the five-story **Ink Brush Tower.** The pillars are inscribed with the Chinese characters for happiness and fortune, while the tower itself bears the inscription *Ta Thanh Thien*, which translates as "writing on the clear blue sky."

To reach the temple, cross the red arc of **The Huc Bridge,** passing the **Dac Nguyet** ("receiving the moon") and **Tran Ba Ding** ("wave-calming") **Pavilions,** which shield the temple from the lake. Beyond Ngoc Son's rather dull entry hall, the middle bay commemorates the temple's three patron saints—Van Xuong, guardian of literature; Quan Vu, master of martial arts; and Lac To, protector of medicinal arts. The innermost bay honors Tran Hung Dao, the 13th-century hero who conducted naval exercises on the lake prior to his celebrated rout of the Mongols.

INSIDER TIP:

Get up early in Hanoi to exercise with the locals. Around Hoan Kiem Lake, you will find tai chi, coordinated aerobics, badminton games, and people walking in silk pajamas.

—CATHERINE WORKMAN
National Geographic grantee

On an island to the south, the landmark **Turtle Tower** is reputed to summon the lake's resident giant softshell tortoises (see sidebar below). An impressive 550-pound (250 kg) preserved specimen is on display at Ngoc Son Temple.

To appreciate the colonial legacy of the French Quarter start at the south end of Hoan Kiem Lake, where the French started to build shortly after the bombardment of the Hanoi Citadel in 1882. Take note of **3 Hang Khay,** perhaps the city's oldest extant colonial building.

Up the east side of Hoan Kiem Lake, you'll pass the **Hoa Phong** ("peaceful wind") **Tower,** a remnant of Bao An Pagoda, which the French razed to make room for colonial structures. Across Dinh Tien Hoang, the whole face of this urban block is consumed by the post office, a rather grim Soviet-inspired edifice sandwiched between two colonial buildings.

Check out the colonial-era octagonal bandstand in nearby **Ly Thai To Park.** In 1954, the Vietnamese named this park in honor of Le Loi's victory there over Ming Chinese invaders in 1427. While named Indira Gandhi Park in 1986, to recognize India's long friendship, it reverted to Ly Thai To Park, in preparation for the city's thousandth anniversary in 2010. ■

Turtle Rescue

Never has Hoan Kiem Lake attracted so much attention as during March–June 2011, when an injured giant softshell turtle was rescued, given treatment, and rereleased in the lake. Previous sightings had been so rare that many people thought the giant turtles were the stuff of legend, but this 375-pound (170 kg) monster is now believed to be one of only four of the species *rafetus swinhoei* in existence, and the only one still alive in Hoan Kiem Lake. Pollution and the introduction of red-eared sliders *(Trachemys scripta elegans)*—a small species of turtle—to the lake were thought to be the cause of the giant turtle's wounds.

Water Puppets

Water puppetry is a thousand-year-old Vietnamese performance art with deep roots in the wet rice agriculture of the Red River Delta. Carved from fig wood, then painted and lacquered to a high, distinctive sheen, the madcap puppets careen over a watery stage, enacting skits drawn from Vietnam's treasury of folklore and history.

Historically, the paddy water of a rice field or a village communal pond served as the stage, but today most shows play out in basins of water at theaters like Thang Long in Hanoi. Unlike marionettes or hand puppets, which are controlled from above, water puppets are manipulated by submerged rods and strings operated by puppeteers standing in thigh-deep water behind the scrim of a stage set. For some of the more rigorous acts, several people work a single pole.

In bygone eras, water puppeteers formed guilds and closely guarded the tricks of their trade from neighboring villages. They were especially secretive with regard to the apparatus that gives a puppet its dramatic flair. What you don't see in the opaque water are the 10- to 13-foot (3–4 m) bamboo rods with pincerlike tools built into each puppet's float.

A system of submerged rods and pulleys control the water puppets' antics on the watery stage.

Though the puppets can be as tall as 40 inches (102 cm) and weigh up to 35 pounds (16 kg), most are slighter, standing about 16 inches (41 cm) high on a buoyant wooden base or float that plows along just beneath the water's surface. The lyrically expressive characters are fashioned in linked segments to maximize their agility and flair, especially through the arms and the head, which occasionally flies off in a scripted decapitation!

INSIDER TIP:

The best place to catch a show is Thang Long, on the east side of Hoan Lake. Even if you don't know Vietnamese, there's enough action to get the gist.

—BARBARA A. NOE
National Geographic Travel Books senior editor

At Thang Long (see Travelwise p. 264), Vietnam's premier venue for the art, a 45-minute performance skitters through 17 episodes drawn from legends and myths, such as Le Loi's return of the magic sword to the golden tortoise of Hoan Kiem Lake and the dance of the four Holy Animals (dragon, lion-dog, phoenix, and tortoise) of Vietnamese mythology. Most sketches also pay tribute to the trials, tribulations, and triumphs of common folk going about their daily business. A traditional orchestra conducts a clamorous sound track while *cheo* (popular opera) singers narrate the dialogue and action.

In nearly every water puppet performance, you'll meet a poor farmer who brags about his ducks until one is snatched by a fox that runs up a tree. You're also likely to see boy puppets swimming after frogs and playing flutes from a perch on the back of a water buffalo.

Water puppet skits exalt the folklife of rural Vietnam—its culture, traditions, and beliefs.

The most beloved character in all of water puppetry is Teu, an ever smiling buffoon, not unlike the Punch of British puppetry, who wears a loincloth and waistcoat and styles his hair in three tufts that sprout from an otherwise bald pate. Uncle Teu is the sharp-tongued master of ceremonies and something of a clodhopper, though he also stands as a symbol of Vietnam's indomitable spirit.

Popular in the north, water puppetry was seldom practiced in the south until modern times. On special occasions, performances at Thay Pagoda (see pp. 91–92) are held on a *thuy dinh* (stage set) that's more than 300 years old.

The French Quarter

However you may regard the French colonization of Vietnam, there's much to admire in the magnificent buildings that survived the occupation. In Hanoi, the French clustered their architectural gems in two districts and on two scales—residential and municipal. Even if you have no sympathy for the *mission civilisatrice* (civilizing mission), you can't help but admire the architectural feats of the French as you gaze at these buildings.

French Quarter
61 C2
tosercohanoi.com

Directly east of **Ly Thai To Park** on Ngo Quyen is an imposing government building, formerly known as the Banque d'Indochine. This 1930 art deco structure is a no-nonsense symbol of financial stability. Note the fusion of East and West in the Chinese characters for happiness and longevity on the building's upper reaches.

Turn right on Ngo Quyen, and on the right you'll find the former palace of the French governor of Tonkin. Shuttered and idle, this 1918 beaux arts structure with a many-petaled portico now serves as a **government guesthouse.** Ho Chi Minh slept here for a short time in 1946.

Visitors today would rather book a room across the street at the **Sofitel Legend Metropole Hotel** *(15 Ngo Quyen;* see Travelwise p. 246), whose guests have included Charlie Chaplin, Graham Greene, and Jane Fonda; they all stayed on the second floor of the 1901 colonial building. Note the immaculate white exterior, the Ionic pilasters, balustraded balconies, and green shutters, a hallmark of colonial French aesthetics.

At the end of the block, turn left on Trang Tien to reach the grande dame of the city's French architectural legacy—the **Opera House.** Built between 1902 and 1911, the still active space (see Travelwise p. 264) is the most opulent of Vietnam's three French-designed municipal theaters. After the Japanese surrender in 1945, some

A bride borrows the majesty of the colonial Opera House as a backdrop for her wedding photos.

20,000 locals rallied at the Opera House, and the Viet Minh seized control of the rally—its boldest demonstration of power to date.

History Museum

The History Museum (Bao Tang Lich Su) is the most powerful French colonial building in Vietnam, a masterpiece of the Indochinese style developed by Ernest Hebrard in the 1920s and '30s. The museum's exhibits, which survey Vietnamese history from 500,000 B.C. to the 1940s, are a worthy complement to the grandeur of the building.

Upon completion in 1932, the building housed artifacts collected by members of the École Française d'Extrême-Orient, whose emblem is embossed on the upper facade of the octagonal tower. Before entering, stroll past the stelae, stupas, and stone gongs on the building's right side for a broad view of its long, balconied back.

Inside, you'll begin your finely presented, artifact-rich journey in the **Stone Age,** with adzes, axes, and skulls, soon encountering the museum's finest objects, the Dong Son drums. Cast in the Red River Delta as far back as two millennia, these bronze drums were used at festivals, to pray for rain, and to rally for war. Note the four frogs perched on the tympanum of the 2,000-year-old Thon Bui drum. To the left of the drum collection is a 2,000-year-old bronze burial jar from Yen Bai, capped with tiny copulating figures.

Also on the first floor, the **Ly exhibits** include a turtle stela with an upright stone slab, raised by Ly Thuong Kiet at the opening of the Linh Xung Pagoda in 1126, some 350 years before Le Thanh Tong inaugurated this genre of statuary at the Temple of Literature (see pp. 76–79). The **Tran exhibits** glorify the battle of Bach Dang River in 1288 with a panoramic 1979 painting and some of the actual stakes used to impale the Mongol fleet. Also look for the goggle-eyed terra-cotta dragons with Jaggeresque lolling tongues.

Upstairs, sandstone **Cham art** rims the rotunda. Look for a replica of Vietnam's most significant Buddhist statue, the Thousand-Hand, Thousand-Eye Goddess of Mercy from But Thap Pagoda in Bac Ninh (see p. 93); it's not marked as a replica, a common oversight at Vietnamese museums.

History Museum

- 61 C2
- 1 Trang Tien & 25 Tong Dan
- 04/3825-2853
- Closed Mon. & noon–1:30 p.m.
- $

baotanglichsu.vn

Colonial Architecture

French colonial architecture is more evident in Hanoi than in any other Vietnamese city, and admiring the shuttered windows and elaborate decorations on the city's elegant buildings is a real treat for visitors. Many of the city's finest buildings, including the History Museum, were designed by Ernest Hebrard (1875–1933), a renowned French architect. A number of these fine old colonial structures have recently been restored to their former glory and now function as embassies and ambassadors' homes.

War Tourism in Vietnam

Ironically, places associated with wars exert a magnetic attraction on visitors to a country. This is especially true in Vietnam, perhaps in part due to the number of movies that have been made about the Vietnam War. Places like China Beach, My Lai, the Cu Chi Tunnels, the demilitarized zone (DMZ), the Hanoi Hilton (Hoa Lo Prison), and Dien Bien Phu feature high on visitors' lists of sites to see.

Visitors to the war museum in Hue on September 2, Vietnam's national day, span generations.

This curiosity is understandable in the case of war veterans, many of whom want to return to the sites that are associated with traumatic memories from decades ago in the hope that such a visit will lay to rest any lingering demons in their minds. Some tour agents specialize in tours for veterans, and there is no shortage of ex-soldiers eager to revisit sites of strong personal significance.

However, this trend does not explain why thousands of regular tourists flock to Cu Chi (see pp. 214–216) each day to see the tunnels that played a big part in the war's eventual outcome. In this case it is the sheer ingenuity of the local people, born out of necessity and a strong urge to survive, that captures visitors' imagination. In Ho Chi Minh City, the War Remnants Museum (see pp. 204–205) is hugely popular, despite (or perhaps because of) the fact that its content is strong enough to draw tears.

From another perspective, it is almost impossible for visitors to Vietnam to avoid visiting sites associated with wars since they are all over the country. Every small village has its war memorial and lines of gravestones that act as a chilling reminder of the devastation this country has suffered.

War tourism is not restricted to foreign visitors. As Vietnam's economy improves and its people find they have enough money to explore their own country, many of them choose to visit sites such as the prisons on Con Son Island (see p. 233), where cruel treatment by French and later American jailers led to an unshakable belief among prisoners in the need for sovereignty. Such visits generate pride and patriotic zeal among young Vietnamese.

Ironic or not, war tourism is big business in Vietnam and a major factor in the steady growth in tourist arrivals to the country.

At the end of the hall is a collection of **Nguyen dynasty artifacts,** including screens, urns, a mandarin's robes, and illustrations of the Nguyen Court from 1895.

The displays continue across the street at 25 Tong Dan, in a building formerly occupied by the **Museum of Vietnamese Revolution.** Exhibits here focus on the 20th-century struggle for independence against the French and Americans.

The Women's Prison

Since being remodelled a few years ago, this is one of Hanoi's most interesting museums. Displays include video clips on various aspects of the lives of Vietnamese women, with themes of family,

INSIDER TIP:

The Vietnamese spend little time rehashing the particulars, or debating the merits of who shot whom, where, and why in a war that's been over for 40 years.

—JON BOWERMASTER
National Geographic author

history, and fashion. The ground floor focuses on their role as street vendors, toting goods on bamboo yokes, while the second floor covers their role in the wars of liberation. The third floor shifts the emphasis to family life, and the top floor presents an eye-catching array of costumes worn by the country's ethnic groups.

Hoa Lo Prison

Hoa Lo Prison was known to Americans as the Hanoi Hilton, a grimly ironic moniker coined by American pilots incarcerated here from 1964 to 1973.

In the 1890s, the French drafted plans for Maison Centrale prison, obliterating a village to make room. Originally built to house 450 inmates, the prison held some 2,000 between 1950 and 1953. A high-rise now occupies most of the former prison grounds, but the old jail's southeast corner was preserved in 1993 as a memorial.

Beyond the main doorway turn right into a room where a diorama and photos detail a colonial-style compound. One picture on the wall shows inmates fettered to wide benches following a 1908 poisoning incident in Ha Thanh; the actual benches are in the next room. In the aboveground cells, jailers shackled prisoners to sloped concrete slabs; oily stains from inmates' hands and buttocks testify to long periods of detention.

Outside, an excavated sewer canal reveals the means of escape for a hundred prisoners at the end of World War II.

In two small **POW exhibit halls,** the museum makes its case for how well the North Vietnamese treated U.S. prisoners and displays "detainees'" toothbrushes, sweaters, beds, and even a volleyball net. The room to the right offers photos of POWs.

The **Death Cell sector** holds several cells, one of two guillotines used by the French, and a metal barrel used for water torture. ■

The Women's Prison
- Map: 61 C2
- Address: 36 Ly Thuong Kiet
- Tel: 04/3825-9936
- Price: $

womenmuseum.org.vn

Hoa Lo Prison
- Map: 61 B2
- Address: 1 Hoa Lo, Hoan Kiem District
- Tel: 04/3824-6358
- Price: $

A Walk Around the Old Quarter

Hanoi's Old Quarter is a warren of shops, still bustling 600 years after dozens of guilds claimed different stretches of road to market their wares. The byways here are no longer a venue for an exclusive kind of product, but the streets are still named for the merchandise *(hang)* purveyed during imperial times. Traditionally, each guild was associated with an outlying village and raised a temple to pray for prosperity.

Business spills out onto teeming sidewalks in Hanoi's Old Quarter.

From the north end of **Hoan Kiem Lake ❶** (see pp. 62–63), walk up busy Hang Dao, where most shops sell clothing and their displays spill out on to the sidewalk. From Friday through Sunday from around 7 p.m. this street, all the way up to Dong Xuan Market, is closed to traffic and the scene of a vibrant **night market,** with stalls set up along the center of the street.

Cross Hang Bo onto Hang Ngang, and look out for No. 48, which was **Ho Chi Minh's residence ❷** *(closed 11:30 a.m.–1:30 p.m.)* during the summer of 1945. In an apartment on the second floor, Ho invoked the United States' Declaration of Independence while writing a speech he would deliver in Ba Dinh Square on September 2, 1945, declaring independence for Vietnam.

NOT TO BE MISSED:

• Ho Chi Minh's residence • Quon Chuong Gate • Bach Ma Temple • traditional two-story home

Downstairs there are photos and letters from the period, while the upstairs is still furnished with the chairs and table at which the speech was drafted.

Continue walking north along Hang Ngang and Hang Duong, noting the narrow storefronts of the buildings known as **tube houses,** most of which date from the late 19th century. Because there was so little

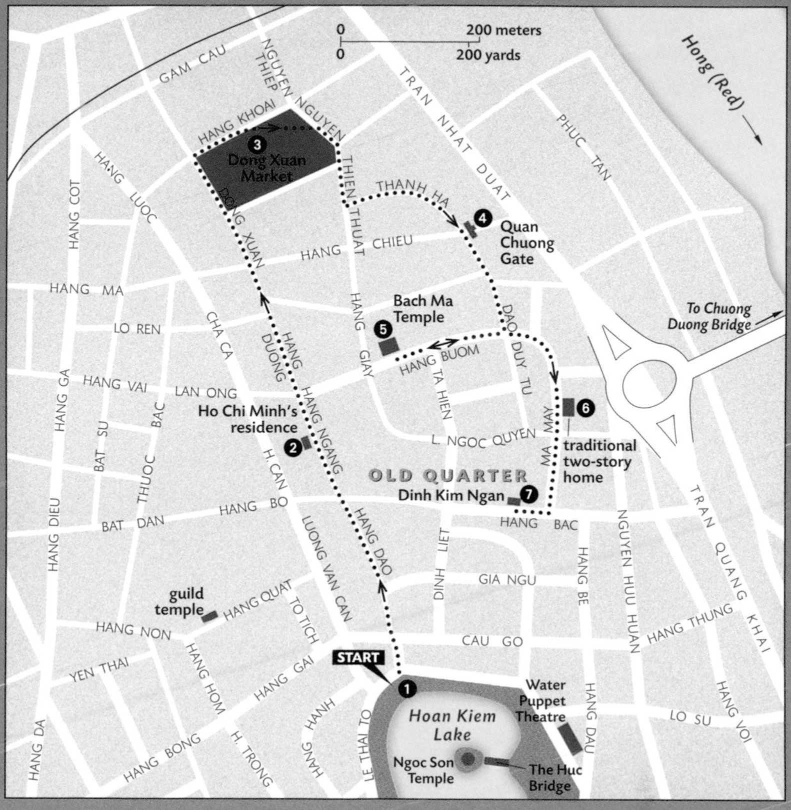

Crossing the Road in Vietnam

Since the traffic never stops, it's extremely difficult to get from one side of the road to the other, and there's a skill to doing it. Find a place near a corner where vehicles are not going too fast. Wait until passing traffic is relatively light, then step out and walk at a steady pace. You'll find that motorbikes and cars veer around you, and miraculously you arrive at the other side in one piece. Take extra care when crossing roads of several lanes, as the speed of approaching vehicles can be difficult to judge.

See also area map p. 61
- Hoan Kiem Lake
- 1 mile (1.6 km)
- 90 minutes
- 42 Hang Bac

space in the old city, and because merchants were taxed according to street frontage, they limited the width of their facades to 7 to 10 feet (2–3 m) and instead built 60 to 200 feet (20–60 m) deep, and sometimes as much as 330 feet (100 m). The country's feudal laws limited tube houses to a single story to thwart would-be assassins using second-floor windows. These days many are stacked five or ten stories high, giving rise to a new term—**rocket houses.**

At 21 Hang Duong is a **merchant's shop** that has remained true to its street's ancient charter. Since the 1930s, but for a hiatus from 1975 to the 1990s, this shop has sold an array of candied fruits—star fruits, apricots, tamarinds, etc. Such treats are prescribed as remedies by practitioners of traditional medicine.

Straight down Dong Xuan, the street's eponymous **market** ❸ fronts a small plaza where colonial authorities built five tin-roofed halls in 1889. The market was rebuilt in 1990, with its preserved original front, but it burned to the ground in 1994. The present structure dates from 1996. A plaque by the main entrance commemorates a 1947 battle between the French and Viet Minh, during

Cosmopolitan spots like this salsa bar breathe new life onto Nha To and surrounding streets.

which the latter destroyed four tanks and sustained one hundred casualties.

Walk through the market, turn right on Nguyen Thien Thuat and then left on Thanh Ha (or Hang Chieu) to approach the **Quan Chuong Gate** ❹. Built in 1749, this triple gate is the only surviving example of 16 gates into a Vietnamese citadel the French destroyed at the end of the 19th century. The gate was originally named Dong Ha, which means "east gate to the Red River."

On Hang Buom (sail), merchants sold sails

INSIDER TIP:

Stroll through Dong Xuan market, filled with all kinds of edible oddities. The tropical fruit is to die for.

—BARBARA A. NOE

National Geographic Travel Books senior editor

for boats that plied the To Lich River, a nearby Red River tributary the French later paved over. At 76 Hang Buom is **Bach Ma** ("white horse") **Temple** ❺ *(closed 11 a.m.–1:30 p.m.)*, one of four temples that protected Hanoi on the north, south, east, and west. Dating from Hanoi's founding in 1010, this eastern guardian is the quarter's oldest structure. The much renovated temple is named for the legendary white horse that showed King Ly Thai To how to orient the walls of his citadel. In the middle bay is a red palanquin that porters tote about the quarter on festival days.

Backtrack along Hang Buom to Ma May. At 87 Ma May is a **traditional two-story home** ❻, built in the late 19th century by a well-to-do practitioner of Chinese medicine. From 1954 to 1999, when the Hanoi People's Committee acquired it, five families lived here. The typical tube house is divided into five bays. The streetside bay is for commerce; the second bay is for storage; the third bay is an open courtyard, also called a heavenly well; the fourth bay is for living quarters; and the fifth bay is the kitchen. This house largely follows this plan, though it includes a second story.

Continue south on Ma May and turn right onto Hang Bac, where many shops still sell their original merchandise—silver. At No. 42 is **Dinh Kim Ngan** ❼ *(closed 11:30 a.m.–2 p.m.)*, one of many communal houses in the Old Quarter that function either as temples or meeting places for the local community. This is where silversmiths used to worship their protective deity, and it still functions as a hub of the community, as well as hosting evening performances of *ca tru* music (see Travelwise p. 264).

West of Hoan Kiem Lake

The area west of Hoan Kiem Lake harbors some of the city's most iconic attractions, from the somber spires of St Joseph's Cathedral to the exquisite Temple of Literature, the recently opened Hanoi Citadel, and the Military History Museum, with its reminders of the country's war-torn past.

St. Joseph's Cathedral

St. Joseph's Cathedral stands at the heart of Hanoi, anchoring the archdiocese's 480 Catholic churches and chapels and 113 parishes. It serves as a vibrant place of worship for Hanoi's 400,000 Catholics.

Built in 1886 by a French missionary, Monsignor Puginier, who wheedled permission from the colonial French government, St. Joe's seeming stone-slab edifice is actually made of brick faced in cement. The facade is bracketed by two square, 103-foot (31.5 m) towers hung with five bells each. Tall stained-glass windows, pointed arches, and high rib-vaulted ceilings call to mind medieval Europe.

The slightly unkempt nave is a casualty of the tropical climate, but the sanctuary glistens, a spectacle of red- and gilt-trimmed wood carving reminiscent of Phat Diem Cathedral (see p. 116) and the imperial aesthetics of Hue architecture. In a further nod to local customs, a red-and-gilt palanquin bearing a statue of the Virgin Mary occupies the left side of the nave.

The cathedral lies at the end of Nha Tho ("church") Street, a short, trendy thoroughfare of cafés, restaurants, and boutiques selling the latest fashion accessories. Tucked between two shops (at #3), a narrow passageway leads into the compound of **Ba Da Pagoda,** whose roots stretch back to 1056 and the reign of Ly Than Ton. In 1946, Ho Chi Minh paid a visit and urged the monks to engage in the struggle for independence.

A short distance up Ly Quoc Su from the cathedral is **Ly Trieu Quoc Su Pagoda.** In the main temple, long tangerine-colored parallel sentences hang from tall hardwood columns. In the right

St. Joseph's Cathedral

- 61 B2
- Nha Tho
- 04/3828-5967
- Closed noon–2 p.m.

The imposing Gothic facade of St. Joseph's Cathedral, at the end of Hanoi's trendy Nha Tho, evokes medieval Europe.

Hanoi Citadel
61 B2–3
9 Hoang Dieu
04/3734-5427
Closed Mon. & 11:30 a.m.–2:00 p.m. daily
$

bay is a gallery of deceased monks, while the left bay contains a gallery of candy-colored statues.

Hanoi Citadel

Listed by UNESCO as a World Heritage site in 2010, Hanoi Citadel is now open to the public after hundreds of years as the exclusive domain of Vietnam's imperial elite. Unlike the Hue Citadel (see pp. 131, 134), which remains intact, the 12-acre (5 ha) Hanoi Citadel is a fragmented collection of monuments.

EXPERIENCE: Drinking in a *Bia Hoi* Bar

An essential Vietnamese experience is to enjoy a few glasses of draft beer *(bia hoi)* with friends at a bia hoi bar. These bars are scattered around the country but are especially noticeable in Hanoi—crowded storefronts where everybody sits on low stools, quaffing locally made beer, nibbling on tapas-type snacks, and discussing everything under the sun.

Bia hoi contains no preservatives, so it needs to be consumed soon after it is made, but with a price tag of around 25 cents a glass, demand is not lacking. For an atmospheric introduction to the art of drinking bia hoi, make your way to **Bia Hoi Ngoc Linh** at 2 Pho Duang Thanh on the western edge of the Old Quarter.

After moving the capital to Hanoi in 1010, Ly Thai To added to the citadel first erected by Chinese governors more than two centuries earlier.

Successive dynasties added more buildings, but the French razed much of the site when they took command of the city in the late 19th century.

The most visible aspect of the complex, at its southern end, is the **Cat Co,** a 60-foot (18.2 m) flag tower with six fan-shaped windows and 36 flower-shaped windows, which was added by the first Nguyen king, Gia Long, in 1805. It is accessed via the Military History Museum on Dien Bien Phu (see p. 75), and you can climb the tower for limited city views.

From the main entrance to the central section of the citadel on Hoang Dieu, visitors turn left to see five significant structures, the first of which is the **Doan Mon,** or central gate, where the ticket office is located. This massive wall, which supports a pavilion topped by a double-layer roof with upturned eaves, is penetrated by five, tunnel-like arches, and once served as the principal entrance to the king's forbidden realm.

Beyond this gate are excavations that have revealed bricks laid down as long ago as the Ly dynasty (1009–1225), and an impressive waterway, thought to be part of an ancient irrigation system. Continuing northward, the next significant remains are two dragon balustrades on a flight of steps that once led to the **Kinh Tien Palace,** which was demolished in the late 1800s.

The next structure, the **D67 Building,** was built in 1967. The interior conjures up the war conferences that took place here in the late 1960s: The names of participants still sit on the table, including General Giap, the military mastermind whose death in

2013 stirred a national outbreak of grief. Deep below the building is a fortified bunker.

North of this building are the **Hau Lau,** the "back pavilion" or "palace of the princesses," and the **Bac Mon** (Northern Gate). Cross the road to the archaeological site at **18 Hoang Dieu** (via a gate to the west of Kinh Tien Palace) to appreciate the enormity of the original site. When foundations were being dug in 2002 for a new National Assembly, priceless artefacts were unearthed that clearly indicated the location of more royal palaces, so the site of the Assembly was moved farther west to preserve this precious heritage.

Other Museums

The **Fine Arts Museum** houses the country's foremost collection of ceramics, sculpture, and painting and is a "must-see" for art lovers. Much of the art on the ground floor originated in Red River Delta pagodas and communal houses. The wood carvings of village festivals, wrestling, and tiger fighting are masterpieces of the form. Also look for the intricately carved doors from Pho Minh and Keo Pagodas. The two upper floors survey fine art painting, which didn't really start in Vietnam until the 1930s. The lacquer and silk paintings are particularly interesting, and the ceramics gallery is in an adjoining annex.

A short walk away, the **Military History Museum** is a tribute to national defense, from the ancient days of arrowheads and breastplates up to Vietnam's recent wars. A highlight is the T-54 tank that crashed through the gates of Saigon's Presidential Palace during the city's fall in 1975.

Museum of Ethnology:

The art and culture of Vietnam's minorities are lionized in the Museum of Ethnology, which proves worth the trip to the city's western fringes. Allow lots of time to take in the stunning open-air exhibitions, where the path leads first to a fenced compound of five **Cham houses.** At the central Thang Lam, peer inside the *garong,* a wheeled trunk used to preserve a dead ancestor's belongings and a box containing the forehead bone.

The most commanding structure is a 62-foot-high (19 m) **Bahnar** (or Ba Na) **communal house,** with pitched roof panels of 1,800 square feet (170 sq m) each. Climb any of the four hewn logs onto the 970-square-foot (90 sq m) bamboo-planked floor, where villagers met for war councils, rituals, and celebrations.

The 138-foot-long (42 m) **Ede house** is remarkable for both its length and its roots in a matrilineal ethnic group, as underscored by none-too-subtle breasts carved into one of the hewn stairways. As conspicuous are the carved penises on the servants of the dead who form a wall of statuary around the nearby **Giarai tomb**.

Inside the museum, dioramas of ethnic activities—funerals, initiation rites—accompany videos of these events. Highlights include a cultural exploration of Vietnam's ethnic majority, the Kinh, or Viet. ■

Fine Arts Museum

- Map: 61 B2
- Address: 66 Nguyen Thai Hoc
- Phone: 04/3823-3084
- Price: $

vnfam.vn

Military History Museum

- Map: 61 B3
- Address: 28 Dien Bien Phu
- Phone: 04/3733-4682
- Hours: Closed Mon. & Fri. & 11:30 a.m.–1:30 p.m.
- Price: $

btlsqsvn.org.vn

Museum of Ethnology

- Map: 61 A3
- Address: Nguyen Van Huyen
- Phone: 04/3756-2193
- Hours: Closed Mon.
- Price: $

vme.org.vn

Temple of Literature

An extraordinary place of worship, Van Mieu (Temple of Literature) is also a rarified expression of the Vietnamese esteem for education and literature, Confucianism in particular. Between 1070 and 1919, students gathered in this 14-acre (5.6 ha) compound to study the master's teachings and strive for recognition as a *tien si* (doctor laureate). Some scholars say the fullest flowering of the philosopher-king was achieved by the Vietnamese.

The Great Middle Gate leads to the Constellation of Literature, known locally as Van Mieu.

Temple of Literature

 61 A2

Entrance at 58 Quoc Tu Giam

 04/6290-8825

 $

Modeled after the Temple to Confucius in Qufu, China, the Temple of Literature was founded by King Ly Thanh Tong in 1070. Six years later, his successor, Ly Nhan Tong, established the nation's first university (Quoc Tu Giam, or "school for the sons of the nation") here, initially for the sons of royalty, but progressively for the sons of mandarins and then for any educationally qualified candidate. In the 14th century, the school's most revered rector, Chu Van An (1292–1370), ushered the university into its golden age. In 1484, the school started to honor each of those who achieved a doctorate laureate by inscribing his name and birthplace on a stone stela, a tradition that would continue through 1779.

In a country that has lost so much to war, it's remarkable that the temple has survived. The Mongols or the Ming Chinese could have razed the shrine during their incursions in the 13th and 15th centuries but didn't, out of respect for Confucius.

Visiting the Temple

The Temple of Literature complex is an oblong of five courtyards accessed via the **Great Portico,** a two-story, three-gated entrance guarded by two mythical lion-dogs that let the good in and keep the bad out. A Chinese inscription on the 300-year-old gate reads, "Among the doctrines of the world, ours is the best and is revered by all culture-starved lands."

Upon entering, you are standing in the **Entrance to the Way Courtyard,** divided into symmetrical halves by a tiled path. Follow the path to the **Great Middle Gate** (Dai Trung Mon), whose name not only refers to its placement between the **Accomplished Virtue Gate** to the right and the **Attained Talent Gate** to the left, but also alludes to a pair of books written by two of Confucius' disciples. The obeisant fish atop the gate represents the deference of students who aspire to become laureates, as carp aspire to become dragons.

The **Great Middle Courtyard** comes next, leading to the **Constellation of Literature** (Van Mieu). In 1802, King Gia Long moved the university to Hue, where he built his own temple of literature. That loss was ameliorated by the erection of this elegant two-story pavilion. The four wooden circles in each window of the belvedere represent the sun.

The third courtyard is the **Garden of the Stelae,** site of the beautiful **Well of Heavenly Clarity** (Thien Quang Tinh) and home to some of the country's most precious relics. The names of 1,306 doctor laureates, who achieved fame between 1442 and 1779 are inscribed on 82 stelae. Each stela details the name, birthplace, and sometimes age of each laureate; the youngest was 16 years old, the oldest 61, though

Five Tips for Visitors to the Temple

1) Allow plenty of time for your visit—it's easy to spend half a day exploring its many corners.
2) Don't miss the turtle stelae, inscribed with the names of those who have successfully passed examinations here.
3) Take time to ponder the temple's one thousand years of history beside the Well of Heavenly Clarity.
4) Enjoy music performed by traditional musicians in the Music Room next to the altar dedicated to Confucius.
5) Give the various souvenir stalls around the temple a miss, as prices are inflated.

most scholars earned degrees in their late 20s and early 30s. The laureates also chiseled maxims for the ages, including this nugget from 1442: "Virtuous and talented men are the life breath of the nation."

During the Vietnam War, authorities entombed the stelae and turtles in sand and concrete to guard against bombings. After the war, the stelae lay more or less abandoned, cracked and sinking into the earth, until 1993, when conservationists built eight elevated pavilions to shelter the relics on either side of the Well of Heavenly Clarity.

Proceed through the **Gate of Great Synthesis** (Dai Thanh Mon) to the **Courtyard of Sages,** flanked by two rebuilt

Temple of Literature

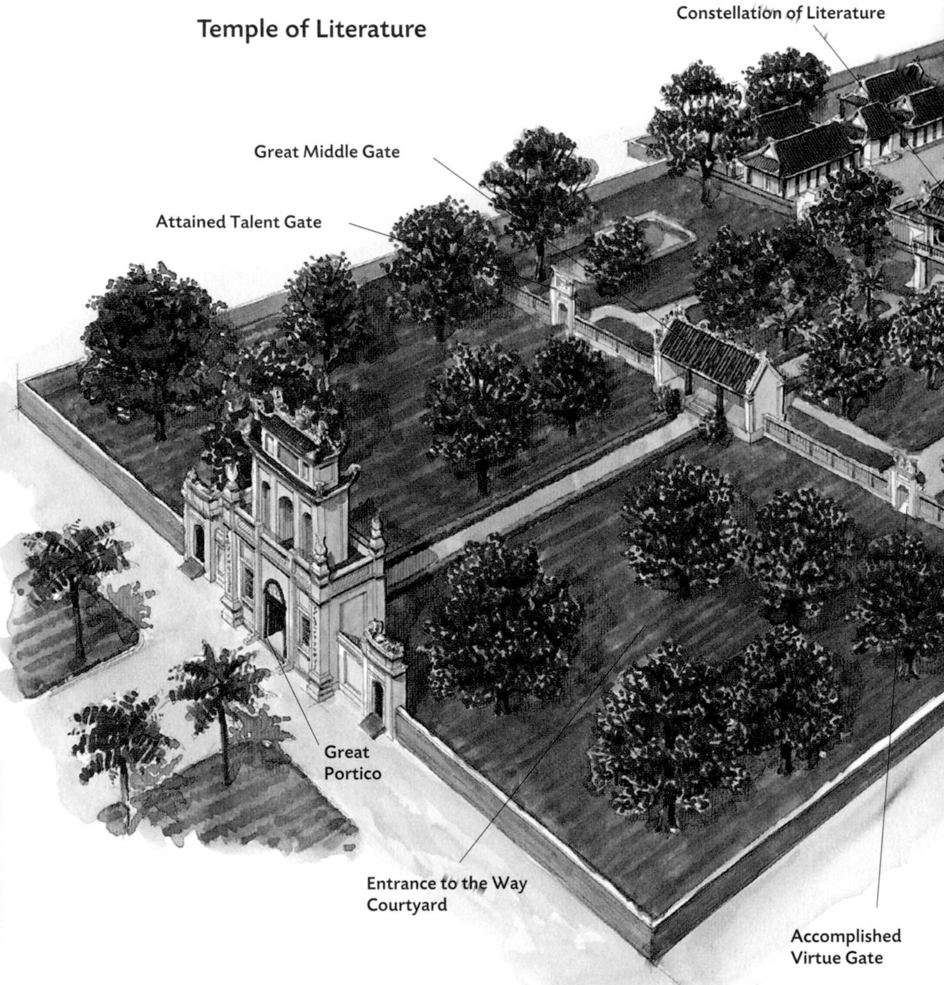

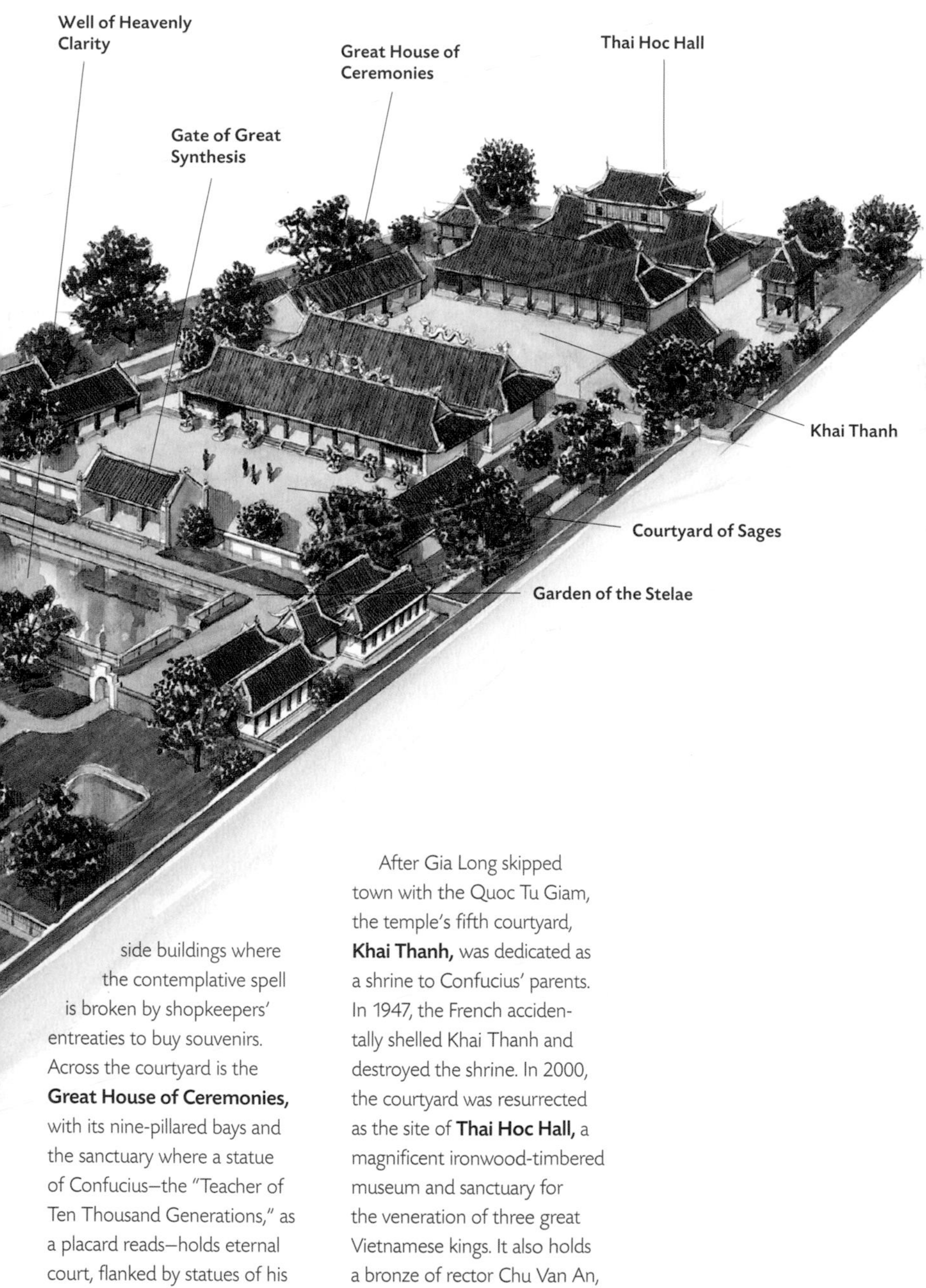

side buildings where the contemplative spell is broken by shopkeepers' entreaties to buy souvenirs. Across the courtyard is the **Great House of Ceremonies,** with its nine-pillared bays and the sanctuary where a statue of Confucius—the "Teacher of Ten Thousand Generations," as a placard reads—holds eternal court, flanked by statues of his four closest disciples.

After Gia Long skipped town with the Quoc Tu Giam, the temple's fifth courtyard, **Khai Thanh,** was dedicated as a shrine to Confucius' parents. In 1947, the French accidentally shelled Khai Thanh and destroyed the shrine. In 2000, the courtyard was resurrected as the site of **Thai Hoc Hall,** a magnificent ironwood-timbered museum and sanctuary for the veneration of three great Vietnamese kings. It also holds a bronze of rector Chu Van An, a preeminent educator. ■

Ba Dinh & West Lake

On September 2, 1945, Ho Chi Minh proclaimed Vietnam independence in a speech here at Ba Dinh Square. Today, a cluster of high-profile attractions—the Ho Chi Minh Mausoleum, Ho Chi Minh Museum, Ho Chi Minh's House, and One-Pillar Pagoda—draw domestic and foreign tourists alike. Although the lines are long and the sites crowded, the square is the holiest place in modern Vietnam. Nearby, West Lake offers a peaceful respite.

Ba Dinh Square
61 A3

Ba Dinh Square

Ho Chi Minh's preserved body lies in a refrigerated viewing chamber in the marble mausoleum that commands the square. If you're unfamiliar with his life story, start your tour instead at the neighboring **Ho Chi Minh Museum** *(19 Ngoc Ha, tel 04/3845-5435, closed Mon. & Fri. p.m., $, baotanghochiminh.vn).* The design of this massive, stark white building is a brutal Soviet interpretation of a lotus flower. Opened in 1990, it is the most bizarre of the many Ho Chi Minh museums in Vietnam Its interior holds photos, handwritten letters, dioramas, and yellowed newspaper clippings, as well as mind-boggling art installations.

The museum's third floor is the most satisfying. Check out the loom, bed, and hammock supposedly used from 1890 to 1895 by Ho's father, the prominent Confucian scholar Nguyen Sinh Sac. Later in life, after a personal rebellion against the ruling clique, Ho's father became a practitioner of traditional Chinese medicine. His pestle and other tools of the trade are on display. The museum also features several examples of art that are surreal, kitsch, or just plain puzzling, such as a huge chain link pierced by a pyramid.

Ho Chi Minh Mausoleum

Thus primed, now join the long line of devotees who've come to see Ho's remains, laid to dubious

Ho Chi Minh's final resting place, a site of pilgrimage

rest in a gargantuan mausoleum of marble quarried from the Viet Cong redoubt of Danang's Marble Mountains. In a number of revisions to his will, Ho repeatedly included a provision for the cremation of his remains and their distribution at undisclosed spots in the country's north, south, and center. The ruling clique had other ideas. Before Ho's 77th birthday, they secretly dispatched a delegation to Moscow to research the possibility of embalming the venerable leader. After Ho died of a heart attack in 1969, his custodians subscribed to the Soviet template and embalmed their founding father for public display, as the Soviets had enshrined Lenin.

The mausoleum, on the west side of the square, opened on August 29, 1975. Inscribed prominently on the mausoleum is Ho's most famous maxim: "Nothing is more precious than independence and freedom." This universal ideal emphasizes Ho's nationalism and echoes the first lines of the declaration that he cribbed from Thomas Jefferson and uttered on Ba Dinh Square in 1945: "All men are created equal. They are endowed by their Creator with certain inalienable rights, among these are Life, Liberty, and the pursuit of Happiness."

More Sights

After exiting the mausoleum, wander north for a glimpse of the **Presidential Palace,** an Italianate Renaissance château built in 1906 as the residence and headquarters of Indochina's governor-general. The palace became known as the house the ascetically minded Ho declined to live in. Today, it is used for affairs of state and is off-limits to the merely curious; photography is forbidden by the stern-faced guards at the gates. Its golden ocher color speaks of its colonial French origins.

Shunning the palace in 1954, Ho moved into three modest rooms in the green-shuttered servants' quarters beyond. Behind the bungalow is a pair of sober gray cars—a French Peugeot

Visiting Uncle Ho

Standing in a long line, wearing respectful dress (no shorts or sleeveless shirts), then filing through the mausoleum in silence under the watchful gaze of Vietnamese soldiers is a strange sensation for most Westerners who pay a visit here. Yet what makes it worth doing is to be in the company of local people, for whom such a visit is nothing short of a pilgrimage, and to sense how powerful the experience is for them. Make the most of the glimpse you get of Uncle Ho's peaceful expression and wispy beard in the glass casket, as visitors are ushered out quickly. Watching the Vietnamese leave with tearful expressions, foreigners might even envy them for having such a hero to revere.

Ho Chi Minh Mausoleum

- 61 A3
- Entrance at corner of Hung Vuong & Le Hong Phong
- 04/3845-5128
- Closed Mon. & Fri., after 11 a.m. most of Sept., & Oct.–Nov.

West Lake
61 A4

400 and a Russian M20 Pobieda—that the Vietnamese president used in the 1950s and 1960s. In 1963, expatriate Vietnamese living in Moscow presented Ho the M20 as a gift.

From the bungalow, stroll around the fishing pond to the square-columned **Stilt House** *(Nha San, closed Mon. & 11 a.m.–2 p.m., $)* that was Ho's home from the time it was built in 1958 until his death in 1969. The house was a tribute to Vietnam's ethnic minorities, for whom Ho long had a beneficent interest. When he returned to Vietnam from China in 1941, after 30 years abroad, he wore the costume of the Nung minority and lived briefly in a Nung home.

Today, you can climb a stairway beside the Stilt House and view the second-floor interior from a walkway that skirts its length. One room holds Ho's office and desk. A second room contains his straw bed, a fan, clock, radio, hat, and books in a glass display case. The open-air ground floor is where Ho often met with colleagues.

From the Stilt House, meander across the grounds past the **One-Pillar Pagoda** (Chua Mot Cot). As quaint as a tree fort, the pagoda is built around a single pillar of concrete, like a lotus flower blooming on a stem. A board inscribed with Chinese characters over the entrance reads *Lien Hoa Dai* ("lotus flower shrine"). The pagoda was the fancy of King Ly Thai Tong, who dreamed that the goddess of mercy, Quan Am, led him to a lotus flower and told the king he would soon be the father of a son. After the king married and sired a son, he erected the pagoda in 1049 in a gesture of gratitude. The French military spitefully razed the original pagoda as they abandoned the country in the 1950s.

West Lake

A couple of blocks north, West Lake (Ho Tay), like Hoan Kiem Lake, is a Red River "orphan," formed when the river shifted

Hanoi's Other French District

The capital city's second French district is anchored by the **Ministry of Foreign Affairs** *(1 Ton That Dam)*, a 1931 blend of European beaux arts and Asian aesthetics. Take note of the two-tiered pagoda-style roofs on the gatehouses that flank the entrance and the vaguely Chinese motifs that bracket the main entrance. French architect Ernest Hebrard designed the building as the Banque d'Indochine's treasury in the 1920s. He also designed many of the nearby villas; once home to merchants and officials, these now serve as embassies and ambassadors' homes.

Wander the wide sidewalks of this neighborhood to fully appreciate the architecture from the 1920s and 1930s. Check out the art deco masterpiece at **10 Ba Huyen Thanh Quan,** which centers on a three-story front stairwell with a long glass panel in the middle of the facade. At **10 Le Hong Phong** is a beautifully restored, jazzy art moderne house, now the Kuwaiti Embassy. The German and Swiss ambassadors live at **47** and **49 Dien Bien Phu,** respectively; the former is bracketed and gabled, with a steeply pitched roof.

course and abandoned this vast body of water. The city's oldest pagoda and one of its four guardian temples lie off either side of a short, leafy causeway that divides the larger expanse of West Lake from Truc Bach Lake, a smaller fragment partitioned by road-building locals.

At the south end of the Thanh Nien Causeway, **Quan Thanh Temple** *($)* honors Huyen Thien Tran Vo, guardian of the northern approach to the city of Thanh Long. Established during the reign of Hanoi founder Ly Thai To (1010–1028), the temple is known for its 4-ton (3.6 metric ton) bronze statue of Tran Vo, cast in 1677. It stands in the back compartment. Devotees lay money at the statue's base, rub its feet, and anoint themselves with blessings.

More impressive are the wooden substructure and 180 panels of gilded landscapes and Chinese poems inscribed in mother-of-pearl on black lacquered wood. The middle compartment is home to a statue of Trum Trung, the 17th-century artisan who upgraded Tran Vo from wood to bronze and forged a 5-foot (1.5 m) bell that hangs in the mirador of the triple-gate entrance. In the first compartment, two phoenixes flank a frieze of warriors engaged in battle before a temple and a netherworld of mythical beasts.

Farther north on Thanh Nien, a **war memorial** set in the sidewalk honors an antiaircraft battery that downed a number of planes during the Vietnam War. On October 26, 1967, it shot down an A-4 piloted by future U.S. presidential candidate, John McCain, who would endure five years as a POW in the notorious Hanoi Hilton (see p. 69) and later champion the normalization of relations between the U.S. and Vietnam.

As its name suggests, the One-Pillar Pagoda is supported by a single pillar (of concrete).

Farther along the causeway on the left is **Tran Quoc** ("protecting the nation") **Pagoda** *(closed 11:30 a.m.–1:30 p.m.),* founded in the sixth century during the reign of Ly Nam De. Its axis extends from an 11-story octagonal tower via a sitting room to the main temple, which holds seven tiers of bodhisattvas and Buddhas. In the courtyard is a bodhi tree cut from the tree under which Sakyamuni received his enlightenment. ■

More Places to Visit in Hanoi

Hanoi Botanical Gardens

This is one of Hanoi's welcome green spaces. More park than botanical garden, it offers a respite from honking horns and clouds of exhaust, with walkways around lakes, under shady trees, and past modern sculptures. Soothe your soul after trudging around Hanoi Citadel or Ba Dinh Square.

61 A3 3 Hoang Hoa Tham, just south of West Lake

Hanoi's Ceramic Wall

This wonderful project, covering 8,312 square yards (6,950 sq m) and stretching almost 2.5 miles (4 km) along the inside of the Red River Dyke, was the brainchild of Nguyen Thu Thuy, an art journalist and champion of public art. As she drove past the drab expanse of bare concrete to work each day, she wondered "Why don't we use ceramic material to decorate this wall?"

Completed to coincide with the city's 1,000th birthday in 2010, it is a true work of collaboration, with artists from Europe, South Korea, and Russia joining renowned Vietnamese artists and schoolchildren to design various sections of the wall. It is the largest ceramic mosaic on the planet. Topics depicted include scenes from Vietnamese history and culture, as well as images of Hanoi and modern art. Though it's a magical sight, it's easier to see from a car than on foot as the roads it runs beside–Au Co, Nghi Tam, Yen Phu, Tran Nhat Duat and Tran Quang Khai–are not pedestrian-friendly.

61 B4–D1 From Au Co to Tran Quang Khai, on the west bank of the Red River

The Ceramic Wall: an artful antidote to concrete

Reunification Park

Every morning, Reunification Park (Cong Vien Thong Nhat), formerly Lenin Park, swells with aging tai chi practitioners. Joggers circuit the pathways all day, and couples canoodle on benches at twilight. Anchoring the park is a large lake, once known as Seven-Hectare Lake. During the colonial era, the site was used as Hanoi's dump. After the French War, Ho Chi Minh played an active role in the site's rebirth as a public space.

61 B1 Entrance on Le Duan

Tay Ho Pagoda

This 17th-century temple sits atop a spit of land that juts into West Lake (Ho Tay), where the mother goddess, Thanh Mau, is said to have revealed herself as a pretty girl to a local mandarin, recited poetry, and then vanished. She's enshrined today in a man-made grotto in one of two temple buildings. Note the 1.6-ton (1.4 metric ton) bronze bell, an industrial stove to burn paper offerings, and the cans of soda and beer stacked on the altar as offerings. Walking in, you pass by stalls purveying temple offerings. Worshippers flock here on the 1st and 15th of each lunar month to request good fortune.

61 B4 Beyond Sheraton Hotel on Xuan Dieu, turn left on Dang Thai Mai. Pagoda is at the end of road, 2.5 miles (4 km) from downtown.

From the limestone wonders of Ha Long Bay to exotic highland villages to the ancient seat of Vietnamese civilization on the Red River Delta

The North

A shrine in bas-relief at one of Ha Tay's pagodas

The North

Beyond Hanoi, the Red River floodplain is a skein of rivers, tributaries, canals, and dikes. Vietnamese culture began percolating here 3,000 years ago and it continues to spring forth. To the northeast, Ha Long Bay lives up to its promised wonders, while to the north and northwest, the interior is rumpled by fantastic limestone and granite mountains inhabited by some of Asia's most colorfully costumed ethnic minorities.

The most popular day trip from Hanoi takes in the Perfume Pagoda (Chua Huong). Although its architecture and statuary don't match those of other nearby pagodas, its setting and grottoes are astonishing. In Bac Ninh, But Thap Pagoda holds Vietnam's best examples of Buddhist art, from both an architectural and statuary standpoint.

With its fascinating communal house and chockablock French architecture, Haiphong is an interesting gateway to spectacular Ha Long Bay. Skip the hotels and spend your nights in any of a selection of air-conditioned boats.

In the country's northernmost province of Ha Giang, the spectacular scenery in

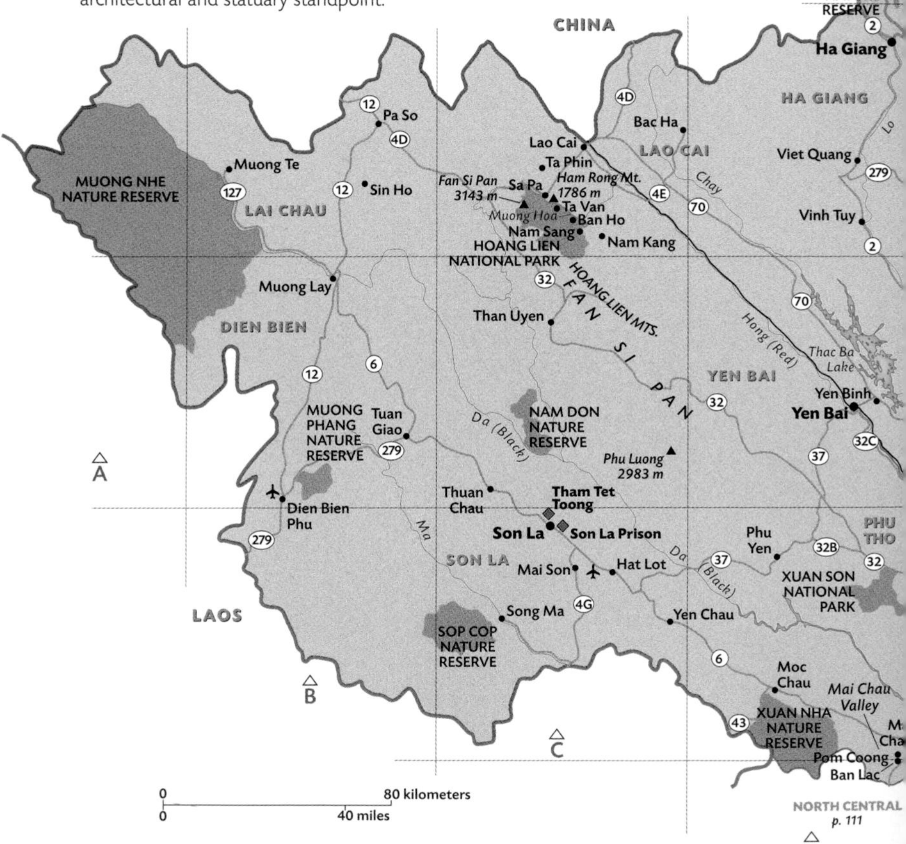

the Dong Van Karst Plateau Geopark makes for indelible memories of jagged skylines and colorful ethnic markets. Off-limits to tourists for decades, this is truly Vietnam's last frontier.

In the far northwest, Sa Pa is a trekker's mecca. Though slightly tarnished by its popularity, the region remains among Vietnam's top five travel destinations, and deservedly so. Its massive granite mountains shelter ethnic minority villages whose costumed denizens look like they've walked through a time warp from the 18th century. Go see them now, as those wardrobes may not be long for this world. ■

NOT TO BE MISSED:

The Perfume Pagoda **88–90**

Watching artisans at work in the handicraft villages **90–91**

Gliding through the otherworldly landscape of Ha Long Bay **96–99**

Jaw-dropping scenery in Dong Van Karst Plateau Geopark **101**

A leisurely boat trip in Ba Be National Park **104–105**

Trekking around Sa Pa **105–108**

South of Hanoi

For all of Hanoi's charms, the area's most compelling pagodas are just a day trip away, nestled among the limestone mountains about 20 miles (30 km) from the city proper, as are numerous handicraft villages. While you can visit the villages and pagodas independently, it's far easier and more rewarding to hook up with a guide or a tour.

Perfume Pagoda

The Perfume Pagoda (Chua Huong) is a complex of 16 separate halls, temples, and grottoes amid a craggy karst landscape southwest of Hanoi. No other landscape in Vietnam so closely mirrors the world of a Chinese ink painting. Nor is any pagoda as popular. International travelers flock to the site, while domestic pilgrims swarm the pathways and halls during a 300-year-old festival held from the 6th to 15th day of the first lunar month (Jan. or Feb.).

Mystical Huong Tich Grotto, dedicated to Quan Am, is the premier attraction at the Perfume Pagoda.

Impressed by the area's natural beauty, the great Vietnamese King Le Thanh Tong (1460–1497) sanctified the locale with a lofty name, Celestial Kitchen, when his hunting party stopped to cook at a small shrine near present-day Thien Tru Pagoda. During the reign of Le Hy Tong (1680–1705), the shrine was improved with terraces and stone steps. The French ravaged the site during their war, but the area's natural beauty and pagoda's fabled reputation ensured renovation.

Three clusters of pagodas and shrines are grouped along two tributaries of the Day River. By far, the most popular route ascends Swallow Tail (Yen) Stream. From Ben Duc Wharf in **My Duc,** female paddlers ferry tourists 2 miles (3 km) up this shallow tributary in aluminum skiffs amid an increasingly beautiful karst landscape.

On the way, you pass the **Trinh Temple,** dedicated to a legendary general under the sixth Hung king who saved the Van Lang Kingdom from Yin invaders. You'll also pass under a red bridge, from which a road leads to a pair of pagodas that form one of the pagoda clusters.

The ferries drop passengers at a wharf below **Thien Tru Pagoda.** It's mostly new since the French War. The Triple Gate was built in 1989, and the beautiful bell tower inside was rebuilt in 1986. Inside the main sanctuary, take a peek at a pair of bas-relief panels of netherworld monkeys and devils.

From Thien Tru, you can either walk 2 miles (3 km) up to Huong Tich, one of Vietnam's most spectacular grottoes and the most attractive element in the pagoda complex, or you can ride up by cable car *($)*.

If you skip the hike, you'll miss a pair of mildly interesting pagodas, as well as countless opportunities to interact with the locals. A little more than half a mile from Thien Tru, a small path to the left leads to the pagoda of **Giai Oan** ("absolution") and its collection of gilded Buddhist statuary in a niche of limestone. A narrow crevice to the right opens into a shallow chamber with some polychromatic statuary.

Back on the main path to Huong Tich, you'll reach **Cua Vong,** a 200-year-old shrine to the green-robed Holy Mother of the Mountains and Forests, where Ho Chi Minh stopped for lunch one day in 1958.

As the climb to Huong Tich wears on, the Buddhist faithful occasionally seek relief by prayerfully clasping their palms to greet other pilgrims with the phrase *Nam Mo A Di Dat Phat* (Glory to the Buddha Amitabha).

The vast maw at **Huong Tich**'s entrance is marvelous. A 1770 inscription of Chinese characters by a Trinh lord describes Huong Tich as the "most beautiful grotto in the southern sky." The entrance is said to resemble the mouth of a dragon; the giant stalagmite inside is its tongue. Deeper inside this grotto, dedicated to Quan Am, two more stalagmites serve as altars for women praying for children. Would-be mothers pat the rocks and mumble, "Come along with me, my little boy (or girl)."

After a survey of the grotto's

Hung Kings Temple

This complex at Nghia Linh Mountain in Phu Tho venerates the legendary Au Co, whose hundred eggs hatched at the site of Ha Temple, thus forming the people of Vietnam. One of the eggs held the first of 18 Hung kings, who worshipped at the site of present-day Thuong Temple. After routing invaders, the sixth Hung king was buried in a hillside tomb. At the foot of Nghia Linh, the 18th king's daughters used the surface of the Gieng Temple well as a mirror when they combed their hair. The temple hosts the Hung Kings Festival (now a national holiday), with parades and activities on the tenth day of the third lunar month each year (usually April).

Perfume Pagoda

- 87 E1
- 38 miles (62 km) SW of Hanoi via Hwy. 6 & Rte. 21B. Boats to pagoda ($$$) travel up Swallow Tail Stream from Ben Duc Wharf in My Duc.
- $

Hung Kings Temple

- 87 E2
- Tran Phu, Viet Tri, 53 miles (85 km) NW of Hanoi

Handicraft Villages

Visitor Information

✉ Handspan Travel, B78 Ma May, Hanoi

☎ 04/3926-2828

handspan.com

Ha Tay Pagodas

87 E2

Visitor Information

✉ Queen Travel, 65 Hang Bac, Hanoi

☎ 04/3826-0860

NOTE: The easiest way to visit Thay and Tay Phuong Pagodas is to join a tour. Check with your hotel.

statuary and fanciful limestone formations, go back down the path and climb the far less arduous stairway to the grotto of **Tien Son** ("fairy mountain"), 650 feet (200 m) north of Thien Tru. The cave entrance is an alluring triangular-shaped passageway of runneled stalagmites, some of which sound like drums when beaten.

Upon your return to Ben Duc, be prepared to tip the ferryboat women. They'll ask for one, and they'll aggressively haunt you if you don't pony up.

INSIDER TIP:

Hit the markets first thing in the morning to see people getting ready for the day—most of Vietnam rises early, so don't miss out!

—JONATHAN A. O'BRIEN
National Geographic grantee

On the return to Hanoi, remain alert for the great numbers of communal houses *(dinh)* off the right side of the dike road. If you're traveling independent of a group, detour for the two dinh in **Binh Da** village, about 12 miles (20 km) southwest of Hanoi.

Handicraft Villages

Villages specializing in a diversity of trades—silk weaving, ceramics, wood carving, woodcut printing, hatmaking, bronze casting, and others—dot the north. Some craftspeople, especially those closer to Hanoi, welcome tourists into their small workrooms and, of course, into their shiny new showrooms.

The best handicraft villages, Bat Trang and Van Phuc, are also the closest to Hanoi. On the Red River 9 miles (14 km) southeast of town, **Bat Trang** ("bowl workshop"; *map 87 E2*) is a 500-year-old village of thatched huts whose pieces are among the collections at the Louvre. Bat Trang reached its artistic peak in the 18th and early 19th centuries, but it has become Vietnam's best known pottery center. A narrow road lined with shops and pottery works winds a half mile (1 km) through the village to an open-air ceramics market. The black paddies stuck to brick walls about town are a coal-clay mix used in the kilns.

For a thousand years, villagers in **Van Phuc** *(map 87 E2)*, 7 miles (12 km) southwest of Hanoi, have been harvesting silkworm cocoons from waffle-like brackets of mulberry branches. One of the best silk workshops is Trieu Van Mao's, a four-generation family operation, where you can watch the looms in action.

Northeast of Hanoi, the road to **Dong Ky** *(map 87 E2)* is lined with four- and five-story homes above showrooms that traffic heavily in garish dragon-backed furniture. Beyond its open-air wood market, the village sawmills churn out furniture. Stop to watch the process, as craftspeople chisel and inlay mother-of-pearl motifs.

Only a few houses actively make woodcut prints in **Dong**

Ho (*map 87 F2;* see p. 55), 22 miles (35 km) east of Hanoi in Bac Ninh Province. Among the most famous is Nguyen Dang Che.

Ha Tay Pagodas

Ha Tay, a suburban province of Hanoi, has several lovely pagodas that display a feast of Buddhist statuary art in lovely limestone settings.

Nineteen miles (30 km) west of Hanoi in the village of Sai Son, the 11th-century **Thay Pagoda** stands at the base of a limestone outcrop. The pagoda forged fame as the *Thay,* or master's pagoda, under the stewardship of the legendary Tu Dao Hanh, a founding father of water puppetry. Water puppet shows are still held during holidays and festivals on a specially built stage in the center of a pond.

The complex features three parallel pagoda buildings that resemble the Chinese character Tam ("three"). Before entering, pause by the singular kidney-shaped stone perched on a lung-shaped pedestal—there to draw badness from the bodies of passersby. The inscribed Chinese characters offer well wishes for health and happiness.

The outer section, used for ceremonies, is a celebration of Tu Dao Hanh, a statue of whom in the middle bay is draped in yellow robes. In the left bay, a pair of Cambodian ambassadors bow at the feet of Ly Than Tong, a 12th-century king believed to be a reincarnation of Tu Dao Hanh. In the right bay, a closed altar house shelters a macabre statue of Hanh, allegedly fashioned from the ashes of his bones and limestone mineral deposits. The jointed statue was rigged to stand on the one festival day of the year when the

Thay Pagoda
87 E2

Thay Pagoda's Thuy Dinh stage has been hosting water puppetry performances for centuries.

Tay Phuong Pagoda
87 E2

door is opened. However, a Tay Son general halted the spectacle 200 years ago, arguing that so lofty a saint as Tu Dao Hanh should not stand for commoners. Don't miss the two 16th-century phoenixes, each carved from a single chunk of jackfruit wood.

Children exit a weathered stone gate between parallel sentences at a Ha Tay pagoda.

The middle pagoda features more impressive statuary. The corpulent guardians of Buddhism *(ho phap)*—known to the Vietnamese as Mister Sternness and Mister Benevolence—date from the 17th century. You'll also find the eight diamond-king bodhisattvas *(kim cuong)*, fierce protectors of the meditating Buddha.

The third pagoda is largely open space where monks teach.

Four miles (6 km) farther west on Tay Phuong mountain in Yen village, **Tay Phuong Pagoda** was established sometime between the third and sixth centuries A.D. In the ninth century, a Chinese proconsul and wizard named Cao Bien refurbished the pagoda to serve as a symbolic jail for a dragon that dwelled within the hill and that might otherwise escape and empower the Vietnamese people. Its present arrangement, also laid out according to the Chinese Tam character, took shape in the 17th and late 18th centuries, with Tay Son dynasty renovations.

In the first hall, or Hall of Prostrations, eight armor-clad diamond kings share tight quarters under a double-tiered roof—common to all three of the pagoda's halls and to Buddhist architecture in general.

In the middle hall, or shrine, terraced altars hold two of the pagoda's 18 arhats, as well as a masterful depiction of the Buddha on Snowy Mountain. The shrine is lit by circular *thi* windows, a form of architecture that plays on both visible and corresponding invisible components. Take note of the truss of ironwood columns on blue stone pedestals, with carved mulberry and banyan leaves, dragons, phoenixes, and tiger heads.

In the back hall, or sanctuary, the remaining arhats provide the pagoda's most interesting congregation of statuary. They date from a renovation in the early 20th century. Each represents a story in the annals of Buddhism. Look for Hiep Ton Gia, the old man who began studying Buddhism late in life and vowed never to lay down until he had learned the entire doctrine.

Tram Gian Pagoda, 12 miles (20 km) southwest of Hanoi in Tien Lu, is laid out in the *noi cong ngai quoc* style, notable for flanking corridors that frame interior halls ("tram gian" means "hundred compartments"). The 800-year-old pagoda's picturesque setting and buildings have long been regarded as a high-water mark in Buddhist architecture, and the bell tower remains captivating.

Bac Ninh Pagodas

Bac Ninh is a suburban province of Hanoi and one of three ancient centers of Buddhism in Vietnam. The province is home to the country's oldest pagoda, **Chua Dau,** though a recent renovation has erased the patina of its venerable charm. Nearby, **But Thap Pagoda** is a masterpiece of architecture and contains the finest ensemble of Buddhist statuary in the country. On an inspection tour of Ninh Phuc Tu Pagoda in 1876, Emperor Tu Duc dubbed the 230-year-old pagoda But Thap ("pen stupa") for its 45-foot (13.5 m) octagonal tower that resembles a pen. From the triple-gate bell tower, a succession of seven houses aligns on a 110-yard (100 m) axis flanked by two corridors of 26 columned bays.

From the **Incense Burning House,** a covered gallery leads to the treasures of the **Superior House,** including the Thousand-Hand, Thousand-Eye Goddess of Mercy, a true masterpiece of Vietnamese wood carving, with 11 faces, 994 arms, and 994 eyes. A trinity of carved Buddhas *(Tam the)* reigns over the hall from the central bay, flanked by a fascinating gallery of emotionally expressive, polychromatic Buddhist deities.

Across an arched stone bridge, a nine-story lotus tower rises from the 17th-century **Virtue Hermitage.** This tower rotates on its axis like a prayer wheel, enabling contemplation of bas-relief depictions of the Pure Land. Outside the right corridor, the bell tower honors the Zen master who inspired the pagoda's founder. Stone balusters girdle the first of its five stories, setting off engraved scenes of fighting tigers, dragons, buffalo, clouds, and a Zen master.

INSIDER TIP:
Try the ethnic minority rice-and-maize alcohol, but beware: It's not for those with delicate stomachs. This is potent stuff!

—SARAH TURNER
National Geographic grantee

Not far from But Thap in Dau, Thuan Thanh District, **Dau Pagoda** is Vietnam's oldest pagoda, probably built in the third century A.D. It once was the most important center of Vietnamese Buddhism. Its three-story Hoa Phong tower houses an 1817 bronze gong and a 1793 bell, accompanied by the statues of followers of the goddess of mercy. ■

Tram Gian Pagoda
Map 87 E2

Bac Ninh Pagodas
Map 87 F2

Visitor Information
- Bac Ninh Tourist, Ninh Xa
- 0241/3831-296 (no English spoken)

But Thap Pagoda
Map 87 F2

Dau Pagoda
Map 87 F2

Haiphong & Ha Long Bay

Haiphong, Vietnam's third most populous city and largest port, is the gateway to Ha Long Bay. The city suffers from this proximity, as most travelers skip its temptations to take in the nearby natural wonder, but Haiphong's cultural assets deserve a stop on any visitor's itinerary. The enchanting Ha Long Bay, meanwhile, was designated a World Heritage site in 1994, an accolade long overdue for one of the world's most stunning natural marvels.

Cat Ba National Park, facing onto Ha Long Bay, is a UNESCO Biosphere Reserve.

Haiphong
87 F2
Visitor Information
18 Minh Khai
098/3222-201
haiphongtourism .gov.vn

Haiphong

Haiphong's lures include a communal hall *(dinh)*, a fascinating pagoda, and a city center replete with French colonial structures in various states of ruin and repair. In addition, the city offers increasingly better accommodations and a contagiously energetic spirit.

If you haven't visited any of Vietnam's 700 dinh, most of which lie scattered around the Red River Delta, be sure to visit the **Hang Kenh Communal House,** on Hang Kenh near the city center. The temple is 106 feet (32 m) wide and 43 feet (13 m) deep, with a roof that sags markedly from the weight of its thousands of tiles. The central bay honors Tran Hung Dao, who routed the Mongols at the nearby Bach Dang River in the 13th century. Originally built in 1717, it was moved to this location in 1841 and was further expanded in 1905. Its main features are the 308 carved wooden dragons on the building's ironwood truss, which are well preserved.

Across town, at 121 Chua Hang, the traditional **Du Hang Pagoda** (aka Phuc Lam Pagoda) includes flourishes from an idiosyncratic monk named Thong Hanh, who dwelt here in 1899. Ten marble statues of distinctive, slightly

Gothic arhats ring a pond that percolates with the gulpings of fat carp. Look among the statues for the exultant bronze Happy Buddha, arms raised in a touchdown-like celebration. Behind it stands Thong Hanh's bell tower. In the main temple, pillars split the central bay into five segments, each adorned by a successively higher altar and a wonderful assortment of religious statuary.

A long sweep of park dominates the **city center.** The French legacy is apparent in much of the surrounding architecture. Off one edge of the park on Tran Hung Dao is Haiphong's lavish **Opera House,** restored in 2005.

Cat Ba Island

Cat Ba is also the name of the town and national park on this karst isle at the southern end of Ha Long Bay. The Cat Ba archipelago was approved as a UNESCO Biosphere Reserve in 2004. Historically a fishing village, the town has spruced up for tourists with a wall of new five- and six-story waterfront hotels. These days, almost as many boat tours of the bay start from Cat Ba as from Ha Long City. While a few boat operators offer tours of the bay out of Cat Ba, most cast off from the town of Ha Long.

From the town of Cat Ba, a paved road winds through a scenic narrow valley in the mountainous interior. Just past Hai Son, a stairway climbs to **Quan Y Cave** *($)*. In 1960, the Vietnamese and Chinese teamed up to build a concrete hospital compound in this spacious cave, thus its moniker—"hospital cave." The groundskeeper is a veteran in his 70s who spent a decade working in the cave and now guides visitors, rendering place-names in English—kitchen, surgery, swimming pool, movie theater.

INSIDER TIP:

Instead of booking your boat tour of Ha Long Bay in Hanoi or Haiphong, head for Cat Ba Island, where you're less likely to find yourself in tour boat "traffic jams."

—DAMIEN SIMONIS
National Geographic author

Quan Y is the most interesting of numerous limestone caves throughout **Cat Ba National Park,** a 24,000-acre (9,800 ha) reserve that covers about a third of the island. The rugged hills rise as high as 1,000 feet (300 m) and provide shelter for the world's last troop of golden-headed langurs *(catbalangur.org)*

The park entrance lies along the island's main north-south artery, 9 miles (14 km) north of Cat Ba. From here, a short trail summits 660-foot (200 m) **Ngu Lam,** where a watchtower offers park vistas. A more ambitious four-hour trek through the park leads past Frog Lake to the village of **Viet Hai,** from which a ferry returns to Cat Ba.

You'll find several appealing

Cat Ba Island

87 G2

Visitor Information

Cat Ba Travel Service, 210 1 Thang 4

031/3888-783

catbatravelservice.com

NOTE: Every morning hydrofoils leave from the pier at the end of Cu Chinh Lan in Haiphong for a 45-minute sprint down the Bach Dang River to Cat Ba.

Cat Ba National Park

87 G2

Hai Son, 10 miles (16 km) NW of Cat Ba town

031/3888-741

$

Ha Long Bay
87 G2
Visitor Information
Queen Travel, 65 Hang Bac, Hanoi
04/3826-0860

NOTE: Most tour boats operate from the piers in Ha Long. From Ben Beo tourist port in Cat Ba, one or two junk ferries depart for Ha Long every morning.

beaches along a promontory east of town. Tourism boosters have run a precarious boardwalk along the cliff, while stairways and paths lead to so-so offshore vistas.

Ha Long Bay

Ha Long Bay, with its sweeping seascape of craggy karst towers that rise hundreds of feet from jade green bay waters, is a spellbinding wonder and a must-see on any trip to Vietnam. Nearly 2,000 distinct islands stud this 620-square-mile (1,553 sq km) offshoot of the Tonkin Gulf. In 1994, UNESCO designated 174 square miles (434 sq km) of the bay a World Heritage site.

According to legend, the bay formed when a dragon plunged into the sea, whipping its tail from side to side in a frenzy that carved the region into a grand archipelago. (The name Ha Long means "dragon descending.") Geologists tell a different story, of course. Over the past 230 million to 280 million years, rainwater and the ocean have eroded the landscape into an array of towers, known as *fenglin*, and clusters of conical crags, known as *fengcong*. At the same time, rising and falling tides have chiseled notched bands into their karst bases, lending a tottering appearance to these primeval expressions of rock. In 2000, UNESCO again inscribed Ha Long Bay on its World Heritage List, citing its geomorphology as a unique asset worthy of mankind's preservation.

Humans moved into the bay area some 25,000 years ago, and several cultures—the Soi Nhu, Cai Beo, and Ha Long—evolved here during the prehistoric era. In 1149, a trading port was established on the coast at Van Don. By the

Junks and a replica colonial French paddle wheeler host travelers on overnight cruises on the bay.

EXPERIENCE: Kayaking in Ha Long Bay

Of course, there's no reason you shouldn't sleep overnight on a junk in Ha Long Bay and spend your days paddling a kayak through the surreal landscape that surrounds you. Apart from the fact that kayaks are eco-friendly, they are also the only way to access the *phong* or cliff-lined, inland lagoons, where a primeval hush prevails. Some karst outcrops in the bay conceal two or even three of these phong, which must be approached at low tide when the caves around them can be entered. Wildlife sightings are not guaranteed, but with luck you'll spot colorful birds, monkeys, reptiles, and several varieties of fish gliding beneath the surface of the clear waters.

Most tours begin with some instruction in paddling techniques and safety procedure, so even complete beginners get a chance to control the kayaks. The staff does much of the paddling, however, allowing visitors the chance to appreciate these special surroundings, and escort boats accompany the group. (See Travelwise p. 265 for kayaking information.)

15th century, when Emperor Le Thanh Tong extolled the bay in verse, the region was firmly rooted in the Vietnamese imagination.

Visiting Ha Long Bay: The bay is best approached from Ha Long City, a Janus-faced port split by the Cua Luc River and linked by an impressive new suspension bridge in 2006. On one side of the bridge, **Hon Gai** is a grimy exporter of coal; on the other side, **Bai Chay** is a gussied-up importer of tourists that sports a bank of new waterfront hotels. The bay is also accessible from Cat Ba Island (see p. 95). While technically an island within Ha Long Bay itself, the latter is so vast, it can feel tangential to the archipelago.

Although Ha Long tourism authorities make much of the islands' grottoes—several of which are admittedly striking—the preeminent Ha Long experience is waterborne. It's about being afloat as much as possible amid a landscape as fantastic as one dreamed up by a five-year-old with a box of Crayolas. Many travelers take to the bay on day-tripping tour boats. Others are tempted by cheap overnight tours, but these are fraught with danger; in 2011, a dozen tourists drowned when their boat sank suddenly in the middle of the night. For a richer experience, book a night's passage on the *Emeraude* (see Travelwise p. 249), a faithful replica of a 1920s French paddle wheeler that crystallizes the romance of colonial Indochina in three stories of terrace-topped splendor. For a more indigenous, if less luxurious, overnight cruise, sign on for a tour aboard one of the junks that suckle up to the tourist pier at Bai Chay.

A junk's bamboo-ribbed sails aren't necessary for propulsion, but they do add a romantic cultural note to a bay excursion. Overhead, eagles soar and dive, plucking fish from a population of a thousand different species.

Though eagles seem as common as butterflies, the islands' resident langurs and other monkeys are more elusive.

But animals aren't the highlight of Ha Long Bay. One comes here for the fantastical karsts, frizzed with short, gnarled vegetation and sculpted over the eons into shapes that resemble swans, kettles, toads, saddles, monsters, and other likenesses. The most dramatic towers are six times higher than they are wide. More breathtaking than individual formations, however, are the karsts from a distance—as a line on the horizon or as boundaries to sight, towering up on all sides like the walls of an arena.

Bai Tu Long Bay

The same geological conditions that created Ha Long Bay also created Bai Tu Long Bay, just to the north, but there's one major difference—almost no tourists. Considering the fact that Ha Long Bay is the country's premier tourist destination, this is a significant difference. The downside is that there are also fewer facilities for tourists, but some tour operators (see Travelwise p. 239) can arrange a visit to this largely unknown gem.

Sightseeing: Tours afford plenty of time for the most popular pastime—mere gazing—but for those who crave the particular, there's no shortage of sights. In recent years, the overnight tour boats have lapsed into a greatest hits collection of stops, so you'll have to shop around for boats willing to ply lesser known waterways. Whatever your itinerary, be sure to visit **Hang Sung Sot** ("grotto of surprises"), generally regarded as one of the two most beautiful caves in the bay. This cave opened to tourists in 1995, though the French pioneered the route for Westerners in the early 1900s, as evidenced by graffiti on the limestone.

A trail leads a half mile (1 km) through the 135,000-square-foot (12,000 sq m) cave, threading through three chambers, each larger than the previous. Grotesque stalagmites and stalactites reveal the usual suspects—turtles, junk sails, monkeys, a Happy Buddha, the roots of molars—and one "special part" of a dragon, luridly lit in red and aimed at a hole in a pocked ceiling of smoothbore craters. The third chamber is breathtakingly cavernous and, while not rivaling Phong Nha (see pp. 118–119) as Vietnam's most magnificent, it does play a worthy second fiddle.

INSIDER TIP:
The 2,000 limestone islands of Ha Long Bay are probably the best-known geographic image the world has of Vietnam.

—JON BOWERMASTER
National Geographic author

Off the overnight-boat track, **Hang Thien Cung** ("grotto of the

The typical tour of Ha Long cruises past several waterborne fishing villages.

heavenly palace") challenges Sung Sot as Ha Long's most beautiful cave and offers up a stone breast in answer to Sung Sot's "special part." In **Hang Dau Go** ("grotto of the wooden stakes"), 13th-century warrior-hero Tran Hung Dao stockpiled the legendary iron-tipped wooden stakes he'd later use to impale the Mongol fleet.

At **Hang Luon** on **Bo Hon Island,** tenders from the bigger boats and, better yet, kayaks, skim the waters beneath its low-slung roof to emerge in a lagoon of sheer-walled majesty that contains some of the bay's best underwater coral gardens. Salt water's corrosive influence also gouged six lagoons at **Dau Be Island.**

Though beaches don't come naturally to these karst islands, swimming is a pastime to be indulged, as the high saline content supports even the leanest bathers with remarkable buoyancy. Depths range from 25 to 40 feet (8–12 m) and can be as shallow as 15 feet (5 m) at many moorings. Most boats dip ladders over their sterns for swimming and, in this land of limited liability, to encourage those brave enough to jump in from the boat's rooftop.

While the beach at **Titop Island** looks suspiciously manmade, the real thrill here comes at the top of a 420-step climb to the summit for a 360-degree, postcard-perfect vista of the bay. The island is named in honor of a Russian cosmonaut who shared this same view with Ho Chi Minh in 1962.

One last cultural note regarding Ha Long Bay: In 1991, a French production company filmed scenes in Ha Long Bay for its epic masterpiece *Indochine*, a hymn to the waning days of the lost colony, starring Catherine Deneuve. Tour boats cruise past one of the movie sets. ■

The Far North

A region of craggy limestone mountains and scenic waterways, Vietnam's far north has much to offer the intrepid traveler. A key draw is the trekking opportunities to the ethnically diverse hill-tribe villages, where traditionally costumed people eke out a living.

Dong Van Karst Plateau Geopark features some of Vietnam's most stunning scenery.

Ha Giang

Vietnam's northernmost province, Ha Giang was off-limits to tourists for years due to a drawn-out conflict with China, and visitors still need a permit, which is regularly scrutinized at checkpoints. However, it's easy to obtain a permit at the immigration office in Ha Giang, and with the province's scenery of limestone hills, the region is destined to increase in popularity.

Though the provincial capital of Ha Giang is in an impressive setting between two mountains, there's little to detain visitors apart from a so-so museum and a bustling market. The fun really begins about 25 miles (40 km) north of Ha Giang, where Highway 4C veers east and climbs into the recently designated **Dong Van Karst Plateau Geopark,** Vietnam's first geopark. This covers more than 900 square miles (2,500 sq km) of limestone peaks reaching around 5,000 feet (1,500 m). The challenging terrain demands a 4WD vehicle or powerful motorbike, but guarantees unforgettable vistas. Signboards at key viewpoints point out the peculiar geological conditions that have created the unusual landscape.

The first viewpoint is at **Quan Ba** (Heaven's Gate), where the sleepy town of

Tam Son and patchwork fields around it are framed by a skyline of endless limestone peaks. Continuing east through **Yen Minh,** the scenery gets ever more dramatic, with villages of White Hmong scattered beside the road to **Dong Van,** Vietnam's northernmost town. At Sa Phin, shortly before Dong Van, look out for **Vuong Palace,** built by the French for a Hmong king.

As with most towns in this part of the country, Dong Van hosts a vibrant **market**, in this case on Sundays, when villagers from miles around trek into town to buy and sell piglets, sugar cane, and bright aprons to embellish their already colorful dress. Another popular attraction, especially for Vietnamese, is the **Lung Cu Flag Tower,** just 14 miles (22 km) north of town, which marks Vietnam's northernmost point and offers sweeping views of rural China.

In the past, visitors to this remote region had to backtrack via Ha Giang, but the road between **Meo Vac** and **Cao Bang** has now been upgraded, making it possible to continue around the northeast of the country. Of all the spectacular views in this region, few can match those between Dong Van and Meo Vac, where the road goes through the **Ma Phi Leng Pass** and offers dizzying views down to the **Nho Que River** set in a steep canyon.

Cao Bang

Also near the Chinese border, Cao Bang is a bustling market town on the fringes of some of Vietnam's least traveled but most spectacular scenery. From Pac Bo Cave in the west to Ban Gioc Falls farther east, the region is a mass of craggy limestone mountains that provide one striking vista after another. As with Dong Van Karst Plateau Geopark, traveling in this region requires a resilient vehicle. Probing the blue highways amid these limestone mountains by motorbike, bicycle, or 4WD is a must.

In February 1941, after 30 years abroad, Ho Chi Minh trekked 40 miles (65 km) from his base in China to **Pac Bo** ("the source") **Cave.** He spent his first week in a hut just inside the border. The hut is gone, but you can climb a steep limestone stairway to the site. More interesting is the nearby cave, where Ho lived that February and March, plotting revolutionary activities with Vo Nguyen Giap and Pham Van Dong, who'd begun to blaze their own legendary paths across modern Vietnam. They ate

(continued on p. 104)

INSIDER TIP:

Ha Giang and Cao Bang Provinces are the best places to see Vietnam's famed karst landscapes, with limestone peaks blanketed in splendid forests.

—SI HE
National Geographic grantee

Dong Van Karst Plateau Geopark

- 87 E5
- Immigration office, 5 Tran Quoc Toan, Ha Giang (for permits)
- 0219/3875-210
- $$$

Cao Bang

- 87 F4

Visitor Information

- Cao Bang Tourist, 42 Kim Dong
- 026/3852-245

Hill Tribes

Beyond the Viet, Chinese, Khmer, and Cham ethnic groups, Vietnam's highlands are home to an additional 50 distinct ethnic minorities with a total population of four to five million. Since 1993, when authorities opened Sa Pa's colorfully costumed hill tribes and their picturesque villages to tourism, trekking in the highlands has become a major draw.

The Red Dao, identifiable by their red headdresses, emigrated to Vietnam from China 300 years ago.

Called *moi* (savages) by ethnic Vietnamese and *montagnards* (mountain dwellers) by the French, the highlanders were largely ignored until the early 20th century, when French growers discovered the rich red earth was excellent for coffee cultivation. During the Vietnam War, highlanders suffered tremendously from bombings and herbicides as the United States tried to stanch the flow of matériel along the Ho Chi Minh Trail. Ethnographer Gerald Hickey estimates the war killed 200,000 central highlanders and destroyed 85 percent of their villages.

After the war, authorities encouraged lowland ethnic Vietnamese (Kinh) to resettle in the highlands in New Economic Zones. As world demand for coffee boomed, so did the demand for coffee plantations. In this climate, highlanders accused the Kinh of encroachment on their land and religious persecution. The resentment occasionally flared into deadly protests.

When the French first made contact in the late 19th and early 20th centuries, they met a primitive people who had one foot in the world of the hunter-gatherer and one in the world of the farmer. Even today, many hill tribes straddle the boundary between ancient ways and modern methods.

Across Vietnam, ethnic minorities share many similarities. Many farmers practice swidden (slash-and-burn) agriculture. They dwell in stilt homes for protection against dangerous wildlife (though threats from tigers and other cats have dwindled). They drink rice wine from communal jars. And they perform blood sacrifice of water buffalo as a way to assert status in the community or mark the inauguration of a new communal hall or house.

Through the centuries, the Vietnamese and highlanders have allied over common causes. In fact, King An Duong was a Tay chieftain who founded the state of Au Lac late in the third century B.C. The Tay remain one of Vietnam's longest standing ethnic minorities. Today, about 1.5 million Tay live across the north, with the greatest concentrations near Cao Bang.

The tribes are most visibly distinguished by dress, especially women's dress. Unlike the men, the women often cling to traditional costumes. Among the Hmong and Dao women, the elaboration of dress is more important than the elaboration of home. Red Dao women wear ornate red headdresses, often decorated with long strings of coins, while Black Hmong women favor black leggings, embroidered tunics, huge loop earrings, and brimless hats.

The Hmong, like many ethnic minorities, branch into subgroups. There are the Black, Red, White, and Flower Hmong. There are the White Thai and the Black Thai. The distinctions have as much to do with differences of customs and dialect as dress. Unlike the Tay, who absorbed the belief systems of the Vietnamese, most Thai maintained their traditional religious beliefs, which focus on ancestor worship and genii, not Confucianism, Buddhism, or Taoism.

In the southern and central highlands, home to 44 distinct ethnic groups, architecture, not dress, is the great attraction. The matrilineal E De (Ede) people near Buon Me Thuot live in thatched stilt homes that stretch as long as 165 feet (50 m), with common areas and sleeping compartments for related families. The communal houses of the Bahnar (Ba Na) people soar 50 to 60 feet (15–19 m) in dramatic thatch pitches. Husbands in both the Bahnar and Giarai tribes live with their wives' families and have no rights of inheritance.

INSIDER TIP:

Hire an ethnic minority Hmong or Yao guide for trekking trips around Sa Pa—you'll gain real insights into highlander life. They can be hired independently or at some Sa Pa hotels.

—SARAH TURNER
National Geographic grantee

EXPERIENCE: Visiting Hill-Tribe Markets

A visit to a hill-tribe market is a must-do on anyone's itinerary for its stunning visual spectacle. Locals dress in their best for market day, which generally means a blaze of bright colors, like the red turbans of the Red Dao or the rainbow-hued dresses of the Flower Hmong. You probably won't be able to resist taking photos, but be courteous; most locals are happy to be snapped, but some may resent having a camera pointed at them.

As for the shopping, that depends on your taste. Piglets, ducks, and cows are popular items among locals, but less so for tourists. Look for the stalls selling garments and accessories; this is where you might find a unique purse, shawl, or embroidered apron to remind you of your visit. Household implements are nice, too. **Sa Pa** holds its market on Saturday and Sunday, **Can Cao** on Saturday, and **Bac Ha** and **Muong Hum** on Sunday.

The residents of Sa Pa are the beneficiaries and casualties of a thriving tourist trade.

Ban Gioc Falls
- 87 F4
- Trung Khanh District
- $$$ (mandatory permit from police office near falls)

fish from a stream that Ho named for Lenin, and at night, beneath the glowering bulk of Karl Marx Mountain, Ho lectured on history and politics.

The shallow cave contains a copy of Ho's wooden bed, and signs below point to where he fished, drew water for tea, and worked at a limestone slab desk. In a museum that's as likely to be staffed as not, exhibits include Ho's bamboo suitcase and Hermes typewriter, and the Nung tunic he wore in 1941.

Farther east, **Ban Gioc Falls** thunder out of China. For years now the Vietnamese and Chinese have been bickering over ownership of the mist-shrouded falls.

Ba Be National Park

Ho Ba Be, north of Hanoi in Bac Kan Province, is Vietnam's largest natural lake and the centerpiece of this national park. The 5-mile-long (8 km) lake is hemmed in by dramatic limestone bluffs, smothered by lush flora, and "guarded" by Pac Ngoi, a 2,597-foot (787 m) sheer promontory to the south.

INSIDER TIP:

If you're going to the northern highlands, consider taking the overnight train to Lao Cai (and minivan on to Sa Pa). You save a day of travel, and you'll get to see the rice fields in the morning.

—SARAH TURNER
National Geographic grantee

The park is home to bears, lorises, and the rare François' langur, a small, reclusive black monkey with distinctive white sideburns. Ba Be is also one of the country's richest butterfly habitats, hosting more than 350 species.

Just over a mile (2 km) from the park entrance, skiffs depart from a ferry landing for tours of the lake, which is fed by three rivers and drained by one. Two five-hour boat trips ply separate rivers, bound for the 1,000-foot (300 m) **Puong Grotto** on the Nang River and **Dau Dang Waterfall.** A leisurely two-hour trip *($$)* tours the lake from end to end. At the north end, the trees are cocooned in tangles of vined growth and rise from the ground like grotesque stalagmites.

At the south end, the clear waters of the Cho Leng River course beneath **Pac Ngoi** and past a Tay village of the same name, which means "mouth of the lake." The Tay settled this area two millennia ago and still occupy wooden stilt houses in the valleys and river bottoms. In all, 3,000 ethnic minority people inhabit 13 villages in the park; more than half are Tay. The Dao, who moved into the area a century ago, live at the mid-elevations, while the Hmong inhabit the uplands.

A paved road rims the lake's south end, opening up beautiful vistas of Pac Ngoi as you reach the bridge. In **Pac Ngoi village,** the Tay provide guest facilities in several stilt homes. Alternatively, you could stay in the state-run guesthouses by the park entrance, but they're nothing special, and you'll have to listen to karaoke on weekend nights.

Sa Pa & Around

Among the big-shouldered mountains of the northwest, Sa Pa is the boomtown hub of Vietnam's most colorfully exotic ethnic minorities. The town is thronged by domestic and international visitors who come to see the elaborate costumes of the Hmong, Red Dao, and Tay people. The town also serves as a base for treks into the region's far-flung villages, where minorities eke out a living as farmers of rice, cardamom, and corn.

Ba Be National Park

- 87 E4
- Park entrance: 27 km (44 km) W of Na Phac on Hwy. 279
- 0281/3894-014
- $

Bac Ha & Beyond

Though it's a long ride east across the Red River Valley from Sa Pa to Bac Ha, a convoy of buses covers the route each Sunday, taking visitors to the weekly market at Bac Ha. The hills around this small town are peppered with hill-tribe villages; the Flower Hmong are the main group. Their presence and wares make this market memorable, as is the Saturday market at Can Cau, about 12 miles (20 km) north of Bac Ha.

First, a caveat about Sa Pa: It has been corrupted by its popularity. Black Hmong women, especially, crowd the doorways of hotels and latch onto passersby, hawking sales of "blankies" in feathery light voices. Hotel rooms have multiplied exponentially since authorities opened the region to tourism in 1993. But go anyway. Hire an inexpensive guide and trek, motorbike, or 4WD your way into the hinterland villages. The ethnic wardrobes are a wonder, and years from now, when the world dresses alike, you will have stunning photographic evidence.

On the Red River, **Lao Cai** serves as the gateway town. You can hop a minibus for the 19 miles (30 km) to Sa Pa. The 90-minute drive unveils steep

Sa Pa

- 86 C4

Visitor Information

- Sa Pa Tourist Information Center, 2 Fansipan
- 020/3871-975
- Closed Sun.

mountain flanks corrugated by terraced rice fields, Sa Pa's signature topographical feature. While other landscapes in Vietnam are more dramatically pitched—the limestone karsts of Cao Bang, for example—residents of those regions lack the allure of Sa Pa's captivating costumes.

Despite its gold rush feel, cloud-bathed Sa Pa retains much of the appeal that prompted a French building boom here in the 1930s. Its mile-high (1,586 m) elevation keeps the heat at bay, though the town is often fogged in. When clear, the views are tremendous, especially from **Ham Rong** ("dragon's mouth"), whose rocky summit sits nearly 700 feet (200 m) above Sa Pa. To reach it, take the trail that starts behind the stone church in the center of town. From the summit, look south into the Muong Hoa Valley, north into the Trung Chai Valley, northwest to Ta Phin, and west to O Quy Ho. Visible in the distance is **Fan Si Pan,** Vietnam's highest peak (see sidebar this page).

Sa Pa is best known for its **market** for area villages, whose costumed residents arrive hauling huge bamboo hampers on their backs. Off Cau May, a stairway flanked by fresh vegetable vendors descends to an attractive market largely dominated by ethnic Vietnamese (Kinh). Turn left at the bottom to find a graphically jarring suite of butcher's blocks that display trays of beet red livers, hearts, and severed heads of cows.

Of interest to travelers is an upstairs room where the region's minorities sell clothes and jewelry. Heavily brocaded blankets, waistcoats, indigo-dyed bolts of hemp, men's caps, and silver bracelets are the big sellers, but shop with discretion. The embroidery on that brocade bag may have been mass-produced in Hanoi. The markets in such remote villages as Bac Ha, east of Lao Cai, and Ban Ho, in the nearby Muong Hoa Valley, are less popular and thus more traditional.

EXPERIENCE: Trekking Near Sa Pa

Whether it's the pull of the energizing chill air and damp mists or the chance to overnight in villages of exotic cultures, there's no doubt that trekking in Sa Pa is the most popular activity for foreign visitors in the hills of northwest Vietnam. Tour operators (see Travelwise p. 239) offer all kinds of treks, ranging from a half-day saunter around the outskirts of town to a week's nonstop trudge through deep valleys and over rugged hillsides, resting nightly in a stilt house in a hill-tribe village.

Looming over Sa Pa, 10,312-foot (3,143 m) Fan Si Pan is a favorite target of trekkers; it requires no ropes or special equipment, but its seemingly gentle slopes and benign climate can be deceptive. The 11-mile (19 km) approach from Cat Cat, a village 2 miles (3 km) south of Sa Pa, passes some very rough terrain, the summit is usually fogged in by cloud, and the round-trip takes a minimum of three to four days. This trek requires levels of endurance well above average.

Farther up Cau May are a new open-air tourist market, across from the sunken public square, and another market on the apron of the **stone church** *(Ham & Phan Xuan Huan)*, built by the French in 1935, and to the west of the sunken public square, behind the tourist office, is an interesting **Culture Museum**, which features videos and useful information about the ethnic minority groups.

Sa Pa Hill Towns: The Black Hmong village of **Cat Cat** is just two miles (3 km) from Sa Pa, so it's easy to visit independently (those farther away require a local guide). You might spot vats of indigo dye, which is essential for Black Hmong dress, and keep an eye open for the bamboo pipes that provide villagers with both water and power.

Sa Pa offers easy access to **Ta Phin,** a Red Dao village about 7 miles (12 km) north, with a so-so granite cave.

To the southeast is the Tay village of **Ban Ho,** on the Muong Hoa River, where guided trekkers can stay in a bamboo-floored, Tay stilt house. As you approach town, you'll spot windowless Hmong homes. After the Xa Pho people, the Hmong are the region's poorest ethnic minority, though the most fancifully attired. Each house centers on the family's simple altar, maybe a sheaf of handmade paper hung from a hook and tacked with the recent good fortune, such as feathers from downed game.

As you stroll village paths, look for bamboo saucers of drying purple cardamom buds, an aromatic spice of the ginger family. Or catch the scent of fragrant white smoke from kilns at the village entrance.

Sa Pa Culture Museum

- 87 E5
- 2 Fansipan
- 020/3871-975
- 11:30 a.m.–1:30 p.m.

As this view from the Topas Eco-Lodge suggests, Sa Pa's greater glories await outside of town.

Dien Bien Phu
✉ 86 B3
Visitor Information
✉ Dien Bien Tourism, 7 Thang 5
☎ 023/3824-410

Other villages near Sa Pa where it is possible for visitors to stay overnight include **Sin Chai, Ta Van,** and **Giang Ta Chai.** In Sin Chai, a Hmong settlement, you might catch weavers at work, while in Ta Van and Giang Ta Chai you'll be able to observe the simple lifestyle of the Dao and Giay communities.

Lai Chau Province: West of Sa Pa, the road to Muong Lay climbs past the Silver Waterfall to 6,600-foot (2,000 m) **Heaven's Gate,** Indochina's highest pass.

Although spectacular, Lai Chau is a remote province with little but the prospect of serendipity to offer travelers. The town of **Muong Lay** sits south of the confluence of the Song Da and Nam Na Rivers. The old town was flooded in 2010 and now lies submerged behind a new dam. A new town has now been constructed beside Highway 12.

Dien Bien Phu

At Dien Bien Phu in 1954, the Vietnamese scored their greatest victory in a modern, set-piece military battle and decisively set the stage for the French withdrawal from Vietnam. Today, the sprawling town that sprouted in the wake of conflict is largely visited by domestic pilgrims and French War buffs.

An old-timer pays his respects to the fallen at Dien Bien Phu.

In late 1953, French soldiers parachuted into this remote valley to cut Vietnamese supply lines and draw out the guerrillas. Gen. Vo Nguyen Giap took the bait and marshaled 55,000 combatants to counter a French force of 16,000. On May 6, 1954, Giap mounted an all-out attack, defeating the French after a 55-day siege and strengthening Vietnam's hand at peace talks in Geneva.

Start your tour at **Dien Bien Phu Museum,** a half mile (1 km) from the town's main fork near the market. One pavilion displays artillery pieces of the kind used by Giap's forces. Another is a graveyard for French matériel, including rusted Willys Jeeps and tanks.

Inside is a panoramic diorama of the valley floor, including the suite of low-lying hills at the core of the French garrison. You'll also find miscellaneous battle relics, including an iron bathtub that French commander General de Castries used in his bunker.

Across the street, ranks of unmarked tombs fill one of several **cemeteries** that hold the 10,000 Vietnamese casualties. Its white granite gate with a mirador bell tower is reminiscent of the triple gates of Vietnam's imperial past. Just inside are listed the names and hometowns of the dead, most from Nghe An and Thanh Hoa, the home provinces of Vietnam's two greatest heroes, Ho Chi Minh and Le Loi, respectively.

Above the museum is a recently restored hilltop redoubt known to the Vietnamese as **A1** and to the French as Eliane 2, with tunnels, trenches, and a massive bomb crater. Across town, **de Castries' command bunker** endures as another vestige of the battle.

Mai Chau Valley

Though the White Thai villages near Mai Chau may lack the colorfully costumed inhabitants of Sa Pa (its rival for trek-minded customers), this valley's bucolic charms, proximity to Hanoi (84 miles/135 km to the northeast), and stilt-house architecture all make for an enriching experience. Nearly every visitor to this fairly remote locale overnights in Ban Lac or Pom Coong, Thai villages situated on the outskirts of Mai Chau town.

INSIDER TIP:

A good trek: 7.5 miles (12 km) from Ban Lac, take a ferry 2 miles (3 km) down the Ma River to Co Loung Village and walk back along the footpath.

—RON EMMONS
National Geographic contributor

With about 75 stilt houses, **Ban Lac** is larger and more popular than neighboring **Pom Coong.** Both villages are touristy, especially Ban Lac, where the space among the stilts is frequently made over as shops for local handicrafts. Beyond here, the commercialism gives way rapidly to more pristine villages.

Most travelers visit on an organized tour, with a homestay included. Usually, host families sleep in a segregated wing of the house, and tourists bunk communally under mosquito tents. As you go upstairs, look for fishtails carved into the wooden door frame of the main entrance. Traditionally, an unmarried son carved a tail for every fish caught, to show off his skills as a provider to prospective in-laws. ■

Dien Bien Phu Museum

✉ 7 Thang 5
☎ 023/3824-971
$ $

Mai Chau

Map 86 D2

Visitor Information

✉ Hoa Binh Tourist, Rte. 6, Hoa Binh, near Mai Chau
☎ 018/3854-374

More Places to Visit in the North

Ba Vi National Park

The landmark mountains of 28-square-mile (73 sq km) Ba Vi National Park rise from a fairly level plain and top out at 4,251 feet (1,296 m). A road summits cloud-wreathed **Ngoc Tan,** where worshippers at **Thuong Temple** pray to the mountain god Tan Vien. On clear days, visitors can soak in vistas of the Red River Delta and Hanoi, 31 miles (50 km) east. The French built 200 villas at Ba Vi during the colonial era. The ruins of a Catholic church and its 36-foot-tall (11 m) bell tower, now smothered by forest, remain popular with photographers. The Muong minority live at the mountains' base, while the Dao dwell higher on the slopes. These forests are also renowned for medicinal plants. *vuonquocgiabavi.com.vn*

87 E2 034/3881-205 **Hanoi Office** Tan Linh commune, Ba Vi District, Hanoi 04/3388-1082

Co Loa

Although Hue is known as the ancient imperial capital of Vietnam, that designation rightfully belongs to Co Loa, founded in the late third century B.C. by King An Duong and occupied by the Ngo dynasty in the middle tenth century. Co Loa means "old snail" and refers to a likeness between the city's concentric walls and the rings of a snail shell. Nine miles (14 km) of earthwork ramparts remain discernible at the original site, 11 miles (18 km) from Hanoi. Inside the citadel, the **Co Loa communal house** stands on the site of the old royal court. Nearby is a **shrine to My Chau,** the king's daughter. Archaeologists have unearthed bronze drums, stone stelae, and tens of thousands of arrowheads, axes, and knives.

87 E2 10 miles (16 km) N of central Hanoi in Dong Anh District $

Lang Son

Eleven miles (18 km) from the border, Lang Son bore the brunt of Vietnam's 1979 conflict with China, hence the relatively new look to a rather old town. Primitive peoples dwelled in caves here 500,000 years ago, and caves remain the attraction. In the three **grottoes at Tam Thanh** *($)*, look for the 18th-century poem inscribed by mandarin border guard Ngo Thi Si.

87 F3 **Visitor Information** Lang Son Tourism, 9 Tran Hung Dao 025/ 3814-848

Son La

In 1908, the French built a penitentiary in this remote province, 203 miles (328 km) northwest of Hanoi. Between 1930 and 1945, **Son La Prison** *(Tien Le, closed 11:30 a.m.–1:30 p.m., $)* housed thousands of revolutionaries, thus consecrating its status as a memorial. Though partly destroyed by a 1952 bombing, its underground cells evoke the torturous past. An interesting on-site **museum** explores the cultures of the province's dozen ethnic minority groups.

86 C2 **Visitor Information** Trade Union Hotel, 6 Thang 4 022/3852-804

Name Changes in the Northwest

Just when you've sorted out Hanoi from Hoi An and Lao Cai from Lai Chau, the government goes and changes it all, and you're no longer such a savvy traveler in Vietnam. Recently, Lai Chau became Muong Lay, Muong Lay became Moung Tra, and Tam Duong became Lai Chau. Let's just hope the locals know where they're going.

A region known for its magnificent cave system, fantastic limestone landscapes, and the home villages of the nation's greatest heroes

North Central

A mandarin statue at Pho Minh Pagoda, near Nam Dinh

North Central

The north-central provinces of Vietnam form a long, slender stem between the great bulge of the Red River Delta and highlands to the north and the beefy belt of the central highlands to the south. The coast offers long stretches of white dunes and unexploited beaches. Inland, limestone mountains crumple the terrain into an alluring landscape of caves, karsts, and bastions of nationalism.

Dramatic limestone karsts define the inland landscape in Ninh Binh Province.

NOT TO BE MISSED:

Visiting the ruins of Vietnam's former capital at Hoa Lu **115**

Rowing through the caves and karst scenery at Tam Coc **115–116**

Ho Chi Minh's birthplace in Hoang Tru near Vinh **117**

The huge stalagmites and stalactites in the Phong Nha Cave **118–119**

Touring the Vinh Moc Tunnels, once inhabited by refugees in the Vietnam War **122–123**

Khe Sanh, a former combat base in the demilitarized zone **125**

Southeast of Hanoi, Nam Dinh Province is a fertile tract of the Red River Delta that warrants a visit for its pagodas and temples. Tran Hung Dao, who repelled the Mongol invasions in the 13th century, hailed from Nam Dinh and expanded a palace at the present site of Thien Truong Temple.

The attractions in Ninh Binh Province have broad appeal. The local tourist bureau touts the karsts of Tam Coc as an inland Ha Long Bay. They're not, but only because Ha Long is in a league of its own. More intriguing is the Phat Diem Cathedral, a hybrid of Asian and Occidental architecture designed by an eccentric Catholic priest in the latter part of the 19th century. In this picturesque landscape, the temple complex at Hoa Lu is an architectural tribute to the country's medieval dynasties.

The attractions in the provinces of Ha Tinh, Nghe An, and Thanh Hoa—Ho Chi Minh's boyhood home, the Lam Kinh Citadel—pale beside competing attractions elsewhere. If you're inclined to skip, here's where to do so. But as you do, note that this infertile region produced two of Vietnam's three greatest heroes—Ho Chi Minh and Le Loi. (Tran Hung Dao is the third.)

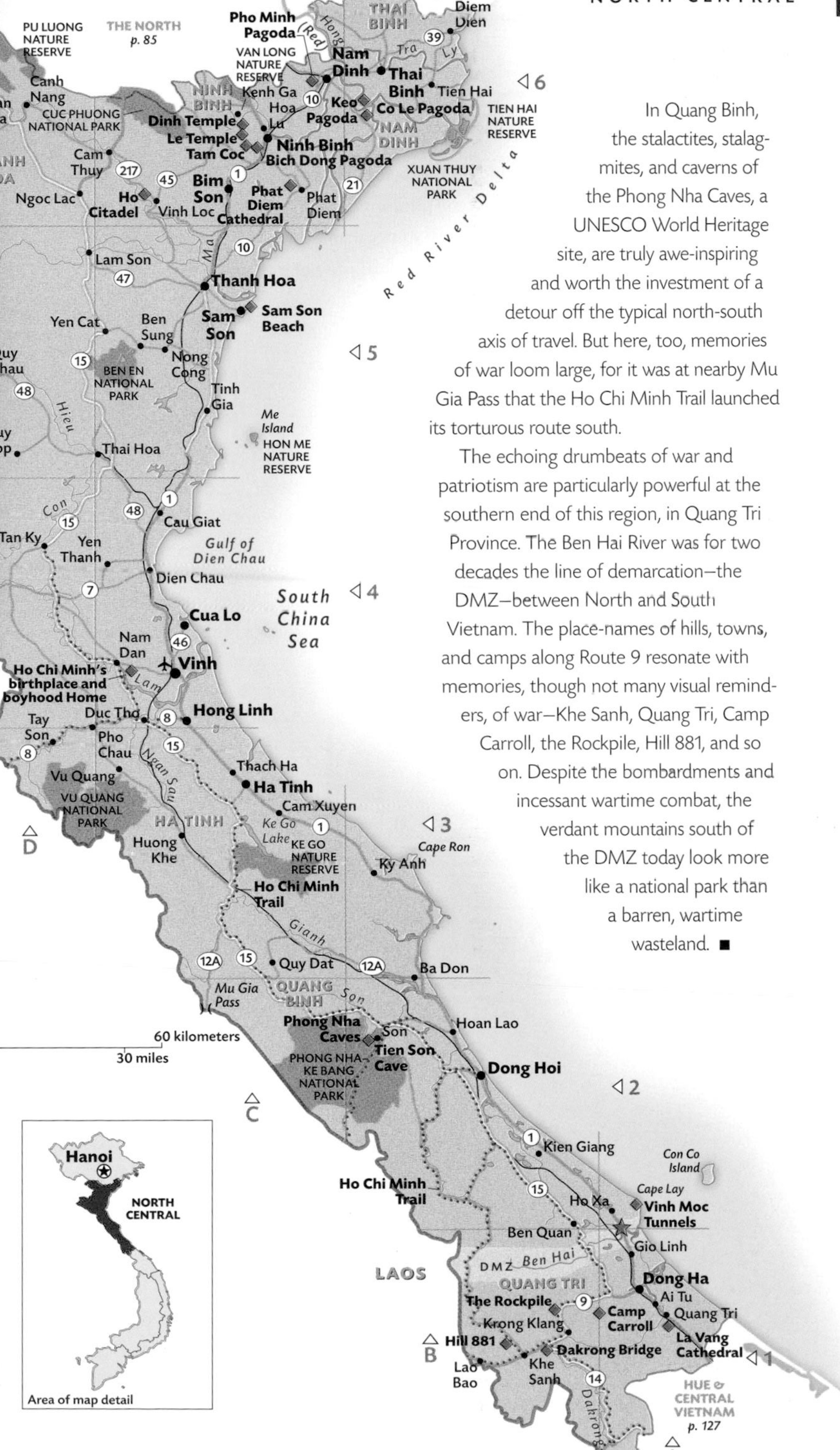

In Quang Binh, the stalactites, stalagmites, and caverns of the Phong Nha Caves, a UNESCO World Heritage site, are truly awe-inspiring and worth the investment of a detour off the typical north-south axis of travel. But here, too, memories of war loom large, for it was at nearby Mu Gia Pass that the Ho Chi Minh Trail launched its torturous route south.

The echoing drumbeats of war and patriotism are particularly powerful at the southern end of this region, in Quang Tri Province. The Ben Hai River was for two decades the line of demarcation—the DMZ—between North and South Vietnam. The place-names of hills, towns, and camps along Route 9 resonate with memories, though not many visual reminders, of war—Khe Sanh, Quang Tri, Camp Carroll, the Rockpile, Hill 881, and so on. Despite the bombardments and incessant wartime combat, the verdant mountains south of the DMZ today look more like a national park than a barren, wartime wasteland. ■

Red River Delta

Nam Dinh, a major city on the Red River Delta, is the gateway to several lovely pagodas in Thai Binh Province, while Ninh Binh is the jumping-off point for Tam Coc, an inland water world of precipitous karst crags reminiscent of the formations in Ha Long Bay. Beyond Tam Coc, several temples and a cathedral warrant a long day of exploration.

Nam Dinh

113 C6

Visitor Information

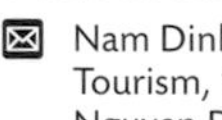

Nam Dinh Tourism, 115 Nguyen Du

035/3849-439

Nam Dinh & Around

Nam Dinh draws few tourists despite centuries-old pagodas and temples that rank among the country's oldest surviving examples. Tran Hung Dao, one of the top three heroes in the Vietnamese pantheon, was born in Nam Dinh, and a cult of his energetic devotees remains prosperous and hard at work, as is amply witnessed by the bustle at area temples.

Pho Minh Pagoda's 14-story tower, built in 1305

A pleasant city of 230,000 with lively, shaded streets, Nam Dinh has made few concessions for travelers. A gargantuan statue of Tran Hung Dao lords over a lake at the city center, looking remarkably like another legendary hero, Le Loi, whose statue stands in downtown Thanh Hoa.

Nineteen miles (30 km) east of Nam Dinh in Thai Binh Province, **Keo Pagoda** *(map 113 B6; $)* is the region's star attraction. Dating from between 1133 and 1154, the pagoda was moved to its present site in 1611 after the Red River flooded its former grounds. Today, the pagoda is celebrated for its architecture and fanciful wooden statuary. More than 20 statues of Buddhist deities occupy the T-shaped entrance to the main temple, and more than 50 statues festoon a succession of altars along the pagoda's main axis. The second temple holds a lacquered miniature boat that's brought out during a major festival here in the ninth lunar month.

Across the Red River, **Co Le Pagoda** *(map 113 B6)* is a 1920 restoration of a pagoda built during the Ly dynasty. Lining the sanctuary walls are impressive relics—a series of devotional tablets, inscribed with Chinese characters in the 12th century. The 95-foot-high (29 m) main chamber is presided over by a painted ironwood Buddha, set on an altar near the ceiling. In front of the pagoda, a 105-foot (32 m) tower of nine tiers stands atop the undulate shell of a tortoise.

Two miles (3 km) northwest of Nam Dinh is **Pho Minh Pagoda,** whose 700-ton (630 metric ton), 14-story tower has somehow kept from sinking into the surrounding floodplain. The 1305 tower dates from the original Ly-built pagoda. Beside it stands **Thien Truong Temple,** where locals fervently worship Tran Hung Dao.

Ninh Binh & Around

The first king of the Dinh dynasty put this area on the map in the 11th century when he moved his government from the ancient capital at Co Loa to this karst landscape 56 miles (90 km) south of present-day Hanoi.

The Dinh set their capital amid the limestone crags at **Hoa Lu,** just north of Ninh Binh town, because it was farther from China and easier to defend. The Ly abandoned the site in 1010 when they moved the capital to Thang Long, now Hanoi. Ruins are limited to a few unearthed sections of citadel wall, palace tiles, simple statues, bones, and porcelain. But the site is worth visiting for two temples built in the 17th century to commemorate the ephemeral dynasties.

Fragrant with jasmine joss and architecturally sublime, the **Dinh** and **Le Temples** boast stout ironwood pillars, lacquered to a high vermilion sheen and gilded with dragons. The pillars stand on stone plinths because, though insect resistant, the wood rots in water. Gilded wood carvings on the trusswork are richly detailed.

Another recently built temple worth visiting in the area is **Bai Dinh Pagoda**, just seven miles (12 km) from Hoa Lu. It consists of an old temple in the foothills and the largest temple complex in the country, sprawling over an entire hillside. Everything about it is on a grand scale, including the largest hall, **Tham The Hall,** which is 193 feet (59 m) wide and stands 111 feet (34 m) high. There's also a 100-ton (91 metric ton) bronze Buddha statue, a 36-ton (33 metric ton) bell in a magnificent bell tower, and 500 statues of arhats carved of local stone.

South of Hoa Lu at **Tam Coc** ("three caves"), you can take a sedate trip up the Ngo Dong River through its eponymous three caves. The rowboats are

Van Long Nature Reserve

Like nearby Tam Coc and Kenh Ga, Van Long is often invoked as another terrestrial Ha Long Bay. The 7,410-acre (3,000 ha) reserve surrounds karst formations that rise abruptly from extant wetlands enlarged by local irrigation efforts. Boats probe the wetlands on tours for birders. Amid this natural splendor, the endangered Delacour's langur is making a last stand.

Ninh Binh
113 C6
Visitor Information
Ninh Binh Tourism, Dinh Tien Hoang
030/3884-101
dulichninhbinh.com.vn/en

Hoa Lu
113 C6
Handspan Travel, 78 Ma May
04/3926-2828
$$$$$ (day tour)
handspan.com

Van Long Nature Reserve
113 C6
Visitor Information
Ninh Binh Tourism, Dinh Tien Hoang
030/3884-101
Boat tour: $$
dulichninhbinh.com.vn/en

Tam Coc
113 C6
Visitor Information
Handspan Travel, 78 Ma May
04/3926-2828
$$$$$ (day tour)
handspan.com

NOTE: Visiting Kenh Ga is best done by signing up for a daylong boat tour ($$$$$) that includes Van Long Nature Reserve (see p. 115).

typically skippered and crewed by women. The distant karst mountains come into high relief, and soon the river tunnels through 417-foot (127 m) **Hang Ca,** the first of the caves, followed by **Hang Giua** and **Hang Cuoi**. The farther you travel upriver, the more dramatic the scenery, as sheer crags rise from either bank.

Just over a mile (2 km) north of Tam Coc via Highway 1 is **Bich Dong Pagoda,** which occupies an interesting if overhyped limestone grotto. To reach this shrine to the Buddha, you'll climb two sets of slippery stairs.

INSIDER TIP: While taking the boat ride through Van Long Nature Reserve's picturesque karst landscape, be on the lookout for monkeys and birds.

—JONATHAN A. O'BRIEN
National Geographic grantee

Farther north along Highway 1, another inland boat trip plies the muddy waters of the Hoang Long River from Ninh Binh to the village of **Kenh Ga** ("chicken canal"), its name a reference to nearby 127°F (53°C) hot springs where locals douse chickens for easier plucking. Village homes perch beneath the crags and on miserly spits that flood during high water. After a quick tour of the watery main street, the sampan will meander into deeper water past limestone hills that supply cement factories.

Seventeen miles (28 km) southeast of Ninh Binh off Highway 1, hundred-year-old **Phat Diem Cathedral** *(map 113 C6)* was the brainchild of Tran Luc, an indomitable Catholic priest more popularly known as Father Six. Parishioners prepared the unstable site by driving thousands of bamboo stakes into the floodplain, followed by layers of earth, gravel, and bamboo rafts.

Graham Greene Legacy

Today, the 5-acre (2 ha) compound comprises the cathedral itself, four chapels, and three man-made grottoes. It was from the 85-foot (26 m) bell tower that novelist Graham Greene watched the Viet Minh battle the French, a scene captured in his 1955 masterpiece, *The Quiet American*. A two-ton (1.8 metric ton) 1890 bell on the tower's upper mirador is audible for miles. From this height, 20 visible church steeples testify to the inroads Catholicism has made here over the past 400 years.

That said, the cathedral looks as much like a Buddhist pagoda as a Catholic sanctuary. Framing the entry is a Buddhist garland of stone lotus blooms. Inside, 52 ironwood columns support a roof that shelters 1,500 for Mass. The vermilion altarpiece has gilt woodwork echoing Hue's Imperial City. Statues of Matthew, Mark, Luke, and John perch atop four pagoda-like turrets that frame the central tower. A huge drum on the tower's lower mirador is another nod to Vietnamese traditions. ■

Vinh

The capital of Nghe An Province, Vinh still lives up to its reputation as the nadir of the North, though that's changing as a rising tide of prosperity reinvigorates a city once infamous among travelers for its downtown ghetto of six-story East German–designed apartment complexes. Still, the main—and only—reason to lay over in Vinh is for access to Ho Chi Minh's birthplace and boyhood home, two bucolic compounds just west of town.

Among the country's most densely populated and least arable provinces, Nghe An has long been a hotbed of discontent, giving rise to generations of revolutionaries, including Ho Chi Minh. He was born in Hoang Tru hamlet, 9 miles (14 km) west of central Vinh.

Ho was born Nguyen Sinh Cung on May 2, 1890, in a simple home his maternal grandfather built in 1883 as a wedding gift for Ho's parents. The thatched home did not survive, but the government reconstructed the birthplace in 1959 to honor the president of what was then North Vietnam.

Ho Chi Minh was born in a thatched house near Vinh in 1890.

Ho Chi Minh Birthplace

Today, the **Ho Chi Minh birthplace** is light on exhibits and none of the explanatory text is in English. But the spacious, rural compound gives a good feel for how Vietnam's rural mandarins lived in the late 19th century.

Adjacent to Ho's birthplace are a temple his maternal grandfather built for the veneration of his ancestors and his grandfather's thatched home. Here, Ho's father, Nguyen Sinh Sac, studied for his doctoral degree, the highest literary honor in Vietnam.

After Sac won the prestigious degree, villagers built a new home for him and his family, just over a mile (2 km) away in Kim Lien. Ho Chi Minh lived here as a boy from 1901 to 1906. With fewer exhibits than the birthplace, **Ho's boyhood home** disappoints. It sits across the road from an equally lackluster **Ho Chi Minh Museum.**

In Vinh, you could look for three restored gates of the citadel on Dau Tan, built in 1831. Apart from that, the main attraction is the beach at Coa Lu, just 10 miles (16 km) away, which is packed on weekends with locals. Literary pilgrims can journey 10 miles (16 km) east across the river into Ha Tinh Province, where Nguyen Du, Vietnam's answer to Shakespeare, was born in 1765. ■

Vinh

Map 113 C4

Visitor Information

Nghe An Tourist, 13 Quang Trung

038/3844-298

Ho Chi Minh Birthplace & Boyhood Home

From Vinh, follow Phan Dinh Phung to Rte. 46. After about 6 miles (10 km), look for signs to Kim Lien, Ho Chi Minh's birthplace is in Hoang Tru hamlet, his boyhood home a mile (2 km) away in Kim Lien.

$ $

Phong Nha Caves

Though celebrated by local people for centuries, the Phong Nha Caves are only now taking their rightful place among the world's most spectacular caverns. A UNESCO World Heritage site since 2003, these limestone grottoes include the largest cave in the world and border the largest contiguous tract of forest in Vietnam, where the age of discovery has yet to end.

Neon highlights the stalactites and stalagmites within Tien Son ("fairy mountain") Cave, one of two great systems in Phong Nha–Ke Bang National Park.

Phong Nha–Ke Bang National Park

113 B2–C2

Son Trach Village

052/3677-021

Boat tour: $$$

phongnhakebang.vn

As far back as the ninth and tenth centuries, the Cham were using these vast, awe-inspiring subterranean chambers as temples. In the 19th century, Nguyen emperor Minh Mang memorialized the limestone caves on one of nine dynastic urns in the The Mieu compound of Hue's Imperial City.

During the Vietnam War, North Vietnamese troops used the caves as a garrison and weapons cache just off the Ho Chi Minh Trail, a fact not lost on the American forces, who heavily bombed the area. Look for the scars of war on the rock face above the cave entrance.

The **Phong Nha–Ke Bang National Park** lies 30 miles (50 km) west of **Dong Hoi.** The city's hotels can arrange transportation to the park, or you can rent a motorbike *($$)* to make the round-trip. From the visitor center, sampans ferry travelers 3 miles (5 km) up the Son River amid a series of picturesque karst crags, soon entering **Phong Nha Cave** through a slot at the base of a sheer, 492-foot (150 m) limestone cliff. In the dry season (Feb.–Aug.), low water levels limit tour boat access 2,000 feet (600 m) into the cave via a 330-foot (100 m) chamber known as Bi Ky.

The sampan puts in at a sandy beach within a stunningly vast chamber, 165 feet (50 m) high and bristling with stalactites and stalagmites. Growing at a rate of half an inch (1 cm) per year, one massive stalagmite stands 56 feet (17 m) high and is 21 feet (6.5 m) in diameter. Over this fantastic formation, an 82-foot (25 m) stalactite tumbles like a woman's hair falls, as locals say.

Illuminated Nature

Back outside, more than 300 steps climb to the mouth of **Tien Son Cave,** a 1,000-yard (915 m) chamber, nearly half of which is open to visitors. Where Phong Nha overwhelms with its vastness, Tien Son is all about fantastic rock formations. As in Phong Nha, the crannies of this cave are illuminated by fluorescent reds, greens, and blues. While the Vietnamese penchant for garish colors trends toward kitsch (e.g., the disco halo about the Buddha's head in venerably old pagodas), in Phong Nha this impulse actually enhances the drama of the formations.

There are two other caves of interest in the park, though only one as yet is open to the public. The first, **Thien Duong Cave** ("paradise cave"; $$$$$), is accessed via a steep stairway leading into a huge cavern that is more than 328 feet (100 meters) wide and tall. Visitors must be accompanied by a guide, and the site is managed by the Sun Spa Resort in Dong Hoi (see Travelwise p. 250). It was thought to be the longest cavern in Vietnam until the 2009 discovery of **Son Doong Cave** ("mountain river cave"), which has been confirmed as the largest cave in the world.

The enormous chambers in this cave could swallow an entire city block, and it is filled with marvels such as 200-feet (60 m) stalagmites and enormous calcite pearls.

World Heritage Sites-in-Waiting

Vietnam has seven sites on the World Heritage List and hopes to add more. Sites under consideration include Ba Be National Park (see pp. 104–105); Cat Tien National Park (see pp. 184–185); Cat Ba Archipelago (see pp. 95–96); and Trang An Scenic Landscapes, which includes Hoa Lu and Tam Coc (see p. 115), and four sacred temples—Bach Ma, Ouan Thanh, Voi Phuc, and Kim Lien (see p. 117).

Unfortunately, the main reason that this cave has remained hidden for so long—its extreme remoteness—is also the reason it is not yet open to the public. However, you can now take a sneak preview at the wonders within by visiting the website, *sondoongcave.org.* ■

Ho Chi Minh Trail

During the Vietnam War, a million North Vietnamese soldiers stole into South Vietnam along the Ho Chi Minh Trail, an elusive 12,000-mile (19,000 km) web of jungle paths and primitive roadways. The road's principal artery plunged south from Mu Gia Pass near the Phong Nha Caves through Laos and Cambodia. Today, the north-south Ho Chi Minh Highway links several sections of the trail.

In 1955, after it became obvious that Ngo Dinh Diem would thwart countrywide elections planned for the following year, a North Vietnamese major began to survey a north-south supply line for the inevitable war. In 1959, more than 400 volunteers started to extend a network of primitive pathways, originally cut by highlanders, as the Truong Son ("long mountain") Trail.

In the early 1960s, the trail comprised simple footpaths, a lane winding through bamboo groves. North Vietnamese soldiers took six months to reach their destinations. By 1968, after years of upgrading, they'd whittled a few months off the transit, but still had to hustle along for 11 to 12 hours a day. By war's end, trucks completed the relatively brisk journey in 23 days.

The U.S. military detected the presence of the supply route almost immediately but was unable to stanch the tide of matériel funneling south for more than a few days at a time. Attempts to interdict soldiers and supplies along the trail sparked the battles at Ia Drang and Hamburger Hill, the siege at Khe Sanh, the air campaigns of Rolling Thunder, Nixon's Cambodian incursion of 1970, and the South Vietnamese incursion into Laos in 1971.

U.S. Bombing Campaign

In 1969 alone, the United States pummeled the trail with 433,000 tons (390,000 metric tons) of bombs. By war's end, the Americans had dropped 1.7 million tons (1.5 million metric tons) of explosives, killing one enemy for every 300 bombs dropped, according to a CIA estimate. Between 1965 and 1971, antiaircraft batteries downed 43 U.S. airmen over Mu Gia Gate. In all, Hanoi claims its soldiers downed 2,500 U.S. planes over the trail; the Pentagon says the Vietnamese brought down 500.

There's no consensus as to why the bombing failed, yet it did. That became obvious to the Americans as early as 1966, when they

EXPERIENCE: Cruising the Ho Chi Minh Highway

The Ho Chi Minh Highway was built to alleviate transportation problems in the country, since the main north-south road, Highway 1, which runs along the coast from Hanoi to Ho Chi Minh City, is frequently damaged by annual rains and a steady stream of heavy trucks. The new highway built in 2000 runs through the mountainous interior of the country, passing remote, rural areas that were previously inaccessible, but as yet the road sees little traffic.

This is good news for independent travelers who want to get off the beaten path and see some of the country's wilder regions. All you need to do is rent a motorbike (make sure it's in good condition) and buy a map. Some of the most beautiful sections of the road are between Hanoi and Vinh, where you'll pass carts pulled by cattle and farmers tending their fields. There is little in the way of tourist facilities along this road, so you'll have to make do with roadside food stalls and simple hotels.

A typical porter along the Ho Chi Minh Trail would keep moving for up to 12 hours a day.

began to mull the option of using tactical nuclear weapons. Strategists discarded the option, arguing the political downside would far outweigh the upside on the battlefield.

So the B-52s rolled on, obliterating huge tracts of the highlands. The campaign killed countless thousands of communist soldiers and petrified everyone else, including the 300,000 laborers who toiled to keep the trail open. As perilous were the snakes, drownings, accidents, and disease. During the early years on the trail, nearly 10 percent of the porters succumbed to malaria. The adversity forged a camaraderie that helped steel the communist forces.

In 2000, Vietnam broke ground on an inland highway along the former Ho Chi Minh Trail to link Hanoi with Saigon. At the time, some suggested the money would be better spent upgrading Vietnam's already existing infrastructure, while others considered the paving of the legendary trail tantamount to consecration of the old jungle footpath. So far, the highway has proven of dubious benefit to the region's ecology and economy.

Quang Tri Province

Bordering the former DMZ (demilitarized zone), Quang Tri Province saw some of the worst fighting during the Vietnam War, with the local citizenry struggling to survive. The Vinh Moc Tunnels, home to hundreds of wartime refugees for years, and the town of Quang Tri bear testimony to the fortitude and resourcefulness of a besieged people and the destruction of war.

Except for a brief respite in 1968, villagers lived in the underground tunnels until 1973.

Vinh Moc Tunnels

- 113 A2
- From Hue, travel 60 miles (100 km) N along Hwy. 1 to Ho Xa, turn E (right), and travel several more miles to the tunnels at Cape Lay
- 054/3816-263
- $

Vinh Moc Tunnels

For six years of the Vietnam War, the mile-long (2 km) tunnel complex at Vinh Moc sheltered hundreds of refugees from a fishing village that had been decimated by U.S. bombing. On three levels, 40 to 75 feet (12–23 m) below the surface, families lived in cramped cells gouged from either side of a 4- to 5-foot-wide (1.2–1.5 m) passage. Vinh Moc is one of 14 tunnel systems in the region north of the former DMZ but the only one accessible today.

Villagers dug their refuge in 19 months and moved underground in December 1967. Except for a brief respite in 1968, they lived here without interruption until January 1973, enduring a barrage of 500 rockets per day on average.

Today, a quarter mile (400 m) of the complex is open to tours. Though some of the uppermost level has collapsed, the deepest sections remain intact. From the visitor center, flashlight-guided tours enter one of 13 portals. Bring your own light.

Unlike Cu Chi's claustrophobic tunnels (see pp. 214–215), Vinh Moc's corridors are a relatively roomy 5 to 6 feet (1.5–1.8 m) high, where planked walls give way to cocoa-colored laterite. The corridor passes small bays that served as family quarters, larger conference chambers, and a maternity ward where 17 children were born. In the deepest chambers, residents drew water from two wells and warehoused supplies that had come down the Ho Chi Minh Trail. At night, they risked discovery by U.S. Navy patrols to ferry supplies to Con Co Island, 17 miles (28 km) offshore. From Con Co, food and ammunition were relayed south.

The tour winds in and out of the tunnels and ends atop a bluff above a beach that King Bao Dai used to frequent.

Quang Tri

Quang Tri, more than Khe Sanh, la Drang, or Hue, resonates painfully in the ears of Vietnamese who recall the ferocious 81-day battle in 1972 that reduced the town to rubble. In the spring of 1972, as North Vietnamese forces advanced on Quang Tri, the South Vietnamese Army decamped from the citadel and joined thousands of refugees fleeing along Highway 1 toward Hue, 35 miles (56 km) south. The communists shelled the melee, wreaking havoc that inspired one correspondent to dub the road the Highway of Horrors. In the early 1950s, after frequent attacks by the Viet Minh, the French had called this stretch of Highway 1 the Street Without Joy.

Approaching Quang Tri from the south, one first notices the ruins of a Catholic church to the right of the highway—a photo op on popular DMZ tours out of Hue. Turn right on Tran Hung Dao, and you'll pass a bombed-out **Buddhist school** whose pocked walls speak to the firepower rained down on Quang Tri. Farther on, the **Cong Trong Gate** breaches the 1824 **citadel** *(Ly Thai Tho, $)*, whose shattered brick walls still rim the grounds. A war memorial stands within, while a decent museum exhibits before-and-after photos of Quang Tri.

Back on Highway 1, near the white bridge, take Le Loi 2.5 miles (4 km) to its dead end at **La Vang Cathedral.** This 1928 church was upgraded to a basilica in 1962. Its bell tower and facade survived the 1972 campaign, and it now also has a glass-walled nave. ■

Quang Tri
113 A1
Visitor Information
Sepon Travel, 189 Le Duan, Dong Ha
053/3855-289
sepontravel.com

Border Crossings

There are now more than 12 international border crossings between Vietnam and its neighbors (Cambodia, Laos, and China), with more opening every year. This is great news for independent travelers who wish to include Vietnam in a grand Southeast Asian circuit. However, some of the crossings are very remote and some border officials and taxi drivers use this remoteness to extract unscheduled payments from travelers. If you are considering crossing a border, use one of the busier ones, such as the border station at Lao Bao, where you can continue on, presumably without any hassle, via Suvanakhet to Vientiane.

A Drive Along the DMZ

Though the former DMZ (demilitarized zone) and nearby mountains fell under the greatest deluge of bombs in the history of warfare until the late 1960s, nature has so persuasively reclaimed the land that it takes a savvy eye to detect wartime scarring. Still, a tour from the Ben Hai River to Khe Sanh is a haunting journey through place-names that resonate for people with even cursory knowledge of the Vietnam War.

A cement-filled sandbag copy of an American bunker during the battle for Khe Sanh

NOT TO BE MISSED:

- **Rockpile** • **Dakrong Bridge**
- **Khe Sanh**

Most DMZ tours (*Sepon Travel, 053/3855-289, $$*) start in Hue and include a trip to the Vinh Moc Tunnels (see pp. 122–123), The first stop is usually at the **Ben Hai River** ❶, the former line of demarcation between North and South Vietnam that runs along the 17th parallel.

A no-man's-land during the war, the DMZ stretched north and south of the riverbank for 3 miles (5 km) in either direction. On the north bank, the restored station of the International Control Commission, jointly staffed by Poland, Canada, and India, stands before a restored gateway to the **Hien Luong Bridge.** U.S. bombers knocked out the French-built planked bridge in 1967. The restored bridge serves as a memorial.

From **Dong Ha,** the tour heads west on Route 9, a road blazed by the French in 1904, toward the Truong Son Mountains. Just shy of **Cam Lo,** a onetime American firebase, a road veers right for **Con Thien** ❷, another U.S. firebase 7.5 miles (12 km) north. In the midst of grueling summer combat in 1967, both *Time* and *Life* splashed images of besieged soldiers at Con Thien on their covers.

West of Cam Lo, a visible trail climbs to the 1,785-foot (544 m) summit of a hill once known as **Firebase Fuller** ❸, from which U.S. artillery hurled shells as far as Khe Sanh, 25 miles (40 km) southwest. Farther along Route 9, a short road to the left leads up to a pepper plantation at the former **Camp Carroll,** named for a Marine captain killed by friendly fire in 1966. Its 22 artillery pieces represented the largest firebase in the hills around Khe Sanh.

Beyond, Route 9 veers around a denuded

UXO in the DMZ

The so-called demilitarized zone (DMZ) that divided Vietnam at the 17th parallel during the Vietnam War is one of the greatest misnomers ever. In fact, the DMZ, a 6-mile-wide (10 km) strip of land straddling the Ben Hai River, had more bombs raining down on it than almost anywhere else in the country. The result is a minefield of unexploded ordnance (UXO) that has claimed more than 10,000 lives since the war ended. Stick to the road while exploring this explosive region.

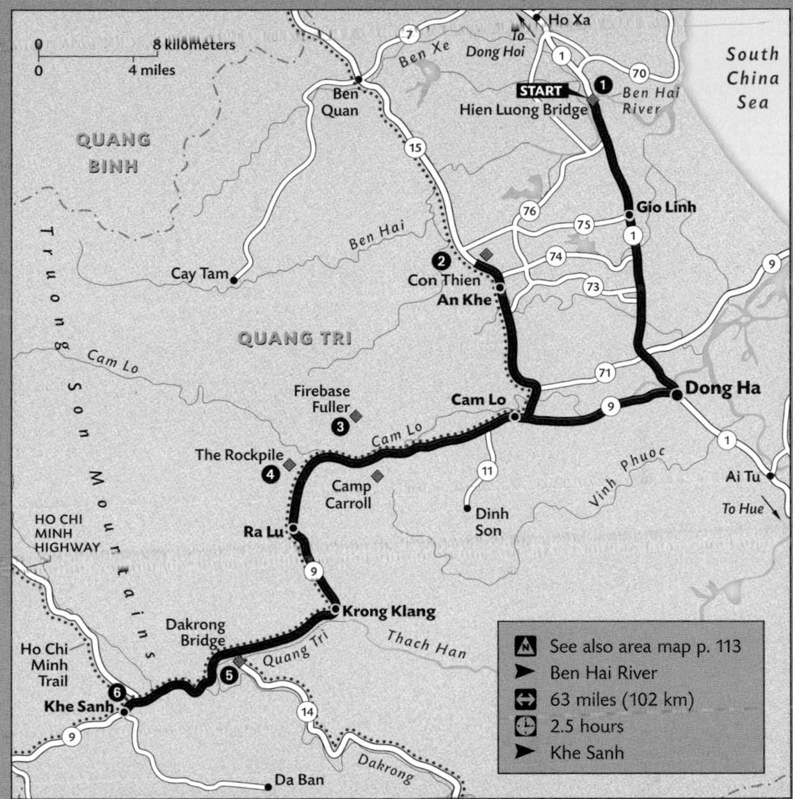

crag to the **Rockpile** ❹, a 755-foot (230 m) hill off the right side of the road. In 1966, U.S. recon troops set up an observation post on the hill. Until abandoning the post in 1968, Marines here directed artillery in support of passing ground troops.

Climbing past the farm villages of the Bru highlanders, the highway beyond Krong Klang now serves trucks hailing from Laos and points farther east on a new route to Burma. At the **Dakrong Bridge** ❺ over the Quang Tri River, a marker memorializes a spur of the Ho Chi Minh Trail that once intersected Route 9 here.

Eight miles (13 km) farther west, the road twists into **Khe Sanh** ❻, site of the largest U.S. combat base in the DMZ and red-hot center of the war between January and April 1968. In late 1967, the North Vietnamese massed an army of 20,000 in the surrounding hills, diverting American attention from the Viet Cong's multipronged Tet offensive in 1968. Over nine weeks, the United States dropped 75,000 tons of bombs on North Vietnamese positions, killing approximately 10,000 soldiers. Incoming mortars and artillery claimed about 200 American lives.

Today, a **museum** *($)* stands at the center of the onetime combat base and airstrip. Outside, next to several helicopters and a tank, cement-filled sandbags replicate American bunkers. Exhibits inside include flak jackets, helmets, weapons, and mess trays salvaged from the base.

Guided tours return to Hue from here.

More Places to Visit in North-central Vietnam

Cuc Phuong National Park

Established in 1962, Cuc Phuong was the country's first national park. Seventy-five miles (120 km) south of Hanoi and 40 miles (65 km) west of Ninh Binh, this is one of the more accessible and visitor-friendly places to experience the country's diverse flora and, with luck, fauna. The big draw is the **Endangered Primate Rescue Center,** a breeding facility that houses 150 primates comprising 15 species of gibbons and langurs. The park also breeds the rare Owston's civet, as well as weasels, otters, and big cats rescued from the wildlife trade. Trails meander past magnificent trees to caves in limestone outcrops and to Muong villages, where guests can overnight in a stilt house.

INSIDER TIP:

At Cuc Phuong National Park, ask to take the Silver Mountain hike. It is strenuous, but it goes to the highest point in the park. The views are spectacular!

—CATHERINE WORKMAN
National Geographic grantee

Langurs—slender, long-tailed monkeys—are rehabilitated at Cuc Phuong National Park.

Visitors can also stay at park-owned bungalows on **Mac Lake.** The best time to visit is in the dry season (Oct.–March); in April and May, millions of butterflies breed here.

cucphuongtourism.com 🅼 113 C6 ✉ 28 miles (45 km) W of Ninh Binh via Hwy. 1; follow the road to Kenh Ga and Van Long Nature Reserve ☎ 030/3848-006 $ $

Ho Citadel

The communist government is surprisingly successful at promoting Vietnam's imperial past and this is a prime example. The Ho Citadel, located near Vinh Loc, northwest of Thanh Hoa, was inscribed as a World Heritage site by UNESCO in 2011. The Ho dynasty lasted only seven years, from 1400 to 1407, but the citadel walls, made of huge blocks of stone and enclosing almost a square kilometer (247 acres), are still standing, with gateways at the cardinal points. All that's left between the walls are a few stone cannonballs and grassland, but UNESCO granted World Heritage status on the basis that the site testifies to the flowering of neo-Confucianism in the late 14th century in Vietnam.

🅼 113 C6 **Visitor Information** ✉ Thanh Hoa Tourist, 25A Quang Trung, Thanh Hoa ☎ 037/3852-517 $ $

Sam Son Beach

Ten miles (15 km) east of Thanh Hoa, Sam Son stretches along the north-central coast. The French colonial government popularized these shores and dunes with a holiday resort in 1907. Today, young Vietnamese couples flock to Trong Mai ("cock and hen") Rock, a natural landmark that memorializes a legend about a fairy who fell in love with a mortal. Before the god of thunder could punish her for this violation, she transformed herself and her lover into stone.

🅼 113 C5

Home to some of Vietnam's most appealing attractions, flush with splendid imperial architecture, an ancient Southeast Asian port, and the ruins of a vanished kingdom

Hue & Central Vietnam

Closed silk lanterns await a buyer's touch and awe.

Hue & Central Vietnam

The chimera of Indochine is rendered most tangible by the central provinces of Vietnam. The cities' imperial and colonial vestiges, the idyllic villages and garden houses, ever present mountains, and pregnant rivers seem to flow as much from an illusion of Vietnam as from the soil and water itself. Vietnam is firing on all cylinders here. When the weather's right, it's as good as good can get.

Neighbors still gather along Hue's sidewalks for Chinese chess and the latest gossip.

Thua Thien and Quang Nam (home provinces to Hue and Danang, respectively) entered the dominion of the Viets in 1306 after a Cham king ceded a huge chunk of his kingdom for the hand of a Vietnamese princess. In the 16th century, a disaffected Nguyen aristocrat heeded the prophecy of a Nostradamus-like character named Nguyen Binh Khiem and migrated south from Thanh Hoa to settle the southern frontier.

While nominally loyal to the powerless remnants of the Le dynasty, the Nguyens fought endlessly with the Trinh, a rival group of northern aristocrats, across a border not too far from the later line of demarcation between North and South Vietnam. The Tay Son routed the

NOT TO BE MISSED:

Nguyen from Hue in 1775, but by 1802, following retaliation by Nguyen Anh (later King Gia Long), the Nguyens unified the country and established their capital at Hue.

Hue's imperial monuments compose one of seven sites in Vietnam inscribed on UNESCO's World Heritage List. Quang Nam is home to a pair of World Heritage sites—the antique port of Hoi An and the Cham ruins at My Son.

Though the weather deters many tourists—from October to January, cloudy skies and rain can plague the city for weeks at a stretch—Hue's tombs, palaces, museums, pagodas, garden homes, colonial French villas, and municipal buildings, coupled with a poetic landscape, are the richest vein for cultural exploration in Vietnam.

South of Hue, Danang is more of a springboard to local attractions—Hoi An, the Marble Mountains, My Son, China Beach—than an attraction in its own right. A beachhead for the great foreign incursions of the 19th and 20th centuries, today Danang is setting itself up as a jaunty commercial center, with international flights landing at its airport and a busy seaport. Hoi An, by contrast, is all about tourism, nostalgia, and the beach. ■

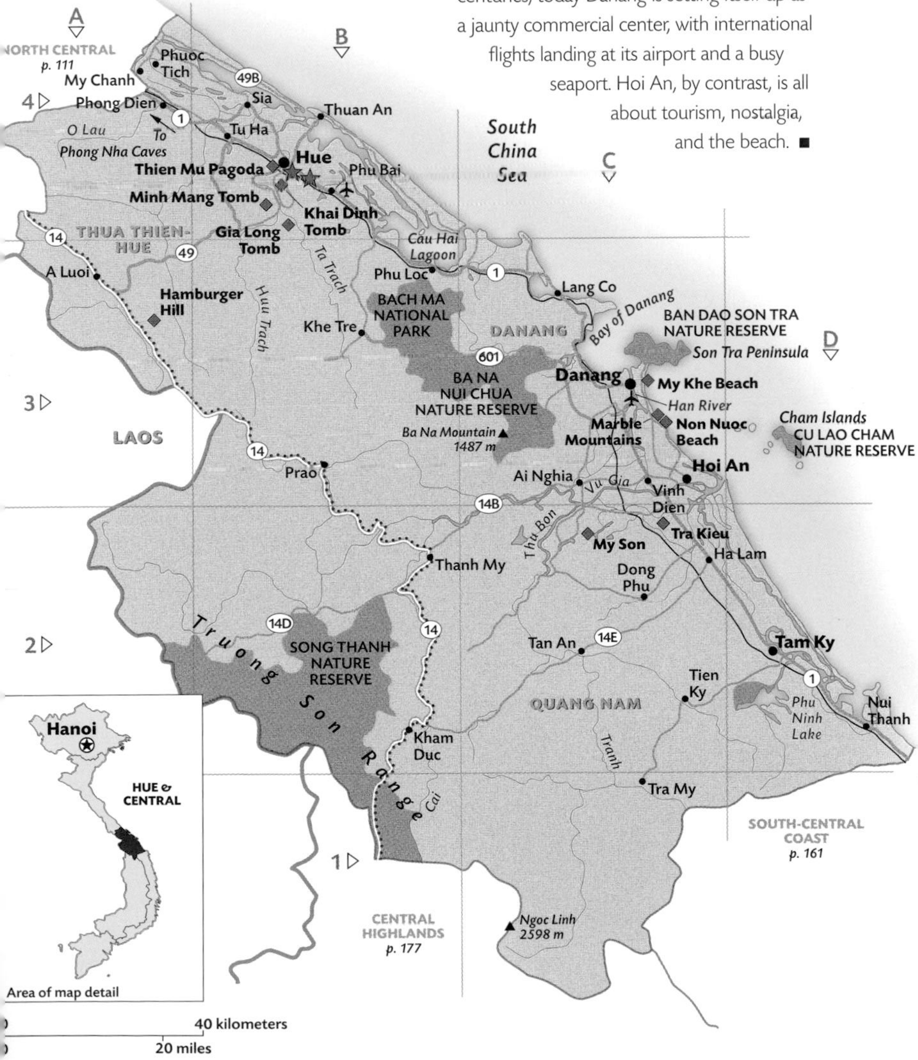

Hue

Though Ho Chi Minh's government extinguished Hue's glory days as the imperial capital of Vietnam in 1945, many architectural and cultural relics of the imperial era have been assiduously preserved. The dervishes of urban renewal have largely ignored the city, leaving its centuries-old pagodas, villas, garden homes, and river with an enduring aesthetic hegemony.

Docents in traditional garb at the Imperial City's Mieu Temple

Hue
129 B4
Visitor Information
Hue Tourist, 120 Le Loi
054/3816-263
huetouristvietnam.com

Mandarin Café, 24 Tran Cao Van
054/3821-281
$$
mrcumandarin.com

Hue is a languorously genteel place whose singularly accented people are not merely behind the times but lost in time. The city is spliced, not divided, by the Perfume River. Life is as vital on the north bank, where the Nguyen kings reigned from within the Forbidden Purple City, as it is on the south bank, where the French laid out their sprawling new district in the late 19th century.

The Forbidden Purple City is contained by the walled Imperial City, where the most resplendent structures and relics survived both the French War and, to a lesser extent, the Vietnam War. Breached by a complement of ten Asian gates, the fortress-like walls of the citadel encompass both walled cities, as well as expansive neighborhoods of leafy streets, parks, museums, markets, and bistros.

The French bequeathed a

graceful European counterpoint on the south bank, with several marvelous art deco buildings and a broad range of villas, churches, and municipal buildings.

Upstream from the citadel, the tower of Thien Mu Pagoda looms over the Perfume River as the city's most prominent landmark. The nearby garden district of Kim Long basks in a timeworn ambience emanating from its houses of columns and panels.

Out along Dien Bien Phu, the level urban terrain rumples into picturesque hills sown by the tombs of the Nguyen kings and lesser royalty and nourished by countless pagodas—perhaps one for every thousand residents.

Hue Citadel

The massive Hue Citadel, which encompasses the grandiose Imperial City and fabled Forbidden Purple City, is an Asian wonderland of palaces, pavilions, temples, ponds, gardens, gates, and halls. Capital of the Nguyen dynasty from 1802 until the abdication of the last emperor, Bao Dai, in 1945, the Imperial City is a sublime interpretation of the larger, more austere dynastic capital at Beijing. Though a catastrophic 1947 fire destroyed many of the 150 royal structures built during the Nguyens' 143-year reign, the most magnificent structures survived and have been restored with such meticulous fidelity to the past that it's hard to tell what's old and what's new.

Gia Long, first emperor of the Nguyen dynasty, broke ground on the colossal imperial complex in 1804, conscripting 30,000 subjects to toil on his architectural fantasy. He soon boosted the daily workforce to as many as 80,000 unhappy laborers, prompting European observers to condemn his despotism.

INSIDER TIP:

Hue's local treat is the *banh khoai*—a small pancake layered with bean sprouts, shrimp, pork, and a quail egg. It's perfect for a snack or with cold beer. Enjoy them at two of the city's best joints: Hong Mai and Lac Thien.

—KRIS LEBOUTILLIER
National Geographic photographer

Bounding the complex is the **citadel** *(kinh thanh)*, a 1.5-square-mile (4 sq km) fortification of 22-foot (6.5 m) walls, ramparts, parapets, and bastions, with a commanding flag tower that fronts the Perfume River. Built on designs by pioneering 17th-century French military architect Sébastien de Vauban, the sheer walls rise from a 13-foot-deep (4 m) stone-lined moat between 130 and 165 feet (40–50 m) wide.

Impregnable as it may seem, the citadel was militarily obsolete even at the time of its construction. Still, Viet Cong and North Vietnamese troops managed

(continued on p. 134)

Hue Citadel

 133

N bank of Perfume River, via Phu Xuan & Trang Tien Bridges; enter at Ngo Mon Gate

A Walk Along Le Loi

After taking control of Hue in 1885, the French ceded the Imperial City to the Vietnamese and made over the Perfume's south bank as a European enclave, where they improved an avenue that King Gia Long blazed in the early 1800s. Today, Le Loi stretches from the railway station to Trang Tien Bridge, its old colonial buildings having borne witness to events that loom large in the history of Vietnam.

Hue is renowned for its music, poetry, cuisine, and residents' distinct accent.

In 1906, the raspberry red **Hue railway station** ❶ *(2 Bui Thi Xuan)* opened as the northern terminal of the Danang-Hue leg of the Transindochinois line. Construction on the railway began in 1899, though the 1,072 miles (1,715 km) between Saigon and Hanoi would not link up until the mid-1930s. Gustave Eiffel's firm designed the White Tiger Bridge north of the station.

Across the Phu Cam Canal, **La Residence Hotel** *(5 Le Loi)* was built in 1930 as the colonial government's guesthouse. Its bowed front, long horizontal lines, porthole windows, and nautical accents are hallmarks of the streamline moderne branch of art deco architecture.

Next door is Hue's **Ho Chi Minh Museum** ❷ *(7 Le Loi, closed Mon & 11:30 a.m.–1:30 p.m., $)*. Its prized relics are trifles—a radio, a pair of watches, cotton shirts—that Ho gave to local supporters. Slightly more profound Ho memorials include the reconstructed house in nearby

NOT TO BE MISSED:

Quoc Hoc High School • imperial monument • Cercle Sportif

Duong No *(5 miles/8 km NE of Hue)*, where Ho (then Nguyen Sinh Cung) lived as a boy from 1898 to 1900, and the house at 112 Mai Thuc Loan, where he lived in 1901.

In 1908, Ho attended the prestigious **Quoc Hoc High School** *(10 Le Loi)*, a national school founded by King Thanh Thai in 1896. A statue of the boy-student stands in the school's main avenue, though access is restricted. Pham Van Dong and Vo Nguyen Giap also studied here. The school's first headmaster, Ngo Dinh Kha, was Thanh Thai's minister of rites and the father of South Vietnam's President Ngo Dinh Diem.

Opposite the school gate is an **imperial monument,** erected in 1920 to commemorate colonial French and Vietnamese soldiers who died in France during World War I; the names are found on the monument's river side. Until recently, the streetside face of the monument was a billboard for Ho Chi Minh's most famous maxim: "Nothing is more precious than independence and freedom."

Continuing along Le Loi, **Hai Ba Trung Secondary School** ❸ *(12 Le Loi)* opened in 1917 as a girls' school complement to Quoc Hoc. Its raspberry red facade, like Quoc Hoc's, is a legacy of Ngo Dinh Kha's tastes.

Farther along, you'll pass the magisterial **People's Committee Building** on your right. Across the street, the streetside ward of Hue's

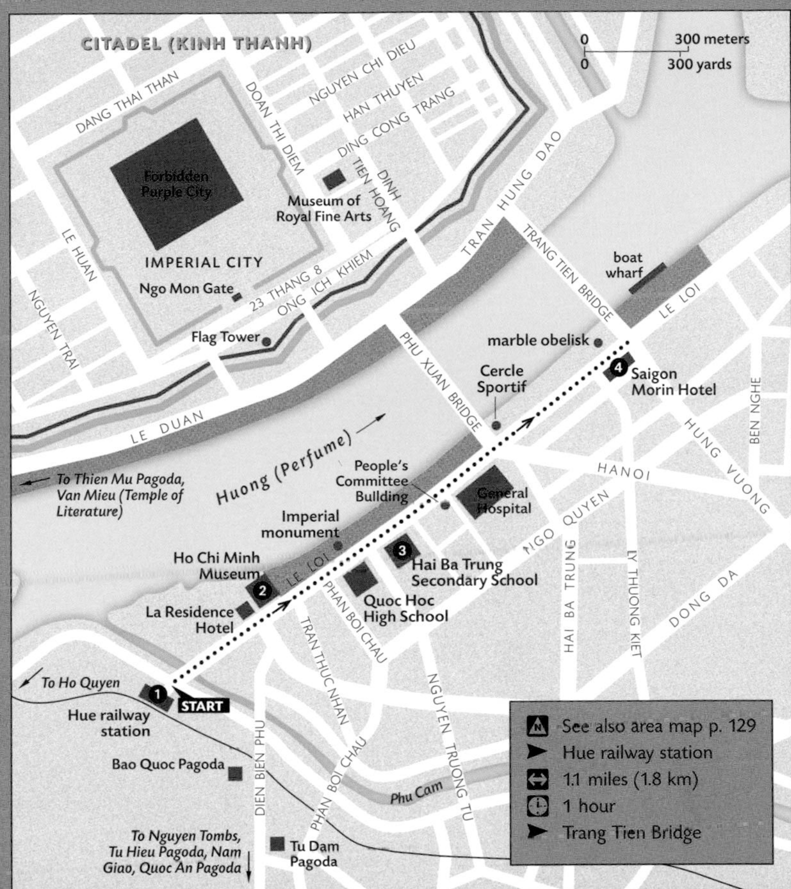

General Hospital was built after the Battle of Hue in 1968.

Across the Hanoi intersection, the **Cercle Sportif** is another streamline moderne design. From **Phu Xuan Bridge,** note the building's pronounced veranda, porthole windows, and bridge-like penthouse on the upper deck. During the colonial era, the Cercle was a leisure club.

Farther east, stretching for an entire city block along Le Loi, the 1901 **Saigon Morin Hotel** ❹ *(30 Le Loi)* was an unfortunate casualty of a Saigon Tourist restoration in the 1990s. Charlie Chaplin honeymooned here with Paulette Goddard in 1936, and writers André Malraux and Somerset Maugham also checked into the Morin brothers' hotel.

Across the street, a **marble obelisk** topped by the Buddhist wheel of law commemorates eight protesters who died on May 8, 1963, during a rally against anti-Buddhist measures enacted by Ngo Dinh Diem. The protests escalated here in Hue and ultimately brought down the Diem regime.

The French-built **Trang Tien Bridge** *(at Hung Vuong)* is mentioned in more than a few melancholy songs about lost love and dreary weather in Hue. The seven trestles of the quarter-mile (400 m) bridge opened to great fanfare in 1900, with King Thanh Thai himself cutting the ribbon.

to hold out inside the citadel for 25 days in a pitched battle against U.S. Marines during the 1968 Tet Offensive. Battle scars remain, though the rubble is fast disappearing as preservationists gradually restore monuments that UNESCO identified in 1992 as a World Heritage site.

from which the emperor presided over state ceremonies. Between the flag tower and the gate are the **Nine Holy Cannon.** Gia Long had these forged from captured Tay Son weapons in 1803.

Cross the **Trung Dao Bridge,** spanning lotus-dotted Thai Dich Lake, and enter into

For nearly 150 years, Nguyen kings reigned from the Palace of Supreme Harmony in Hue.

Imperial City

133

Enter the citadel at Ngo Mon ("noon") Gate, 23 Thang 8

$$

NOTE: Court Music Performances are held in the Royal Theater, Imperial City; daily at 10 a.m. & 2 p.m., ($$).

Into the Imperial City:

The Imperial City, a second walled and moated city with a 6,700-square-foot (603 sq m) perimeter, follows the same layout as Beijing's Forbidden City. Tree-shaded paths, crumbling palaces, and flowering gardens make for a pleasant stroll.

Enter through the **Ngo Mon ("noon") Gate,** the 190-foot-wide (57 m), U-shaped entrance once reserved for the sole use of the emperor. Atop the gate's 15-foot (4.5 m) brick foundation is the **Belvedere of Five Phoenixes,** the **Esplanade of Great Salutations,** where mandarins stood in ranks of nine during court ceremonies. The emperor, who declared himself the Son of Heaven, ruled from the **Thai Hoa Palace** (Palace of Supreme Harmony) beyond the courtyard. The sole furnishing in this tiled expanse of lacquered vermilion columns and gilded wood carvings remains the throne, elevated on terraces beneath a canopy representing the heavens.

Behind the palace, the wartime toll is made painfully obvious by

INSIDER TIP:
While visiting Hue, take time to visit Bach Ma National Park (see pp. 149, 152) for its plentiful wildlife, spectacular trees, and flowering vegetation.

—LOIS K. LIPPOLD
Douc Langur Foundation director & National Geographic grantee

huge swards of green space where other royal structures once stood, including 21 acres (8 ha) of the **Forbidden Purple City,** a third walled enclosure that was off-limits to all but the emperor, his wives, concubines, and eunuchs.

The extant **Left** and **Right Mandarin Halls** once flanked the now vanished Can Chanh Palace, a second throne room where the emperor conducted daily business. The mandarins wore court dress when meeting with the emperor. Now, tourists don mandarin attire for photo ops in the left hall; the right hall displays works from the Hue Museum of Royal Fine Arts (see p. 143).

The Splendor of The Mieu

Behind and to the left of the Palace of Supreme Harmony, a leafy avenue leads toward the restored **Chuong Duc Gate.** To the left before the gate is **The Mieu,** a temple Minh Mang built in 1821 to worship his father, Gia Long. The interior is a stunning indulgence of vermilion columns and gilded wood carvings. Its ten bays are dedicated to the veneration of the Nguyen emperors. Although the French overlords first balked at the inclusion of emperors Ham Nghi, Thanh Thai, and Duy Tan, each of whom had been deposed by the colonial masters, the three rebels were duly accorded their bays in 1959.

Across the courtyard, the **Nine Dynastic Urns** stand before the **Hien Lam Pavilion,** the tallest and, to some, the most beautiful structure in the city. The pavilion memorializes those who've helped perpetuate the dynasty. Still more intriguing are the urns. Cast between 1835 and 1837, these 2-ton (1.8 metric ton) vessels served both to collect heaven's mandate and to celebrate the country's beauty and dynastic stability. The hips of each urn are embossed with 17 separate depictions of plants, landscapes, animals, boats, and weapons that form a lexicon of Vietnamese culture. Each is dedicated to one of the Nguyen emperors and stands opposite his bay in The Mieu.

If possible, cap your visit to the Imperial City by attending a

Imperial Cuisine

Hue cuisine is revered throughout Vietnam as the ultimate gastronomic experience. Developed by the emperors of Hue, imperial cuisine consists of at least seven courses. Each dish is prepared using a wide range of ingredients and is presented like a work of art. You can play at being an emperor yourself and sit down to a royal feast, complete with costume, at upscale hotels like the Saigon Morin (see Travelwise p. 253).

Thien Mu Pagoda

 129 B4

From the citadel, follow Kim Long SW beyond railroad bridge

concert of court music (*nha nhac;* see p. 57), a ritual genre once performed at coronations, funerals, and other royal events.

Thien Mu Pagoda

The seven-story tower of Thien Mu ("heavenly lady") Pagoda is Hue's defining landmark, as you will clearly see from the plethora of images on postcards, T-shirts, paintings, and myriad other souvenirs. Thankfully, the pagoda's setting, storied history, and relics make good on its promise as a precious place.

Thien Mu's tower is as much a landmark to Hue as the Eiffel Tower is to Paris or the Empire State Building to New York City.

In 1601, a female mystic decreed that whoever founded a pagoda on this bluff above the Perfume River would also found a great dynasty. Nguyen Hoang gambled on the mystic's prophecy, and his lineage, all the way down to Vietnam's last emperor, Bao Dai, stood as a testament to her wisdom.

From Kim Long, a stairway climbs to four pillars inscribed with Chinese characters that praise Buddhism and the pagoda. The **Phuoc Duyen** ("source of happiness") **Tower** stands 70 feet (21 m) over the pagoda's trapezoidal terrace. A stela to the right details the tower's construction in 1844, while a stela to the left is inscribed with Thieu Tri's poetry.

In 1710, Lord Nguyen Phuc Chu ordered casting of the 8-foot (2.5 m) bronze bell framed within a six-sided pavilion to the left of the tower. Then, in 1715, Chu engraved a hymn to himself and Buddhism on a stela perched atop the sculpted marble tortoise in the pavilion to the right of the tower.

Buddhist guardians flank each portal in the triple-gate entrance to the courtyard. Once through, look back up to see helmeted Ho Phap, guardian of the law, standing above the Taoist jade emperor.

Beyond, the **Temple of the Great Hero** shelters a gallery of statues. In the vestibule, a glass case holds a smiling bronze Di Lac Buddha, while farther in you'll find the ten netherworld kings and a fine collection of 18 clay brown arhats in ceramic robes with gray tracery. Above one threshold, a bronze, black-haired Sakyamuni sits before another iteration of Di Lac and a sanctuary of Buddhas of the past, present, and future.

However superb the statuary, though, there's no relic at Thien Mu more emotive than the one garaged in the monk's apartment building. This robin's egg blue Austin sedan ferried Thien Mu's Thich Quang Duc to the Saigon intersection where he set himself ablaze in 1963 (see p. 47).

Other Pagodas

A Chinese monk, Giac Phong, founded **Bao Quoc Pagoda** *(off N end of Dien Bien Phu)* at the end of the 17th century. In 1747, Lord Nguyen Phu Khoat chartered the pagoda with a royal decree and inscribed the name board that hangs in the main sanctuary. Later in the 18th century, the Tay Son king Quang Trung stored arms and gunpowder in the pagoda. Beyond the name board and a bronze bell cast during Gia Long's reign in 1808, few of the pagoda's relics survived a fire that broke out during fighting at Tet in 1968. But do check out Giac Phong's three-story pink stupa beyond the main hall. At the bottom of the steep stairway is the 15-foot (4.5 m) **Ham Long** ("dragon's jaw") **well.** Though murky these days, its water was once famed for its freshness and clarity and was reserved for the king.

About a half mile (1 km) south on Dien Bien Phu, **Tu Dam Pagoda** has served as a rallying point for Buddhist causes nationwide since the 1930s. Inside the triple gate, a two-story conference hall stands to the right of an expansive courtyard, designed to accommodate throngs of people. The bodhi tree inside the gate grew from a sprig cut in the 1930s from the bodhi tree under which the historical Buddha is said to have received his enlightenment. Following Thich Quang Duc's example in Saigon, a monk immolated himself in this courtyard in 1963.

At the south end of Dien Bien Phu, turn right on Le Ngo Cat. About a half mile (1 km) from the turn are the gates to picturesque **Tu Hieu Pagoda.** Tu Hieu owes its present stature to imperial eunuchs who, fearing oblivion after death, offered money and land to the pagoda in 1848. In return, the monks allotted a graveyard to the eunuchs and pledged to honor their souls. Inside the triple gate, the crescent lotus pond dates from an 1894 restoration. Beyond the main sanctuary, Quang Hieu Duong Hall honors Le Van Duyet (see p. 209) and Quan Kong. This pagoda is also renowned as

Hue's Pagodas

More than 300 pagodas sow the seeds of Buddhism in and around Hue, enlightening the city's reputation as the soul of Vietnam. While their statues and wood carvings do not rival those of the finest northern pagodas, their pleasant settings and feng shui channel chi like nowhere else in the country.

Bao Quoc Pagoda
Map 133

Tu Dam Pagoda
Map 133

Tu Hieu Pagoda
Map 133

Quoc An Pagoda
133

Nguyen Tombs
133
Minh Mang, Tu Duc, or Khai Dinh: $

the "root pagoda" of Thich Nhat Hanh, who lived here as a novice and is now one of the most celebrated teachers of Buddhism in the West after the Dalai Lama.

Turn left at the end of Dien Bien Phu and then left again at Dao Tan to reach **Quoc An Pagoda.** Like Bao Quoc and Tu Hieu, Quoc An was laid out in the square shape of the Chinese character for mouth *(khau).* Four buildings surround an interior courtyard of potted bonsai, with the main sanctuary at front, a hall to worship the pagoda's benefactors at rear, and a reception hall and monks' quarters to either side. Quoc An is one of Hue's oldest pagodas, founded in 1684 by the monk Nguyen Thieu from Guangdong, China.

Nguyen Tombs

The tombs of the Nguyen dynasty kings are in fact grandiose temple complexes, anchored by burial sites and complemented by palaces, pavilions, stela houses, courtyards, gates, ponds, and gardens. Built between 1814 and 1931, the seven tombs were laid out south of the citadel according to the ancient Asian art of

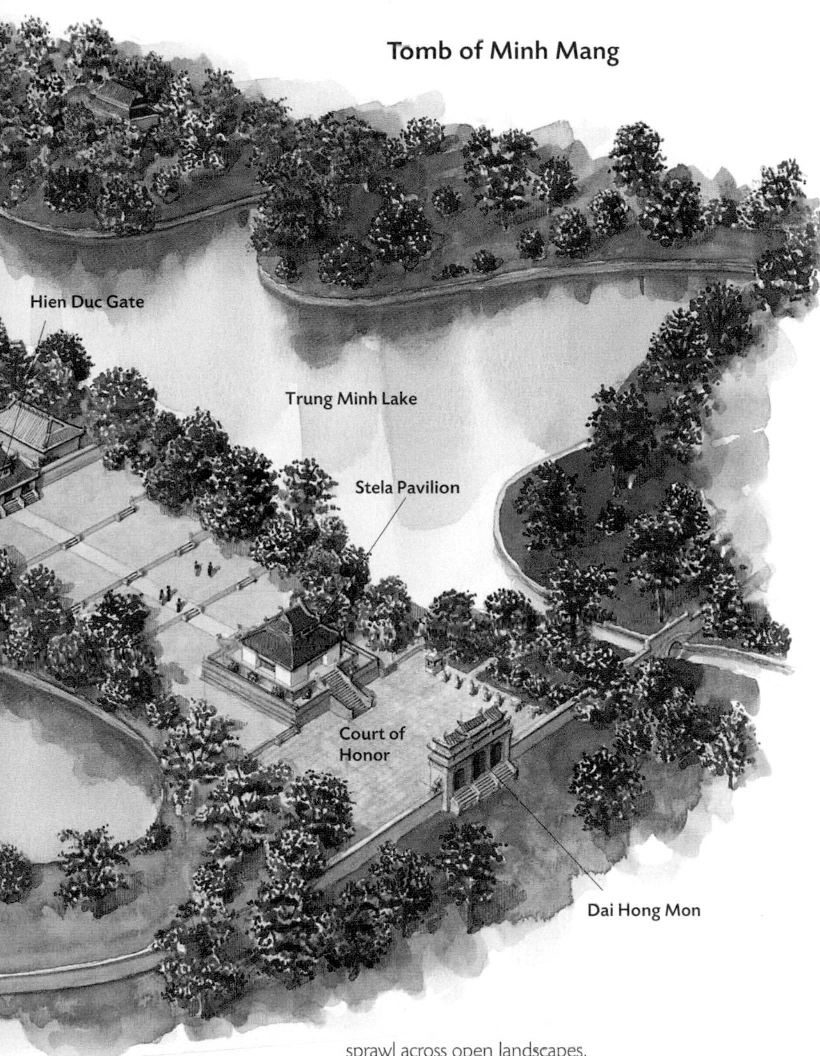

phong thuy, known in the West as feng shui.

Most visitors to Hue confine their explorations to the tombs of Minh Mang and Tu Duc, which are the most majestic and best preserved. The other tombs would rate as major tourist attractions were it not for the proximity of these grand neighbors. Unbound by walls, the monuments to Gia Long, Thieu Tri, and Dong Khanh sprawl across open landscapes, inspiring intimate links with the natural environment. Khai Dinh is a fusion of Asian and Occidental styles. Duc Duc was buried closer to town, on the spot where his corpse accidentally fell in transit.

The Nguyens, who often succumbed to Chinese influence, modeled their eternal cities on the Ming dynasty tombs. Their geomancers strived to nestle the structures within the protective confines of hills, with a dominant

NOTE: To reach every tomb but Duc Duc's, which lies closer in on Duy Tan, you'll turn right at the south end of Dien Bien Phu. Turn left on Minh Mang to reach **Thieu Tri'**s and **Khai Dinh'**s tombs.

Stay straight and take Le Ngo Cat to its end, then turn left on Huyen Tran Cong Chua to reach **Tu Duc'**s and **Dong Khanh'**s tombs. Both **Minh Mang'**s and **Gia Long'**s tombs are accessible via sampan ferries across the Perfume River or via the bridge that crosses the river along Minh Mang. The entrance to Minh Mang's tomb lies a couple hundred yards from the bridge.

The route to **Gia Long'**s is more complicated and follows an unmarked path along the river.

elevation in the near-distance to serve as a hedge against ill winds and a lower hill at the rear to cushion the complex. To the extent possible, they laid out the major monuments—triple gate, court of honor, stela house, temple, and burial site—along a common axis, known as the Way of the Spirit. The statues of mandarins, horses, and elephants that flank the court of honor stand in service to the king after death. Not every tomb subscribes exactly to the model, though Minh Mang's does so with remarkable fidelity.

Minh Mang (*r.*1820–1841): From the **Great Red Gate** (Dai Hong Mon), shut since Minh Mang's corpse passed through in 1841, the Way of the Spirit channels through the **Court of Honor,** ascends a stela house raised on three terraces, then ambles across another courtyard, past two more gates and bridges, and through a temple and a pavilion to its terminus at Minh Mang's tumulus, almost a half mile (1 km) later. A wall, 10 feet (3 m) high and more than a mile (1,750 m) long, encircles 40 structures and a parkscape.

The emperor dragooned 3,000 soldiers and laborers into work on the tomb in 1840. From the **Pavilion of Light** (Minh Lau), Minh Mang watched the tomb take shape. After he died, his son Thieu Tri enlisted 9,000 soldiers and workers to finish the job, which they did in 1843. Until French soldiers plundered this tomb and others in 1885, the **Temple of Infinite Grace** (Dien Sung An) held the emperor's most prized personal possessions. Written by Thieu Tri, the Chinese inscriptions on the **stela** detail Minh Mang's merits and accomplishments, including a reference to the king's 142 offspring.

Tu Duc (*r.*1848–1883): Tu Duc sired no children, despite having 103 concubines. He nevertheless begot a fairyland for his eternal rest before succumbing to smallpox. His tomb caught the eye of French filmmakers, who used the **Xung Khiem Pavilion,** where Tu Duc wrote poetry, in the 1992 epic *Indochine.*

A 4,950-foot (1,500 m) wall encloses 50 distinct elements, including a theater and lake. Following its construction in 1867, the king used the compound

Visiting the Dead

Ancestor worship is an essential element of all Southeast Asian cultures, and Vietnam is no exception. Thus visitors to the country may witness the Vietnamese paying their respects to the deceased in a variety of locations, including the imperial tombs in Hue, the Ho Chi Minh Mausoleum (see pp. 80–81), the cemetery at Dien Bien Phu (see pp. 108–109), and at graveyards of the Giarai tribe.

as a retreat from stormy political straits, for it was on his watch that Vietnam ceded the bulk of its autonomy to France. Beyond the **Khiem Cung Gate,** six major halls mirror the larger imperial compound in Hue. To the right and left are houses for the military and civil mandarins. Tu Duc lodged in both **Hoa Khiem Palace,** where his cult is most active today, and **Luong Khiem Palace,** on the other side of the courtyard. *Khiem,* used in all named elements of the tomb, means "modesty." **Minh Khiem Royal Theater** is one of Vietnam's oldest theaters but is no longer in use today.

The **Court of Honor, Stela House,** and Tu Duc's **tomb** align on an axis beside the Khiem Cung compound. Stroll around the finger of **Luu Khiem Lake,** and you'll pass the tomb of Tu Duc's queen and arrive at the tomb of Kien Phuc, an adopted son of Tu Duc, who ruled from 1883 to 1884.

Gia Long (*r.* 1802–1819):

Gia Long incorporated far fewer man-made structures in the design of his eternal city. The grace notes here are mostly natural. A constellation of 42 hills, big and small, surrounds his tomb.

Beyond **Minh Thanh Temple,** dedicated to the memory of Gia Long and his wife, the first Nguyen emperor and his wife lie side by side in mausoleums of dark blue stone, riddled with scars from wartime fighting. Statues of mandarins in the **Court of Honor** were also damaged, though they, as well as some of the animal

At King Tu Duc's tomb, all named structures contain the word *khiem* (modesty).

appendages, have been restored. Twin obelisks across Long Lake herald **Thien Tho Mount,** the tomb's screen.

Khai Dinh (*r.* 1916–1925):

Khai Dinh's tomb mounts a steep hillside in terraces of cement, concrete, slate, and marble. Such austerity was at odds with the lavish personality of the king, but consistent with his embrace of the trappings of Western civilization.

Inside **Thien Dinh Palace,** the walls of the first room are bedecked in mosaics of ceramic and glass. Panels of the four seasons depict bamboo for winter, the plum blossom for spring, the lily for summer, and the chrysanthemum for fall, while panels in a two-tiered frieze contain the eight precious objects (scroll, lute, wine gourd, etc.), complemented by such modern motifs as a tennis racket and alarm clock. The king's remains are entombed in a vault 30 feet (9 m) beneath this statue.

Dong Khanh (r. 1885–1888): After Dong Khanh's death, King Thanh Thai rehabbed a temple the previous king had built to worship his father's memory. Inside, much of the temple's decor are gifts from the French and carry a subtext of supremacy, from the tricolor stained-glass windows to a lithograph of a Napoleonic battle scene and a pillow used when smoking opium.

Thieu Tri (r. 1841–1847): As at the tombs of Gia Long and Dong Khanh, this complex lacks a surrounding wall. From its wide **Court of Honor,** the axis mounts a second terrace where Thieu Tri's accomplishments, written by his son Tu Duc, occupy a timeworn shelter. Beyond the commanding stone obelisks, three bridges span **Ngung Hy Lake** to Thieu Tri's tumulus.

Duc Duc (r. 1883): Duc Duc, his son Thanh Thai, and his grandson Duy Tan are all revered in **Long An Temple,** a complex that's fallen on hard times. Duc Duc's altar occupies the central bay, flanked by altars and bronze busts of his son and grandson.

The French armed forces used the compound as a garrison during their war, and at least one of the bunkers remains. Duc Duc is buried in a detached compound behind the palace, without attendant statues or a stela. His son and grandson are interred nearby in simpler tombs. ■

Stone mandarins stand eternally at attention in the Court of Honor at Khai DInh's mausoleum, a familiar sight at Nguyen kings' burial sites.

More Places to Visit in & Around Hue

Hon Chen Temple

Shrines, stelae, altars, and spirit houses cling to the side of a picturesque bluff above the Perfume River at Hon Chen Temple. The Cham worshipped Po Nagar (see pp. 164–165) here a thousand years ago. The Viets absorbed the goddess into their tradition and continue to worship her as Thien Y A Na. During the third and seventh lunar months, the goddess' cult throngs the temple grounds to perform sacred rituals. King Dong Khanh embraced the goddess as a patron saint and enlarged the temple in 1886. Dong Khanh himself is also worshipped at the temple.

✉ 6 miles (9 km) W of Hue, accessible via river; join a boat tour or hire sampan *($)*

Museum of Royal Fine Arts

Widely considered Vietnam's most elegant palace, **Long An Palace** also rates as one of the country's finest museums and houses the grandest collection of Nguyen dynasty relics. Its two-tiered roof is a hallmark of Hue architecture. Inside, 128 ironwood pillars partition the gallery into seven bays, with wings at either end. Glass paintings lean off the capitals of six columns in the vestibule, each inspired by a poem King Thieu Tri wrote and sent to China for illustration. Exhibits include imperial robes, porcelain, furnishings, screens, coins, gongs, and ceremonial weapons.

Ⓝ 133 ✉ 3 Le Truc, Hue ☎ 054/3524-429 (no English spoken) $ $

Nam Giao Esplanade

The Nguyen kings prayed for the well-being of their dynasty and country at this monument, laid out in 1806. The esplanade comprises three superimposed terraces: The lowest–man; the square middle–Earth; and the circular terrace 15 steps above–heaven. Until 1942, the kings paraded to this site annually (after 1890, every three years) in a procession of great fanfare. Before making sacrifices, the king fasted for three days in the **Fasting Palace,** which still stands in a walled enclosure next to the esplanade. Planted by mandarins and royal family members, pines stand as emblems of eternity and nobility.

✉ From 5 Le Loi, follow Dien Bien Phu S a little over a mile (2 km) to its end

Temple of Literature

After Gia Long assumed the throne in 1802 and moved the capital to Hue, he ordered construction of another temple of literature to complement Hanoi's venerable Van Mieu (see pp. 76–79). The wars demolished the temple's seven ironwood structures, but the triple gate remains, as do 32 stone stelae, borne by tortoises and inscribed with the names of 293 successful candidates. Two more stelae stand under separate covers.

Ⓝ 133 ✉ Follow Kim Long along river from White Tiger railroad bridge, past Thien Mu Pagoda. Temple is on right, just over 2 miles (3.7 km) from bridge

Tiger's Arena

Between 1830 and 1904, the Nguyen kings pitted elephants and tigers in mortal combat in this arena (Ho Quyen). The arena is ringed by two concentric brick walls with an interior diameter of 144 feet (44 m). Two stairways climb to the tribune where the king and his retinue sat. Opposite, five doors at the base of the arena wall open onto pens for tigers and panthers. Elephants entered through a 13-foot (4 m) door beside the tribune. Before combat, the tigers were weakened through starvation, declawed, and their mouths sewn shut, so that the elephant, a symbol of royal prestige, invariably prevailed.

Ⓝ 133 ✉ From train station, turn left, follow Ben Ngu Canal to Bui Thi Xuan, along river; arena on left side, 1.5 miles (2.5 km) from train station

Garden Homes

While the Nguyen kings indulged their architectural fantasies in the Forbidden Purple City and the sumptuous mausoleums south of the Perfume River, the aristocrats of Hue cultivated the urban landscape with hundreds of garden homes. Hunkered behind tall hedges and minded by a serried rank of areca palms, these homes are a pure expression of the Vietnamese sensibility of living space.

Vietnam's scholar-mandarin class resided in homes set amid gardens with due regard to feng shui.

The garden home's roof is a vast, hipped realm of flat terra-cotta tiles, four insulating layers deep. Suites of doors stretch across the facade. Inside, ironwood and jackfruit pillars do the work of walls, partitioning the living space into bays. Timberwork tenons often include elaborately carved dragons, waves, flowers, and other traditional motifs. The Vietnamese refer to such a home as a *nha ruong* (house of panels), for the squares and oblongs of exquisite wood carvings and mother-of-pearl inlay that hang from the truss.

The charm of a garden home lies not merely in its physical appearance but in its metaphysical accord. Builders invariably summoned masters of feng shui (known in Vietnam as *phong thuy*—wind and water) to position the structure with regard to the ancient art of placement. Ideally, a garden home should face south, the most auspicious direction for living. In front of the principal entrance, the owners erect a *binh phong* screen as a hedge to thwart the entry of malevolent spirits. Some nha ruong are so naturally ensconced in their surroundings, it's tempting to believe that they've always been there and that the earth has simply eroded around them.

Unlike the venerable merchants' homes

of Hoi An (see pp. 154–155), which stand in a frozen parade of architecture along a cluster of downtown streets, the garden homes are less visible. They're clustered in a number of Hue neighborhoods, particularly the Kim Long and Vi Da Districts, crouched behind hedges and within garden foliage.

The garden homes of Hue are crouched behind walls and hedges.

Urban Estates & Land Reform

These homes once stood as the centerpiece of modest urban estates. However, land reform measures after 1975 divvied up many of the properties. The privations of the late 1970s and early 1980s forced many home-owners to sell chunks of land. The homes have persevered, a bit worse for the wear, but now they're more threatened than ever.

As Vietnam's economy booms, people naturally want something modern, clean, and utilitarian. So, the descendants of the aristocrats are cashing in on their storied homes, selling off the timbers for as little as $2,000. One developer swooped in and bought 17 nha ruong, which he dismantled and rebuilt as the Nha Trang Sailing Club. The nouveau and nostalgic riche from Saigon are buying and rebuilding in the south.

A French organization has identified more than 800 nha ruong in the province—more than 200 in the city of Hue. One hundred of these are viable candidates for preservation, not as fusty relics inhabited by otherwise bereft families but as living and breathing opportunities. "B&Bs," suggested Antoine Erout, director of the program run by Nord Pas de Calais, "restaurants, cafés, galleries."

EXPERIENCE: Visit Hue's Top Garden Homes

Hue's Kim Long district holds several garden homes, conveniently clustered near each other for the traveler. Their peaceful and harmonious ambience shouldn't be missed by any visitor to Hue. Perhaps the most impressive is An Hien, once owned by Tu Du, a high-ranking mandarin under Emperor Gia Long; its massive pillars and tiled roofs create three attractive bays, though its current role as a café seems to diminish their effect. The doors and beams are richly carved. As with all garden homes, nearby Lac Tinh was designed in accordance with the principles of feng shui, and the four separate houses set in a half-acre (2,000 sq m) garden create an elegantly refined atmosphere. A third garden home, Y Thao, is only about 50 years old, but its traditional design and carefully positioned rocks in the garden set the ideal stage in which to savor some Hue specialties (the house functions as a private restaurant). The best way to visit these homes is on a tour with Hue Tourist or Mandarin Café (see p. 130).

Central Vietnam

The triangle formed by Hoi An, Danang, and My Son yields myriad charms for tourists, from the ambience of Hoi An's Old Town to the tropical pleasures of the beach at Danang and the ruins of a legendary kingdom at My Son. The region's pagodas and villages layer on additional diversions, as do the Truong Son mountains, which plunge into the ocean along the border between Quang Nam and Thua Thien Provinces.

Hoi An's preeminence as a trading port diminished after its river silted up in the 19th century.

Just north of the provincial border lies Bach Ma National Park, famous for its ruinous colonial villas, spectacular forests, and 25 feet (7.5 m) of annual rain. Also located here is Phuoc Tich, one of Vietnam's ethnic Viet villages, a pretty village with foliage-draped pathways and examples of domestic architecture.

Danang's urban charms are few, but the Cham Museum is the best place to view the art of this vanished kingdom. And the Bay of Danang is truly one of a kind.

South of Danang, on the way to Hoi An, a unique pagoda experience awaits at the Marble Mountains, where a combination of hilltop vistas, grottoes, and shrines evokes a sense of timelessness.

In Hoi An, itself, the old trading port's merchants' houses, assembly halls, and museums collectively exude a magnetism that's more powerful than any individual site.

China Beach

Near Danang, the U.S. Marines built an R&R center on a fine stretch of sand that Americans once knew as China Beach. The section near the city is now called My Khe Beach, which is popular among locals, and the stretch south of town is called Non Nuoc Beach, where several exclusive resorts now attract well-heeled tourists. There are no longer any vestiges of the bygone R&R era, and the Vietnamese re-branding of China Beach is now complete.

From either Danang or Hoi An, the Cham ruins of My Son are an easy day trip. The ruins might disappoint, but the towers nestling in a jungly setting make for a singular Cham experience.

Phuoc Tich

Phuoc Tich is a Vietnamese (Kinh) village of traditional garden homes *(nha ruong),* family temples, and pagodas, embraced by a loop of the lovely green O Lau River. Sadly, many of the houses in the village are decaying through neglect as most of the young have left to work in the big cities.

Phuoc Tich was founded in 1470 by a group of settlers from Nghe An Province. In the 19th century, pottery kilns fired up an era of wealth that made the construction of its many garden houses possible. In recent years the traditional craft has been revived and there are a few places producing pottery in the village.

Cultural historians stumbled upon Phuoc Tich in 2003, and in 2009 it was recognized by the Ministry of Culture as a national relic. However, little has been done to accommodate tourists, though the mostly elderly residents are hospitable and tend to fawn over the odd foreigner who pays a visit.

Today, 37 of Phuoc Tich's 117 homes are classified as garden homes. You'll find neither a tourist trail nor a navigable road. Instead, park at the village gate and stroll the rutted dirt tracks, keeping the O Lau to your left. The hedged pathways, groves of bamboo and bananas, and gardens evoke the timeless grandeur of the Vietnamese village like few other places

Past the ruined pottery works stands the 200-year-old home of **Truong Cong Bac,** possibly the village's oldest. As such, it may also serve as something of an architectural template, as most of the village's nha ruong, which date from the 1870s, share structural similarities. Here, the typical nha ruong centers on a colonnade of jackfruit pillars that divide the interior space into three bays beneath a sloping roof, with wings on either end. Eighteen wooden doors swing through nine doorways across the home's facade.

At the home of **Le Tran Phu,** floral designs trace across many panels, while mother-of-pearl inlay adorns others. At the home of **Ho Dinh Lan,** a mandarin who ruled this village and others in the early 1900s, the fan-shaped name

Phuoc Tich

Map 129 A4

Visitor Information

Hue Tourist, 120 Le Loi

054/3816-263

huetouristvietnam.com

Mandarin Café, 24 Tran Cao Van

054/3821-281

$$

mrcumandarin.com

Danang
129 C3
Visitor Information
32A Phan Dinh Phung
0511/3550-111
danangtourism.gov.vn

INSIDER TIP:

On the Hue-to-Danang train, take a seat on the left side and enjoy spectacular ocean views as the train chugs through the Hai Van Pass. This memorable ride costs only a few dollars.

—KRIS LeBOUTILLIER
National Geographic photographer

board over the central bay was a gift of King Duy Tan. The wooden side panels have carvings of writing brushes and lutes. In the home of **Ho Van Te,** intricate wood carvings cover the joints in the first compartment. The common *ba thuy* wave motif is often accompanied by a dragon's head. Also look amid the rafters for *Tho*, the Chinese character for longevity.

Danang

Vietnam's fourth largest city, with a population of about one million, Danang serves as a gateway to Hoi An, My Son, and the Marble Mountains. Its Cham Museum houses the country's best sculpture, and its egg-shaped bay, bracketed by the Hai Van headlands and Monkey Mountain on the Son Tra Peninsula, yields a spectacular seascape.

Cham Museum: Built in 1915, this palatial museum *(2 Thang 9, tel 0511/3470-114, chammuseum.danang.vn, $)* displays some 300 terra-cotta, sandstone, and bronze sculptures from that kingdom's capitals and temples. Most famous is the **Tra Kieu Dancer,** a lithe *apsara* draped in hallmark loose belts and bead necklaces. Attendants strum the vina, an ancient Indian

The Bay of Danang is now recognized as one of the world's most beautiful waterways.

EXPERIENCE: Bird-watching in Bach Ma National Park

More than 350 bird species have been sighted at Bach Ma National Park, making it one of the best destinations in the country for birders. In fact, the park was established in 1991 in part to offer protection for the rare and endemic Edward's pheasant *(Lophura edwardsi)*, which is also the park's symbol. Other resident rare species include the rufous-throated partridge, the silver pheasant, the crested argus, and the red-vented barbet, though they are so reclusive that they are more likely to be heard than seen.

Of the many trails within the park, bird-watchers will want to flock to the **Pheasant** and **Rhododendron Trails.** In addition, there's a known site for the Annam partridge on the main road, about 2 miles (2–3 km) downhill from the park headquarters, while the area around the guesthouses at the summit is a good spot for silver-breasted broadbills, short-tailed scimitar babblers, and sultan tits.

instrument. In the same gallery is the tenth-century **Tra Kieu Pedestal,** wrapped in a frieze with figures that detail scenes from the life of Krishna.

In the left wing, three steps climb the **Pedestal From My Son E1,** whose niches hold a popular turbaned flute player and a harpist with a distinctive chignon. Note the apsaras who serve as telamones on the risers, especially the spread-eagled dancer at center. Also in this gallery, see the seventh-century statue of **Ganesha** dipping his trunk in a bowl of sweets—the oldest complete Cham sculpture.

Visiting the Town: From the museum, a walking tour follows the **Han River** along Bach Dang, past the new Dragon Bridge, which actually breathes fire, as far as the cable-stay, swing bridge. Turn left, then left again, and return to the museum along Tran Phu, passing a 1923 Gothic **cathedral** with a Gallic cock atop its 230 foot (70 m) steeple.

If you cross any of the bridges over the river and keep heading east, you'll arrive at My Khe Beach and a coastal road that runs south to the Marble Mountains and Hoi An.

Bach Ma National Park

The ruins of a thriving French resort from the 1930s and '40s form the architectural centerpiece of this 85-square-mile (220 sq km) park, adding a haunting, ghost-town atmosphere to this area of stunning natural beauty. With an average annual rainfall of 25 feet (7.5 m), Bach Ma is Vietnam's rainiest place. But during the drier spring and summer months (Feb.–Aug.), the lush tropical forest is a first-rate destination for day hikes, birding, and swimming in cascade pools.

In 1932, the French broke ground on the upper flanks of 4,800-foot (1,440 m) Bach Ma

(continued on p. 152)

Bach Ma National Park

- 129 B3
- 054/3897-360
- $

bachmapark.com.vn

NOTE: No regular buses run to Bach Ma National Park, and there's only occasional demand for a traveler's café bus from Danang or Hue. By private vehicle, travel S from Hue along Hwy. 1 for 25 miles (40 km) to Phu Loc and turn right for the 2-mile (3 km) ride up Rte. 6 to park reception. You can take your own car but not a motorbike into the park.

Driving the Mandarin Road

Between Hue and Danang, the Mandarin Road negotiates three mountainous spurs that peak at Hai Van, the 1,637-foot (496 m) Pass of the Clouds by the Sea. The road was conceived under the Ho dynasty of the 15th century to provide a way for scholars to journey to the capital for the mandarin exams. In the 19th century, Gia Long upgraded the route as an artery between Gia Dinh (Saigon) and Thang Long (Hanoi).

The stretch of Highway 1 between Hue and Danang is one of Vietnam's most scenic drives.

South of Hue's **An Cuu Market,** a hodgepodge of houses cum shops cling to the edges of the heavily trafficked Mandarin Road, more commonly known as Highway 1. Once the congestion eases, you'll pass French pillboxes adrift in the rice fields, followed by Phu Bai Airport, a former U.S. Marine base.

Across the Truoi River, an old French railway station marks the center of **Loc Dien ❶**, a collection of hamlets 16 miles (25 km) south of An Cuu that had its 15 minutes of fame in September 1965 when *Life* ran a 10,000-word feature about eight men from this village who'd been "marked for death" by the Viet Cong.

Beyond Loc Dien, the Truong Son Mountains skew east, and Cau Hai Lagoon opens up views to the east. Three miles (5 km) along, a pink-marble marker memorializes a branch of the **Ho Chi Minh Trail ❷** (see pp. 120–121), down which men and matériel traveled in 1975.

NOT TO BE MISSED:

Lang Co • Elephant Springs • Hai Van Pass • Bay of Danang

East of Phuoc Tuong Pass, turn right at Thuy Ta hamlet *(32 miles/51 km S of An Cuu)* for a 2.5-mile (4 km) run to the **Elephant Springs ❸** *(Suoi Voi, $)*. A boulder decorated with a curved cement trunk and broken tusks minds a series of cascades and swimming pools in this steep-sided ravine.

Heading farther south on Highway 1, threading Phu Gia Pass, the reward is a vista of **An Cu Lagoon,** crowded by mountains and sown with fishing weirs. The road swings down onto a long, narrow spit at **Lang Co ❹**, whose true glory only reveals itself once you look back at it from the headlands. The beach at Lang Co is one of Vietnam's most spectacular.

Stay to the right as you leave Lang Co, avoiding the Hai Van Tunnel (see sidebar right), to start up into the headlands. At an elevation of 1,627 feet (496 m), the road crests at **Hai Van Pass** ❺ amid a cluster of French forts and two imperial gates, the latter built during the reign of Minh Mang and inscribed with Chinese characters that read, "Gate of the Clouds by the Sea" and "Most Grandiose Gate in the World."

Two miles (3 km) beyond the pass, the tantalizing crescent of beach below serves a **leper colony.** Once ministered to by the Sisters of St. Paul, the dozens of families are now mostly cured though still subject to quarantine. Rumor has it the colony is destined for relocation as developers froth over the obvious possibilities.

Across the Cu De River Bridge, turn left and merge onto the 7-mile (11 km) boulevard that borders the **Bay of Danang.** From the restroom facility parking lot you can check out a stretch of **Xuan Thieu-Nam O Beach** ❻, where the first contingent of U.S. combat troops came ashore in March 1965. The Marine base sprawled along this beach, though few traces remain. A mile (2 km) farther, end at Xuan Thieu Restaurant, just north of which is a concrete slab Marines poured as the foundation of a service club. Look for the graffiti signature of American soldier Ortiz Vasquez.

Hai Van Tunnel

Though the Hai Van Pass on Highway 1 between Hoi An and Danang offers great coastal views for tourists, it has always been recognized as a bottleneck for traffic. This problem led to the construction of one of the world's longest tunnels (over 4 miles/6 km), which opened in 2005, cutting 6 miles (10 km) and about 30 to 40 minutes off the journey. All vehicles must pay a toll fee; motorbikes, bicycles, and pedestrians are prohibited entry.

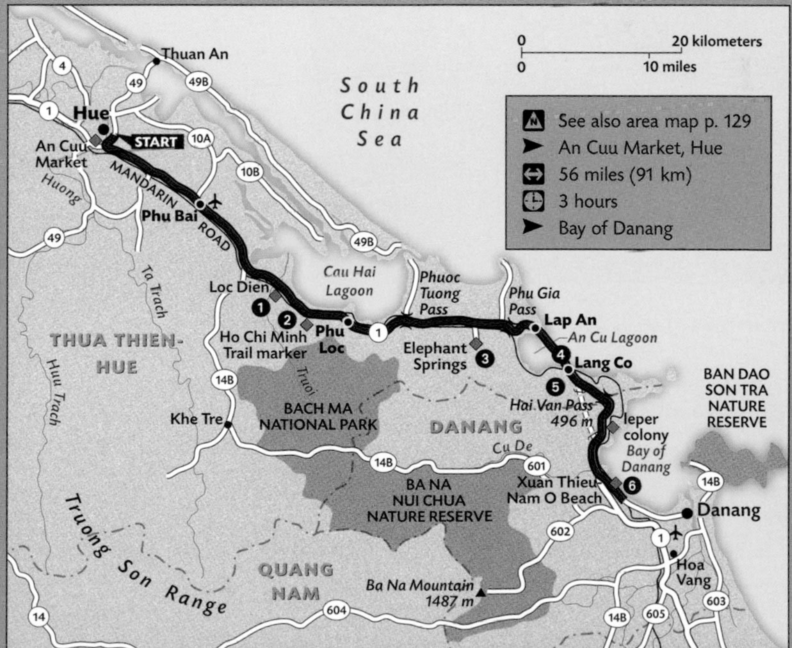

Marble Mountains

- 129 C3
- Take coastal road 5 miles (8 km) S of Danang, turn right on Huyen Tran Cong Chua; entrance on right a little farther along
- $

as a refuge from the sweltering weather in Hue, 34 miles (54 km) northwest. By 1942, they'd clustered 139 villas, a hospital, a market, parks, a swimming pool, tennis courts, and two hotels on the hill. During the Vietnam War, the villas were largely destroyed in heavy fighting between U.S. soldiers and the Viet Cong.

Check in at the visitor center, from which rangers ferry *($$)* vanloads of tourists 10 miles (16 km) up a narrow, winding road to the ruins and back. From the summit parking area, a paved stone pathway climbs a third of a mile (0.5 km) to an octagonal summit house. Off one side of the path, steep stone steps lead to a onetime American helicopter base. Not far from the bottom step, an unmarked cave entrance marks a Viet Cong hideout.

Visitors read a Chinese tablet at a Marble Mountains pagoda.

Visitor Information

- 32A Phan Dinh Phung
- 0511/3550-111

danangtourism.gov.vn

If the clouds aren't roosting about the summit, the views are long and inspiring. Below the summit, a trail drops 1.25 miles (2 km) through evergreen monsoon forest to an orchid nursery. The trails are fairly well marked, and it's best not to stray too far. Wartime ordnance still remains, as evidenced by an exhibit in the visitor center.

Bach Ma is renowned for its wildlife, though the grandest fauna is all but gone. Elephants last trod this region in 1995, and rangers last spotted tiger tracks in 2001. The park's deeper recesses still shelter Asiatic black bears, leopards, and saola, a rare deer species.

Marble Mountains

South of Danang, the Marble Mountains compose a cluster of five limestone and marble outcrops, famous for their grottoes, pagodas, and role as a Viet Cong redoubt during the Vietnam War. The peaks yield sweeping views of the strand American soldiers dubbed China Beach (see sidebar p. 147). At the base of one mount is a 500-year-old stonecutters' handicraft village known to locals as Lang Da ("stone village").

The first emperor of the Nguyen dynasty named these outcrops the Ngu Hanh ("five elements"), after the essential elements of water, wood, earth, metal, and fire. **Thuy Son** ("water mountain") is the most rewarding. There are two steep stairways up the mountain, and a lift *($)* beside the first. At the base of the second stairway, stop in at **Tam Son Pagoda.** Atop the stairs, at the triple gate to **Tam Thai Pagoda,** turn left for a short climb to **Vong Giang** ("river watchtower"), which offers views south to the sister peaks, Danang's Han River, and the Quang Nam rice fields.

INSIDER TIP:

For an authentic look at the real Vietnam when visiting Hoi An, wake before dawn and wander the narrow streets, discreetly observing people preparing for their day.

–DON MANKIN
National Geographic author

Behind Tam Thai, a path leads through a stone gate to a two-level cave the Viet Cong used as an operations center and first-aid station. The upper level, **Hoa Nghiem,** includes an altar and adjacent stela that dates from 1640. In the lower level, **Huyen Khong,** where sunlight streams down from gaps in the ceiling, is a large seated Buddha.

From Huyen Khong, head back through the gate to the circular entrance to **Van Thong Cave.** Another stone gate leads down to **Linh Ung Pagoda,** behind which is the Tang Chon Cave, where ancient standing and sitting Buddha images are also illuminated by shafts of light that pierce the limestone. From here, climb up to the seven-story tower at **Xa Loi Temple,** for its sweeping coastal views, then either take the lift or stairway back down.

Hoi An

Hoi An is a dreamy old Southeast Asian trading port, renowned for its timeworn merchants' homes, grid of riverfront streets, and Chinese assembly halls. While the rival 17th-century ports of Malacca and Penang evolved into modern cities, Hoi An lost its raison d'être in the late 19th century after the silting of its river shunted commercial activity to nearby Tourane, now Danang. The town consequently ossified and now ranks as the best preserved port of a bygone era in Southeast Asia. This prompted UNESCO to inscribe the site on its World Heritage List in 1999.

Though the Old Town dates largely from the late 16th to early 18th centuries, Hoi An's otherwise dubious claim as an ancient town is partly justified by archaeology that proves the Sa Huynh people used it as a port as early as the second century B.C. Before the Vietnamese gained control of the area in the 14th century, Cham merchants had developed the port into the kingdom's primary trading center, though no extant structures date from that era. Accepting an invitation from the Nguyen lords, the Japanese and Chinese settled on either side of a waterway spanned by the Japanese Bridge (see p. 157). Portuguese

Hoi An
129 C3
Visitor Information
10 Tran Hung Dao
0510/3910-911
hoiantravel.com

Sinh Café, 587 Hai Ba Trung
0510/3863-948

NOTE: The tourist office sells Hoi An Tourist tickets ($$) good for admission to any five attractions, including an old home, assembly hall, museum, and one other attraction, but not two of any one category. Additional tickets are available for more sites. Tickets can be purchased at one of five stalls in Old Town.

A wood-carver applies finishing touches to his version of the Happy Buddha.

merchants came calling in 1535; the Dutch, English, and French followed suit in the 17th century. While the Europeans left little trace of their tenure, the Japanese and Chinese played fundamental roles in the development of the port then and the town's enduring appeal today.

The town's attractions center on one of three main streets. Tran Phu, the oldest and best known, historically linked the Japanese Bridge and Quan Kong Temple, across from the market. The Nguyen Thai Hoc route opened in 1841, and the riverfront Bach Dang in 1886.

Merchants' Houses: Along Tran Phu and south toward the river, the Chinese merchants' homes are the single most potent ingredient in the spell cast by Hoi An. Nearly all claim 17th- or 18th-century pedigrees, which may be so, though the present structures date from 19th-century reconstructions. It may seem odd that most of these old Chinese homes are in the half of town settled by the Japanese. But after a shogun issued a decree in 1635 restricting overseas maritime activities, the Japanese community died off. None of their houses survive, though the floor plans of later homes built by Chinese merchants do resemble those of older homes in Kyoto, Japan. The Japanese influence also endures in woodwork trusses, which include Chinese and Vietnamese aesthetics in a fusion fundamental to Hoi An's fame.

The tourist bureau has placed the following three homes on its register, so they're the most heavily visited. Be prepared for the "hard sell" in each location, as the people who explain the features of each house also try to sell old coins and embroidery to supplement the owners' income. Old Town is a trove of similar homes, now restaurants, hotels, and shops.

Hoi An Homes: On Nguyen Thai Hoc, a sixth generation Vietnamese family lives in **Tan Ky House,** a home their ancestors acquired from Chinese merchants out of Fujian Province. Like most homes in Old Town, this is a corridor house, not unlike the tube houses of Hanoi's Old Quarter (see pp. 70–71). At 10 to 12 feet (3–3.5 m), these houses are typically wider than Hanoi's, but the run of rooms from front to back is similar—shop, living room, open courtyard, sleeping quarters, and kitchen. The shop is raised slightly higher than succeeding rooms, a good omen, as income is more likely to run downhill. *Tan Ky,* as it's embossed in Chinese characters on the name board in the living room, means "progress." The triple-beam construction of the living room ceiling is distinctly Japanese, while crab motifs in the woodwork are Chinese. The flooring is Vietnamese, made from Bat Trang bricks and stone slabs from Thanh Hoa.

Across the Japanese Bridge is the 1780 **Phung Hung House** *(4 Nguyen Thi Minh Khai),* whose balconies evoke China, four-sided roof Japan, and three bays Vietnam. Eight generations of the same Vietnamese family have occupied the house, selling medicine, silk, and porcelain from their shop. During a 1999 flood, water rose 5 feet (1.5 m) in the house. In 1964, the floodwaters climbed 8 feet (2.5 m), and the family hosted more than one hundred stricken neighbors on the second floor. The same Chinese family has occupied the **Quan Thang House** *(77 Tran Phu)* since the 18th century.

Hoi An Tailors

Hoi An has developed a reputation for its silk and tailoring, and with prices cheaper than in Hanoi or Ho Chi Minh City, this is a good place to order a new dress or suit. Though bargaining over prices is acceptable, generally you get what you pay for, so avoid the cheapest places. One reliable outfit is A Dong *(62 Tran Hung Dao).*

Assembly Halls: Hoi An's Chinese settlers predominantly came from five of China's southern provinces, and each rallied in their own assembly hall, which served as both temple and guesthouse to transient Chinese merchants. These halls are sometimes referred to as pagodas, but are not temples to Buddha.

The red-faced Quan Kong takes center stage at the **Cantonese Assembly Hall** (aka Quang Trieu Pagoda; *176 Tran Phu*). Kong was a second-century Chinese general revered in temples throughout Vietnam and East Asia. His telltale red face symbolizes loyalty and righteousness.

Calligraphy and silk art lure shoppers to Hoi An's centuries-old storefronts.

The goddess of the sea, Thien Hau, occupies the bay to Quan Kong's left, accompanied by two grotesque assistants, one of whom points at his eyes, the other at his ears, underscoring their ability to see and hear across the waters for a thousand miles.

Down the street, the **Chinese Assembly Hall** *(62 Tran Phu)* still serves as a language school for the local Chinese population.

The most opulent hall is the **Fujian Temple** (aka Phuoc Kien; *46 Tran Phu*), which is set far from the street, through a single-door gate and a lower courtyard, then a garishly modern triple gate. The principal deity here is Thien Hau, a wise choice for a seafaring people. Continuing east on Tran Phu, look into the colorful **Quan Cong Temple** (aka Ong Temple), directly opposite the market.

Built in 1875, the **Hainan Assembly Hall** *(10 Tran Phu)* honors 108 Chinese merchants murdered in 1851 by a rogue skipper in King Tu Duc's navy, a massacre detailed in Chinese characters on the entry hall storyboard. Next door is the **Minh Huong Temple,** dedicated to ancestor worship.

Phuc Ba is the principal deity at the **Trieu Chau Assembly Hall** *(157 Tran Phu).* More compelling, however, is the intricately carved woodwork that frames the altar, with crab and woman motifs that clearly speak to the work's Chinese origins, if not its antiquity, which stretches back 250 years.

Other Sights: The collection at the **Museum of History and Culture** *(7 Nguyen Hue)* features bronze bells, Sa Huynh ossuaries, Cham artifacts, and a pair of wooden shutters from a wine house at 46 Nguyen Thi Hoc. At the **Museum of Trade Ceramics** *(80 Tran Phu),* artifacts from shipwrecks and old pottery fragments anchor the contents. The house itself, particularly the balcony doors and woodwork panels, is a prime example of a traditional wood house. So is the **Museum of Sa Huynh Culture** *(149 Tran Phu),* whose building is a fusion of corridor-house and French architecture. Here, you'll find Sa Huynh burial jars and other artifacts unearthed in nearby sand dunes. Upstairs, the streetside room highlights artifacts from the French War, while the back room exhibits Vietnam War paraphernalia, including a hand-drawn map of Hoi An used in a 1969 attack.

Past the museums, at the end of Tran Phu, the **Japanese Bridge** spans a stream that flows into the Thu Bon. Historically, the stream divided the Japanese district, which stretched down present-day Tran Phu, from the Chinese district. The bridge was built in the middle of the 17th century, as was an adjacent **Taoist temple.** The latter was dedicated to a god who the bridge builders hoped might exorcise a subterranean beast whose thrashing tail was believed to be the cause of earthquakes in Japan. The beast's head was beneath India, but its heart was beneath Hoi An, hence the temple. At either end of the wood-planked bridge is a pair of statues, monkeys on one end and dogs on the other, which are believed to represent the years construction was started and finished. The name board of Chinese characters on the bridge was hoisted by one of the Nguyen lords in 1791. The characters denote the span as the "faraway people's" bridge.

My Son

Like Cambodia's Angkor Wat and Thailand's Ayutthaya, My Son is Vietnam's opus in the canon of ancient Southeast Asian holy lands. Standing in a lush valley 28 miles (45 km) west of Hoi An, the 1,500-year-old brick-built temple complex lay forgotten for centuries until rediscovery by the French in 1898. Archaeologists stripped the temples of their most valuable sculptures, which are now on display in Danang's Cham Museum and in the history museums in Hanoi and Ho Chi Minh City. But this UNESCO World Heritage site retains an incomparable ancient resonance.

My Son served as the heart and soul of its culture for a

My Son

129 C2

Visitor Information

My Son Sanctuary Management Board, Duy Xuyen District, Quang Nam

0510/3731-309

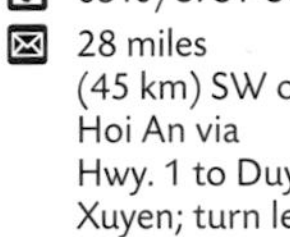

28 miles (45 km) SW of Hoi An via Hwy. 1 to Duy Xuyen; turn left and go last 12 miles (20 km) to site

$ (includes transportation from booking office to towers)

EXPERIENCE: Cooking Classes in Hoi An

If, like most visitors to Vietnam, you are delighted by the subtle tastes and thoughtful preparation of Vietnamese cuisine, consider learning how to prepare a few dishes yourself so that you can enjoy them (as well as impress your friends) back home. **Red Bridge Cooking School** *(visithoian.com)* in Hoi An offers half-day, full-day, or evening courses, all of which will have you rolling up your sleeves and tying on an apron for a hands-on experience.

The cooking school sits in an attractive location 2.5 miles (4 km) from the city center. Students are taken there by boat and shown around the organic herb garden before visiting the local market to buy ingredients. Students then spend 2 to 3 hours learning how to make classic dishes like *pho* (beef noodle soup) and *cha ca* (fish in clay pot), finally self-evaluating their success by eating the prepared dishes. Evening classes are conducted at **Hai Café** in the town center (see Travelwise p. 252).

thousand years. King Bhadravarman founded the first temple here late in the fourth century, and except for a 200-year gap between the eighth and tenth centuries, My Son was the holy epicenter of the Cham world. Every Cham king built here. After a Cham king married a Vietnamese princess in the 14th century and ceded a huge chunk of his kingdom, My Son drifted into obscurity and the grip of jungle growth. After rediscovery, a French archaeologist identified 14 groups of 71 ancient relics.

Through 1945, the French exhumed, studied, catalogued, and, on occasion, restored these monuments. Twenty years later, the Viet Cong used My Son as a base, and the U.S. launched a bombing campaign that ruined many structures, including two magnificent *kalans,* or temples, in the designated A and E complexes. Today, 20 of the 71 Cham relics are more or less intact, most clustered in the B, C, and D groupings. Most visitors take guided tours *($$$)* from Hoi An; you can also rent a car. Go early to avoid crowds and the heat.

INSIDER TIP: Vietnam's youth under 25, who make up one-third of the population, infuse the country with energy and optimism.

—JON BOWERMASTER
National Geographic author

At the **BCD cluster,** note how seamlessly the Cham put together these temples. An enduring mystery of Cham architecture is how they managed to construct brick towers with seeming disregard for mortar. Some have suggested that the Cham may have baked one 100-foot (30 m) tower in situ, while others reason the bricks are fastened by vegetal resin and a mortar derived either from powdered lime and brick or from clay.

Architectural Styles

In all, Cham builders employed seven distinct architectural styles, all of which are represented at My Son. In the **C group,** the intact **C1 kalan** tower was built toward the end of the tenth century in a style now dubbed the A1 My Son style. Its roof is saddle-shaped, a departure from the classical norm, which rose in a three-story steeple. The hollowed-out interior leaves little room to maneuver, but these interior spaces were the province of Brahmans, not worshippers. The Cham believed their deities actually dwelled within the statues sheltered by these temples. The statue of Siva from this tower is now on display at Danang's Cham Museum (see pp. 148–149).

In the neighboring **B group,** the **B5** *koshaghara* (storehouse) tower mirrors C1's saddle-shaped roof and exhibits many features of the A1 My Son style, notably in the elegant pairs of pilasters. Between the pilasters, note how the figures stand on a lotus balanced on an elephant's head. The Cham carved this art directly onto the spongy brick after

Encroaching vegetation makes its claim on 1,500-year-old Cham temples in My Son's C Group.

construction; the sandstone heads were obviously attached later. B5 also features a pair of elephants in bas-relief, their trunks wrapped around a coconut tree.

French archaeologists believed that the two long *mandapas,* or assembly halls, belonged to a distinct group they labeled **D group,** east of the B and C groups. But later studies showed that these mandapas, D1 and D2, were built for pilgrims who used the halls to prepare offerings for temple visits. The mandapas' tile roofs long ago collapsed, and their interiors today house statuary that hasn't been taken to other museums.

From the D temples, cross the Suoi The stream and turn right to reach the largely ruined **A group** temples. The commanding peak before you is 2,460-foot (750 m) Rang Meo ("cat's teeth").

The most heartbreaking loss at My Son is the **A1 kalan tower,** which stood 79 feet (24 m) high and 32 feet (10 m) wide. It was the masterpiece of the complex and stood for nearly a thousand years until a U.S. bombardment in late 1969. A photo of the ruined tower is on display in the museum near the lower 4WD terminal. The 13 heaps of ruins are otherwise overgrown with vegetation.

Outside the BCD cluster, the path winds to the left past the **G group,** which recently underwent extensive restoration and reconstruction. Farther along the path is the **E group,** the oldest complex at My Son. The **E1 kalan** was also a casualty of the 1969 bombing. Between E1 and the also damaged E4 are the bomb craters. Luckily, E1's magnificent pedestal and pediment had been removed long before the war and are on exhibit at Danang's Cham Museum. **E7,** used as a library during My Son's heyday, is the most intact structure in this cluster. Before it stands one of the site's 31 stelae. ■

More Places to Visit in Central Vietnam

Ba Na Mountain

In 1919, the French founded a hill station atop 4,879-foot (1,487 m) Ba Na to escape Danang's sweltering heat. Attractions include the world's longest (16,500 feet/5,042 m) and highest (4,230 feet/1,291 m altitude gain) cable car route *($$$)*, hiking paths, the colonial villa ruins, and a handful of waterfalls. The view from the summit takes in the Han River and the ocean.
danangtourism.gov.vn 129 C3 **Visitor Information** Danang Tourism, 32A Phan Dinh Phung 0511/3550-111

Cham Islands

Nine miles (15 km) off Hoi An are seven lightly touristed islets. Coral abounds in the crystalline waters off Lao ("pear"), the largest islet. Each spring, islanders harvest birds' nests, used in soups and medicine. The slow boat from Hoi An takes 2.5 hours, while a speedboat makes the trip in 30 minutes.
ntravel.com 129 D3 **Visitor Information** 10 Tran Hung Dao 0510/3910-911

Son Tra Peninsula

This mountainous peninsula brackets the Bay of Danang to the west and My Khe Beach to the south, its bights rapidly filling with resorts. Dominating the headland is 2,274-foot (693 m) **Monkey Mountain,** the centerpiece of a reserve that shelters endangered Javan silvery gibbons. Son Tra is also home to the forlorn **Spanish Tomb,** a 40-foot (12 m) ossuary containing the remains of Spanish and French soldiers who died during the 1858–1860 Danang campaign.
129 C3 Spanish Tomb: From Han River Bridge, follow Ngo Quyen, turn onto Yet Kieu, proceed 5 miles (8 km) to Tien Sa

INSIDER TIP:

If you visit Danang, check out the new Ban Dao Son Tra Nature Reserve, home to the largest population of the endangered douc langur ever found.

—LOIS K. LIPPOLD
Douc Langur Foundation director & National Geographic grantee

Tra Kieu

From the 4th to 11th centuries, the Cham capital was at Simhapura ("lion citadel"), on the site of modern-day Tra Kieu, about 10 miles (16 km) northeast of My Son; visitors from Danang can stop here on the return trip. Only some ramparts, banisters, and traces of the wall remain, but the main gallery at Danang's Cham Museum (see pp. 148–149) is filled with sculptures unearthed here, including the Tra Kieu Dancer. *hoiantravel.com* 129 C2 **Visitor Information** 10 Tran Hung Dao 0510/3910-911

Cham Culture Today

Though these days the Cham are physically indistinguishable from the Vietnamese, recent years have seen a resurgence of Cham culture and many crumbling towers, especially along the central coast, have been restored to their original condition. The Kate Festival (Cham New Year), which takes place around October, focuses around the Po Klong Garai towers (see pp. 170–171) and involves traditional Cham music and dance as well as a colorful procession.

A region of alluring golden-sand beaches and turquoise water that resonates with echoes of the kingdom of Champa

South-central Coast

Sea stars cluster on Phan Thiet beach.

South-central Coast

An arc of six seaside provinces, from Quang Ngai in the north to Binh Thuan in the south, this coast's sandy shores and scenic promontories are helping to redefine the face of Vietnam to the rest of the world. Until the 14th century, this area was the domain of the Cham people, whose magnificent towers command knolls up and down the littoral. Most of the region's attractions, like the population itself, hug the shore.

Traditional boats, their latticework sealed with tree pitch, anchor near Mui Ne.

Don't look for azure waters or placid bays here: The south-central coast fronts a long fetch of the Pacific where the surf is more dramatic than sublime. Do look for coconut palms that crane over dazzling white sand, for freshets that burst from the flanks of riotously verdant headlands, and for coastal roads that course through fishing harbors jostling with fancifully painted boats.

Nha Trang is the crown jewel in Vietnam's constellation of beach resorts and the only city along the coast with a nightlife to complement its sunny appeal. Its municipal beach is internationally renowned, its islands kissed by some of the country's most beautiful coral reefs.

As beautiful as the south-central coast is, it was also a frightening battleground, particularly during the Vietnam War. The Americans built an air base at Phan Rang; a combat base at Chu Lai, north of Quang Ngai; and a massive logistical base at Cam Ranh Bay. At My Lai in Quang Ngai Province, the war reached its nadir in two little hamlets where a powerful memorial now commemorates the notorious 1968 massacre.

North of Nha Trang, the little-visited Khanh Hoa coast boasts the white sands of Doc Let and Van Phong Bay, which intrigued Jacques Cousteau. My Lai is also here.

The surviving Cham towers are nowhere more collectively appealing than they are at Po Klong Garai, near Phan Rang, which remains home to half of Vietnam's ethnically identifiable Hindu Cham people. Phan Rang

NOT TO BE MISSED:

The sun, sea, and sand at Nha Trang's beautiful beaches **164**

Snorkeling around the islands off Nha Trang **166–167**

The My Lai memorial **168–169**

The beautiful Po Klong Garai towers **170–171**

Riding the waves at the hip resort of Mui Ne **171**

The fabulous views from the Vung Tau statue of Jesus **174–175**

also claims Ninh Chu, one of Vietnam's finest and less touristed beaches.

Farther south, the rain-shy seaboard of Binh Thuan Province has surfed a tidal wave of mostly tasteful development, especially near Mui Ne, since the mid-1990s. Just north of the provincial capital of Phan Thiet, the Po Shanu towers herald the former kingdom of Champa, whose land eroded under the relentless Vietnamese march to the south.

Though geographically more southern than south-central, Vung Tau is where the beach party really kicks off. Known as Cap St.-Jacques to the French, who popularized its coastal charms in the late 19th century, Vung Tau now draws mostly Vietnamese beachgoers. A stone's throw from Ho Chi Minh City, it makes a fine diversion and great starting point for a coastal tour. ■

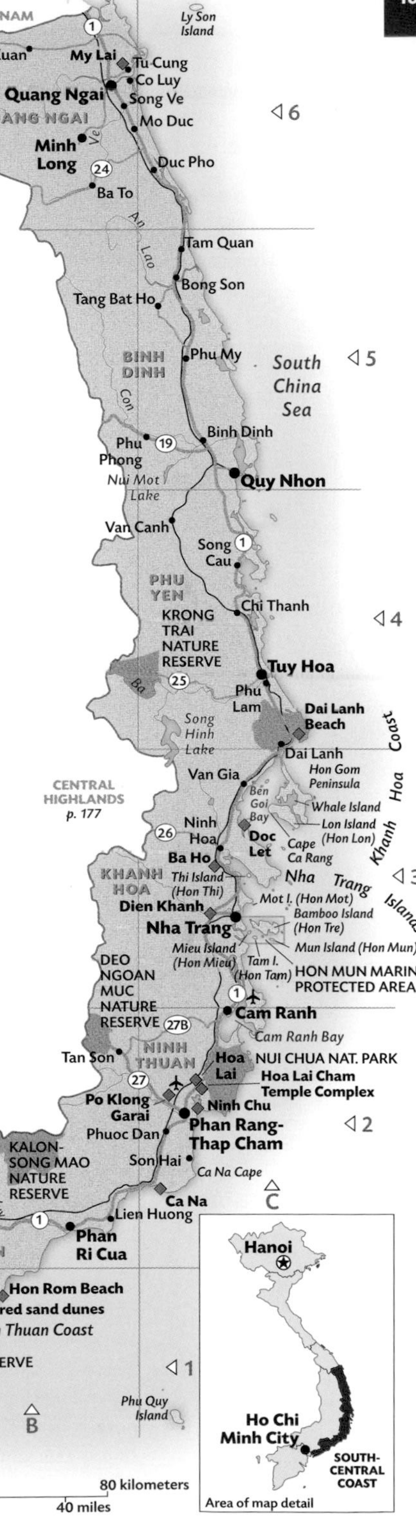

Nha Trang & the Islands

Nha Trang's gorgeous beach, happening nightlife, indolent ambience, and nearby islands as well as the Khanh Hoa coast are an antidote to the freneticism of Saigon and the cerebral demands of pagoda-hopping. Still, with its grand complex of Cham towers and two fine museums, Nha Trang can toss a few cultural curveballs beyond the beach.

The Po Nagar Cham towers

Nha Trang
163 C3
Visitor Information
Khanh Hoa Tourism, 1 Tran Hung Dao
058/3528-100
nhatrangtourist.com.vn

Po Nagar Cham towers
2 Thang 4, near Xom Bong Bridge

Nha Trang

Nha Trang's beach is a 4-mile (7 km) crescent of toasted sand and turquoise water, flanked by a pair of promontories. Tran Phu skirts its length, dividing an ever expanding wall of hotels from palm-happy esplanades that overlook the shore. On the southern promontory, five of **Bao Dai's villas** once served Vietnam's final emperor as a getaway. Today, the French colonial buildings are guest-houses. To the north, on **Hon Chong** promontory, stone steps descend to a jumble of rocks where fabled fairies once frolicked and played chess. One boulder bears the "handprint" of a voyeuristic male fairy who lost his balance while spying on naked female fairies.

Po Nagar Cham Towers: Inland from Hon Chong, on a bluff above the Cai River, these towers *($)* are the city's most august attraction. The site is named for the ten-armed mother goddess who taught the Cham how to plant rice and weave. Javanese raiders sacked the original wooden structures in A.D. 774. Within a decade, however, the Cham had built their first stone structure and a *mandapa* (assembly hall) whose saddle-shaped roof rested atop 24 columns. The roof is gone, but 14 columns remain.

The most impressive of four extant towers is a 74-foot (22.5 m) 11th-century *kalan* (temple) known as **Thap Ba** ("tower of the lady"). Draped in yellow robes, Po Nagar reigns from within its sooty black interior. The statue, its pedestal, and its stela were sculpted from a monolith in 965, though Po Nagar's head was lopped off by the French in 1946 and replaced by a Vietnamese-looking surrogate. Note the Sanskrit-style Cham lettering on the lintel and jambs, as well as the graceful *apsara* dancer above the lintel.

On the back of the saddle-roofed **northwestern tower,** a cross-legged figure rides the back of an elephant, holding a spearhead and a weapon thought to symbolize the god Indra. Though a statue of a robed Po Nagar now sits in this tenth-century tower, as well as a *linga-yoni* (sacred stone), historically this space venerated Sandhaka. The **south temple,** with its saddle-shaped roof, exalted Ganesha.

More Sights: Across the Cai River, a gleaming white Buddha presides over the city from his perch above **Long Son Pagoda.** From the sanctuary, stone steps climb to the 80-foot (24 m) landmark, erected in 1964 to protest South Vietnam President Ngo Dinh Diem's repression of Buddhism. Its base holds bronze busts of eight monks who immolated themselves in 1963, each framed in a halo of flames. Below reclines a massive Buddha cut from local stone.

The **Alexandre Yersin Museum** *(10 Tran Phu, closed Sat. & Sun. p.m. & 11 a.m.–2 p.m., $)* honors the doctor (1863–1943) who spent much of his life in Nha Trang and discovered the pathogen that sparked the 1896 bubonic plague. The museum offers a compelling narrative, well-written captions, and fine exhibits, such as Yersin's library and his instruments. Hand-drawn maps detail Yersin's 1892–1894 explorations, including his 1893 discovery of the site that later became Dalat.

Party Town Extraordinaire

Nha Trang is certainly Vietnam's best known beach resort, but it's not just the sun and surf that draw the visitors. The city also happens to be the best place to party in Vietnam, and a cluster of bars in the budget district and along the beach, such as Louisiane Brewhouse (see Travelwise p. 254), provide the music and drinks to put people in the mood. Some places stay open all night, and hardened party-goers head straight from the bar to the beach once the sun is up.

Heading out to the Nha Trang islands

Oceanographic Institute
South end of Tran Phu, near Nha Trang Port
$

Nha Trang Islands
163 C3
Visitor Information
Khanh Hoa Tourism, 1 Tran Hung Dao, Nha Trang
058/3528-100
nhatrangtourist.com.vn

Across town, a 1923 French colonial building anchors the **Oceanographic Institute.** The museum's central attraction is a humpback whale skeleton, unearthed by northern villagers in 1994. One gallery holds 8,000 pickled sea creatures, while a second-floor gallery in the old building displays antique maps, a globe, and a collection of 18th-century seafaring books, presumably left behind by the French.

Nha Trang Islands

In pleasant weather, a fleet of beamy wooden boats motors to a cluster of largely deserted, rock-rimmed islands, where they moor among splendid coral reefs for snorkeling and tie up at islands for various activities. The city's most popular pastime, these day trips tend to reach a feverish party pitch by midday.

Several tour operators run boats out into the bay, each with a band, a buffet lunch, and buckets of beer. These fun-loving party boys will answer questions about flora or fauna but much prefer to whoop it up with passengers. Hiring your own boat is another affordable option; ask for info at one of the tour shops on Biet Thu.

The largest island is **Hon Tre,** which rises 600 feet (180 m) above the bay and is also connected to the mainland by cable car *($$$$$, including admission to Vinpearl amusement park).* The huge amusement park features a water park and lots of games, making it a good day out for families with young kids.

Four miles (6 km) southeast of the pier, **Hon Mun** is the premier snorkeling venue. A garland of buoys protects the island's 350 coral species from boat anchors, while some thousand fish species flit to and fro over the fantastic formations. In the distance, **Hon Yen** ("swallow island") is a source of salangane nests, the principal ingredient of bird's nest soup.

At noon, the tour boats bunch together off **Hon Mat** for lunch and happy hour partying. Crews set up a floating bar and pass out shots to guests hanging on to life belts.

Hon Tam offers a sandy swimming beach, parasailing, water-skiing, and other water sports. You can also rent a shady cabana.

Closest to shore is **Hon Mieu,** where fishermen in colorful boats bring in their catch. Restaurants tempt the hungry with fresh fish and waterside terraces. On the far side of the island, **Tri Nguyen** is home to an aquarium, worth visiting if your boat calls at the pier.

Jacques Cousteau

The world-renowned marine biologist explored the undersea realm of the Khanh Hoa coast and Van Phong Bay in 1933 as a sailor in the French navy. The French were mapping the bay, known then as Port Dayot, in preparation for a naval base that was never built. The area's coral and marine life fired Cousteau's imagination and led him toward his lifework.

Khanh Hoa Coast

North of Nha Trang, the seaboard of Khanh Hoa Province is a largely undeveloped region of white-sand beaches, rustic peninsulas, rocky promontories, and streams that gush from the coastal mountains.

Fifty miles (80 km) north of Nha Trang, **Dai Lanh** is a half-mile (1 km) swath of powdery white sand between a crystal clear bay and a range of low, green mountains. This much beloved beach is even embossed on one of the Nguyens' Nine Dynastic Urns at The Mieu in Hue (see p. 135).

Just south, a road shoots across long, sandy **Hon Gom Peninsula** as far as the fishing village of Dam Mon. Beyond the coast guard station, 11 miles (18 km) from Highway 1, the peninsula bulks up into roadless, thicket-covered headlands.

Offshore, a French ecotourism company has built a clutch of quaint bamboo bungalows around the beach at **Whale Island** (see Travelwise p. 256). A 3-mile (5 km) trail loops through bushy wilds inhabited by barking deer and parrots.

Farther south, casuarinas and coconut palms lean over the white sands of **Doc Let,** Khanh Hoa's grandest peninsula. The 4-mile (7 km) strand is bracketed by a shipyard to the south and Cape Ca Rang to the north. Offshore is **Hon Lon,** the province's largest island.

Inland from the peninsula, 10 miles (16 km) south of Ninh Hoa, a stream flows into a series of small swimming holes at **Ba Ho** ("three lakes"). The first pool is 700 yards (650 m) from the trailhead.

Near Ba Ho, boats ferry day-trippers from Da Chong Pier to **Hon Thi,** an island with ostriches and deer, while nearby **Orchid Stream Island** offers several swimming holes. On **Monkey Island,** monkeys, dogs, and bears frolic in circus acts. ■

Khanh Hoa Coast
163 C3–C4

Visitor Information
Khanh Hoa Tourism, 1 Tran Hung Dao, Nha Trang
058/3528-100

nhatrangtourist.com.vn

Whale Island
163 C3
2 Me Linh, Nha Trang
058/3840-501

whaleislandresort.com

NOTE: Nha Trang boat tour operators include **Con Se Tre** (100/16 Tran Phu St., tel 058/3527-522), **Mama Linh Boat Tours** (23C Biet Thu, tel 058/3522-844), and **Hanh Café** (10 Hung Vuong, tel 058/3527-466).

My Lai

Eight miles (13 km) northeast of Quang Ngai are the hamlets of Tu Cung and Co Luy, better known worldwide as My Lai. In four hours on March 16, 1968, a U.S. Army unit raped, tortured, and murdered 504 Vietnamese civilians, the majority of whom were women, children, and the elderly. The site of the My Lai massacre is now a memorial to the dead and presents the most emotionally charged couple of hours you're likely to spend in the country.

Cement figures memorialize the 504 villagers massacred at Tu Cung and Co Luy hamlets, known collectively as My Lai.

My Lai
163 B6

Son My Memorial
Tu Cung hamlet
$

The massacre erupted as a perfect storm, fueled by tin-pot leadership, frustrated GIs, and a U.S. military policy that condoned free-fire zones. My Lai was not the only American atrocity of the war, but it was the most horrific, the most exposed, and the most thoroughly documented. That documentation forms the core of a memorial museum that opened in the village of **Son My,** at Tu Cung hamlet, in November 2005, replacing a smaller museum.

The hall is an austere, square edifice of dark stone blocks, as windowless and dour as a mausoleum and thus perfectly suited to its contents. It sits on the edge of the Thuan Yen sub-hamlet of Tu Cung, overlooking a 5-foot-wide (1.5 m) irrigation ditch where rogue American soldiers gunned down 170 people. Up a dark flight of exterior stairs, an interior stairway brings you to the upper-level gallery and a black granite wall that lists the names, ages, and genders of the dead.

The most arresting display begins on the wall to the left of the inscribed names, where 51 photos graphically detail that day's events, from the arrival of the helicopter-borne troops to the V-for-victory sign flashed by Lt. William Calley in the wake of the operation. These color photos shocked the world after they ran in *Life* magazine in 1970. Prodded by British documentary makers, the U.S. Army released the black-and-white photos in 1988—the huddled group of 15 women and children just prior to execution, the two boys cowering in the road moments before they were shot dead, and the many corpses strewn across the road. Beyond the photos is a heartbreaking diorama of soldiers shooting civilians at the irrigation ditch.

Other exhibits include a diorama depicting a bird's-eye view of Tu Cung hamlet, which the GIs knew as My Lai 4, and yellowed clippings of worldwide newspaper coverage of the atrocity, including photos of a girl, Vo Thi Lien, who survived the massacre and became a key subject of subsequent propaganda tours. Look as well for the small red slipper worn by a four-year-old girl named Truong Thi Khai, killed at Thuan Yen.

Outdoor Memorial

Outside, cement footpaths wind among the reconstructed foundations of Thuan Yen's **19 destroyed homes.** The paths are textured with boot treads, villagers' footprints, and bicycle tire tracks, as the muddy paths probably looked that morning. A metal placard beside each foundation lists the names, ages, and genders of the people who lived there and died nearby.

As you wander these paths, look for bullet scars in the coconut palms, a flourishing bodhi tree that survived the torching of the village, and two plots of 21 graves. The irrigation ditch has been encased in cement in order to maintain its 1968 proportions. At the center of the outdoor memorial is a concrete statue, erected in 1982, of a woman holding a dead baby in one arm while lifting the other arm in defiance. This figure, as well as the figures of two cowering boys at her feet, was based on the photos.

Beyond the compound, a narrow path runs behind the former memorial hall and curves left across the rice fields to **Tu Cung.** Most of the massacre's survivors still live in this sub-hamlet. Fewer than 100 yards (90 m) from the far edge of the rice field is a collection of stone markers. Off the right side of the path is the foundation of a watchtower where GIs positioned machine guns and shot 102 people. Farther down this path on the right is the silk-cotton tree where 15 women and children were shot after a photo was snapped. In the courtyard of the house across from the tree is the well into which a 72-year-old man was thrown and then shot. ■

Personal Touch

Since 2000, the My Lai museum's curator has been a woman named Kieu, whose mother survived the onslaught at Co Luy by hiding in a bunker with her sister and mother.

Phan Rang to Vung Tau

The coastline stretching south from Phan Rang, the provincial capital of Ninh Thuan, to Vung Tau, a resort town on the Mekong Delta, offers tourists myriad delights: the country's greatest concentration of Hindu Cham people and wonderfully preserved 13th-century towers in Phan Rang; sunny weather and steady winds for beachgoers along Binh Thuan's coast; one of Southeast Asia's largest recumbent Buddhas; and vestiges of Viet Cong history.

Sledding the red sand dunes just north of Mui Ne is a popular pastime.

Phan Rang

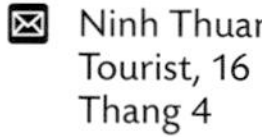

163 C2

Visitor Information

Ninh Thuan Tourist, 16 Thang 4

068/3822-627

ninhthuantourist.com

Phan Rang

Phan Rang, home to the greatest concentration of Cham people, boasts an attractive market building on Thong Nhat and a grand boulevard that leads to the beach. April 16th Boulevard (16 Thang 4) was named for the day in 1975 that North Vietnam won control of the city from South Vietnam.

At the end of the boulevard, Yen Ninh parallels **Ninh Chu,** a 6-mile (10 km) beach of steeply pitched brown sand, once the favorite of Phan Rang native and South Vietnamese president Nguyen Van Thieu and now a draw for domestic travelers, with amusement park–themed resorts.

In Thap Cham, 6 miles (9 km) west of Phan Rang, the **Po Klong Garai** temple *($)* features Vietnam's finest cluster of towers. Dedicated to a 12th-century king who engineered an effective irrigation system, the 13th-century towers include a 70-foot (21 m) *kalan* with an intact roof and original bas-relief statues, a gate tower, and a saddle-roofed *mandapa* with buffalo horn accents.

Over the door of the three-story kalan is a bas-relief of the temple guardian, Po Klaun Tri, a six-armed dancing Siva, while superimposed on the vestibule gable are four arcatures with flame-shaped flourishes, hallmarks of 13th- and 14th-century architecture. Each roof corner supports smaller towers capped with lotus buds. Inside, the superimposed statue of a local king stares from the *linga.*

Every year during the popular Kate New Year Festival in October, a procession of worshippers carries King Po Klong Garai's garments to the temple complex.

Nine miles (14 km) north of town, the two restored towers of the **Hoa Lai** Cham temple rise alongside Highway 1. The pilasters show fine decorative details, including images of Garuda and a deity riding atop a tiger, but the site is walled off from the road.

Binh Thuan Coast

Until the mid-1990s, the Binh Thuan coast barely blipped on anybody's radar screen as a destination. Now, thanks to the most dependably sunny weather in Vietnam and its proximity to Ho Chi Minh City, the booming beachfront between Mui Ne and Ke Ga has emerged as Nha Trang's archrival for sunseekers. Famous as well for dragon fruit *(thanh long),* fish sauce *(nuoc mam),* and sand dunes, the arid region packs a clutch of interesting relics from the Cham and French colonial eras.

North of Phan Thiet:

It took a 1995 solar eclipse to draw tourists to **Mui Ne**'s 12-mile (19 km) swath of plush sand and prize open the eyes and wallets of developers. Thankfully, the latter eschewed sterile high-rises in favor of low-rise garden resorts, which run chockablock between the water and a palm-shaded shoreline road. Development has now begun on Hon Rom beach, just northeast of Mui Ne village; it is connected directly to Phan Thiet by a broad highway that runs parallel to the main beach at Mui Ne. Steady winds make both beaches ideal for wind- and kitesurfing.

On the cusp of Vietnam's richest fishing grounds, Mui Ne

Binh Thuan Coast

163 B1

Visitor Information

Binh Thuan Tourist Association, 97 Nguyen Dinh Chieut

062/3741-093

bta.vn

EXPERIENCE: Kitesurfing at Mui Ne

During the last decade, kitesurfing (or kiteboarding as it is also known) has become one of the world's most popular extreme sports; it now numbers more than a million aficionados worldwide. Already established as Vietnam's windsurfing center, Mui Ne has become the prime spot to practice this activity, with winds of over 12 knots on more than 200 days a year.

Equipment can be rented at places like **Jibe's Beach Club** *(90 Nguyen Dinh Chieu, www.windsurf-vietnam.com),* a cool beachside bar that also hosts spontaneous parties at night, and instruction is available, too. So if you don't know your chicken loop from your pigtails, here's the place to find out. There are several safety procedures you'll need to master before you get to ride the waves, but once you're out there, you won't want to come back in a hurry.

Kingdom of Champa

The Indian-influenced kingdom of Champa flourished along the south-central coast from the 600s until the destruction of its capital by the Vietnamese in 1471. The Cham artistic and archaeological legacy perseveres today in its sandstone sculptures and the powerful stone temple towers at Phan Rang, Nha Trang, My Son, and scattered sites along the country's littoral.

Their descendants are physically indistinguishable from the Vietnamese, though many wear a red-check headdress or the trappings of Islam. Unlike the Viets, who struggled within China's mighty orbit, the Cham took their cultural cues from India. Their gods were the Hindu gods Siva, Brahma, and Vishnu. Their script was Sanskrit. They adopted the caste system as a social infrastructure. But they were not immune to other cultures. By the 800s and 900s, the influence of Buddhism began to pepper Cham art, and later, many migrated to Islam.

Archaeologists sent the best Cham pieces, like this seated goddess from My Son, to Danang's Cham Museum.

The Cham warred on and off with the Chinese, who first sacked the fledgling Cham capital in 446 and made off with tons of gold. The Javanese destroyed the Po Nagar temples near present-day Nha Trang in the 700s. Yet the Cham thrived, expanding north and south from central Vietnam. By the 900s, the Cham ranked with the Khmer as the leading regional powers after China.

Most research into Cham culture centers on art, thanks largely to a bounty of extant sculpture. Little is known about their society, religion, or language. Marco Polo mentions them in his travels, as did Arab traders, who prized Cham sandalwood, cinnamon, ivory, rhinoceros horn, and glazed ceramics.

As the newly independent Vietnam matured, the Cham exerted tremendous influence, particularly among the educated elite between the 11th and 15th centuries. However, the kingdom's loose confederation of principalities would ultimately prove no match for the Vietnamese, who, bucking their Chinese overlords in the tenth century, set their sights on Cham territory.

In response, the Cham moved their capital south from Indrapura to Vijaya, in today's Binh Dinh Province. While they gave up lands around present-day Hue for the hand of a Vietnamese princess in 1306, they also scored victories, killing a Tran king in 1377 and winning the riches of various Vietnamese cities throughout the 1300s.

Retribution was harsh. The greatest of all Vietnamese emperors, Le Thanh Tong, razed Vijaya in 1471, decapitated 40,000 Cham people, and deported another 30,000, thus ending 1,100 years of Hindu primacy on the eastern edge of Southeast Asia.

The Cham limped on with nominal autonomy for several hundred years, but the great age of temple building was over. By 1653, the Vietnamese were settled as far south as Cam Ranh, leaving the Cham to make do with just two provinces. King Minh Mang extinguished the last flickerings of the Cham state in 1832.

itself is a fishing village devoid of any real attractions but for its spectacular fleet of sky blue boats, moored off the town's crescent beach. (Similarly attractive are views of Phan Thiet's fleet from Tran Hung Dao Bridge.)

Just north of the village, **red sand dunes** rise like a misplaced patch of Arabian landscape. The dunes are a mecca for ski buffs, who coast the furrowed slopes on plastic sleds rented by local kids.

Farther north, *so do* bushes speckle the savannas beyond the beach at **Hon Rom,** and 175-acre (70 ha) **Bau Trang** ("white lake") offers a fetch of clear waters amid a sea of white dunes. Locals refer to the highest dune as **Bui Trinh Nu** ("virgin hill"), a dubious moniker now that 4WD tours comb the area. Lotuses bloom along the lakeshore in April, yielding seeds for sweetmeats and soups.

Eleven miles (18 km) west of Mui Ne, closer to Phan Thiet, the three towers of **Po Shanu** stand atop Ba Nai Hill, at the southern border of the vanished kingdom of Champa. Built in the eighth century, they're among the oldest surviving Cham towers and are notable as an architectural bridge between Cham and Khmer styles. The 50-foot (15 m) kalan to the south is dedicated to a son of Po Nagar (see pp. 164–165), while the whole complex pays homage to Po Shanu, a Cham queen famed for her talent, virtue, and tact.

Just a short distance on either side of the towers are two manicured golf courses that perhaps reflect modern man's shift from spiritualism to recreation. To the west, the fairways of Sea Links Golf Course look out over the ocean, while to the west, Ocean Dunes Golf Course was designed by Nick Faldo and has won several awards. Both courses feature luxurious resorts on their grounds.

Phan Thiet: In Phan Thiet proper, **Van Thuy Tu Temple** shelters the 72-foot (22 m) skeleton of a fin whale that washed up nearby in 1893. With great reverence, the villagers buried the whale along the shore, exhuming the skeleton three years later. Though the Vietnamese reject few creatures as a food source, they won't dabble in whale, believing they protect fishermen at sea.

INSIDER TIP:
Remember, temples are sacred places: Show respect by covering knees and shoulders.

—JUSTIN KAVANAGH
National Geographic International Editions editor

The Ca Ty River flows through Phan Thiet, passing a landmark water tower with Chinese motifs built in the colonial era. An eighth of a mile (200 m) upstream of the bridge at Le Hong Phong is the **Duc Thanh School.** As a fledgling nationalist in 1911, Ho Chi Minh taught Chinese and *quoc ngu* (see p. 50) to students at this private school. Today, the varnished benches and sloped

Po Shanu
163 B1
Ba Nai Hill, Phu Hai
$

Van Thuy Tu Temple
54 Ngu Ong, Phan Thiet
$

Duc Thanh School
41 Trung Nhi, Phan Thiet
$

Ta Cu
163 B1
Visitor Information
Ta Cu Tourist
062/3867-484
tacutourist.com

Long Phuoc
163 A1
16 miles (26 km) N of Long Hai
$

Vung Tau
163 A1
Visitor Information
Vung Tau Tourist, 29 Tran Hung Dao
064/3856-445
vungtautourist.com.vn

desktops fitted with inkwells evoke a bygone era. Across the street, a 1986-built **Ho Chi Minh Museum** holds a hodgepodge of interesting memorabilia.

Ta Cu

One of Southeast Asia's largest recumbent Buddhas—160 feet (49 m) long and 33 feet (10 m) high—reclines against an upper flank of Ta Cu Mountain, off Highway 1, 19 miles (30 km) south of Phan Thiet. To reach the statue, you can either hike two hours—a 1,500-foot (475 m) climb through the 60,000-acre (25,000 ha) **Ta Cu Nature Reserve**—or spend ten minutes in a cable car (*$$*). The car docks below the 19th-century **Linh Son Truong Tho Pagoda** and three towering Buddhist deities dressed in flowing robes. While the pagoda is only so-so, the view of the Binh Thuan countryside, **Ke Ga lighthouse,** and the coast are worth the trip.

Bamboo Coracles

The bamboo basket coracle is a familiar sight along Vietnam's south-central coast. Fishermen propel these boats by churning a single oar. It takes a week to weave the strands of a basket boat and seal the bamboo lattice with a pitch derived from the *dau trai* tree. The boats sell for about 2–3 million dong, or $100–$150 each. Boatbuilders often make boats on the grounds of the Van Thuy Tu Temple and in the streets of Phan Thiet.

Long Phuoc

Though they hardly compare to the tunnels of Cu Chi (see pp. 214–215), the tunnels of Long Phuoc open yet another hatch on Viet Cong tenacity. These tunnels burrow 2 miles (2.5 km) beneath ground once patrolled by U.S. soldiers and Australians, who operated from a base at Nui Dat, 1,000 feet (300 m) from the present museum. In 1993, the original tunnels were cased in cement and opened to the public. A quarter-mile (400 m) tour of the works takes you past underground cells and, close to the surface, gun slits from which the Viet Cong would ambush passing patrols. The first of Long Phuoc's three tunnels was dug in 1948, while the longest stretch (1.25 miles/2 km) was started in 1963.

Vung Tau

Vung Tau is Vietnam's version of Atlantic City—a coastal resort with proximity to a metropolis, whose beach is less appealing than its history and whose aura is more festive than sublime. The town crouches between Nui Nho ("small hill") and Nui Lon ("big hill"), which hold the area's two big cultural attractions—a giant statue of Jesus and the White Palace. Vung Tau itself is borne up by a clutch of noble colonial buildings and a pleasant seaside ambience.

The French colonials popularized Vung Tau as Cap St.-Jacques

The statue of Giant Jesus has drawn visitors to Vung Tau since the early 1970s.

in the late 19th century and built the **Bach Dinh** ("white palace") on the site of a demolished imperial fort, renowned for firing the first shot of the resistance against the French in 1859. Built in 1898 as a resort for the French governor-general, the palace later served as a jail for the deposed emperor, Thanh Thai. Set amid a frangipani grove, the palace is now a **museum** *(Tran Phu, $)* whose main galleries display blue-and-white porcelain pottery salvaged from a ship that wrecked nearby in 1690.

In town, stroll **Tran Hung Dao** past two-story French colonial buildings, built between 1911 and 1915. Turn left into Thong Nhat for **Vung Tau Catholic Church,** designed by a French architect and built in 1942 with Indochinese flourishes. At the south end of the street, an enormous statue of Tran Hung Dao stands on a plinth in the middle of a small park.

Heading south out of town on Ha Long, you'll hug the hills past the rocky beach of **Bai Dua,** a colonial-era lighthouse, and a succession of pagodas and temples. Standing at the tip of the promontory, the 92-foot (28 m) **Giant Jesus** implores the sea with outstretched arms. This landmark statue was raised in the early 1970s. An interior stairway climbs to an observation deck on Jesus' shoulders for fantastic views.

Development is mushrooming along **Bai Sau** ("back beach"), a 3-mile (5 km) swath of brown sand and decent surf. Farther north along the coast, the beaches of **Long Hai** are less crowded and offer greater water clarity. ■

More Places to Visit Along the South-central Coast

Ca Na

Ca Na, some 20 miles (32 km) south of Phan Rang, is a bay of startling clarity, jumbled boulders, and white sand that most travelers catch as a lunch break on the Highway 1 run up the coast from Ho Chi Minh City to Nha Trang. If you're looking to give other tourists the slip, this could be a good place to do so, though be warned that there's not much in the way of facilities. A few budget hotels dot this arid landscape of rocks and cactuses, but the barreling traffic along Highway 1 saps much of the charm of its natural beauty.

163 C2

Cam Ranh Bay

At Cam Ranh, two sandy peninsulas embrace 23 square miles (60 sq km) of water in a harbor frequently hailed as the best in the world after Sydney, Australia. The United States built a massive supply depot on the larger peninsula during the Vietnam War, though scant evidence remains of this sprawling complex. In early April 1975, some 100,000 South Vietnamese refugees converged on the largely abandoned base ahead of the southward marching communists. Discovering the bay would soon be in peril, U.S. Navy ships, having just off-loaded many of the refugees, reembarked them to ferry them to points farther south and west. Beyond its historical relevance, the bay's principal attraction is its natural splendor. Nha Trang's airport is now located just north of the bay.

163 C2

Quy Nhon

This seaside town of 300,000 souls in Binh Dinh Province is a popular getaway for domestic tourists because of its broad swathe of golden beach, though there's no shade and the sea is generally murky. It sees few foreign visitors so promises a more authentic Vietnamese experience than places like Mui Ne or Nha Trang. There are plenty of sleeping and eating options, but English is not widely spoken. The **Thap Doi Cham Towers** in town are worth a visit, and the beaches south of town, pristine as you could wish, are fun to explore by motorbike or car with driver.

163 C5 **Visitor Information**

Binh Dinh Tourist, 10 Nguyen Hue

056/3892-524

Diving Responsibly

These days a high percentage of visitors to Vietnam include a diving trip in their itinerary, but the increasing popularity of this activity poses a severe threat to the environment.

Coral reefs are extremely delicate and are easily damaged, so it's important for divers to act in a sensitive manner to avoid destroying these beautiful natural environs that they come to see.

You can start before you even enter the water by asking your boat captain where he intends to drop anchor, and make sure it is not directly above any coral. When you get below the surface, take care not to touch the corals, as the slightest contact can damage them.

Be particularly aware of your fins, as the surge they create when you kick water can harm delicate organisms within the coral reef.

Finally, as with all wild animals in their natural habitats, don't feed the fish. They may be cute and curious as to your presence among them, but feeding them can disturb their eating patterns.

A rugged region of evocative hill-tribe architecture, timeless landscapes, wildlife sanctuaries, and colonial ambience

Central Highlands

Elephant ride at Yok Don National Park

Central Highlands

Along Vietnam's western border with Cambodia and Laos, the Truong Son Mountains dominate the rugged topography of the central highlands. Waterfalls plunge through evergreen forests. In timeless hill-tribe villages, ethnic minorities preserve age-old traditions in longhouses and towering, blade-roofed communal houses. Coffee is the king cash crop. But nature reigns supreme at ten reserves and national parks.

Vegetables suited to the temperate climate thrive in the mile-high fields around Dalat.

The old French hill station of Dalat is all most travelers see of these highlands. You have to approach this city with discretion, however. If your first impression is made by the market, or the town center, or the gaudy attractions that have turned Dalat into the honeymoon capital of Vietnam, there's a tendency to wonder what all the fuss is about. But as soon as you start to wander the streets lined by old colonial villas and take in the hilly vistas and steep ravines cultivated with vegetables, its charms can captivate.

Outside Dalat and throughout the highlands, waterfalls command attention. Too few are left to their pristine charms and instead are "enhanced" with reinforced concrete flourishes, tourist elevators, and the proximity of karaoke culture. Fortunately, the natural majesty of some cascades, like Dambri Falls near Bao Loc, retain the ability to impress.

In the national parks at Yok Don, Chu Mom Ray, and Cat Tien, Vietnam's most emblematic fauna—the Indochinese tiger, Javan rhinoceros, and Asian elephant—are making a last stand. These endangered animals prove elusive, but the scenery and sublime silence, in a country that does not place a premium on quietude, are invigorating. The central highlands' tallest peak, Ngoc Linh, tops out at 8,523 feet (2,598 m) in Ngoc Linh Nature Reserve north of Kon Tum.

Vietnam's Coffee Lands

Farther south in Buon Ma Thuot, the capital of Vietnam's coffee industry, cafés and wholesalers peddle countless brands of Robusta, Arabica, and Culi bean coffee. The premium brands retail at about $2 per pound.

Until the early 20th century, the modern world had hardly intruded upon the primitive peoples who inhabited the highlands. Stimulated by the region's rich red earth, the French cultivated the plateaus with coffee plantations, forcing the locals into the first of a long string of losing propositions. During the war, the United States garrisoned the highlands in a futile attempt to stem the tide of matériel flowing down the Ho Chi Minh Trail.

Highland place-names still call to mind momentous wartime events—Ia Drang, Pleiku, Buon Ma Thuot. But today the area is winning more welcome notice as one of Vietnam's most naturally enticing and least plumbed regions. Unlike the highly touristed northern

NOT TO BE MISSED:

Dalat, gateway to the central highlands **180–183**

Feeling the spray on your face at one of the highland waterfalls **184, 185**

The wildlife at Cat Tien National Park **184–185**

Getting a caffeine fix in Buon Ma Thuot, Vietnam's coffee capital **188**

An elephant ride in Yok Don National Park **189**

Overnighting in a communal house near Kon Tum **191–192**

highlands near Sa Pa, few Western tourists trek to the hinterland homes of Bahnar (Ba Na), Giarai, and E De (Ede) highlanders near Kon Tum, Pleiku, and Buon Ma Thuot. Though these groups lack the compelling wardrobes of their northern cousins, the architecture of their villages is unrivaled among Vietnam's ethnic minorities. ■

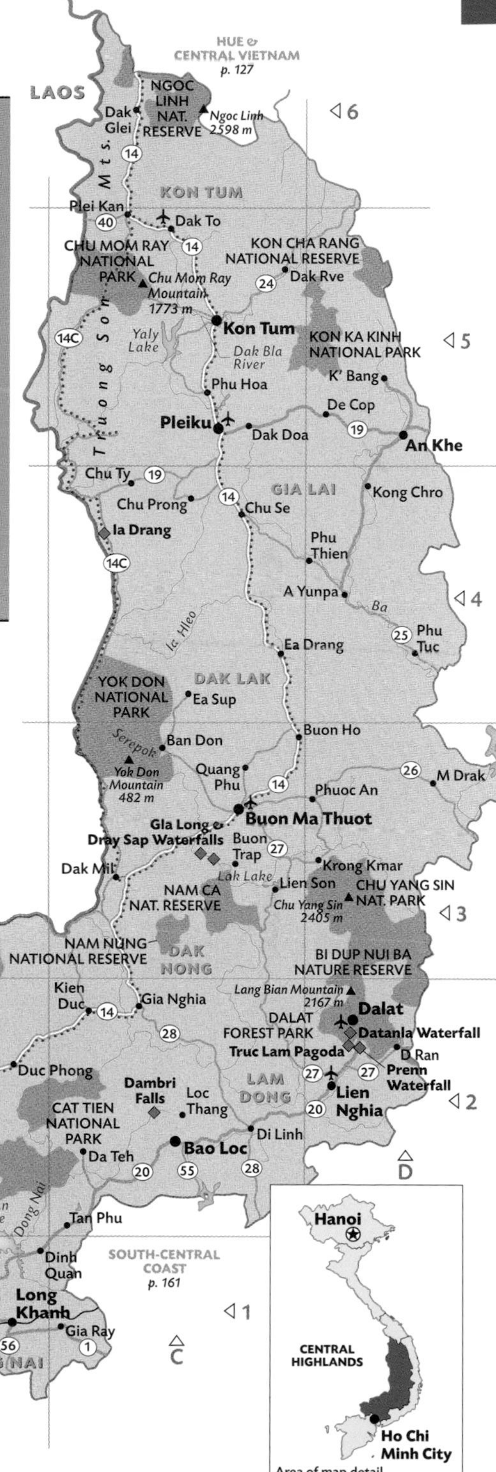

Dalat & Around

Perched on a plateau 5,000 feet (1,500 m) above sea level, Dalat remains the geographic antidote to the swelter and smog of Ho Chi Minh City, 190 miles (300 km) to the southeast. Its fresh air, pine-clad hills, and mild temperatures—an average daily high of 59°F (15°C) in winter, 80°F (27°C) in summer—have earned Dalat the moniker "City of Eternal Spring." As an added bonus, Dalat's treasury of colonial French villas and châteaus is unrivaled in Vietnam.

The last king of Vietnam, Bao Dai, used this nautical moderne villa as his summer palace from 1938 through World War II.

Dalat
179 D2
Visitor Information
7,3 Thang 2
063/ 3822-125

During an 1893 exploration, Alexandre Yersin, the doctor who discovered the plague pathogen, also identified the plateau as an ideal location for a health resort. After an initial burst of enthusiasm, interest in Dalat waned, until the 1920s when the colonial government opened the sumptuous Lang Bian (now the Dalat) Palace Hotel and a golf course and dammed the Cam Ly River to create the Grand Lac (now Xuan Huong Lake). In 1932, a cog railway conquered the steep pitches between the coast and the hill station, and from the mid-1930s through World War II, a building boom speckled the hillsides with hundreds of villas inspired by architecture in Normandy, Brittany, and other French provinces.

French Legacy

The villas and an abundance of colonial structures are the essence of Dalat's charm and its least exploited resource. Begin at the lavishly restored **Dalat Palace Hotel** (*12 Tran Phu, S of Xuan Huong Lake;* see Travelwise p. 256). In 1942, a Vichy French governor stripped the architectural confections from the hotel's opulent exterior and made it over with the art deco facade that endures today. Inside, however, Victorian grandeur still reigns, in the heavy drapery, the chandeliers, the monumental lobby fireplace, and some fine reproductions of European masterpieces.

Traveling east on Tran Phu, continue along Tran Hung Dao, where the richest vein of villas fans away from the colonial governor's château atop the hill. Norman villas include Tudor-like wood detailing on the facade, while heavy, ground-floor stonework characterizes Breton villas. **16 Tran Hung Dao** is the former home of Paul Veysseyre, Dalat's most prominent colonial architect, and now functions as the Dalat Cadasa Resort. The restored Landaise-style villa at **27 Tran Hung Dao** is the former home of a Michelin rubber plantation director. As you continue up Tran Hung Dao, Lang Bian Mountain dominates the northern horizon.

At 4 Hung Vuong, the **Lam Dong Museum** features a collection of archaeological exhibits from the seventh- to tenth-century Funan culture, as well as ethnic minority exhibits, including photos of a buffalo sacrifice and a skewer used in such a ceremony. The collection was recently moved from a 1930s villa into a new building.

INSIDER TIP:

In Vietnam, don't be afraid to negotiate the price of anything and everything.

—CATHERINE KARNOW
National Geographic photographer

Follow the signs to **Dinh 1,** one of Bao Dai's residences. This rambling colonial structure enjoys excellent views over the city, while inside the conference room, the period furnishings and revealing photographs are worth a look.

Loop back toward town along Quang Trung and check out the **Corsican villa** across from No. 4. This villa's turreted wings flank a gallery punctuated by three stone

Lam Dong Museum
- ✉ 4 Hung Vuong
- ☎ 063/3822-339
- 🕒 Closed Sun. & daily 11:30 a.m.–1:30 p.m.
- $ $

Dinh 1
- ✉ Hung Vuong
- 🕒 Closed 11:30 a.m.–1:30 p.m.
- $ $

The Last King

Though frequently cited as Vietnam's last emperor, King Bao Dai (1913–1997) never ruled any state but Vietnam, and there only as a puppet. History remembers him as a playboy who indulged in women, sports cars, speedboats, airplanes, hunting, golf, and a sumptuous suite of villas in the mountains and along the south-central coast. His mother was a peasant who became a concubine, and his alleged father was King Khai Dinh, who preferred to keep his distance from women.

As a sovereign, Bao Dai meant well, but he lacked the wherewithal to wrest control from his French overseers or the resolve of his revolutionary peers. After he abdicated in 1945 to Ho's government, he led an affluent life near Cannes, France. He married a French woman and converted from Buddhism to Catholicism. He is buried in the Passy Cemetery west of Paris.

The crazy yet enticing Nga Guesthouse and Gallery is part hotel, part gallery, and altogether hallucinatory.

Dalat Railway Station
1 Quang Trung
063/3834-409

Crazy House
3 Huynh Thuc Khang
063/3822-070
$
crazyhouse.vn

Bao Dai's Summer Palace
1 Trieu Viet Vuong
063/3826-858
$

arches. On the left turret, a Cham *apsara,* or Khmer dancer, struts her stuff in bas-relief.

Farther along Quang Trung on the left is the 1938 **Dalat Railway Station,** inspired by the *gare* in Deauville, Normandy. Its two marquees jut from either end of a triptych of gables. Bombing during the Vietnam War in the 1960s closed the line, though the engine from its 10-mile (16 km) cog stretch supposedly remains operative in Switzerland today. The Japanese engine on the tracks is for show, but a Russian diesel *($$)* does ferry passengers 4.5 miles (7 km) to and from the village of **Trai Mat**.

From the station, follow Nguyen Trai to Yersin and look up to the right for the château built as a **maternity clinic** for French and high-society Vietnamese women who wanted to give birth in a temperate climate.

Heading west on Tran Phu, look for the 155-foot (47 m) steeple atop the **Dalat Cathedral** *(15 Tran Phu),* built between 1931 and 1942. Manufactured in Grenoble around the same period, its stained-glass windows filter the late afternoon sun into bursts of lush color against the salmon pink interior walls.

West of the Lake

Follow Tran Phu west to Pasteur Street and loop up around Le Hong Phong to another clutch of French villas. Before road's end, turn left on Huynh Thuc Khang and stop at the Hang Nga Guesthouse and Gallery, or **Crazy House,** a fantasy of a guesthouse/art gallery conjured up by a Moscow-trained Vietnamese architect named Hang Nga. The house is actually a compound of ferroconcrete villas shaped like molten tree trunks, entwined by giraffes and bridged by concrete spans. Writhing stairways of fabricated stumps climb the insides of these villas to rooms with jigsaw puzzle–piece beds and grotesque artwork—bears, eagles perched on giant eggs and acorns. Open to visitors, this apogee of kitsch is a must-see.

Less surprising is **Bao Dai's summer palace,** near the end of Trieu Viet Vuong. From 1938 until the end of World War II, the last emperor vacationed in this nautical moderne villa. The flat-roofed château is incised with a grid of coping, a hallmark of the style. Inside the 26-room villa, wander from the reception room to the festivities room, with its

30-foot (9 m) banquet table, then upstairs to the roped-off private chambers of the royal family, all with original furnishings.

Down Pasteur, a dirt track on the left takes you to **Lam Ty Ni Pagoda** *(2 Thien My)* to meet Dalat's most eccentric personality, a monk/artist named Vien Thuc. The pagoda's sole occupant, Thuc moved here in 1964 as a 19-year-old. Today, larger-than-life cement busts watch over the garden, each a representation of Thuc in the trademark knitted cap he wears like an open hood. In a studio out back, thousands of his paintings, calligraphy, and Zen poems lean framed and stacked against the walls or draped from hooks. The pagoda is named for the garden where the Buddha was born.

City Center

Across the Cam Ly River dam is the less lovely heart of town. The facade of the main **market,** built in the 1960s, describes a short arc before a run-of-the-mill victory monument in Hoa Binh Square. Atop the stairs to Khu Hoa Binh, the long, rectangular building to the right was the city's first market, now a movie cinema.

Below the market, follow Xuan Huong Lake's north shore and turn left on Tran Nha Tong to the **Dalat Palace Golf Club,** one of Vietnam's oldest and best golf courses. First laid down in 1922, it was upgraded to an 18-hole championship course in the 1990s.

Past the steepled tower of the Teachers' Training College, Bui Thi Xuan leads to **Linh Son Pagoda.** Completed in 1941, the pagoda once sheltered an offbeat, ascetic monk named Vien Ngo, who cloistered himself in the log cabin behind the main hall for five years. The bell tower no longer houses the bell, as its walls would crack whenever the bell was rung. In the main hall, an enormous bronze of Sakyamuni is framed by an ornate wood carving of dragons and bats.

EXPERIENCE: Pursue Adventure Sports

Dalat's highland location, at an elevation of 4,900 feet (1,500 m) and with an average temperature of 64.5°F (18°C), makes it ideal for energetic activities. As a result, in recent years the town has emerged as the country's premier adventure sports destination.

Some of the activities offered are relatively easy, such as paddling a kayak around Tuyen Lam Lake and enjoying the pleasant views, or taking a gentle horse ride through pine forests. Other activities like canyoneering require a high level of fitness and good sense of balance. One activity gaining in popularity is a mountain-bike ride downhill from Dalat to Mui Ne or Nha Trang, which takes a couple of days and passes through some glorious scenery.

A reliable company in Dalat that organizes these activities is Phat Tire Ventures ***(109 Nguyen Van Troi, phattireventures.com).***

Around Dalat

While international travelers extol the delights of Dalat proper, domestic tourists fancy the region's sylvan charms. Honeymooning couples throng viewing

Dalat Palace Golf Club
✉ Phu Dong Thien Vuong
☎ 063/3823-507
dalatpalacegolf.vn

Linh Son Pagoda
✉ 120 Nguyen Van Troi
☎ 063/3822-893

Cable Car to Truc Lam Pagoda

Robin Hill
063/3837-938
Closed 1st Mon. of month & 11:30 a.m.–1:30 p.m.
$

Cat Tien National Park

179 B2–C2

Visitor Information

Cat Tien Ecotourism Center
061/3669-159
Entrance: $; half-day guide: $$$

catthiennationalpark.vn

sites below a half dozen nationally renowned waterfalls and dress up for pony rides and pictures at the Valley of Love. Kitsch and crowds notwithstanding, several of the waterfalls merit attention, as does a popular Zen monastery.

Just south of town, Highway 20 tops Robin Hill, where you can ride a cable car down to **Truc Lam Pagoda,** a Zen monastery built in 1993 on Tuyen Lam Lake. The flying eaves of its two-tiered roof echo the aesthetics of Zen temples in Japan. Inside, a bronze-painted Sakyamuni holds a single lotus flower beneath a cement frieze that details the story of his life. The 80 monks and 60 nuns rise at 3:15 a.m. for meditation followed by three hours of daily chores.

INSIDER TIP:

In Cat Tien National Park, sleep over at Crocodile Lake, so you have a chance to see wildlife in the late afternoon and early morning.

—JONATHAN A. O'BRIEN
National Geographic grantee

You can also approach the pagoda and lake by road; it's 3 miles (5 km) south of Dalat via Highway 20. A couple hundred yards farther south, a long stairway leads to **Datanla Waterfall** (Thac Datanla; $), which tumbles down rock chutes lined by a path. More impressive is 30-foot (9 m) **Prenn Waterfall** *($)*, another 3 miles (5 km) south, though its appeal is marred by pushy vendors and couples dressed up like bunny rabbits.

Just over a mile (2 km) from downtown Dalat is **Cam Ly Waterfall** *(36 Hoang Van Thu, tel 063/3824-145, $)*, whose name pops up in a treacly song that goes, "Oh, Dalat. Can you hear Cam Ly sobbing for its first broken love?"

The treacle reaches a fever pitch at the **Valley of Love** *(Dap 3 Da Thien, tel 063/3821-448, $)*, 4 miles (7 km) north of town, where young couples ride ponies, play dress-up, and race toy speedboats on the Da Thien reservoir.

A little farther north, **Lang Bian Mountain** *(tel 063/3839-088, $)* peaks in three summits, the tallest of which is 7,109 feet (2,167 m). You can walk or drive to the top. At the massif's southern foot, the K'Ho ethnic minority of **Lat village** sound ceremonial gongs for tourists.

Cat Tien National Park

This 179,000-acre (72,000 ha) preserve of wetlands, grasslands, evergreens, and bamboo forest lies off Highway 20, 105 miles (170 km) southwest of Dalat. The restricted northern tract harbors the critically endangered Javan rhinoceros and perhaps a small population of Indochinese tigers, while Asian elephants, gaur, civets, muntjacs, and Siamese crocodiles inhabit the park's southern reaches. Cat Tien was recognized as a biosphere reserve by UNESCO in 2001, and is listed as a World Heritage site.

Visitors usually stay overnight in plain but comfortable guesthouses near park headquarters on the Dong Nai River. Branching off a sealed road that leads from headquarters are the park's dozen trails, each less than 6 miles (10 km) round-trip. Rangers ask visitors to refrain from entering the forest unguided, though the reasons may have more to do with revenue than safety.

From headquarters, tour boats *($$$$/hr.)* ply the river, which winds through the park for 56 miles (90 km). On night safaris *($$$)*, jeep lights scour the forest for muntjacs, porcupines, and wild boars. At the **Crocodile Lake** ranger station, a 3-mile (5 km) hike from the park road, lucky guests sometimes spot gaur (a type of wild ox) and crocodiles. Towers here and at **Bird Lake** enable birders to spot standouts among the park's 348 bird species.

The fauna may be hit or miss, but the park's majestic trees are accessible. Near headquarters, the **Lagerstroemia Trail** winds amid these speckle-trunked trees, which tower as much as 230 feet (70 m). One *thitpok* tree *(Tetrameles nudiflora)* on this trail is 500 years old, its buttressed roots sprawling far out across the forest floor. Another featured specimen is the **Uncle Dong tree,** an *Afzelia xylocarpa* named for celebrated Vietnamese leader Pham Van Dong, who visited the park in 1987 and advised locals to care for the forest.

Cinder cones and steep-sided conical hills evince the region's volcanic origins. In the dry season, a Dong Nai tributary tumbles through porous volcanic rocks at the **Ben Cu Rapids,** among three accessible sets in the park. Locals use these rocks to build farmyard walls.

Dambri Falls: Near Cat Tien, in the midst of a forest 11 miles (18 km) northwest of Bao Loc, Dambri Falls *(map 179 C2; Dalat visitor information: 7,3 Thang 2, tel 063/3822-125)* drop more than 295 feet (90 m), including one awe-inspiring cascade.

A glass elevator shuttles sightseers up and down 130 feet (40 m) of the falls, or, if you are feeling fit and energetic, you can get your daily workout in by climbing the more than 245 stairs. In the ethnic Ma language, *dambri* means "cascade of the lion," while in Coho it means "the stream of hope." ■

Cat Tien's *thitpok* trees tower more than 200 feet (60 m) above the forest floor.

A Last Stand for Vietnam's Elephants & Tigers

The knell is tolling for Vietnam's best known wild animals—the Asian elephant and the Indochinese tiger. Conservationists in the region concede these species are biologically doomed here and hope the requiem will serve as a clarion call to conservationists in neighboring Laos and Cambodia, where populations of tigers and elephants remain viable.

Less than 100 Indochinese tigers remain in Vietnam's highlands, as poaching and other infringements continue to exact a heavy toll.

The loss of Vietnam's wild elephants and tigers is heartbreaking. At the end of the Vietnam War in 1975, approximately 2,000 Asian elephants roamed Vietnam's highlands and central plateaus. Today, only around 100 animals survive.

The reasons for this are many, and it's the same sad story across Asia: poaching, a burgeoning human population, habitat degradation, logging. In Vietnam, one of 13 Asian countries that still harbor wild pachyderms, coffee, pepper, and tobacco plantations have backed the animals into increasingly smaller islands of forest. While more than 50 percent of neighboring Cambodia remains forested, the percentage is half that in Vietnam.

The elephants, for one, are not going down without a fight. In the 1990s, rampaging herds and the odd rogue trampled dozens of villagers to death in a series of isolated incidents throughout the highland provinces. In 2005, the government heralded a plan to administer a trio of conservation zones for the elephants, an announcement many conservationists greeted as too little too late.

Fate of the Tiger

Tigers face similar challenges in Vietnam, particularly from poaching. Nearly three-quarters of them wind up at pharmacies in China, where the flesh, bones, and skin are coveted for medicinal qualities and command a huge price tag. Fewer than 100 Indochinese tigers stalk the hinterlands of Vietnam. Sadder still is the case of the Javan rhinoceros, whose last stand in the country is now over. A few had been living in Cat Tien National Park, but the last one was shot in 2010 and its horn removed, so it is now officially extinct in Vietnam. This leaves the Javan rhino in the unenviable situation of being one of the most critically endangered species on our planet, with a population of less than 50 surviving in a national park in Java, Indonesia.

Culturally, elephants and tigers have loomed large in Vietnam's history. In the 15th century, King Le Loi's elephant cavalry stunned the horse cavalry of their Ming antagonists and won the country's independence after a 20-year occupation by the Chinese. In the 19th century, the Nguyen emperors pitted elephants and tigers in deadly combat in an arena in Hue (see p. 143) and worshipped the majestic elephant at a nearby temple. Vietnam's ethnic minorities built their houses on stilts to guard against attack by tigers and other wild animals.

While elephant and tiger numbers dwindle, wildlife biologists have been thrilled by the discoveries of giant muntjac, a species of barking deer, and the saola, a species of long-horned rain forest animal that's as big as a sheep and sometimes described as a kind of cow or antelope. Discovered in 1993, the saola is likely to be the last new species of large mammal brought to the world's attention. Scientists believe that 500 to 1,500 of these animals live in the forests of Vietnam and Laos.

INSIDER TIP:

Consider hiring a guide in national parks, as park rangers know the animals' habitat and can lead you to memorable sightings.

—RON EMMONS
National Geographic contributor

EXPERIENCE: Seeing the Tigers

Along the border with Cambodia, south of Laos, Chu Mom Ray National Park ***(map 179 C5; visitor information, Kon Tum Tourist, 2 Phan Dinh Phung, Kon Tum, tel 060/3862-703)*** **is the most remote of Vietnam's national parks. The government designated the 136,000-acre (55,000 ha) tract a national park in 2002, and it is home to the country's largest population of Indochinese tigers, as well as the kouprey, a kind of wild ox. The park also shelters such precious timber as ironwood, margosa, and sindora.**

However, this border area is considered sensitive due to occasional conflicts between ethnic minorities and government officials over land rights, so the park is currently off-limits to foreign visitors. Other national parks where small numbers of tigers are believed to roam are Cat Tien (see pp. 184–185) and Cuc Phuong (see pp. 126, 190), though sightings are as rare as winning the lottery. Sadly, to be sure of seeing one of these beautiful creatures in Vietnam, you'll need to visit them at Hanoi Zoo ***(Thu Le, Ba Dinh).***

Buon Ma Thuot & Around

On the northern edge of the southern highlands, Buon Ma Thuot is the capital of Dak Lak Province and the hub of Vietnam's booming coffee industry. Most visitors use the town as a base for excursions to waterfalls southwest of the city, Lak Lake, Yok Don National Park, and villages of the E De (Ede) ethnic minority. But the city does offer some mildly interesting sights if you've a couple hours to spare.

The Serepok River sustains resident wildlife at Yok Don, Vietnam's largest national park.

Buon Ma Thuot

179 C3

Visitor Information

53 Ly Thuong Kiet

0500/3852-246

Ethnography Museum

182 Nguyen Du

0500/3850-426

$

At the heart of town is the **Victory Monument,** a bland war memorial of a tank, an arch, and a column at the intersection of Le Duan and Phan Chu Trinh. From the monument, head a mile (2 km) north to reach the small E De settlement of **Ako Dhong,** which includes a street of longhouses in hedged, rectangular plots. The E De compose about 14 percent of the Dak Lak Province population.

Back toward town, turn right on Phan Boi Chau to the intersection with Nguyen Trai to reach **Khai Doan Pagoda,** built in 1952 to memorialize Bao Dai's mother. Inside, a sprawling bodhi tree shelters a pure white statue of the Buddha. The pagoda marries E De longhouse architecture with such imperial hallmarks as the two-tiered roof and dragon balustrades on either side of the central stairway.

The **ethnography museum,** housed in a brand-new facility, provides an interesting introduction to the history, environment, and people of the area. It features a gallery of Sedang, Giarai, and E De costumes worn at festivals, judicial proceedings, weddings, and other rituals.

Beyond Buon Ma Thuot

Twenty miles (30 km) south, several waterfalls jockey for attention in the wet season, including **Gia Long** and **Dray Sap,** the most scenic. Another watery wonder lies 32 miles (52 km) southeast of Buon Ma Thuot: **Lak Lake** *(map 179 C3),* the largest lake in Vietnam's central highlands. King Bao Dai built a summer villa here in the 1930s. Tourism authorities have since turned the old place into a small hotel, known as the **Bao Dai Villa** *(tel 00500/3586-184).*

Yok Don National Park

Yok Don National Park borders Cambodia in country that once nurtured wild elephants. While the herds have dwindled to a few dozen animals at best, elephants remain the draw here, either for treks in Yok Don or rides in nearby Ban Don.

Hire a guide to explore the dry deciduous forest and 1,581-foot (482 m) **Yok Don Mountain** by elephant, foot, or even motorbike. Sightings of wild boars, deer, and monkeys are rare, while even some of the park's veteran guides have yet to spot the park's half dozen tigers or several dozen wild elephants.

Across the Serepok River, a 2-mile (3 km) upstream trek from the park's garden leads to the **Seven Branches Rapids.** In dry season, one can rock-hop to one of the midstream monkey-inhabited islands. Downstream, guided hikes lead to white water at the **Buddhist Rapids,** named for a vanished pagoda.

Just outside the park is **Ban Don,** a Mnong Bubong village of Laotian people that until recently housed the region's legendary elephant hunters.

The village's most famous resident was **Y Thu Knul,** an elephant hunter and trainer who netted 444 pachyderms before he died at age 89 in 1924.

About a mile (1.5 km) from the village, **Knul's tomb** stands amid others trimmed with elephant motifs, including the tomb of his daughter and son-in-law, Ma Krong, another renowned *chasseur des éléphants,* as is written on his tomb.

Unfortunately, the village itself has now become a touristy village featuring short elephant rides and stalls selling souvenirs. However, in the spring they hold elephant races here as the focus of a riotous festival. Check with Ban Dot Tourist Center for dates. ■

Vietnamese Coffee

With nearly 500,000 acres (200,000 ha) under cultivation in the province, Dak Lak now harvests a third of Vietnam's annual coffee output.

Germany buys the biggest share of the crop, which amounted to 1.5 million tons (1.35 million metric tons) in the 2012–2013 season. Vietnam is the world's second largest coffee exporter after Brazil. French missionaries planted the first bean plants here in 1857.

Dray Sap & Gia Long

✉ Dray Sap: 17 miles (28 km) SW of Buon Ma Thuot via Ho Chi Minh Hwy.; go to Km 739 and turn right
Gia Long: 4 miles (7 km) beyond Dray Sap along same secondary road

$ Dray Sap: $

Yok Don National Park

Map 179 C3–C4

Visitor Information

✉ 25 miles (40 km) NW of Buon Ma Thuot via Rte. 681

☎ 0500/3783-049

$ Half-day trekking tour: $$$$$
Elephant trek: $$$$$/hr.

Ban Don

Map 179 C3

Visitor Information

✉ Ban Don Tourist Center

☎ 0500/3783-020

EXPERIENCE: Ecotouring in Vietnam

As defined by the International Ecotourism Society, ecotourism is "responsible travel to natural areas that conserves the environment and improves the well-being of local people."

One means of being responsible is by choice of boat.

A great number of international travelers are keen to minimize their impact on the environment, but unfortunately many tour companies use the concept of ecotourism simply as a marketing tool without applying its principles in reality. As a comparatively young country in terms of tourism development, Vietnam is yet to fully embraced the principles of sustainable tourism, although the government has introduced new laws to offer greater protection to the nation's natural and cultural heritage.

Fortunately there are several examples of environmentally friendly initiatives in Vietnam. Projects such as the **Endangered Primate Rescue Center** at **Cuc Phuong National Park** (see p. 126) offer visitors the chance to learn about the habits of gibbons and langurs, while providing a sheltered environment for these endangered creatures. Other examples are the banning of traffic in **Hoi An**'s town center (see pp. 153–157), which allows visitors to wander around the historic buildings without being disturbed by noise and exhaust fumes, and kayaking in **Ha Long Bay** (see p. 97), which lets visitors enjoy this spectacular environment without adding to pollution in the region. One of the most eco-friendly activities is cycling, and the growth in popularity of cycling holidays is another hopeful sign for the future of responsible travel in Vietnam.

INSIDER TIP:

Ecotour or *ecotourism* does not mean environmentally friendly in Vietnam. Tourist companies have found that saying eco-anything attracts tourists and can increase what they charge.

—LOIS K. LIPPOLD
Douc Langur Foundation director & National Geographic grantee

Travelers need to do their part as well. You can help minimize your negative impact on places by cutting down on carbon emissions by flying as little as possible, traveling in small groups, hiring local guides, and buying local products (avoiding those made of endangered species, hardwood, or coral). In addition, since a considerable share of your vacation expenses goes to hotel owners and tour operators, find out what they are doing to minimize their impact, such as disposing of waste water in ways that do not harm the environment.

Yet ecotourism is not just about don't do this, don't do that. It is also about learning about the culture you are visiting. Seek out opportunities for genuine cultural exchange, for example, when you go trekking or visit markets. Consider volunteering on a local project that will enable you to share your skills.

For more suggestions on how you can help protect the environment and links to environmentally sensitive tour operators, visit *responsibletravel.com.*

Kon Tum Province

The province of Kon Tum is peppered with more than 600 ethnic minority villages and 200 alluring *nha rong* (communal houses), whose blade-shaped thatch roofs soar as high as 56 feet (17 m). Most visitors venture into this accessible highlands region from the provincial capital of Kon Tum on the Dak Bla River.

Eight ethnic minority groups live in Kon Tum Province, including the Sedang (the most populous contingent), the Giarai, the Rongao, and the Bahnar (Ba Na). French missionaries began converting highlanders to Catholicism in the 19th century, and in 1913 they built a large **wooden church** in town at the east end of Nguyen Hue. In deference to, or perhaps to entice, the Bahnar, the French lofted the church on a familiar footing of short stilts. Inside, Bahnar textiles drape the sanctum, and prayerful mottoes are written in the Bahnar language. Behind the church, nuns tend to local orphans.

Two blocks north on Tran Hung Dao, a bishop and two dozen priests live in a defunct **Catholic seminary.** Built in 1935, the structure calls to mind an alpine hotel. On the second floor is a museum devoted to the region's ethnic minorities.

Kon Tum

Within Kon Tum township, eight nha rong play a central role in the community. West of Phan Dinh Phung, along Ba Trieu, is **Plei To Nghia,** a village that moved its 1968-built nha rong to its present location in 2003. As with every rong, the crest of this 52-foot (16 m) structure is rimmed with vertical stakes that symbolize the skewers used in buffalo sacrifices, a gruesome ritual Francis Ford Coppola filmed for the memorable climactic scene in the 1979 film *Apocalypse Now.* The roof's distinctive blade shape serves to protect occupants against supernatural harm.

Inside, the jaw and skull of a bull sacrificed during construction of the hall hang above the door. Many highland groups still sacrifice buffalo on auspicious occasions, believing

Kon Tum Province

179 C5–C6

Visitor Information

Kon Tum Tourist, 2 Phan Dinh Phung

060/3862-703

Kon Tum is a hub for the province's 635 villages of ethnic minority people.

Gia Lai Province
179 C5
Visitor Information
Gia Lai Tourist, 2 Le Loi
059/3824-645
gialaitourist.com

that the screams of the buffalo, as it writhes in agony, will wake the deities. The longer and harder the buffalo screams and suffers, the better.

On the eastern edge of town, two more nha rong rise in the villages of **Kon Tum Kopong** and **Kon Tum Konam** ("upper" and "lower" Kon Tum). Five miles (8 km) southeast of Kon Tum, across the Kon Klor suspension bridge, is **Kon Kotu,** home to 60 families of 350 Bahnar and one of the loveliest nha rong in the area. The thatch of this hall is matted in bamboo, which extends the life of the roof and guards against sparks from the frequent ceremonial fires in the adjacent courtyard. The Kon Tum Province tourist office can arrange an overnight stay in this rong.

On the way back into town, turn left into **Kon Jri** ("apricot village"), where two stepped tree trunks climb to the terraced porch of another rong. The men are obliged to use the seven-stepped ladder on the right, while the women use the five-stepped ladder on the left. In this traditionally matriarchal society, the five steps signify quicker, preferential access for women.

Ten miles (16 km) west of Kon Tum, the Giarai village of **Ro Lay** also features a nha rong, as well as a fascinating cemetery rife with animist traditions. Following a death, the Giarai will mind the staked burial mound every day for a period of three, five, or seven years. Several members of the same family may occupy the same tomb, and their prized possessions, such as a sewing machine or bicycle, may be placed in the tomb area. They then hold a ceremony to "abandon the grave." After sacrificing a water buffalo, villagers mount carved wooden figures of moping men and copulating couples atop the fence posts. Objects placed atop the mounds offer clues as to who is buried beneath—a jar for a single person, a canteen for a soldier, a teapot for a woman, and bicycle tires for a youth.

Farther west, Highway 24 winds toward a vast reservoir of the Dak Bla River. The lofty peak to the northwest is 5,816-foot (1,773 m) Chu Mom Ray.

Villages of Gia Lai

Adjacent to Kon Tum Province, Gia Lai Province is laced with many ethnic minority villages, populated mainly by the Giarai and Bahnar peoples, but provincial authorities have dampened the region's tourism potential with overly restrictive access privileges and an insistence on using guides to visit. ■

EXPERIENCE: Trekking Around Kon Tum

Kon Tum is the most liberal of the highland provinces and as such is the best place to go trekking. Kon Tum Tourist (see p. 191) can assist in arranging overnight stays in the towering communal houses of the Bahnar tribe, as well as white-water rafting trips on local rivers and visits to Giarai graveyards filled with enigmatic carvings.

Ho Chi Minh City (aka Saigon), a city of vibrant nightlife, colonial and wartime vestiges, museums, temples, and a heady pace of life

Ho Chi Minh City

A statue of Vietnam's great leader presides in the park next to Ho Chi Minh City Hall.

Ho Chi Minh City

The West's love affair with Vietnam is nowhere more passionate than it is in Saigon, District 1 of the larger municipality known as Ho Chi Minh City. This booming metropolis nets about 40 percent of the country's revenue from international travelers. Its heady growth rate and low cost of labor are as alluring to foreign businessmen as its legendary opium dens and taxi girls were to previous generations.

The city owes its origins to the Khmer, who had dwelled here for centuries before the Viets developed an appetite for the fertile Mekong Delta. In 1698, the Nguyen lords established the prefecture of Gia Dinh, with mandarin Nguyen Huu Canh as founding father. After the French arrived in 1859 and founded the colony of Cochinchina, they adopted Saigon, a locally popular alternative to Gia Dinh, as the name of their capital.

In its first 20 years as a colonial capital, Saigon blossomed. The French laid out wide boulevards flanked by kapok and tamarind trees that now tower above the avenues. They built a monumental cathedral, an opera house, palaces, and villas, as if their tenure were to last a millennium.

By the 1870s, travelers had begun to wax lyrically about the city as the Pearl of the Orient, the Paris of the East. Today, you'd be hard-pressed to refer to this urban frenzy in such genteel terms, but its former glories and architectural gems, many all but subsumed by agglomerations of shanty shops, can still dazzle.

Officially, close to seven million people pack the city's 19 urban districts, 5 rural districts, and 770 square miles (2,000 sq km), though on-the-street estimates put that number closer to ten million. Its history is shallower than that of Hanoi or Hue. Its pagodas, temples, museums, and scenic beauty are wanting in comparison. But its café society, its nightlife, and the ambience stoked by its markets, hotels, and business climate are inimitable. As "mythalopolis," the city also doesn't disappoint, especially if you're attuned to the French or American legacy. It's not at all difficult to conjure the ghosts of French legionnaires,

NOT TO BE MISSED:

The Municipal Theater & Notre Dame Cathedral 196–197, 200

Trendy Dong Khoi 198–199

The historic Reunification Palace 201–203

Exploring the cavernous Ben Thanh market 203–204

Remembering the past at the War Remnants Museum 204–205

Relaxing in the zoo & botanical gardens 206–207

The Chinese-influenced Jade Emperor Pagoda 208

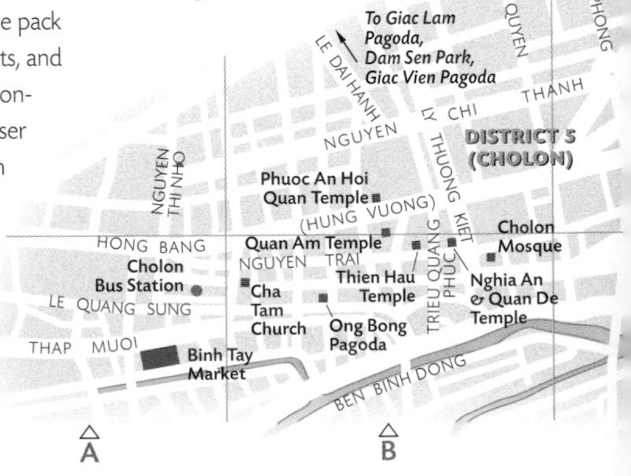

American GIs, or Saigon bar girls flooding old rue Catinat, since renamed Dong Khoi.

The grand monuments of Lam Son Square—the former opera house, the Continental and Caravelle Hotels—evoke Saigon's legendary renown. Though it's far less common these days to spot a bulbous-fendered Citroën or a Peugeot 404 prowling these streets, the descendants of rickshaw coolies still spin down the city's byways on their cyclo pedicabs.

The echoes of war resonate profoundly at the city's top three tourist attractions—the War Remnants Museum, Reunification Palace, and Cu Chi Tunnels. The war may no longer be the big story in Saigon and across Vietnam, but it certainly helps drive the tourist trade. ■

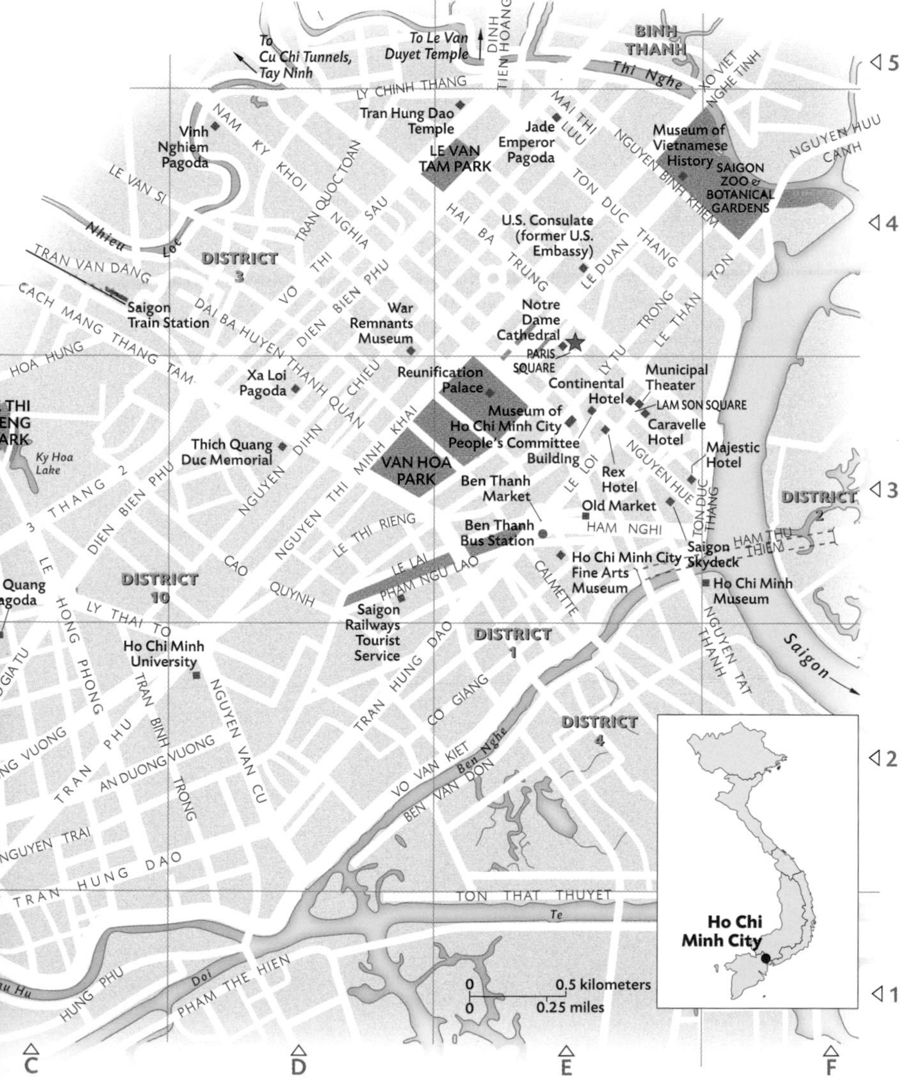

Lam Son Square Neighborhood

The Saigon of myth and memory truly resonates in and around Lam Son Square, home to the city's storied hotels, a colonial French opera house, and the cinematic heart of the city. It's still possible to take its pulse from the terrace of the Continental Hotel, where the French colonials sipped their *citron pressé* and absinthe, and the Saigon Saigon bar on the tenth floor of the Caravelle Hotel makes an ideal perch for a late afternoon cocktail.

Lam Son Square
195 E3

British writers Graham Greene and Somerset Maugham both stayed at the 1880-built **Continental** (*132–134 Dong Khoi;* see Travelwise p. 258) and alluded to it in their writings. In Greene's *The Quiet American*, the two lead characters first meet in the Continental, and a bomb explodes in Lam Son Square.

In 1964, a real bomb exploded on the fifth floor of the **Caravelle Hotel** (*19 Lam Son Sq.;* see Travelwise p. 257), a ten-story hotel that opened on Christmas Eve 1959 with fanfare, Italian marble, and bulletproof glass. The bomb didn't kill anyone, but it damaged nine rooms and windows of cars parked below. During the Vietnam War, CBS and ABC operated bureaus here.

The **Municipal Theater,** with its broken mansard roofs and arched facade, has reigned over the square since its debut as the Saigon Opera House on January 1, 1900. It once housed the legislature of South Vietnam. Restored for its 100th anniversary, the 800-seat hall again serves as a performing arts center.

The Caravelle Hotel towers over the landmark 1900 Municipal Theater.

Notre Dame Cathedral

Notre Dame (Duc Ba) Cathedral, on the north end of Dong Khoi, is the grandest expression of French Catholic architecture in Vietnam. It boasts two matching bell towers that rise 187 feet (56 m) above Paris Square (Cong Xa Pari). Once visible from afar, these towers are now hemmed in by new developments that are transforming the city.

French architect Jules Bourard designed the cathedral in the mid-1870s, and a French cleric laid the cornerstone in 1877. It opened to worshippers three years later, with bricks imported from Marseilles, granite from nearby Bien Hoa, and a construction tab of 2.5 million francs. Its six bells weigh nearly 30 tons (27 metric tons).

As in the Vatican's basilica, Notre Dame's nave is divided by a double colonnade and centered

INSIDER TIP:
The Caravelle Hotel's legendary Saigon Saigon bar, with its panoramic city views, is the place to enjoy cocktails as the sun goes down.

—BARBARA A. NOE
National Geographic Travel Books senior editor

on a semicircular apse. The design departs from form with a vaulted Gothic ceiling. A series of niches along either side of the sanctuary houses the Stations of the Cross and statues of the patron saints. While the statuary is not especially satisfying, commemorative stones cemented to the walls are deeply evocative of the church's colonial past. Beginning around World War I, parishioners began placarding the walls around a favorite saint—Anthony in particular—with expressions of gratitude such as

To Say or Not to Say

Go ahead and say it: Saigon. Wary travelers often stick to the politically correct Ho Chi Minh City—since 1976 the name of the vast municipality that encompasses Saigon. But the two lovely syllables of the old name are not verboten. Communist officials routinely use the name. The river remains the Saigon. Buses still flash "Saigon" as their destination. The largest state-run tourist company is Saigon Tourist. The three letter airport code is SGN. In fact, the city's District 1 officially remains Saigon. So go ahead and say it.

Merci and *Reconnaissance*. After the colonials departed and the Vietnamese assumed command of the congregation, the gesture continued, albeit in Vietnamese.

Stained glass from the Lorin Company of Chartres originally lit the niches. Replacement glass from Grenoble in the 1940s and '50s delivered such motifs as St. Theresa before a map of Indochina and St. George slaying the dragon.

The Vietnamese have gradually infused the staid Catholic decor with fanciful modern touches. Blue neon halos one niched saint, white neon beyond the apse spells out *Ave Maria*, and fluorescent tubes hang vertically in the nave.

In 1962, the Vatican elevated Notre Dame to basilica status,

(continued on p. 200)

Municipal Theater

195 E3
7 Lam Son Square, District 1
08/3829-9976

Notre Dame Cathedral

195 E4
Paris Square

A Walk Along Dong Khoi

If Lam Son Square is the heart of legendary Saigon, then Dong Khoi is its marrow. This street inspired the city's reputation as the Paris of the East. Here's where war-weary GIs whooped it up with the city's racy bar girls. The French knew the street as rue Catinat. The South Vietnamese called it Tu Do ("freedom"). Now named Dong Khoi ("general uprising"), it is home to the city's poshest shops and profound echoes.

Start at the **Main Post Office** ❶ in Paris Square, across from **Notre Dame Cathedral** (see pp. 196–197, 200). Designed by Gustav Eiffel's firm and built between 1886 and 1891, the post office's vaulted interior and skylights echo the railway stations of 19th-century Europe. Symmetrical wings flank a grand pavilion and arched entryway with a marquee. The escutcheons on the first-floor piers bear the names of Benjamin Franklin, Alessandro Volta, André-Marie Ampère, and other notables who made their mark in electricity. Inside, a map from 1892 depicts an era when marshland separated Saigon and Cholon. On the opposite wall, a 1936 map details the colonial telegraph lines.

Boutique Saigon

The city center's boutiques displaying the latest fashions, chic furniture, and fine art with price tags in the thousands of dollars are sure signs of Saigon's recovery from the war-torn years. In fact, the city seems to have come full circle since French colonization. Wearing the newest outfit or toting the latest cellphone is the short-term ambition of the city's high-flying youth. If you'd like to indulge yourself, head for Khai Silk *(107 Dong Khoi)*, which sells exclusive outfits from one of the city's top designers, or Apricot Gallery *(50–52 Mac Thi Buoi)*, which features striking artwork by some of Vietnam's most eminent artists.

NOT TO BE MISSED:

People's Committee Building • Rex Hotel • Lam Son Square

Leaving the post office, turn left and start down Dong Khoi. The 100-yard-long (90 m), two-story building at **164 Dong Khoi** ❷ was built in 1917 to house the colonial Surete, the national security arm of the French police. Its roll of inmates reads like a who's who of Vietnamese nationalists, including future prime minister Pham Van Dong.

Turn right on Le Thanh Ton, passing trendy boutiques, and go on to the head of Nguyen Hue for a gander at the 1908 **People's Committee Building** ❸. Still referred to locally as the Hôtel de Ville, the ornate structure also served as the French colonial city hall. Though a treat to see from outside, the interior of this former apartment building is inaccessible to tourists.

Beyond a statue of Ho Chi Minh at the top of Nguyen Hue stands the **Rex Hotel** (see Travelwise pp. 257–258), which once hosted press conferences by the US military known as the "Five O'Clock Follies." Check out the rooftop terrace for a sweeping view that, to the south, includes the distinctive, protruding helipad of the Bitexco Financial Tower, where this walk ends.

Follow Le Loi east from the fountain in front of the Rex, pause to take in **Lam Son Square,** then turn right on Dong Khoi. When the French decamped from the country in the

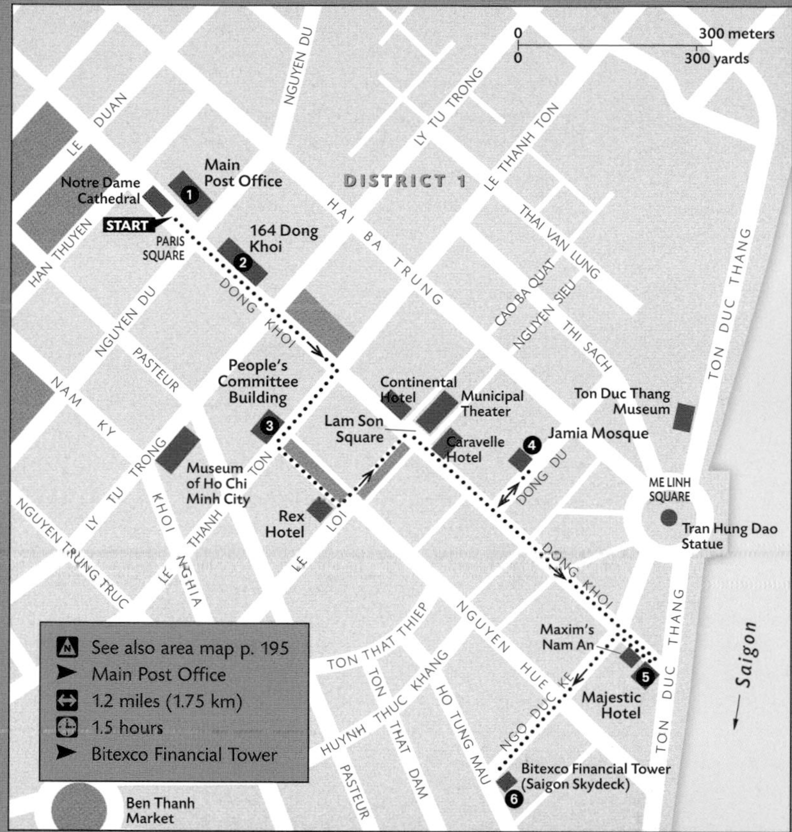

mid-1950s, it is said the legionnaires paraded up this street, singing songs made popular by the French chanteuse Edith Piaf.

As Tu Do, this infamous street was the go-go girl bar district that figures in so many American movies about wild, wartime Saigon. Today, the much revamped thoroughfare brims with chic boutiques, art galleries, fancy restaurants, and stylish cafés.

Turn left on Dong Du and walk half a block to the 1935 **Jamia Mosque** ❹ *(66 Dong Du)*. One of several active mosques in the city, the Jamia sits in the shadow of the Sheraton Hotel. Backtracking to Dong Khoi, check out the appealing window displays of the many fancy boutiques and art shops as you make your way toward the river.

At the foot of Dong Khoi, the signature arcade of the 1925 **Majestic Hotel** ❺ (*1 Dong Khoi;* see Travelwise p. 258) sweeps up from the sidewalk to an attractive facade of wrought-iron balconies. Inside, the plush lobby retains a nostalgic and still-alluring aura of yesteryear.

Retrace your steps to Ngo Duc Ke and turn left, then cross Nguyen Hue and walk to Ho Tung Mau. On this corner is the **Bitexco Financial Tower** ❻**,** home to the new signature feature on the city's skyline, the **Saigon Skydeck** (see p. 204). Take the elevator to the 49th floor, 584 feet (178 m) above the streets, and see how many sights you can identify from this lofty perch, including all of those you have passed on this walk.

Museum of Ho Chi Minh City
195 E3
65 Ly Tu Trong, District 1
08/3829-9741
$
hcmc-museum.edu.vn

though its exalted designation didn't spare the structure from wartime scarring. Check the exterior walls for damaged bricks, splattered by bullets when the war came to downtown Saigon.

In late 2005, pilgrims flocked to the statue of the Virgin Mother in Paris Square, persuaded the statue was shedding miraculous tears.

Museum of Ho Chi Minh City

The comprehensive Museum of Ho Chi Minh City takes a long, Michener-esque view of the settlement known first as Gia Dinh, then Saigon, and now Ho Chi Minh City. Exhibits peer back at prehistoric times, linger over the colonial era, and indulge the city's ties to revolutionary activities against the French and resistance to the Americans.

The museum is housed in a magnificent French imperial palace, designed by architect Alfred Foulhoux in the 1880s. Foulhoux had designed the palace as a museum, but upon its completion in 1880, the French governor of Indochina retained it as his residence.

Today, brides and grooms come to be photographed amid the grandeur of the main foyer. Sadly, the interior does not live up to the exterior promise, and the tired displays are in dire need of a makeover.

First Floor: To make sense of the city's chronological development, start in the **room at the back and to the left on the ground floor.** Here you'll find a few clues to the region's nature and archaeology, such as a stuffed crocodile, crumbling burial jars, and a few ornaments like bracelets and earrings believed to be 2,500 years old. The **second room** features the city's geography and administration, where map aficionados can feast on a series of charts that show how the city progressed after the Vietnamese subsumed its Khmer inhabitants in the late 16th century and founded the prefecture of Gia Dinh in 1698. That name remained in place until 1863, four years after a French attack put Vietnamese autonomy on long-term hold.

The **third room,** beside the entrance, shifts the focus to Saigon's role as a trade center. Exhibits are mostly photos of the city's port and railway station, though weights, measures, and life belts

EXPERIENCE: Sightseeing From a Cyclo

The cyclo, a three-wheeled rickshaw with a seat in front, is one of Vietnam's most distinctive forms of transportation. Unfortunately, it is also a dying breed, being squeezed off the streets by the motorbike, which is now the most common form of Vietnamese transportation. The main use of cyclos these days is for short shopping trips from the market, as the vehicles can be piled with produce. Yet they are also an ideal way of sightseeing in cities like Ho Chi Minh City, once you have got over the initial shock of moving through the chaotic traffic. The best way is to get someone from your hotel to negotiate a route and an hourly rate with a rider, then sit back and get your camera ready to shoot the sights.

Patriotic art, like the Museum of Ho Chi Minh's mural depicting the fall of Saigon, is de rigueur at most Vietnamese museums.

add a touch of realism. Fortunately interest picks up to the right of the entrance, where, in the **fourth room,** you can learn about the region's traditional handicrafts, such as pottery, weaving, and bronze casting, as well as the city's growth as an industrial center. Probably the most interesting display on the ground floor is in the **fifth room,** where mannequins wear the traditional wedding costumes of the Viet, Chinese, Cham, and Khmer.

Second Floor: Upstairs is all about the revolutionary struggle, and the **sixth** and **seventh halls** are neatly divided into two periods—1930–1954 and 1954–1975, chronicling victories first against the French and then against the Americans. As you might expect, the tone is somewhat partisan, and any potential objectivity is compromised by references to "puppet regimes" and the unquestioned heroism of certain participants.

One artful exhibit centers on an enlarged photograph of combat boots strewn across a South Vietnamese road in 1975—the flotsam of South Vietnamese soldiers who didn't want to be caught wearing the incriminating footwear. In a glass case beneath the photo is a mishmash of wartime booty picked up on "Liberation Day," including a billy club, mess kits, shoes, rifles, field telephones, gas masks, and plaques.

Reunification Palace

On April 30, 1975, a Russian-built tank commanded by a North Vietnamese colonel bashed through the gates of

Reunification Palace

- Map: 195 E3
- Address: 135 Nam Ky Khoi Nghia
- Phone: 08/3829-4117
- Hours: Closed 11 a.m.–1 p.m.
- Price: $

South Vietnam's Independence Palace, delivering a dramatic coup de grâce to both a war and a nation. The victors renamed the building Dinh Thong Nhat ("reunification palace") and left the structure and its contents intact as a time-warped memorial to the Great Spring Victory. Today, the palace is the city's main tourist draw and a haunting relic of a vanished state.

Though the current building dates from 1966, the site's relevance as a capitol winds back to 1868 when the French laid the cornerstone of a palace, a romantic flight of Second Empire and Greek Revival architecture, for the governor-general of Indochina. In a failed 1962 coup d'état, two pilots bombed the renamed Independence Palace, dooming the structure to the wrecking ball.

In his design of the new palace, a South Vietnamese architect worked the shapes of the Chinese characters for good fortune, education, and consistency into the building's floor plan and facade. The dominant exterior motif is a stone curtain of bamboo segments that shades floor-to-ceiling windows. Inside, a grand stairway rises through the five-story core of the 95-room palace.

At the palaces's completion in 1966, President Nguyen Van Thieu took up residence. His thumbprints are all over the building today, from the parquet dance floor on the rooftop terrace to the back issues of *Tennis World* in the library.

A tank on the Reunification Palace grounds symbolizes the April 1975 victory and war's end.

Touring the Palace: Visitors are not allowed to roam freely and must join a guided tour.

The cabinet room, dining room, and conference room on the **first floor** are worth a cursory peek. On the **second floor,** in the president's office, are framed seascapes of Ninh Thuan, the south-central province where Thieu was born. A now closed passage leads from this room down a private stairway to the palace's underground bunkers. In the **lobby,** four dragons encircle a round red carpet that depicts the Chinese characters for longevity. In the grandest space, the **Credentials Presenting Room,** the president received foreign ambassadors before a gorgeous, 40-piece lacquer painting of 15th-century Vietnam.

On the **third floor** in the casino, the president gambled with cronies around a bar cut like a whiskey barrel. Nearby is a 42-seat cinema. From the rooftop **terrace,** you can look down on the helipad and two painted red circles that commemorate a pair of bombs dropped by a South Vietnamese pilot who showed his northern stripes in the closing days of the war. The view down Le Duan leads to the botanical gardens and past the site of the former U.S. Embassy, which was destroyed in the mid-1990s to make way for a more modern and less emblematic U.S. Consulate.

The visit's highlight is the warren of concrete corridors and war rooms in the **basement,** an eerie time capsule of electronics, maps, and avocado-colored telephones. In the **radio room,** big black knobs and round meters trick out the industrial gray casings of equipment by GE and Motorola.

The ground-floor **kitchen** is filled with mixers, Zenith woks, and Electrolux dishwashers. An interesting **photo gallery** on this level offers a snapshot of the war and history of the building, as does a worthwhile half-hour documentary.

Palace Grounds: Outside on the parklike grounds, neither of the tanks is the one that smashed through the gates in 1975. (That famed one rests in Hanoi.) Likewise, the F-5E is genuine, but not the one that bombed the palace on April 8, 1975.

INSIDER TIP:

The Reunification Palace underground war room, with its old communications equipment and enormous maps, provides an eerie glimpse into the war-torn past.

—BARBARA A. NOE
National Geographic Travel Books senior editor

Ben Thanh Market

This market stands atop a swamp that was drained and filled in the early 20th century. The previous market sat on the banks of the Ben Nghe River, and merchants traded there until the French authorities launched this new commercial center.

Opened in 1914 and capped by a landmark clock tower atop the south gate, the 3-acre (1.2 ha) market is divided into quadrants by two main aisles crisscrossed by smaller aisles. Main gates front each quadrant, and 12 additional gates provide access.

Ben Thanh Market

195 E3

Quach Thi Trang Sq., District 1 (intersection of Le Loi, Ham Nghi, Tran Hung Dao, & Le Lai)

Saigon Skydeck
195 E3
Bitexco Financial Tower, 2 Hai Trieu
08/3915-6868
$$$
saigonskydeck.com

War Remnants Museum
195 D4
28 Vo Van Tan, District 3
08/3930-5587
Closed noon–1:30 p.m.
$
baotangchungtich chientranh.vn

Start beneath the **clock tower,** where a color-coded schematic details the market's wares. On the south side, the largest department peddles clothing. Footwear, handbags, and sundries claim the next largest share of space, followed by food counters frequented by shoppers and connoisseurs alike.

The 1,200 kiosks range from small cubbyholes to spreads along the main aisles. Though you'd expect to bargain for items in any other Vietnamese market, prices are fixed at Ben Thanh, indicating how much it's geared toward tourists. Buyer beware: Arabica coffee beans that sell for $2 per pound in Buon Ma Thuot are hawked here at five times that price, and the brand-name accessories are knockoffs.

On the north side, stroll from east to west and back again amid a cornucopia of vegetables, tubs of seafood, and busy butchers' chopping blocks.

Book Pirates

The Vietnamese skill in making copies is evident in books that are sold by vendors at a fraction of what they would cost back home. On close inspection you'll find that virtually all these books are photocopies (albeit very good ones) rather than originals. While this option may please tourists who can pick up a travel guide for peanuts, spare a thought for writers who receive nothing for their pains.

Saigon Skydeck

With its tapered design and protruding heliport near the summit, the imposing 860-foot (262 m) **Bitexco Financial Tower** has rapidly become Saigon's foremost icon since the building's opening in 2010. Located on the 49th floor, at 584 feet (178 m) above ground level, the Saigon Skydeck offers the traveler a 360-degree panorama of the downtown area and many of the city's outlying districts. There are telescopes pointing in every direction, old photos of unchanged places down below, touchscreens offering information, and, of course, a souvenir shop.

You'll probably be able to pick out some of the city's major sights such as the Municipal Theater, the People's Committee Building, and the tips of the spires on Notre Dame, though the rest of the cathedral is blocked by high-rise buildings. Yet what might come as a shock is the number of entire blocks in the city center that have been razed and are being redeveloped. New high-rise towers such as this one and Times Square on nearby Dong Khoi are transforming the city's skyline at an astonishing rate.

War Remnants Museum

Many provinces and cities throughout Vietnam memorialize the nation's struggle against the French and Americans with

A gallery at the War Remnants Museum features photos of victims of torture and execution.

museums, but none speak with as much impact or devastation as this place, formerly known as the Museum of American and Chinese War Crimes. Despite its anti-American message, this museum is one of Vietnam's most popular among Western visitors.

The United States spent $130 billion on the war and abandoned billions of dollars worth of equipment in Vietnam. Some of it stands on the museum grounds: a 175-mm cannon able to hurl a projectile 20 miles (32 km); an M-48 tank, one of 370 in country at the war's height in 1969; and an emblematic Huey (UH-1 Bell helicopter).

The **main hall** is a monolith of granite-faced concrete suspended above an open floor. Inside you'll find photo after gruesome photo—some of them Pulitzer Prize winning—depicting American brutality in the war. Among them are images of the My Lai massacre and the deformative effects of Agent Orange, white phosphorous, and napalm.

Other halls hold more photos, including the **Requiem Exhibit.** All of the photos here are by correspondents who died during the conflict, including Larry Burrows, Henri Huet, Dana Stone, and Sean Flynn, the son of actor Errol.

The final gallery explores the worldwide protests against the war. The most touching exhibit is a collection of medals, including a Purple Heart donated to the museum by an American Army sergeant with an inscribed brass plaque that reads: "To the people of a United Vietnam. I was wrong. I am sorry."

The museum is certainly not unbiased in its representation of events in Vietnam in the 1960s and '70s. Nonetheless, it drives home the fact that wars are devastating and that civilians are the biggest losers. ■

Northeast of City Center

The area northeast of the city center claims a few worthwhile sights. Though somewhat unkempt, the botanical gardens and adjacent zoo offer an oasis of green space in this vast cityscape, while the Museum of Vietnamese History and Temple to the Hung Kings, just inside the gardens' main gate, make for a fascinating introduction to Vietnam's past. The Jade Emperor Pagoda and Le Van Duyet Temple, meanwhile, attract scores of devotees.

An elephant gets up close and personal with a visitor at the Saigon Zoo and Botanical Gardens.

Saigon Zoo & Botanical Gardens

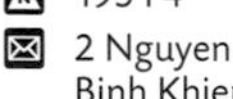

195 F4

2 Nguyen Binh Khiem, District 1

08/3829-3728

$

saigonzoo.net

Saigon Zoo & Botanical Gardens

Under the auspices of French botanist J. B. Louis Pierre, the Saigon Botanical Gardens opened in 1865 as a proving ground for the imported plants—cocoa, coffee, vanilla, rubber—French colonists hoped to cultivate in Vietnam for export to the homeland at a handsome profit. The **bonsai garden** boasts exquisite specimens of Far Eastern flora that have been under cultivation for as long as 50 years. But it's as an **arboretum** that the park achieves its real glory. Flanking the wide main avenue are rows of majestic African mahogany trees that top out at more than 100 feet (30 m). Other species of trees labeled in Latin and Vietnamese but alas not in English include bodhi, flower, pagoda, plum, queen's, tamarind, tea shade, *thitpok,* wild jackfruit, and yellowwood.

The park also penned wild animals from tropical Vietnam for export to zoos in France. The zoo features the usual suspects—giraffes, elephants, hippos—and one rather glorious multidomed monkey cage. The pens betray the poverty of their hosts. The zoo is a casualty of hard times that started during World War II when occupying Japanese forces used the park as a barracks. Still, conditions are improving yearly.

Other Sights

The **Museum of Vietnamese History** is housed in a light-filled building topped by a pagoda-style roof that is very similar to its namesake in Hanoi, though unfortunately the displays inside are not as informative as those of its northern sister. Nevertheless, for an overview of the country's complex and turbulent history, it provides a reasonable introduction. In exhibits spanning 13 halls, the museum presents a collection of artifacts that detail Vietnam's history, from the discovery of 500,000-year-old teeth from *Homo erectus* to the Nguyen dynasty of the 20th century.

The **third hall,** spanning the Chinese occupation from the first century B.C. to the tenth century A.D., features a series of dioramas. The first depicts the legendary battle on the Bach Dang River in 938, in which Ngo Quyen impaled the invading Chinese fleet on thick wooden stakes planted in the river mud, a tactic used with similar success to repel Mongol invaders three centuries later. Three stakes from that later conflict are on display in the **fifth hall,** which showcases artifacts from the Tran dynasty.

The exquisite, meticulously arranged dioramas are worth a dedicated visit to the museum. So, too, are the mummified remains of a 60-year-old woman that are displayed with traditional Vietnamese burial garments and jewelry in their own alcove.

In addition to artifacts from the Vietnamese dynasties, the museum also houses worthy collections of Cham art, stone sculpture from Cambodia, and various art made by Vietnam's ethnic minorities. In the **seventh hall,** look for the two 1,600-year-old wooden statues of the Buddha, carved by people of the Oc Eo culture. A Roman coin retrieved from an Oc Eo site demonstrates that these Mekong Delta denizens were trading with, and influenced by, cultures as far away as Rome.

The museum also hosts six daily performances by the **Saigon Water Puppet Theater** *(10 a..m.–4 p.m., on the hour, except for 1 p.m., $)*. These modest shows will either whet your appetite for, or encourage you to skip, the more grandiose production at Hanoi's Thang Long Theatre (see Travelwise p. 264).

INSIDER TIP:

Use a few simple phrases of Vietnamese; nothing gets a bigger smile than a well-placed *cam on* (thank you) or *troi oi* (oh my!).

–JONATHAN A. O'BRIEN
National Geographic grantee

Museum of Vietnamese History

- 195 E4
- 2 Nguyen Binh Khiem, District 1
- Closed Mon.–Sat. 11 a.m.–1:30 p.m.
- 08/3829-8146
- $

Jade Emperor Pagoda
195 E4
73 Mai Thi Luu, District 3

Jade Emperor Pagoda

Built by Saigon's Cantonese community in 1909, the Jade Emperor Pagoda is a surreal Taoist temple, populated by a singular collection of statuary and the best wood carvings in the city. Its signature mauve facade and jade green pantiles induce wild expectations that are fulfilled by the temple's equally fanciful contents. It is one of the best temples in town.

A statue of the jade emperor, Ngoc Hoang, presides over the main sanctuary of the colorful temple named in his honor.

Devotees flock to the temple to burn paper votives in a stove in the **courtyard** and sandalwood joss at an array of **indoor altars.** Don't miss the outdoor **crescent pool,** brimming with scores of turtles of various shapes and sizes.

A secondary interior doorway is flanked by a pair of parallel sentences that hang from the mouths of sculpted bats. The heavy wooden doors are carved with Taoist warriors who breathe fire from the mouth and nostrils.

Intricate carvings in ebony-stained hardwood frame the bays between columns throughout the **main hall.** A pageant of Asian characters decks out the wide bay before the main altar, dedicated to Ngoc Hoang, the jade emperor. His towering, bearded attendants lean toward each other in textural detail made possible by their papier-mâché construction.

In an **annex temple** to the left of the main hall, women pray for fertility in a niche dedicated to Kinh Hoa, a deified maternity specialist, who's flanked by a host of husbands. On the left and right, a bumper crop of baby statues clamber in play about the laps, thighs, and sleeves of fruitful ceramic mothers.

Beyond this niche, Than Hoang lords over a **hall of tortures,** flanked by high-hatted papier-mâché guards painted black. In this chamber's middle hall, carved panels depict various means of retributive torture in the netherworld. While the ten kings of the netherworld write maxims above, devils feed onerous humans to flames, cut off their heads, and impale them on beds of spikes.

Back through the main hall, climb the stairs up the right side of the temple to a room dedicated to Quan Am. Here you'll find the best view of the chaotic pitches, crests, and flying eaves of the pantiled roofs.

Le Van Duyet Temple

This tomb and temple complex honors the charismatic eunuch Le Van Duyet (1764–1832). The complex lies deep within a largely untouristed part of the city and attracts mostly a domestic following, who come to pray for luck, health, and myriad other desires.

Le Van Duyet was a eunuch since birth, though it's unclear whether he was a hermaphrodite or was castrated in preparation for a life of royal service. In the early 19th century, he engineered a naval victory against the Tay Son and helped usher the deposed Prince Nguyen Anh to the throne as Emperor Gia Long. Later, Duyet ruled southern Vietnam as viceroy and defied King Minh Mang's order to persecute Christians.

Inside the mausoleum's triple-gate entrance, the viceroy and his wife lie buried under egg-shaped concrete mounds. Minh Mang ordered the desecration of the original graves to avenge Duyet's disobedience. The viceroy's loyalists then massacred Minh Mang's agents. Minh Mang then razed the citadel of Gia Dinh, now Saigon. Perhaps as a gesture of penance, Minh Mang's successors restored the site in 1841 and 1847.

The temple comprises three main halls, built in 1925 to replace the previous bamboo structures and extensively renovated in 2008. It is often busy with devotees making offerings and ringing resonant gongs. In the **second hall,** massive whale jawbones arch from the mouth of a mythical beast, while in front are elephant tusks. A glass case to the left holds the carcass of a tiger that reputedly prowled the temple grounds during the colonial era. After a Frenchman killed the tiger, locals preserved it, believing the animal to be an agent of Duyet's security.

On a platform altar to the left is a portrait of Phan Thanh Giang, one of Duyet's administrators, whom worshippers also honor here. A portrait of a cheerfully optimistic Duyet sits on the central altar.

In the **third hall,** dragons spiral around tall cement columns that rise above sumptuous red Nguyen dynasty altars with gilt carvings. The glass cabinets are filled with robes, donated by local devotees, for Le Van Duyet, his wife, and Phan Thanh Giang. ■

Lodging in Saigon

While Vietnam is supposedly a classless society, visitors to Saigon are inevitably grouped into rich or poor by where they stay. Well-heeled tourists head for the five-star hotels and fancy mid-range places located around the city center. By contrast, budget travelers make a beeline for the cheap lodgings and dormitories around De Tham and Pham Ngu Lao, about a half mile (1 km) west of the city center, where the cheaper restaurants, souvenir shops, and tour agents also help stretch the dong a bit further.

Le Van Duyet Temple

- Map: 195 E5
- Address: 1 Phan Dang Luu, Binh Thanh District
- Phone: 08/3841-2517

Cholon

Cholon ("big market") is the hyperactive, commercial heart of Ho Chi Minh City and its Chinese population. Historically notorious as a den of thieves, opium parlors, gambling halls, and brothels, the district remains gritty, and cash is still king, though the heavy hand of Hanoi stifled the obvious vice after 1975. The most fulfilling dividends are to be found in the flamboyant temples, wonton soup, and exposure to the feverish pitch of life on the streets.

The ethnic Chinese heart of the city pulses with commercial opportunities.

Cholon

 194 B1–B2

District 5, bounded by Tau Hu Canal to S, Nguyen Van Cu to E, Nguyen Chi Thanh to N, & Nguyen Thi Nho to W

Cholon surged into prominence in the late 18th century as a haven for ethnic Chinese refugees from Bien Hoa and the Mekong Delta, whose established loyalty to the Nguyen lords sparked retaliation by Tay Son generals. The Chinese named their settlement De Ngan, after the embankments they built as a hedge against flooding along the Tau Hu Canal, which feeds the Saigon River. In 1874, Cholon merged with Saigon, and today it comprises District 5.

On Thap Muoi, along the district's western border, **Binh Tay Market** is a massive, two-story Chinese market with pagoda-style roofs at the four corners and a clock tower above the main entrance. In the open courtyard, statues of lion-dogs stand guard over goldfish ponds that surround a monument to the Chinese merchant who founded the market in 1930. The market stalls cluster by wares, with big departments for incense candles, bags, fabrics, household aluminum, and sealing wax. Most residents will steer you here for the best buys in the city.

Cholon's Temples

The district's spiritual pulse beats loudest at a fairly dense cluster of temples between Nguyen Trai and Huong Vuong. These temples are not nearly as frequented by tourists as the temple cum assembly halls of Hoi An (see pp. 155–156), but they're equally picturesque and just as storied.

In the heart of the quarter at **Thien Hau Temple** *(710 Nguyen Trai),* devotees worship the eponymous goddess of the sea, whose robed statue in the temple's back compartment is flanked left and right by the goddess of fertility and the protector of fishermen. The temple's signature adornments are hundreds of exquisite ceramic puppets, congregated in 200-year-old friezes that crest the roofs of the entry hall and inner galleries. The long coils of sandalwood incense that hang here and at temples elsewhere in Cholon will burn for a month.

Heading east on Nguyen Trai, as you cross **Trieu Quang Phuc,** make a quick detour south along this shop-filled road. The aromas of traditional Chinese medicine, drying in bushel baskets and brimming from bags plopped on the sidewalk, make for a wonderfully pungent experience. Inside the shops, look for the practitioners of traditional medicine as they diagnose the yin and yang imbalances of customers who won't have far to go to fill their prescriptions. Some of the medicine is packaged, but much of it—the roots, bark, herbs, funguses, seeds, and other organic substances—is stored in voluminous wooden hutches that line the walls.

A little farther east on Nguyen Trai, the Taoist deity and Buddhist bodhisattva Quan Cong presides over **Nghia An and Hoi Quan Temple** *(676 Nguyen Trai)* from a large glass display case in the temple's central compartment. Quang Binh, the pink-faced youth who symbolizes justice, and Chau Xuong, a warrior-saint, stand in glass-cased octagonal pavilions to the right and left, respectively.

This temple has recently been subject to an extensive renovation, which makes it one of the most photogenic temples in Cholon. Note the magnificent carving of a temple scene over the main doorway and the beautifully crafted bas reliefs of tigers and mandarins on the walls. The columns are embossed with gilt Chinese script and bordered by intricately carved frames, while the door and window panels with their depiction of

INSIDER TIP:

One of the best meals you will ever have is a bowl of steaming hot *pho,* or noodle soup, made right on the street. The chicken soup *(pho ga)* is delicious.

—CATHERINE KARNOW
National Geographic photographer

Giac Lam Pagoda
- 194 B2
- 565 Lac Long Quan
- Closed noon–2 p.m.
- 08/3865-3933

delicate birds, bamboo, and bonsai are a delight to behold.

Across the street is the **Cholon Mosque** *(641 Nguyen Trai)*, built in 1932 by the district's Indian residents. While the mosque lacks a telltale dome or principal minaret, the four slender towers that rise from the building's corners are distinctively Middle Eastern, as are the ogee-style arches that frame the bi-level terrace. After the Indian population decamped during the war, the city's 5,000 Cham Muslims appropriated the mosque.

On the other side of Thien Hau Pagoda, off Lupong Nhu Hoc, the 1740 **Quan Am Temple** *(12 Lao Tu)* was dedicated to the eponymous goddess of mercy by the district's Fujian Chinese congregation. As at Thien Hau Temple, the roof is lined with miniature ceramic figures. Quaint mosaic-faced Asian gates and pagodas line the crests of the two-tiered entry hall. Inside, a gold-faced Thien Hau occupies the choice throne at back. On the other side of the wall, Quan Am faces a pantheon of Chinese deities, who dwell in seven bays.

South on Chau Van Liem and west on Hai Thuong Lan Ong stands **Ong Bong Pagoda** *(264 Hai Thuong Lan Ong)*. People from two districts of Fujian Province may have built the temple in 1765, as evidenced by a date scratched into a bronze bell at the site. Beneath a vast span of distinctive pink roofs, worshippers pay homage to both Ong Bong, the guardian of happiness and virtue, and the jade emperor.

For a religious counterpoint, stroll to the west end of Tran Hung Dao to **Cha Tam Church** *(25 Hoc Lac)*. Father Tam is buried beneath a marble slab on the portico. More intriguing is the church's cameo in Vietnam's political past, for it was here, on November 2, 1963, that President Ngo Dinh Diem and his brother, Nhu, surrendered to troops loyal to a short-lived junta of South Vietnamese generals. The Ngos were executed soon after soldiers escorted them from the church.

Beyond Cholon

Founded in 1744, the **Giac Lam Pagoda** is an exceptional pagoda in a cityscape that lacks

Chilling Out in Saigon's Cafés

When the French colonized Vietnam, they did their best to re-create the café culture for which their country is famous, and they were so successful that these days visiting cafés is very popular among Vietnamese as well. As the country's biggest city, Saigon has the widest choice of restaurants, bars, and cafés, and despite fierce competition, most of them do a good trade. The drink of choice for most Vietnamese is *ca phe da*, or iced coffee, which is usually strong enough to make your hair stand on end.

Knowing that most clients enjoy people-watching, many café owners position their sidewalk seating facing outward to afford their patrons a prime view of the street action.

venerable Buddhist sanctuaries. Its wealth of wood statuary, columns, parallel sentences, and intricately carved frames rival the appeal of northern pagodas.

In 1799, Giac Lam's master launched a six-year restoration project that raised 98 columns of precious wood decked with 86 parallel sentences inscribed with gilded Chinese calligraphy. The enlarged pagoda diminished its contents' prestige, however, so the master also called for new jackwood statues.

Most of the 113 statues reign from terraced altars in the **main hall.** Along either wall, nine 32-inch (80 cm) wooden arhats, carved in the early 19th century, roost above older 20-inch (50 cm) versions of the same characters. Between the arhats, the ten kings of the netherworld (five to each side) stare at mirrored tablets to maintain solemn composure.

The Amitabha Buddha atop the **main terrace** dates from 1744. After the statue was carved, it was coated in clay paper, painted in vermilion (a brilliant red pigment made from mercury sulfide), and then gilded. Below this statue is a 1757 bronze of the Nine Dragons, the most precious piece in the pagoda's collection. On the **lowest terrace,** two bodhisattvas flank the Amitabha Buddha. They face the dharma guardian, who stands within the outer wall beside his grotesque companion, Tieu Dien. Armed with a sword, the guardian protects the Buddha, the dharma, and the monks.

Vietnamese Buddhists venerate spirits who dwell in the loftiest trees.

Twenty-three name boards hang from the ceiling, and 28 chiseled screens frame the columns. Outside, the stupas nearest the sanctuary mark the graves of the pagoda's patriarchs, or abbots. The seven-story hexagonal tower was completed in 1993. ■

Outside Saigon

Two of Saigon's great sightseeing venues lie outside the city. No ground from the Vietnam War is as hallowed as the tunnel-ridden earth of Cu Chi, which draws returning servicemen, history buffs, and the merely curious alike to tour this Viet Cong stronghold. Near Tay Ninh, meanwhile, stands a stupendous temple devoted to Cao Dai, a religion founded in the early 20th century that blends the tenets of several beliefs.

A tour guide in Cu Chi demonstrates the fine art of concealment.

Cu Chi Tunnels
221 D4
08/3794-8767
$
cuchitunnel.org.vn

Cu Chi Tunnels

Cu Chi played host to 18,000 peasant guerrillas who waged war from 125 miles (200 km) of hand-dug passageways and chambers. It was in Cu Chi that the Viet Cong (VC) planned their momentous assault on Saigon during the 1968 Tet New Year celebrations. In 1990, the government opened two tunnel sections to the public, including the command center at Ben Duoc, an area known to U.S. soldiers as Ho Bo Wood, and Ben Dinh.

Cu Chi's peasant soldiers started burrowing into the district's clay ground in the late 1940s during the French War. By 1967, they'd excavated a network of tunnels, aid stations, kitchens, theaters, dormitories, weapons caches, wells, printing shops, and other chambers. So well hidden was this three-tiered network, 10 to 30 feet (3–9 m) underground, that the 25th U.S. Infantry (aka Tropic Lightning) unwittingly situated its base partially above the tunnels just northeast of Cu Chi town.

The U.S. Army sent volunteers known as tunnel rats into this Viet Cong netherworld to root out intelligence and destroy the guerrillas' base. During Operation Cedar Falls in 1967, Army bulldozers razed more than 4 square miles (11 sq km) of neighboring forest to deprive the VC of cover. At the war's height, more than 200,000 shells rained down here each month, transforming Cu Chi into the "most bombed, shelled, gassed, defoliated, and generally devastated area in the history of warfare," according to British journalists Tom Mangold and John Penycate in their 1985 book *The Tunnels of Cu Chi*. Though bombing disabled some 70 percent of the tunnels, Cu Chi remained a staging area for VC operations throughout the war.

Visiting the Tunnels: Most day trips out of Ho Chi Minh City visit the reconstructed tunnels at **Ben Dinh,** 31 miles (50 km) northwest of the city, and at busy times tour groups can be large. The tunnels at **Ben Duoc,** 12 miles (20 km) farther out, are less crowded, but you'll need to make it clear to the tour company where you want to go. The first stop on a guided tour is often at a camouflaged 10-by-12-inch (25 by 30 cm) hatch atop a **tunnel entrance.** A guide wearing fatigues and a floppy green bush hat will wriggle down the hole and then pop up, holding the hatch overhead for Cu Chi's signature photo op.

Nearby, a larger hatch covers a **booby trap** of bamboo spikes driven into the bottom of a pit. The VC cooked up grisly ways to kill and maim GIs, as an exhibit of eight booby traps makes painfully obvious. American GIs fell prey to traps both outside and within the tunnels.

Playing Soldier

If you've ever wondered what it's like to fire a deadly weapon of war, both Ben Dinh and Ben Duoc offer target ranges. Here, for a dollar a pop, visitors can fire their wartime weapon of choice—an M-16, AK-47, Chinese carbine, shotgun, or any of several other makes.

Above ground, the tour winds past an American **M-41 tank,** disabled by a mine in 1970, as well as mannequins of VC cadres, resting in hammocks and working in excavated weapon-making shops. The guerrillas mined a good deal of gunpowder from duds dropped by American bombers and hurled from artillery cannon.

Though some **tunnels** have been enlarged for tourists, following in the guerrillas' footsteps often means crouching or crawling through close, humid, bell-shaped corridors. Guides presume that everyone wants to go into the tunnels, but if you are at all prone to claustrophobia, decline politely and rejoin the group later. The earthen walls retain the consistency of cement, a natural attribute that made the district particularly well

NOTE: The easiest way to visit the tunnels is on a tour (easily arranged through your hotel), often combined with a visit to the Cao Dai Great Temple into a convenient day trip.

Cao Dai Great Temple
✉ Long Hoa, 3 miles (5 km) SE of Tay Ninh

Visitor Information
✉ Tay Ninh Tourist, 210B 30 Thang 4
☎ 066/3822-376

suited for tunneling. As excavated earth was a dead giveaway of tunneling activity, the guerrillas would dispose of freshly dug dirt by raking it into rice fields and pouring it into streams and bomb craters.

Cao Dai Great Temple

In October 1926, a civil servant and mystic named Ngo Van Chieu settled near Tay Ninh with 300 followers and founded Cao Dai ("high palace"), a unique belief that elaborates on the traditional Vietnamese blend of Buddhism, Confucianism, Taoism, and ancestor worship with elements of Christianity and other religions. In the early 1930s, the new religion's high priests began channeling instructions via séance for construction of this magnificent temple that took two decades to complete.

INSIDER TIP:
John Tue and his Trails of Indochina company *(trailsofindochina.com)* are the most knowledgeable guides to all of Southeast Asia.

—JON BOWERMASTER
National Geographic author

An architectural fusion of East and West, the temple is as long and lofty as a cathedral, with towers bracketing the facade, a domed tower over the sanctum, and a fourth tower in the rear. Staring from a third story mirador on the facade is the divine eye, which symbolizes both the spirit of God and the light of the heart. Above the eye, Buddha sits atop a tiger, recalling the year when construction began. The female statue on the left tower honors the first woman ordained into Cao Dai. The man to the right is Le Van Trung, the first Cao Dai pope, whose clerical hierarchy mirrors that of Catholicism.

Just inside, the patron saints—French writer Victor Hugo, Chinese revolutionary Sun Yat-sen, and 16th-century Vietnamese poet Nguyen Binh Khiem—are depicted as signatories to the Divine Contract of the Third Amnesty. The Cao Dai believe God revealed himself to mankind in three great revelations. Moses was a witness to the first; Christ, Sakyamuni, and Muhammad to the second; and Cao Dai to the third.

In the nave, sacred dragons swirl around pink Corinthian columns, while the holy lion-dog, tortoise, and phoenix dwell in bas-relief on ceiling medallions. Overhead are sky blue vaults puffed with clouds and stars. Before the sanctum are six gilded red chairs for the cardinals and a throne for the pope. Framing the sanctum is a screen populated by statues of eight Cao Dai deities, including Sakyamuni in the most prominent position, Jesus Christ, and the red-faced Quan Cong.

Ranks of costumed devotees pray here four times every day *(6 a.m., noon, 6 p.m., & midnight).* Visitors can observe the precedings from the galleries above the nave. ■

More Places to Visit In & Around Ho Chi Minh City

At Dam Sen Park, visitors escape the daily grind with Vietnamese-style amusements.

Dam Sen Park

Vietnam's answer to Disneyland, Dam Sen is jam-packed with kiddie and adult attractions. A monorail circuits a large, central lake from which recreational fishers haul catch to local grills for on-site consumption. The tropical garden features many birds and animals, and elephants are available for rides. There's a water park too, and even a musical water show located behind the European flower garden. All in all, it's an ideal place for a day out with young kids.

194 B2 3 Hoa Binh, District 11
08/3963-4963 $ (not including rides)

Giac Vien Pagoda

Weathering away on the edge of Dam Sen Park, Giac Vien is the city's second oldest pagoda and looks it, though it retains a woebegone appeal. The pagoda had an inauspicious start as a guard shack and meditation hut for the monk overseeing restoration at nearby Giac Lam (see pp. 212–213) in 1799. By 1850, the hut had grown into a pavilion and then a pagoda in its own right. The sanctuary mirrors that of Giac Lam. Many of the same deities—the dharma guardian, Tieu Dien, the ten netherworld kings, the five personalities, the arhats, and others among the pagoda's 153 statues—pack the terraces and altars, all lacquered to a water puppet sheen. A multicolored disk halos Amitabha's head. Notice the carved wooden screens between the columns, including 18 arhats astride buffaloes, pigs, cows, a dragon, and other mythical animals, as well as fruit widely cultivated in the south, such as coconut, mangosteen, durian, and rambutan.

194 B2 247 Lac Long Quan, District 11

Ho Chi Minh City Fine Arts Museum

The fine arts museum occupies a grand colonial building with stained-glass French doors and fanlights, a flared roof, and lots of balconies. Once home to a wealthy businessman, the foursquare palace opened as a museum in 1991.

The **first floor** is used for temporary exhibitions, and the **second floor** concentrates on revolutionary art, which is mostly forgettable, though it includes a wonderfully redemptive gallery with a nine-panel lacquer masterpiece by Nguyen Gia Tri (1908–1993), a pioneering student of the Indochina School of Fine Arts. The **third floor** features bronze and wood statues of Buddhist deities and genii, 19th- and 20th-century ceramics, a fine wooden statue of Confucius, funereal statues from the central highlands, Cham sculpture, and Theravada art from the ethnic Khmers of the Mekong Delta.

195 E3 97A Pho Duc Chinh, District 1 08/3829-4441 Closed Mon. $

Ho Chi Minh Museum

Unfortunately, this museum holds the same photos, yellowed newspaper clippings, and meager contents that plague every other Ho Chi Minh museum in the country. This one is mostly a photo gallery, with the odd trifle cased in glass—a radio that broadcast news of Ho Chi Minh's death in 1969 to a Saigon resident, carpenter tools that built a temple to Ho in Soc Trang. Known as the Dragon House for the two mythical beasts crawling along the roof crest, the building is a classic colonial structure with distinctive wraparound verandas on the first two stories. In 1911, Ho embarked from this wharf to struggle for Vietnam's independence from abroad.

195 F3 1 Nguyen Tat Thanh, District 4 08/3940-2060 Closed Mon. $

Tran Hung Dao Temple

This tidy, well-heeled temple honors Tran Hung Dao, the general who routed the Mongols from Vietnam in the 13th century. A suite of doors opens across the front of the brick-faced sanctuary. Inside, a pair of whale jawbones curve from the mouths of lion-dogs before the altar. A small statue of Tran Hung Dao stands on the middle altar, with a larger bronze to the rear. Paintings along the roof detail the general's triumphs. A neighboring museum, built in 1929, covers the history of the Tran dynasty.

195 E4 36 Vo Thi Sau, District 1

Vinh Nghiem Pagoda

This pagoda's seven-story tower, dedicated to Quan Am, is the first landmark along the main route from the airport. The pagoda was built between 1964 and 1971 with assistance from the Japan-Vietnam Friendship Association, hence the telltale uplift to the tower's eaves. Despite its modernity and outsize proportions, the sanctuary is dazzling. A colossal trinity of Buddhas at the rear is painted a glossy gold. Vermilion panels on the many altars bear gilded images of famous pagodas and temples from around the world. In the vestibule, arhats save people from netherworld torments, teach devotees, and meditate in a wonderful series of color illustrations.

195 D4 339 Nam Ky Khoi Nghia, District 3

Xa Loi Pagoda

On June 11, 1963, Buddhist monk Thich Quang Duc immolated himself at the intersection of present-day Cach Mang Thang Tam and Nguyen Dinh Chieu. Today, the site bears a memorial to Duc's protest against the repressive South Vietnamese regime. Nearby is Xa Loi Pagoda, from which he set off that morning. The pagoda centers on an unattractive seven-story tower that was modern in Duc's day. Inside, a massive gold-painted Buddha presides over a largely empty hall. Near the ceiling, 14 illustrations depict landmark events in Sakyamuni's life. The panes of the pagoda's stained-glass windows are the colors of the Buddhist flag.

195 D3 89 Ba Huyen Thanh Quan, District 3

The Mekong Delta—vast, watery, timelessly grand, and the country's premier rice basket

Mekong Delta

Rice is harvested by hand in the paddy fields of An Giang Province.

Mekong Delta

After its 3,000-mile (4,800 km) journey from the Tibetan Plateau, the Mekong River splays across southern Vietnam in a watery web, emptying into the South China Sea through nine branches known as the Cuu Long ("nine dragons"). Its rivers, channels, and canals irrigate a land as large as Holland, spreading alluvium over rice fields that yield three crops a year. Despite its flatness, the landscape is quietly impressive in places.

Produce distributors and retailers stock up by boat at the Cai Rang floating market.

NOT TO BE MISSED:

The wacky temple established by the coconut monk near My Tho **223**

Cruising out of Vinh Long through narrow waterways, visiting floating markets **223–224**

A Mekong Delta homestay among fruit orchards **226**

Climbing Sam Mountain near Chau Doc for a view of the pancake-flat delta **227–228**

Exploring the beaches and temples around remote Ha Tien **230–231**

The beautiful beaches of Phu Quoc Island **232**

Until the 13th century, the 15,000-square-mile (44,000 sq km) tract was densely forested and barely populated. Chinese and Vietnamese pioneers stepped up settlement in the late 17th century, taking political control from the Khmer residents. The darker skinned Khmer still inhabit the region. Their distinctive pagodas, with steeply pitched red roofs and hornlike finials, are the delta's signature architectural flourish.

To the northeast, the Mekong roils between My Tho and Ben Tre like a superhighway, churning with rice barges, ferries, and sampans. Its shorelines and islands teem with fruit orchards and cottage industry manufacturers of coconut candy and cane sugar.

In Vinh Long, the waterways are less commercialized, and the floating market caters to local buyers, not tourists. These narrow channels bristle with verdant walls of water palms, banana plants, and other vegetation, while orchards and bonsai gardens flourish in the spongy alluvium.

The floating market is the delta's great attraction. The one at Cai Rang, upstream from Can Tho, is the most colorful and bustling. As a city, Can Tho, with its hopping riverfront and clutch of good restaurants, offers a flavor and a charisma worth indulging for a few days. This is the delta's premier destination.

Chau Doc is next best place to uncork the region's possibilities. From the summit of Sam

PHU QUOC NATIONAL PARK
Bai Ong Lang
Duong Dong
Phu Quoc Island
Bai Vong
Ham Ninh
Bai Truong
Bai Sao
An Thoi
Bai Khem
To Tho Chu Islands
A

Mountain, the delta reveals itself as an amphibious marvel, part water and part land. From Chau Doc to Ha Tien, the scenic landscape, with its sugar palms, luminous paddies, and mountainous horizons, exudes a primeval majesty. At Ba Chuc, the beauty is marred by ten separate killing fields, where the Khmer Rouge massacred Vietnamese in 1978.

The quiet cities of Ha Tien and Rach Gia, notable for history, peaceful pagodas, and beaches, front the placid Gulf of Thailand. They serve as gateways to Phu Quoc, a rugged island rimmed by white sand and clear waters that is quickly becoming a favorite beach destination for Vietnamese and foreigners alike. ■

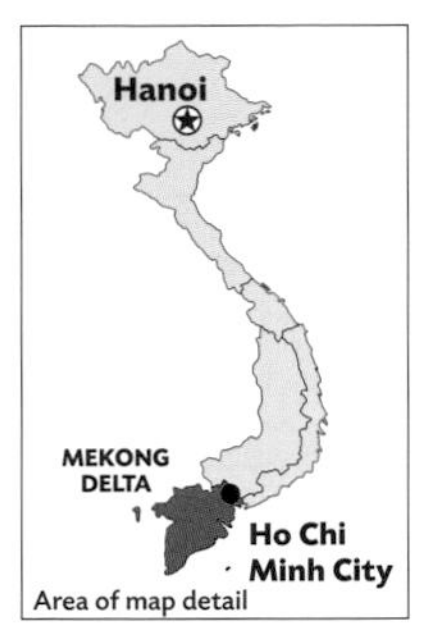

Delta Towns

Known as the breadbasket of Vietnam, the densely populated Mekong Delta is dotted with bustling towns, all connected by a network of watery highways and byways that offers glimpses into the day-to-day life of the delta's farmers and fishermen. Vinh Long and Can Tho are particularly noted as gateways to the world of the picturesque, colorful floating markets, while Chau Doc seduces visitors with its rugged, outlawish charm.

A Buddhist devotee makes obeisance at Vinh Trang Pagoda in My Tho.

My Tho & Ben Tre
221 D3
Visitor Information
Tien Giang Tourist, 8, 30 Thang 4, My Tho
073/3873-184
tiengiangtourist.com

My Tho & Ben Tre

The Tien branch of the Mekong River divides the towns of My Tho and Ben Tre, 43 miles (70 km) southwest of Ho Chi Minh City, though a new bridge now spans this divide. Visitors board boats to explore narrow, mud brown waterways and fertile islands, and to call on cottage industry makers of candy, honey, and sugar. In Ben Tre, the coconut monk's peace pavilion is singularly eccentric, while My Tho's Vinh Trang Pagoda fuses Occidental and Asian architecture.

This region's proximity to Ho Chi Minh City guarantees it a steady stream of visitors. Most arrive on tours booked in the city, though it's possible to book your own, more expensive trip through the tourist offices on 30 Thang 4 in My Tho or with a private operator who has managed to dodge the rigid licensing restrictions.

Tour boats call at **Unicorn, Dragon,** and **Tortoise Islands,** where the attractions are similar (restaurants, orchards, coconut candy) and proprietors are ready at their cash registers. Whenever possible, stay on the water in My Tho.

At **Phoenix Island,** the so-called coconut monk (see sidebar below) struck a blow for kitsch with construction of his fanciful open-air temple complex in the 1960s. Multicolored cement dragons spiral up nine columns, one for each branch of the Mekong. A bridge spanning two towers, one for Hanoi and one for Saigon, represents the monk's hopes for peace. A space capsule on another tower served as an elevator to the monk's meditation perch.

Vinh Trang Pagoda *(60A Nguyen Trung Truc, My Tho)* is worth a detour from the river. While the pagoda dates from 1850, its grandest flourishes date from the early 1930s. The facade is an amalgam of Roman arches, French grills, Japanese tiles, and Chinese and Gothic calligraphy. Inside, the carved altar screen and 18 arhats all date from 1907.

Vinh Long

In the heart of the delta, Vinh Long occupies the midsection on a long wedge of an island defined by the two main branches of the Mekong—the Tien and the Hau. While the town itself lacks appeal, it serves travelers as a decent launch for waterway exploration. The Cai Be floating market can be disappointing, but the channels themselves will fulfill your expectations of a delta trip.

From the pier beside the Cuu Long Tourist office, tour boats start out across the Co Chien arm of the Tien branch of the Mekong, which splits upstream beneath the **My Thuan Bridge.** (The bridge offers stellar views of the vast delta.) Along the Dong Phu waterway, your boat will thread the upper end of **An Binh Island.** Nurseries and orchards thrive on its fecund banks, and feeder streams tempt detours from the usual route. This channel is thick with sampans and barges, which ferry mounds of unhusked rice between splints wedged in the hull to maximize the load. Glaring eyes are painted on either side of the boats' prows to deter malevolent water spirits.

Past the Dong Phu Market, you'll enter the main branch of the Tien and soon reach Cai Be village and its mundane **floating market.** Yams, onions, and other produce dangle from upright staffs lashed to the sides of the large sampans, signaling each boat's concealed payload to buyers, who paddle out in skiffs. The big boats peddle more than produce, as you'll see from the firewood and

Coconut Monk

Ong Dao Dua was called the coconut monk because he allegedly spent several years meditating and eating nothing but coconuts. In the 1960s he devised a new religion called Tinh Do Cu Si, a blend of Buddhism and Christianity. The monk attracted a host of young American devotees, including journalists Sean Flynn and John Steinbeck, Jr.

Vinh Long

221 D3

Visitor Information

Cuu Long Tourist, 1 1 Thang 5

070/3823-529

cuulongtourist.com

Can Tho
221 C3
Visitor Information
Can Tho Tourist, 50 Hai Ba Trung
0710/3824-221
canthotourist.vn

sculpted topiary perched on the cabin roofs.

Cai Be itself is a collection of sheds, shops, and houses, dominated by an august Catholic church. Onshore here and at a number of scripted stops, pathways parallel the riverbank and plunge at right angles through orchards of papayas, longans, bananas, and pineapples.

Up the Cai Muoi channel on An Binh lies the quaint villa of a Vietnamese official in the colonial administration. A blend of French and Vietnamese architecture, this house marries the tall hardwood pillars, panels, and bay of a *nha ruong* (see pp. 144–145) inside with the arched gallery windows and pilasters of a French facade.

For mainland delights in Vinh Long, walk from the pier to check out the palatial villa at 2 Le Van Tam. Note the colorful bas-relief wreaths above its massive wooden doors. The **military museum** on Phan Boi Chau is worth a look, and you can stroll out back to see several tanks, an F-5A, an A-37B, and a Huey helicopter. A couple of miles south of the tourist office along the river is a seldom visited temple of literature *(van mieu).*

The Growing Coastline

The Mekong River has a huge impact on all the countries it flows through, and none more so than Vietnam. Alluvial deposits dragged down from China, Thailand, Laos, and Cambodia make the delta fertile enough to produce much of the country's agricultural needs. Silt carried to the river's many mouths also drifts down to the country's end at Cape Ca Mau, where accumulated deposits cause Vietnam to grow by about 160 to 330 feet (50–100 m) each year.

Can Tho

Connected to Saigon by frequent flights and the longest cable-stay bridge in Southeast Asia (1.68 miles/2.75 km; opened in 2010), Can Tho is the capital of the Mekong Delta, with a population of more than a million. This seductive river city nestles against its channel of the Mekong with an esplanade built for strolling, a restored French market, and a suite of restaurants with superb views. Down the channel, floating markets provide an alluring incentive to roll from bed at the crack of dawn and hit the water. An excellent in-town temple and one exquisite house just outside town offer opportunities to escape the riverbanks.

At the heart of town is **Ninh Kieu Park,** a riverfront esplanade that stretches along Hai Ba Trung between the wharf and the old city fish market, now made over as a tourist market. Built by the French in the 1930s, the airy, attractive market houses kiosks of tourist trinkets and a very good café and restaurant on the water. That same progressive impulse razed the old riverside city market

INSIDER TIP:

It's best to negotiate and hire your own boat and driver to cruise the delta. Travel some of the side canals to get an up-close-and-personal look at delta life.

—KRIS LEBOUTILLIER
National Geographic photographer

and opened up the space for pavilions, benches, and gardens. In the evening, neon bands light the rooflines of pavilions and markets, a hokey gesture unless you let yourself be charmed by it.

Midway between the market and wharf, **Kuang-Tsao Temple** (aka Ong Temple) shelters a niche for Quan Kong and a rich collection of wood carvings. Prosperous Chinese immigrants imported columns, rafters, and ornaments from Guangdong and built the temple between 1894 and 1896. The carved and painted rafters under the front eaves are especially attractive, as is the vividly painted carving of a sumptuous Chinese palace hung from the truss. In the niche to the right of red-faced Quan Cong is the god of earth, and to the left is the honor graduate Dong Vinh.

In town, at the intersection of Hoa Binh and Phan Dinh Phung, is the magisterial **Can Tho Museum,** while farther south on Hoa Binh is the **Munirang Syaram Pagoda,** one of 400 Khmer pagodas on the delta. In 1948, this 19th-century pagoda was wholly made over in painted, molded cement. Its austerely appointed halls are less inspiring than the Khmer temples at Soc Trang and Tra Vinh (see p. 234).

Can Tho Museum

- 1 Hoa Binh
- 0710/3820-955
- Closed Mon., Tues–Thurs. 11 a.m.–2 p.m., Sat.–Sun. 11 a.m.–6:30 p.m.

Merchants display the Mekong Delta's bounty each morning at floating markets.

EXPERIENCE: Try a Homestay in the Delta

The Vietnamese are a friendly people and easy to get along with; however, they do not usually invite short-time visitors to their country into their homes. Fortunately, several tour operators have set up a system of homestays, by which tourists may spend a day or more living in a typical Vietnamese home and learning about the lifestyle of their host family. Available throughout the country, these homestay programs are particularly successful in the Mekong Delta, where the houses are often located in an idyllic rural environment surrounded by fruit orchards or rice paddies.

The facilities available at a homestay tend to be very basic—bathrooms, for example, often consist of nothing more than a bucket shower and squat toilet—but such minor inconveniences pale in comparison to the rewards gained by joining a family meal and experiencing some cultural interaction—at least as far as language limitations allow. For more information, contact one of the tour companies listed in Travelwise (see p. 239).

Duong Home

26/1A Bui Huu Nghia, Binh Thuy Ward

 0710/3841-127

Noon–2 p.m.

$

A treat awaits in the Binh Thuy Ward, where you'll find the **Duong home,** built in 1870 and featured prominently in the 1992 French film *The Lover*. Two sweeping stairways meet on a terrace before a suite of five green-shuttered doors crested by arches and pediments. Inside, ironwood colonnades divide the open space into five bays, tastefully appointed with marble-topped tables, platform beds, massive mirrored hutches, chandeliers suspended from floral medallions, and an antique vase reputed to be 500 years old. The carved wooden screens between the columns are as elaborate as a pagoda's. The current owner, Duong Minh Hien, is a descendant of the home's builder, whose portrait hangs inside above the central door.

On the River: After dawn, traffic along the river thickens with a potpourri of puttering long-tail boats, sampans oared by standing women, and barges sunk to the gunwales with cargo of dredged mud and gravel. Four miles (7 km) downstream from Can Tho, the **Cai Rang floating market** draws hundreds of waterborne buyers and sellers from nearby farms and villages. If you shove off from Can Tho before 7 a.m., this market won't disappoint. The anchored produce boats dangle fruits and vegetables from tall bamboo staffs lashed to the cabins as buyers glide up to purchase watermelons (five for a dollar), longans, pineapples, cabbages, guavas, bananas, pomelos, and other local goodies. Six miles (10 km) farther down the channel, the **Phong Dien floating market** specializes in fruit and sees fewer tourists. Buyers at both markets are mainly seeking bulk sales, though the pineapple salespeople will cut and sell fresh fruit on a stick to tourists.

On the return trip to Can Tho, consider stopping at the riverside **Cao Dai temple** above My Khanh. You can't miss the well-maintained church, with its distinctive pair of tiered towers bracketing the facade and signature all-seeing eye. Its vaulted sky blue ceiling is lofted by cement columns painted like turquoise candy canes. Ten more columns coiled in orange-scaled dragons cluster about a gilt-framed eye. If the church is closed, the on-site caretaker might be cajoled into unlocking the doors.

Nearby is **My Khanh Tourist Village,** a cluster of bungalows set amid a sapodilla orchard that caters to local tourists, hence the caged monkeys. The restored hundred-year-old house was moved to the property in 2002.

Chau Doc

En route from Can Tho to the town of Chau Doc, the exuberantly verdant delta flaunts some of its fabled rice fields. Seven miles (11 km) east of the Cambodian border, Chau Doc is a commingling of Vietnamese, Khmer, Cham, and Chinese people. Driving the local economy are the many *ca ba sa* (catfish) farms that clog the river and waterways. The region's bizarre mix of pagodas, temples, and mosques underscores its reputation as a seedbed of ardent religious devotion. That said, as a frontier town, Chau Doc was one of the last to be settled by the Vietnamese and still retains a bit of wild woolliness. Smugglers on motorbikes occasionally blaze through town, trafficking in cigarettes and CDs, and the incidence of AIDS among women, mostly Cambodian, who work in the sex trade is reportedly high.

Attractions are comparatively weak. On Tran Hung Dao near the market, **Dinh Chau Phu** is a 1926 communal hall dedicated to local hero Thoai Ngoc Hau (1761–1829), a military administrator of the Nguyen dynasty. He was responsible for the construction of the Chau Doc Canal, which defines the border with Cambodia, and he is buried in an elaborate tomb at the foot of Sam Mountain. On the other side of the market, a festively headdressed Quan Cong holds court in one of the least interesting temples to the Taoist deity and Buddhist bodhisattva, built in 1972.

Con Tien Island

A bridge to the north of Chau Doc connects the town with Con Tien Island. The island and the village of Chau Giang are home to ten pretty mosques and a large percentage of the 15,000 Cham Muslims who live in the area. The Cham villages are bucolically charming, but offer little as tourist destinations. Most people visit these villages on a tour that also includes a visit to fish farms, where pontoon houses float on empty barrels above huge cages of catfish.

Sam Mountain: Rising from the floodplain 3 miles (5 km) southwest of Chau Doc, 755-foot (230 m) Nui Sam

My Khanh Tourist Village
- 335 Lo Vong Cung
- 0710/3846-260

mykhanh.com

Chau Doc
- 221 C4

Visitor Information
- An Giang Tourist, 563/29 Tran Hung Dao, Long Xuyen
- 076/3954-432

(Sam Mountain) represents the region's most compelling attraction. The high road from Chau Doc—fittingly called Mountain Road—winds amid the granite outcrops to an unassuming military base at the summit, where you're free to poke around for views northwest into Cambodia and southeast over the delta. The views affirm Vietnam's self-perception as a country of water and earth.

At the foot of the mountain, eccentric **Tay An Pagoda** elaborates on traditional Buddhist architecture with Hindu and Islamic flourishes in a riot of tangerine, purple, aqua, and lime green. The pagoda dates from 1847, but its current look took shape during a 1958 restoration. A pumpkin crowns its central tower, and seven cobras in bas-relief flare off the Middle Eastern arch on the portico. Inside, more than 200 wood statues, glossed in vibrant colors, bedeck altars, shelves, and pedestals. You'll find the whole cast of characters—the jade emperor, the arhats, the four celestial kings, the dharma guardians, and many manifestations of Buddha. Look on the right side of the temple for a Grinch-like character with a yellow sword and inside the main door for a gang of statues done up in leafy garb like the Jolly Green Giant.

The flanks of Sam Mountain provide fabulous views across the delta and into Cambodia.

Farther up Mountain Road, the **Ba Chua Xu Temple** is a magnet for pilgrims who come to pray before a local goddess known as the Holy Lady. The clearly obese Holy Lady is a deity whose likeness was found on Sam Mountain by Khmer invaders in the early 19th century. The statue's weight foiled their plans to plunder the relic. Later, nine virgins managed to carry the Holy Lady as far as the mountain's base, where villagers promptly raised a temple. The current structure was last rebuilt in the early 1970s. Access to the temple is through a reception hall as big as a railway station, testifying to the swarms of devotees who flock here, especially during the festival in the fourth lunar month. Today, the diva reigns in robes of sequined silk before a disco-light halo. The neighboring three-story building was built as a repository for the robes and finery offered to the lady by devotees.

Just up the road is the 1930s **tomb of Thoai Ngoc Hau** (1761–1829), the mandarin cum engineer who first exploited the area's rich soil and spurred commerce on the delta with construction of its canals. He and his two wives are buried in the courtyard. ■

Plight of the Boat People

In the years after the fall of Saigon in 1975, an exodus of more than one million refugees took to the seas in tiny, overcrowded boats, sailing toward the promise of a better life outside Vietnam. They came to be known as "boat people," and for a time in the late 1970s, they gripped the world's attention.

Fearful of reprisals by the victorious North Vietnamese and National Liberation Front (Viet Cong), the first wave of 131,000 South Vietnamese refugees escaped as Saigon fell—some 6,500 by helicopter and plane, others by land, and many more by boat.

While the dreaded bloodbath did not happen, the communists were loathe to forgive or forget those who remained in Vietnam and who'd allied themselves with the South Vietnamese government during the Vietnam War. They imprisoned thousands of those who hadn't fled in "reeducation camps," while making a shambles of the country's economy with the miserable policies of command economics.

Meanwhile, the government in Hanoi sought favors from its two wartime allies, the Soviet Union and China. Because the Soviets were more geographically removed and less of a threat to Vietnamese independence, and because Vietnamese antipathy toward China runs deep, Hanoi favored the U.S.S.R.

Chinese Invasion

The growing Soviet-Vietnamese relationship worried China. On Feb. 15, 1979, the Chinese government announced its intentions to invade Vietnam, giving two reasons: the mistreatment of Vietnam's ethnic Chinese minority, and the Vietnamese occupation of the Spratly Islands, claimed by China. Two days later, Chinese tanks rolled into North Vietnam. A brief incursion ensued, after which the Chinese troops withdrew, claiming their punitive mission had been achieved. Both sides, however, claimed victory.

The Vietnamese closed the businesses of ethnic Chinese, seized their gold, and began relocating 1.5 million into so-called new economic zones. Continual poverty and an exodus ensued. This second wave of refugees spawned an international crisis and worldwide appeals.

A vessel overloaded with boat people weighs anchor after Malaysian authorities refuse to grant them refuge in November 1978.

Similar to their predecessors, the refugees embarked on deadly seas, subject to typhoons, hunger, starvation, and attacks by Thai pirates. Their reception in neighboring countries was hardly welcoming. Many Southeast Asian governments turned away the boat people. In the first six months of 1979, Malaysia towed about 58,000 refugees out of its territorial waters. Some estimates say that as many as 500,000 to 600,000 people perished in the exodus.

The lucky ones who made landfall in Malaysia, Singapore, Thailand, Hong Kong, and the Philippines were herded into refugee camps, where they idled for months, sometimes years, awaiting resettlement elsewhere. By the mid-1990s, the number of people fleeing Vietnam had dwindled. Many camps were closed. In 2005, the last refugees in the Philippines were granted asylum in Canada and the U.S. At long last, the plight of the refugees had ended.

Along the Gulf of Thailand

Lined with sleepy fishing villages and sandy strands, the stretch of coastline from Ha Tien, near Vietnam's border with Cambodia, to Rach Gia, the provincial capital of Kien Giang, is a quiet, idyllic place known for its Khmer heritage—reflected in the people and in numerous peaceful pagodas—and the increasingly popular beach destination of Phu Quoc Island.

The coastal waters of the Gulf of Thailand are placid in comparison to those of the South China Sea.

Ha Tien
221 B3
Visitor Information
Kien Giang Tourist, 190 Tran Phu
077/3862-231

Ha Tien

In Vietnam's remote southwest, Ha Tien is the last stop along the seaboard before Cambodia. Few travelers push beyond Chau Doc to this quiet border town, although this trend is likely to change with the opening of the border to Cambodia and the introduction of express boats to Phu Quoc Island.

With permission from the Khmer court, Cantonese merchant Mac Cuu settled Ha Tien in the 1670s and built a port visited by traders from as far away as The Netherlands. Envious Thai pirates repeatedly attacked the port, prompting Mac Cuu to strike an alliance with the Nguyen court. After the enterprising merchant died at age 81 in 1735, the deal he struck held fast for seven generations, whose members all enjoyed the privileges of titled nobility.

They're buried in terraces of hillside graves a half mile (1 km) northwest of town behind the **Mac Cuu Temple.** Cuu himself occupies the loftiest eternal perch, on Nui Lang, a short climb worth making for views of the extensive rice paddies and rolling coastal hills. Ringed by a stone wall, the temple honors Cuu, his sons, and their wives at various altars. Original murals from 1846 honor locals who restored the place.

Closer to town on Mac Thien Tich, 300-year-old **Quan Thanh Temple** harbors the red-faced, beard-dragging Quan Cong and four colossal, armed attendants. Aggressively protuberant dragons coil up two of its columns. The murals above the doors to the side galleries and the granite threshold in the open-air courtyard all reputedly date from the original building. Be on the lookout for tortoises, which have free run of the temple's heavenly well.

About 4 miles (6 km) west of Ha Tien, gulf waters lap the brown-sand strand at **Mui Nai** *($)*, the only beach of note in the area. A clutch of nicely situated hills lends the beach a feng shui feel, while deck chairs and seafood restaurants tempt visitors to linger.

Two miles (3 km) farther along Mac Thien Tich, a monument of a clenched fist at the base of **Thach Dong cave** memorializes the 130 people murdered nearby during a 1978 raid by Pol Pot's rampaging Khmer Rouge troops. You may choose to skip the humdrum pagoda within Thach Dong's vertical expanse, but do visit the overlooks on the far side of the cave. Views stretch down the rugged coast to Cambodia, just over a mile (2 km) away.

Rach Gia

Rach Gia's fame flared briefly in 1868 when the first great Vietnamese nationalist, Nguyen Trung Truc, attacked the French garrison here and briefly held the town (see sidebar right). The coastal town has quieted since then and mainly plays host to travelers bound by ferry or plane to Phu Quoc (see sidebar p. 232). Rach Gia isn't much of a magnet, though you could while away an afternoon traipsing from the communal house to a Khmer temple and a pagoda.

The town sits on an islet in the Cai Long River, centered on a statue of Truc at Le Loi and Ham Nghi; the urban sprawl, however, spills over to the river's north and south banks. You'll find the market and hotels on the north bank.

Also on the north bank is Truc's **communal house,** at 18 Nguyen Cong Tru near the ferry terminal. Inside the 1963 temple are ceremonial weapons and altars topped by portraits of Truc. Two bas-relief murals depict him on the deck of the *Espérance* and in the Rach Gia garrison. A glass display case holds timbers from the ship.

North of the market on Quang Trung, the path to **Phat Lon Pagoda** starts from an ornate Khmer gate and skirts a *naga* (divine serpent) balustrade supported by statues of the mythical bird Garuda. Beneath the hornlike finials and steep pitch of the roof, a frieze of Sakyamuni's life story wraps around the main hall above a decent statue collection.

Across town on Thich Thien An, **Tam Bao Pagoda** centers on a courtyard and a square lotus pond. Outside is a statue of Muchalinda, the seven-headed naga king who used his hood to shelter the meditating Buddha from heavy rainfall.

Resistance Leader

From 1861 to 1868, Nguyen Trung Truc led the first great resistance movement against the French. In December 1861, the 22-year-old swashbuckler boarded, burned, and sank the French warship *Espérance*. Six years later, his forces overran the Rach Gia garrison and held the town for six days. The French later captured Truc on Phu Quoc and executed him in the Rach Gia marketplace in 1868.

Rach Gia
221 C3
Visitor Information
Kien Giang Tourist, 190 Tran Phu
077/3862-231

Visitor Information
26 Nguyen Trai, Duong Dong
077/3994-181

EXPERIENCE: Motorbiking Around Phu Quoc

Many visitors to Phu Quoc are more than content to spend their time lounging on its soft-sand beaches, never venturing far from their resort. However, the large island is worth exploring, and the best way to do so is by motorbike. Most hotels and guesthouses have motorbikes for rent, but you should inspect the bike carefully—especially the brakes and lights—before agreeing to take a particular model.

Apart from a few paved roads along the west and east coasts, the rest of the island's roads are no more than rutted or packed laterite. Be prepared to return after a day's exploration covered in a film of red dust.

There are several routes to choose from. For diverse scenery, travel west from Duong Dong to the village of **Ganh Dau** in the northwest corner, then return through the densely wooded hills and pepper plantations of the island's interior to the capital. If you love views of sand and surf, follow **Bai Truong** to the southern end of the island, then return up the east coast, stopping off for a dip at **Bai Sao** ("star beach")—lightly developed and bracketed by promontories, its dazzling white beach offers superb swimming.

Phu Quoc
220 A3
Visitor Information

Kien Giang Tourist, 137 Nguyen Hung Son, Rach Gia
077/3862-103
visitphuquoc.info

NOTE: Express boats serve Phu Quoc from Rach Gia and Ha Tien, though many travelers take one of several daily flights from Ho Chi Minh City to the new international airport in the center of the island.

Phu Quoc

Off the southern coast of Cambodia, the island of Phu Quoc is fast emerging as Vietnam's premier destination for sea and sun. It's no wonder: The 237-square-mile (593 sq km) island is lapped by the limpid waters of the Gulf of Thailand and fringed with the country's finest beaches, while the mountainous interior harbors a national park, thousands of monkeys, and nationally famous pepper plantations. The island is best explored by motorbike, available for rent at the hotels (see sidebar above).

In the early 19th century, the future king Gia Long rallied here before routing the short-lived Tay Son dynasty to win back the country for the Nguyens. In the early days of the French resistance, Nguyen Trung Truc used Phu Quoc as a base. More recently, during the Vietnam War, South Vietnam imprisoned 40,000 Viet Cong guerrillas at Coconut Tree Camp on the island's south tip.

A handful of facilities along the river in Duong Dong distill 1.5 million gallons (6 million L) of world-famous *nuoc mam* (fish sauce) annually. But unless you're a gourmand or can visit for more than a few days, spend your time in search of the perfect beach. *Phu quoc* means "beautiful country," and these strands are Vietnam's only serious rivals to the jewels of Thailand and the Indian Ocean.

Bai Truong ("long beach") is a ruler-straight 12-mile (20 km) stretch along the western shore. The burgeoning resort scene is encroaching from Duong Dong, but its southern reaches remain the province of fishermen, who tie up at shoreline coconut trees.

Also on the west side, several resorts cling to **Bai Ong Lang.** Offshore rocks offer decent snorkeling here, though the fishscapes are much better off smaller islands to the north and south. ■

More Places to Visit Around the Mekong Delta

Ba Chuc

Between Chau Doc and Tri Ton, the countryside opens up on vast rice plains, hemmed by ranks of sugar palms *(thot not)*. Khmer pagodas abound, signaling a proximity to Cambodia that had devastating consequences for the people of Ba Chuc. Between April 18 and 30, 1978, the Khmer Rouge embarked on a series of killing sprees that claimed the lives of 3,157 villagers. At a **memorial** on the fringes of town, a glass-walled tomb holds the skulls of 1,159 victims, segregated by age. These bashed and fissured bones testify to the brutality of the massacre. A nearby gallery exhibits cudgels, daggers, and spears used in the attacks, as well as horrific photos of bludgeoned and impaled victims. The Khmer committed their atrocities at ten nearby sites, including the **Phi Lai Tu Communal House,** a short stroll from the memorial. In the back hall of this house, two red painted lines on the wall indicate where 150 people had been shackled before execution.
221 B3

Con Dao Islands

Since colonial days, the islands of Con Dao, 112 miles (180 km) southeast of the delta, earned notoriety as Poulo Condore, where the French and later the Saigon regime jailed inmates in deplorable conditions. This environment would serve as a think tank for Vietnamese nationalists (including Pham Van Dong and Le Duc Tho), who buoyed each other's spirits with lessons in Marxism, literature, science, and language. Today, tourism centers on the island of **Con Son,** where the Saigon regime held captives in so-called tiger cages during the Vietnam War at **Phu Son** ("rich mountain") and **Phu Hai** ("rich sea") **prisons.** The island also lures visitors with beaches and the forest-sea ecosystem of **Con Dao National Park.** The park boasts 2,500 acres (1,000 ha) of coral reef. Dugongs—sea cows related to Florida's manatees—feed on nearshore sea grass, while thousands of hawksbill and green sea turtles nest here from June to September. Here, Marco Polo anchored following a storm in 1294, and composer Camille Saint-Saëns finished his opera *Brünhilde* in 1895. New luxury hotels promise a bright future for the islands, which are accessible by daily plane service from Saigon.
221 E1 **Visitor Information** Vung Tau Tourist, 29 Tran Hung Dao, Vung Tau 064/3857-527

INSIDER TIP:

Phu Quoc Island is a perfect spot to chill out for a long weekend. Cheap, sleepy, and slow, it's beach life as it was meant to be.

—KRIS LeBOUTILLIER
National Geographic photographer

Hon Chong Peninsula

Between Ha Tien and Rach Gia, Hon Chong is surrounded by clear, tranquil seas that wash gently onto sandy brown beaches. The turreted Green Hill guesthouse *(tel 077/3854-369)*, which has a few immaculate rooms, lords over the premier beach at **Bai Duong.** Farther down the oceanfront road, the **Sea and Mountain Pagoda** crouches at the base of limestone outcrops. A grotto tunnels through to the beach, where the landmark Father and Son Islands rise just offshore. Unfortunately, the Father, one of two huge rock pillars, collapsed in 2006. Stop by any of the fishing villages to hire a boat for exploration.
221 B3 **Visitor Information** 190 Tran Phu 077/3862-231

Long Xuyen

The district capital of An Giang Province, Long Xuyen lies midway between Can Tho and Chau Doc on the Hau River. If you've somehow missed the floating markets at Can Tho, there's one here. Otherwise, most sites line Nguyen Hue between the river and Highway 91. A statue of **Ton Duc Thang,** the Long Xuyen native who succeeded Ho Chi Minh as president of Vietnam in 1969, stands in one of the boulevard's rectangular parks. Beyond, two long arms clasp a cross atop the steeple of the **Catholic church.** On the same side of Nguyen Hue, Nguyen Huu Canh stands as the tutelary spirit in the **My Phuoc Communal House,** founded in the early 18th century.

221 C3 **Visitor Information**
563/29 Tran Hung Dao, Long Xuyen
076/3954-432

Soc Trang

Soc Trang merits a secondary place on the tourist circuit for its handful of Khmer pagodas, including **Khleang** and especially **Doi** ("bat"), where thousands of fruit bats cling to the trees, sleeping by day and feeding by night—but never, rumor has it, from the pagoda's own fruit trees. Inside the 16th-century sanctuary, some of the Buddhist texts are incised on palm leaves.

221 D2 **Visitor Information** Soc Trang Tourist, 104 Le Loi 079/3822-024

Tra Vinh town

Most visitors to Tra Vinh are day-trippers out of Vinh Long, heading for **Ba Om Pond,** a clear blue pond surrounded by oddly rooted dipterocarps and tamarind trees. The same majestic trees shade nearby **Ang Pagoda,** one of the province's 140 or so Khmer pagodas. Another is **Hang Pagoda,** renowned for the storks that settle amid the trees at dusk. The colonial French developed a resort at **Ba Dong,** a 6-mile (10 km) strip of white sand that is one of the delta's few beach destinations. Be forewarned, however: The war-ravaged roads turn the 34-mile (55 km) jaunt from Tra Vinh town into an ordeal.

221 D3 **Visitor Information** Tra Vinh Tourist, 64–66 Le Loi 074/3858-556

A Khmer monk steps into his room for morning meditation in Tra Vinh.

Travelwise

A goldfish cyclo

TRAVELWISE

PLANNING YOUR TRIP

When to Go

While Vietnam lies in the tropics, that doesn't necessarily mean the weather is always tropical. With the exception of the extreme south (below Phan Thiet/Mui Ne), winter can bring long bouts of rain and temperatures in the 60s Fahrenheit (high teens Celsius) that can feel even colder due to the high humidity. By the end of January, you can usually start banking on the sun and warmer temps from north to south. (See more on climate on pp. 28–29.) October through December is the high season in Hanoi and Ho Chi Minh City, and the weather is delightful. However, these same months are the worst time to visit the south-central coast around Nha Trang, as rain is frequent and hours of sunshine are limited.

Between mid-January and mid-February, the country's transportation network strains with travelers headed home for the Tet lunar new year (see p. 35). Unless you've booked a domestic flight long in advance, you'll likely be put on standby. The same holds true for the railways. The traveler cafés operate buses along the popular routes, and there's usually space there. However, that's changing as more affluent Vietnamese can now afford the more expensive tourist buses.

What to Bring

Men should wear trousers when visiting a pagoda, as shorts will offend the monks. Women should wear shirts that cover the shoulders. A handful of temples and pagodas will deny admission to anyone dressed inappropriately.

Locals often cringe at the sloppy appearance of foreign backpackers, whom they refer to pejoratively as *tay ba lo* (Westerners with bags). While Vietnamese dress casually at home, they tend to dress smartly when in public.

Between November and February in the central and northern provinces, you'll need to bring a sweater or polar fleece jacket. You could bring expensive rainwear, but the widely available cheap ponchos make more sense, especially if you're traveling by motorbike. Bring English-language reading materials, as bookstores offer little choice.

A wide-brimmed hat is a good idea. Even if you're trying to tan, the midday glare can be oppressive. Vendors throughout Vietnam hawk sunglasses, but the lenses are cheap and offer little protection. Bring your own.

Also bring your own sunscreen. Unless you buy sunscreen at a big chain hotel, you risk paying top dollar for some other cheap ointment with zero SPF.

Photographic supplies, such as memory cards and batteries, are widely available, though film is difficult to find.

Outside of upscale hotels and restaurants, toilet paper can be scarce, especially in rural areas. Consider bringing spare tissues.

Insurance

Before leaving home, check with your insurance carrier regarding coverage limits. You may want additional coverage that includes an emergency evacuation.

Travelers cannot as yet drive rental cars in Vietnam. When you rent a car, you'll be hiring a driver as well, and he'll assume any responsibility for accidents. If you putter about on a rental motorbike, however, you'll be liable for damages. Driver's insurance is not readily available. If you do get into an accident, and it's your fault, the other driver will likely demand payment on the spot.

Hotels usually post a disclaimer that leaves you responsible for the security of your own possessions, unless you check them with the front desk. Most mid-range and luxury hotels provide in-room safes for valuables. On-site theft is not an issue, as access to most hotels is very difficult for would-be thieves.

Entry Formalities

Visa

Unless you're from Scandinavia, Japan, the Republic of Korea, or elsewhere in Southeast Asia, you'll need to obtain a visa for entry to Vietnam. The easiest way is to get a visa on arrival, which costs around $60–$70, depending on which agency you use. The government website at *vietnamvisa.govt.vn* is a reliable choice. The visa can be extended twice, at a cost of $25 per extension, for an additional stay of up to 60 days.

If you overstay your visa, be prepared to explain why to the Department of Immigration of the Ministry of Public Security in Hanoi or Ho Chi Minh City.

Travelers can obtain visas from consulates at the following overseas embassies:

United States
1233 20th St. NW, Ste. 400,
Washington, DC 20036
Tel 202/861-0737
Fax 202/861-0917
vietnamembassy-usa.org

Australia
6 Timbarra Crescent, O'Malley,
ACT 2606
Tel 02/6286-6059 or 6290-1556
Fax 02/6286-4534
vietnamembassy.org.au

Canada
55 Mackay Street,
Ottawa, ONT K1M2B2
Tel: 613/236-0772

Fax: 613/236-2704
vietem-ca.com

United Kingdom
12–14 Victoria Rd.,
London W8 5RD
Tel 20/7937-1912
Fax 20/7937-6108
vietnamembassy.org.uk

Customs

Travelers age 18 and older may import up to 400 cigarettes, 100 cigars, 0.2 pounds (100 g) of tobacco, and 3 pints (1.5 L) of liquor duty free. For more information, see *customs.gov.vn.*

Vietnamese law prohibits the import of literature and materials that might provoke violence or debauchery or contradict Vietnam's customs and traditions. Restricted items include pornography, toxic chemicals, fireworks, and toys that might negatively impact education or social security.

Vietnam restricts the export of antiques; even artificially aged objects that look antique may pose a problem. If you buy that statue of a Cham *apsara,* be sure to carry a receipt with the name and phone number of the shop.

When leaving Vietnam, no outbound declaration is necessary if you leave with less than $7,000/11 ounces (300 g) of gold and 15 million dong (about $1,000).

In most cases, DVDs and CDs breeze through customs, although officials reserve the right to screen content for several days.

Drugs & Narcotics

Vietnam bans all restricted drugs, so be sure to have a note from your doctor if you're carrying prescription substances that may interest people who aren't ill. You may notice people openly doing hits from bamboo bongs throughout Vietnam, but they're smoking a kind of tobacco, not the other stuff. The days of opium dens are long past in Saigon, but many tourist shops sell opium pipes and pillows as souvenirs.

HOW TO GET TO VIETNAM

By Airplane

In 2004, United Airlines became the first U.S. carrier to fly direct to Vietnam since 1975. The next year, Continental Airlines and American Airlines launched service from the United States, via code-sharing deals with Vietnam Airlines and Japan Airlines.

More than 40 international carriers fly into Ho Chi Minh City's Tan Son Nhat Airport; nearly 30 carriers fly into Hanoi's Noi Bai Airport.

It takes 15 to 16 hours to fly nonstop from New York to Hong Kong, then an additional 2 or 2.5 hours to fly from Hong Kong into Hanoi or Ho Chi Minh City, respectively. The flight time from Paris to Ho Chi Minh City is 13 hours, while from Sydney it's 8 hours.

Some of the major carriers are as follows:

Air France
Hanoi: 04/3825-3484
HCMC: 08/3829-0981
British Airways
Hanoi: 04/3934-7239
HCMC: 08/3930-2933
Cathay Pacific
Hanoi: 04/3826-7298
HCMC: 08/3822-3203
China Airlines
Hanoi: 04/3824-2688
Japan Airlines
Hanoi: 04/3826-6693
HCMC: 08/3848-5146
Korean Air
HCMC: 08/3824-2878
Lufthansa
HCMC: 08/3829-8529
Qantas
Hanoi: 04/3933-3026
HCMC: 08/3930-2939
Singapore Airlines
Hanoi: 04/3826-8888
HCMC: 08/3823-1588
Thai Airways
Hanoi: 04/3826-7921
HCMC: 08/3829-2809
United Airlines
HCMC: 08/3823-4755
Vietnam Airlines
Hanoi: 04/832-0320
HCMC: 08/832-0320

Noi Bai Airport, Hanoi

Noi Bai Airport *(tel 04/3826-7163, hanoiairportonline.com)* is 28 miles (45 km) from central Hanoi. A brand-new terminal is scheduled to open in late 2014. You can change money in the airport or make a withdrawal from one of several ATMs.

There are three ways to get into Hanoi: by taxi ($15–$20/300,000d–400,000d; agree on a rate up front as they don't use meters), by the Vietnam Airlines bus, VA bus ($2/40,000d), or by public bus (25 cents/5,000d). Each leaves from just outside the main terminal, and the ride takes about 40 minutes.

Tan Son Nhat Airport, Ho Chi Minh City

Tan Son Nhat Airport (SGN; *tel 08/3848-6711, saigonairport.com*) is 5 miles (8 km) from downtown Ho Chi Minh City. After passing through immigration and clearing customs, stop by the SASCO (Southern Airport Services Co.) desk for tourist information. SASCO provides free information and free maps, can change money or direct you to an airport ATM, and can book you a hotel room, limo, or tour.

A taxi to Saigon (District 1) costs about $7–$8 (140,000d–160,000d). Minivans are available to taxi larger groups for slightly higher rates. You can also take public bus 152 to the Ben Thanh Market for about 25 cents (5,000 dong) every 15 minutes between 6 a.m. and 6:40 p.m. These distinctive green buses stop outside the domestic terminal. It takes about half an hour in light traffic to reach the city by bus.

GETTING AROUND

By Bicycle

Outside Saigon and Hanoi, a rental bicycle is a cheap, safe, interactive way to get around. Many hotels and traveler cafés rent bikes for as little as a dollar a day.

By Car

Traveling by car in Vietnam can be a hair-raising experience. Road rules devolve into a sort of vehicular Darwinism, as right of way often falls to the bigger vehicle. Many drivers flout basic safe driving practices, speeding to make up for lost time or perhaps passing in the face of opposing traffic. Police have been cracking down on such scofflaws and speed demons, and the experience is a lot tamer than it was, for example, in the 1990s, but road travel remains the least welcome part of a visit.

Tourists don't actually drive cars in Vietnam. Instead, they rely on the navigational skills and road savvy of hired local drivers. A car and driver costs about $60 (1,200,000 dong) per day. You can make arrangements at nearly any hotel, one of the established tour operators, or any of the traveler café cum agencies in Ho Chi Minh City's Pham Ngu Lao District. If you require a car for a multiday excursion, you'll be asked to pay about $10 (200,000 dong) per day for the driver's food and lodging.

By City Bus

Public buses ply numerous routes through Saigon and Hanoi. Clean, air-conditioned, and incredibly cheap (about 25–50 cents/5,000d–10,000d) for a typical ride), they are proving a decent means by which to navigate the cities. The buses in Ho Chi Minh City *(tel 08/3854-6110)* run from 4:30 a.m. until 7 p.m. or later, depending on the route. At rush hour, buses sweep through stops along the most popular routes every five to eight minutes.

By Cyclo

The most charming means of transportation is the cyclo, a three-wheeled pedicab that succeeded the rickshaw as the human-powered option. The rate is about $4–$5 (80,000d–100,000d) per hour, but you'll need to bargain hard. Get your hotel to help you with this.

By Jitney

Small buses and vans—jitneys—go pretty much anywhere in this densely populated country. The jitneys are as cheap as the local bus, but can be excruciatingly crowded. A jitney also vacillates between recklessly high speeds, when the driver is trying to make up time, and fits and starts, when the conductor is trolling for more passengers to cram aboard. These vehicles should be a last resort.

By Local Bus

Most Vietnamese travel by local bus. It's cheaper than the Sinh tour bus (see p. 239), but there are no assigned seats, and your legroom may be compromised by a couple of sacks of rice. While some are air-conditioned, most aren't. Most permit smoking.

The best place to pick up a local bus is at the city or town bus station *(ben xe)*, usually found on the outskirts of smaller towns and up to several miles from the centers of larger cities. Be forewarned: As soon as you enter a bus station, you'll be mobbed by a half dozen facilitators. Ignore them and head to the ticket counter. Make sure your ticket includes an allowance for luggage, as the bus conductor might try to hit you up for more money if your luggage takes up a lot of room.

You can flag down a local bus on the highway, but you'll have to haggle with the conductor for the best price, which is likely to start at two to three times the local rate.

By Motorbike

You can rent your own motorbike (actually 125cc scooters) from the traveler cafés in most cities. Be warned: Wearing a helmet is now compulsory.

Usually the renter will ask to hold your passport as security. Rental motorbikes cost about $5 to $6 (100,000d–120,000d) per day. There's no insurance, so you're liable for anything that goes wrong. Unless you're a very savvy driver, it's not advisable to rent your own bike in Saigon or Hanoi.

Motorbike taxis are ubiquitous in the big cities. The market rate for a motorbike taxi is about $1 per mile or 10,000 dong per kilometer.

Settle on a price before you hop on the bike.

By Metro

In 2010, ground was broken on a new metro system in Hanoi that will have five interlinked routes. It will not be complete until 2020, but the first stage is scheduled to open in late 2015.

By Plane

Vietnam Airlines' modern fleet offers the best way to get around the country. In the 1990s, the carrier upgraded to ATRs, Fokkers, and Airbuses. The airline flies 22 domestic routes between 15 cities, with hubs in Ho Chi Minh City, Hanoi, and Danang. The flights are inexpensive ($100/2,000,000d between Ho Chi Minh City and Hue), and fares remain the same regardless of the time of purchase.

Fortunately for travelers, seat availability is rarely a problem, even up to the day of departure. (This does not hold true during the

Tet lunar new year.) Don't be dismayed by reports that a flight is fully booked. You can be sixth on a waiting list for a flight that later leaves with 14 empty seats—a common scenario.

Jetstar Pacific and Vietjet Air are competing airlines with slightly lower fares than Vietnam Airlines. They both offer a half dozen daily flights between Ho Chi Minh City and Hanoi and at least one daily flight to Danang from either city.

Vietnam Airlines
Hanoi: 04/3832-0320
Danang: 0511/3821-130
HCMC: 08/3832-0320

Jetstar Pacific Airlines
Hanoi: 04/3584-4494
HCMC: 08/3955-0550

Vietjet Air
Hanoi: 04/3584-4494
HCMC: 08/3547-4174

By Taxi

Taxis are a cheap and convenient way to get around. In the major cities, any portion of the first half mile (1 km) costs around 60 cents (12,000d). Each subsequent half mile costs less than a dollar. In Ho Chi Minh City and Hanoi especially, this is the safest and most comfortable way to travel.

Be on your guard for scheming hacks who've rigged their meters to move at double the pace. If you notice the meter running out of synch with your distance, ask the driver to stop immediately and end the ride. If you choose to make a stand, tell the driver you're going to call the police (*goi canh sat*—pronounced goy kun saht). If he is scamming you, he'll back down at the threat.

By Tour Bus

Among tour bus operators, Sinh Tourist Open Tour *(tel 04/3926-1568)* is the only way to go. Its clean, modern, air-conditioned buses make multiple daily trips up and down Highway 1, with stops in Hue, Hoi An, and Nha Trang. You can hop off at any designated stop, stay as long as you like, and resume your journey all on the same ticket. The $45 (900,000d) ticket includes two side trips. One spur leads from Nha Trang up into the highlands for Dalat, while another trails south along the coast to Mui Ne.

By Tour Company

Traveling to and learning more about any destinations beyond Vietnam's most popular tourist haunts can be frustrating. Fortunately, tour guides come relatively cheap, from just $5 to $10 (100,000d–200,000d) for a walk around Hanoi's Old Quarter to hundreds of dollars a day for upscale tours that include food and lodging. Hundreds of licensed tour companies across the country vie for business. In Hanoi alone, Vietnam Tourism lists more than 200 operators. For more information, see *vietnamtourism.com/e_pages/service/company.asp*. A select few boast established reputations among foreign travelers. Some of the more reputable agencies include:

Exotissimo, Central Plaza Building, 17 Le Duan, District 1, Ho Chi Minh City, tel 08/3827-2911, fax 08/3827-2912, exotissimo.com. Owned by the same company that built the Emeraude in Ha Long Bay and La Residence in Hue, Exotissimo caters to luxury and high-end adventure travelers. Its luxury tours stop at the country's finest hotels, while its adventure tours emphasize biking and trekking.

Handspan Adventure Travel, 78 Ma May, Old Quarter, Hanoi, tel 04/3926-2828, fax 04/3926-2792, handspan.com. This popular company is owned by three Vietnamese who cut their teeth at the Green Bamboo, a onetime travel powerhouse here. They own their own junk on Ha Long Bay. With more than 40 guides, they do private and group tours, mainly in the north.

Queen Travel, 65 Hang Bac, Old Quarter, Hanoi, tel 04/3826-0860, queentravel.vn. This long-established company runs a number of day tours around Hanoi, as well as offers custom-made tours throughout the country for small groups or couples. The knowledgeable staff is happy to recommend an itinerary according to your interests.

Sinhbalo Adventure Travel, 283/20 Pham Ngu Lao, District 1, Ho Chi Minh City, tel 08/3837-6766, sinhbalo.com. This super-efficient setup specializes in customized tours such as bicycle expeditions along the Ho Chi Minh Trail *(cyclingvietnam.net)*, motorbike tours, long-distance boat cruises, and kayaking in the Mekong Delta. The owner is an insatiable adventurer who is constantly exploring new destinations.

By Train

Hanoi and Ho Chi Minh City are linked by the 1,072-mile (1,726 km) Reunification Express line, known during the colonial era as the Transindochinois line. The line parallels the coast and takes in some fantastic scenery, with the loveliest stretch lying between Hue and Danang. As romantic as that may sound, however, riding the rails can get tiresome. The trains are old, noisy, uncomfortable, and prone to long stalls. That said, the railway is always preferable to the highway.

In the north, southbound trains leave from the Hanoi railway station *(120 Le Duan, tel 04/3825-3949)* for the 32-hour express or 40-hour regular train to Ho Chi Minh City. From Tran Quy Cap station (adjacent to the Hanoi railway station), trains run up several different spurs to Haiphong, Lang Son, and Lao Cai (Sa Pa).

In the south, northbound trains leave from the Saigon railway station *(1 Nguyen Thong, tel 08/3843-6528)*, headed for Hanoi and points in between, including Nha Trang, Danang, and Hue.

Several ticket classes are available on the 32-hour express. A soft bed in an air-conditioned, four-berth compartment costs $88 (1,726,000d), while a hard bed in a six-berth compartment costs $75 (1,511,000d). A soft seat costs $57 (1,141,000d). Cheaper hard seats await on the slow train.

PRACTICAL ADVICE

Communications

Post Office

The post office *(buu dien)* is a fixture in every town, even in out-of-the-way tourist destinations like Bach Ma National Park. While it offers a cheap and efficient means of shipping, you'd be foolish to send anything of value through the system, which has a bad reputation for pilfering from packages and envelopes.

Ho Chi Minh City's main post office stands across from the Notre Dame Cathedral in Paris Square. Hanoi's main post office commands a whole block of Dinh Tien Hoang, on the eastern shore of Hoan Kiem Lake. Most clerks speak English.

You can also leave your letters and packages with hotel reception for delivery.

Telephone

Traditionally, the post office has served as the best place to make international calls. Unfortunately, many clerks do not let foreigners place collect calls. It's not clear why; it simply may be that there's not much in it for them. However, you can call collect from a hotel or private residence.

In the big cities and many of the tourist towns, it's as cheap as a few pennies a minute to place international calls from Internet shops. Calls to the United States average about 10 cents per minute. For the best possible connection, go early or late when the ADSL lines are less crowded. It's even cheaper to buy your own calling card (many of the Internet shops sell them) or dial out on Skype or Yahoo Messenger.

Mobile phone coverage is excellent. Though it may cost you $150 (2,400,000d) to buy a phone, the per-minute charges are cheap, and incoming calls are free.

In 2008, an extra digit was added to all numbers. In almost every case it is a 3, but in some cases it is a 2, 4, 5, 6, or 7. Some area codes have also been changed.

For directory information, an English-speaking operator is available at 1080 for pennies per call. You'll reach an operator in the province from which you're calling. If you're after a number in another province, dial that area code, preceded by a 0.

To call Vietnam from abroad, dial the international access code (011 from the U.S., 00 from Europe) then 84 (Vietnam country code), then the area code minus the first 0 and number. To call abroad from Vietnam, dial either 171 00 or 00 followed by the country code (1 for Canada, 44 for the U.K., 1 for the U.S.) followed by the area code minus the first zero (if relevant) and the number.

Internet

Outside of the most remote rural villages, the Internet is available nearly everywhere. Internet shops are crowded with teenagers exchanging instant messages. The rates are ridiculously cheap, at about 40 cents per hour. If you've brought your own laptop, most shopkeepers will pull an Ethernet plug from one of their units so you can plug in.

Ethernet and Wi-Fi fees in the country's best hotels are as expensive as they are in the U.S., at about $15 per 24 hours; many places, however, offer free Wi-Fi.

It's possible to dial into the Internet from virtually any phone line. The number is 1269, and the password is vn1269. Unlike in the United States, where you pay a monthly subscription to an ISP, there's only one dial-up ISP here, and it doesn't cost anything but the local call to dial in.

Conversions

Vietnam uses the metric system for weights and measures. An older Chinese system is also used, but unless you're buying and selling gold, you won't have much contact with it.

Electricity

Vietnam's current runs at 220V, which tends to work just fine with most modern electronics. If you need access to 110V, you'll have to bring your own converter or buy a unit here. Many electronic supply stores sell converter boxes, but most are big and heavy—fine if you're staying put for a while but otherwise a bear to travel with.

With rare exceptions, most hotel sockets can accommodate the two flat pins on plugs from the U.S. The same slots also take the two standard round pins on most Vietnamese devices. You'll occasionally run across a socket that demands three pins.

The power grid is very reliable in the big cities and surprisingly good elsewhere.

Holidays

The Tet lunar new year (see p. 35) dwarfs all other Vietnamese holidays, so much so that you wonder whether the country celebrates any others. In Saigon, streets are gridlocked at night during Tet as celebrants congregate for dance and music performances. In smaller cities and towns, the holiday is still boisterous though hardly on the same scale. For the first three days of Tet, many shops and restaurants remain closed. If you plan to be here for Tet, expect limited services over the holiday.

The Vietnamese also celebrate Saigon Liberation Day on April 30, International Labor Day on May 1, and the National Day of the Socialist Republic of Vietnam on September 2.

See p. 265 for a rundown of popular festivals.

Liquor Laws

You must be 18 to buy alcohol, although no one checks.

Media

Magazines

Regional and international magazines such as *Newsweek, Time,* and *The Economist* are available at a few bookshops and hotels in the major cities.

The Word (wordvietnam.com) is a popular English-language monthly with up-to-date reviews, listings, and features about various travel destinations. *AsiaLife (asialife magazine.com)* is another compendium of tourist-related listings in magazine format. The *Saigon Times* also publishes a weekly magazine that provides news for business travelers and tourists.

Newspapers

You'll find day-old copies of *The International New York Times* and *USA Today* in select bookshops and hotels, as well as from sidewalk vendors in Ho Chi Minh City and Hanoi.

The *Vietnam News* and the *Saigon Times* are the major English-language dailies. Both are state-run entities with restricted content, but the papers do a good job of keeping their fingers on the pulse of what's up and coming in the country.

Radio

You'll find some English-language programs on the state-run radio station at 105.5 FM. But you'll be far better connected to world events by tuning in a shortwave to the BBC, VOA, or Radio Canada.

Television

Most hotels, from high-end to budget, offer satellite television with a wide range of channels, including CNN, BBC, HBO, MTV Asia, and National Geographic.

Money Matters

Dong

Vietnam's official unit of currency is the dong (pronounced dowm). The currency is rather unstable, with a current exchange rate of about 20,000 dong to the dollar. The state issues 500, 1,000, 2,000, 5,000, 10,000, 20,000, 50,000, 100,000, 200,000, and 500,000 dong notes. While the old currency was paper, newer 50,000, 100,000, 200,000, and 500,000 notes are printed on a very durable plastic that lasts about four times as long. The downside is that it folds awkwardly, and you have to carry so much of it. The state also issues coins in 200, 500, 1,000, 2,000, and 5,000 increments, but locals aren't used to carrying them, and cyclo/motorbike drivers may balk at taking coins in payment.

U.S. Dollars

Though Vietnamese merchants will always accept their own currency, there's an ingrained preference for U.S. dollars that goes back to the 1970s and '80s when the government devalued the currency on several different occasions. The newer the bills, the better. Merchants will often reject notes with slight blemishes.

Exchange

Most banks in cities and towns are set up to exchange Western currency for Vietnamese dong. There's no surcharge for the exchange of currency notes, but you'll lose 1 to 2 percent when exchanging traveler's checks for Vietnamese cash. Remember that most banks close between 11:30 a.m. and 1:30 p.m. Many hotels will also exchange currency, but at less favorable rates. Some jewelry shops will exchange dollars at slightly better rates than the banks.

Credit Cards

Many Vietnamese hotels, restaurants, and shops accept credit cards, but in most cases, you'll have to pay a 3 percent surcharge for the privilege.

ATMs

ATM withdrawals are the best way to handle money in Vietnam. Traveler's checks are increasingly less attractive, as you have to pay surcharges to cash them. But ATMs are proliferating in the major tourist hubs, as well as secondary cities and towns.

Tipping

Vietnam is not a tipping culture. Vietnamese people don't tip each other. But there is an expectation that foreigners will tip, especially if the foreigner is American. Cab drivers don't expect tips, though they do expect that you won't ask for change if it's a matter of a few thousand dong. There's a higher expectation among waitstaff and a still higher expectation from bellhops, who'll be pleased with 10,000 or 20,000 dong (50 cents–$1) for toting your luggage. Tour guides do work for tips. Some will ask for the tip, especially boat paddlers at places like Tam Coc and the Perfume Pagoda.

Opening Times

Businesses tend to open early, by 8 a.m., and close by 4:30 p.m. But there's a long lunch break every day, from 11:30 a.m. to 1:30 p.m. Restaurants and bistros, obviously, stay open through lunch.

Some museums, catering to Western tastes, stay open during the lunch break, but most close. Since Sunday is the busiest museum-going day, many close on Monday to rest and recuperate. Be sure to check schedules ahead of time.

Passports

Be prepared to surrender your passport to hotel clerks. In larger cities more dependent on tourism, they're less likely to insist on holding it overnight. But in places like Chau Doc and the highland towns, where paranoia is still prevalent, the police insist on knowing who's in town. Thus, hotel clerks are obliged to bring everyone's passport to the cops at 10 p.m. It's a crummy practice, because if you change hotels often, you're bound to forget it, and the clerks are bound to forget to tell you.

Religion

Although nominally communist, the Vietnamese are largely free to worship as they please. There have been reports of persecution against Christians in the central highlands. The government's motivation in those situations seems to be more politically oriented than religious.

The vast majority of Vietnamese are enmeshed in a culture strongly influenced by Buddhism, Confucianism, Taoism, and ancestor worship. That said, about 8 percent of the population is Catholic, and churches are widespread, visible, and active.

Many of the Mekong Delta Cham people are Muslim.

Restrooms

Public bathrooms in Vietnam are often less welcoming than their Western counterparts. While the days of squat treads and basin holes are largely over, many bathrooms still forgo paper wipes for water nozzles. Be sure to carry spare tissues, even when visiting the best museums.

In the countryside, a query about the location of a bathroom is sometimes dismissed with a wave of the hand, which may be interpreted as "among the bushes." In an emergency, most Vietnamese will open their facilities to you. Ask for the *ve sinh* (pronounced vay sin), and they'll help you find your way.

Time

The time difference from Greenwich Mean Time is +7 hours. From New York, it is +12 hours (one hour less during daylight saving time).

Tourism Offices

Despite their resemblance to visitor bureaus, Vietnam's provincial tourism offices function as state-run rivals to private tour companies. Like Saigon Tourist, these offices often own and manage several hotels. They maintain staffs of tour guides and vehicles for hire. Except for offices in the larger cities, their services are largely geared to domestic tourists, not international travelers.

As information sources, these folks can be rather useless. They often don't speak English, so basic information is hard to come by. Vietnam Tourism's website *(vietnamtourism.com)* is a decent source for general information.

The best firsthand sources are local travel agents. In Hanoi and Ho Chi Minh City, local agents keep longer hours than state-run agents, their English is usually better, and they're often far more savvy than state-run operators. If you're desperate for additional information in a remote region, call the biggest hotel; its reception staff will likely speak passable English.

Traffic

Since traffic never stops, it's extremely difficult to cross the street, but there's a skill to it. Select a place near a corner where vehicles are not going too fast. Wait until traffic is relatively light, then step out and walk at a steady pace. You'll find that motorbikes and cars veer around you and miraculously you arrive at the other side in one piece. Take extra care when crossing several lanes, as the speed of approaching vehicles can be difficult to judge.

Travelers With Disabilities

As a country that still ranks among the poorest in the world, Vietnam's accommodations for travelers with disabilities are predictably scarce. Even the pavement is often uneven, and crossing the street via wheelchair can be a nightmarish proposition. Domestic flights do not use jetways but require a walk across the tarmac and up a flight of mobile stairs.

EMERGENCIES

Phone Numbers

Emergency: 115
Fire: 114
Police: 113
Directory assistance: 1080
International operator: 110
Time: 117

Embassies & Consulates

Foreign embassies and consulates in Vietnam provide a range of services, including passport renewal, provision of federal income tax forms, and limited emergency services. What they won't do is help find your luggage, issue driving permits, intercede in disputes with local hotels, or let you stay at the office if stranded. They can offer advice in such circumstances, however.

United States

U.S. Embassy
1st Floor, Rose Garden Tower,
170 Ngoc Khanh, Hanoi
Tel 04/3850-5000
Fax 04/3850-5048
vietnam.usembassy.gov
Walk-in: Mon.–Thurs. 8:30–11:30 a.m. & 1–3:30 p.m.; closed on local/U.S. holidays
Tel 04/3850-5000, ext. 6133

U.S. Consulate
American Citizen Services
4 Le Duan, District 1,
Ho Chi Minh City
Tel 08/3520-4200
hochiminh.usconsulate.gov
Walk-in: Mon., Tues., Thurs., & Fri. 8:30–11:30 a.m.; closed Weds. and local/U.S. holidays

Australia

Australian Embassy
8 Dao Tan, Ba Dinh District, Hanoi
Tel 04/3831-7755
Fax 04/3831-7711
vietnam.embassy.gov.au
Hours: Mon.–Fri. 8:30 a.m.–noon, 1–5 p.m.

Australian Consulate General
20th floor, Vincom Center, 47 Ly Tu Trong, District 1, Ho Chi Minh City
Tel 08/3521-8100
Fax 08/3521-8101
hcmc.vietnam.embassy.gov.au
Hours: Mon.–Fri. 8:30 a.m.–noon, 1–5 p.m.

Canada

Canadian Embassy
31 Hung Vuong, Hanoi
Tel 04/3734-5000
Fax 04/3734-5049
canadainternational.gc.ca/Vietnam
Hours: Mon.–Thurs. 8 a.m.–noon, 1–5 p.m.; Fri. 8 a.m.–1:30 p.m.

Canadian Consulate General
The Metropolitan, 10th Fl.,
235 Dong Khoi, District 1,
Ho Chi Minh City
Tel 08/3827 9899
Fax 08/3827 9935
Hours: Mon.–Thurs. 8–11 a.m., 1–5 p.m., Fri. 8 a.m.–1:30 p.m.

United Kingdom

British Embassy
Central Building, 4th Fl.,
31 Hai Ba Trung, Hanoi
Tel 04/3936-0500
britishembassyhanoi.clickbook.net
Hours: Mon.–Fri. 8:30 a.m.–12:30 p.m., 1:30–4:30 p.m.

British Consulate General
25 Le Duan, District 1,
Ho Chi Minh City
Tel 08/3829-8433
Fax 08/3822-1971
Hours: Mon.–Fri. 8:30 a.m.–noon, 1–4:30 p.m.

Health

Vietnam presents no particular health dangers to travelers in the country, though a few years ago the country was hit hard first by severe acute respiratory syndrome (SARS) and then by Asian bird flu. For a while tourist numbers, which had been climbing steadily, plummeted, but thanks to swift and efficient action by the government, these problems were resolved. These days few visitors experience anything worse than a touch of sunstroke or an upset stomach due to change of climate or diet.

Vietnam does not require any vaccinations of travelers. For travel to Southeast Asia, the Centers for Disease Control recommends vaccinations for hepatitis A and B, Japanese encephalitis, rabies, and typhoid, as well as a course of antimalarial drugs.

Inoculation against hepatitis A and B is especially important, as the disease is prevalent. Typhoid is another advisable inoculation. This disease is often spread through fecal contamination of water, a risk when eating street food in Vietnam.

Few expats bother with antimalarial drugs or inoculation against Japanese encephalitis. If you're planning a highland trek or think you might come into contact with dogs, consider an inoculation against rabies.

In bistros, soup stalls, and rice shops, utensils (chopsticks, forks) are typically kept in holders at the table. Vietnamese diners often just wipe down such utensils with a napkin before dining. Better yet, bring your own chopsticks, as well as antibacterial fluid for cleanup.

Always drink bottled water. The Vietnamese boil water for their own consumption and presumably use this water to make ice. Since you can't always be sure, it's better to avoid ice unless you're eating at a high-end place.

Medical Services

Vietnam's hospitals are generally good, especially for outpatient care, though less comfortable than Western hospitals if you must stay overnight. Doctors are not paid well and, unfortunately, tend to respond better when patients pay them an incentive. The same is true of nurses. Most expats make do with the international clinics, which are widespread in Ho Chi Minh City and Hanoi.

Safety

Vietnam is an exceptionally safe place to travel. In 2005, a major insurance carrier singled out the country as one of the six safest destinations for travel worldwide. Violent crime is not an issue.

The greatest safety hazard posed to travelers is the traffic. Only in recent decades has the country begun to install traffic lights, and old, bad driving habits die hard. The situation is improving, but use extreme caution when crossing the street.

Robbery can be a problem, especially in downtown Saigon. Women should not wear gold hoop earrings or anything else that might tempt a drive-by thief on a motorbike. Leave your purse in the hotel room. Don't carry cameras by straps; keep them in a bag.

Though at present Vietnam has no official tourist police force, it is likely that one will soon be introduced. One good sign is that police officers are now assigned to assist tourists crossing the street in hot spots like Ben Thanh market.

If you do need to report a scam or any form of harassment, the Ho Chi Minh City police office is at 161 Nguyen Du. The emergency hotline is 99398.

FURTHER READING

Fiction

A Good Scent from a Strange Mountain, by Robert Olen Butler (Grove Press, 2001). Pulitzer Prize–winning collection of short stories written with a Vietnamese sensibility.

Paradise of the Blind, by Duong Thu Huong (HarperPerennial, 2002). A grim novel about a young woman's relationship with her family in postwar Hanoi of the 1980s.

The Beauty of Humanity Movement, by Camilla Gibb (Penguin, 2010). A powerful cross-generational novel that revolves around the Vietnamese national dish–*pho.*

The Quiet American, by Graham Greene (Penguin, 2002). First published in 1955, this novel remains vital reading. The story charts the love triangle between a detached journalist, his Vietnamese mistress, and an idealistic American.

The Sorrow of War, by Bao Ninh (Riverhead, 1996). Tells the story of the war's impact on a North Vietnamese soldier, without any nationalistic trumpeting.

The Tale of Kieu, by Nguyen Du, translation by Huynh Sanh Thong (Vintage, 1973). This nationally renowned epic poem details the tragic story of a girl who sells herself as a concubine to save her family.

Nonfiction

Birth of Vietnam, by Keith Taylor (Univ. of California Press, 1983). This academic work is peerless in its appreciation of Vietnam's roots.

A Bright Shining Lie: John Paul Vann and America in Vietnam, by Neil Sheehan (Vintage, 1989). This Pulitzer Prize–winning biography serves as a monumental history of the U.S. war in Vietnam.

Dispatches, by Michael Herr (Vintage, 1991). Reflects the grit, passion, and insanity of the war.

A Dragon Apparent, by Norman Lewis (Trans-Atlantic Publications, 1995). A travel-writing tour de force by a master of the genre who explored Vietnam in the waning days of French colonialism.

Fire in the Lake, by Frances Fitzgerald (Vintage, 1973). An insightful look at Vietnamese culture.

The Girl in the Picture, by Denise Chong (Penguin, 1999). Intimate life story of the napalmed girl who appeared on the front pages of the world's newspapers one day in 1972.

Ho Chi Minh, by William J. Duiker (Theia, 2001). Compelling portrait of the leader admired and respected by Americans who knew him intimately between the end of World War II and the partition of Vietnam in 1954.

Over the Moat, by James Sullivan (Picador, 2004). The story of a young American's romance with a woman from Hue during the last days of the U.S. trade embargo.

Reporting Vietnam (Library of Vietnam, 1998). A two-volume, 1,500-page anthology of American journalism and nonfiction about the war.

A Rumor of War, by Philip Caputo (Owl Books, 1996). Searing memoir by a U.S. Marine who marched into the rice paddies with the convictions of a 1960s idealist and marched out with his world turned upside down.

Sacred Willow, by Duong Van Mai Elliott (Oxford University Press, 1999). This saga relates how a scholarly family coped with the upheavals of Vietnamese society over four generations.

Shadows and Wind, by Robert Templer (Penguin, 1999). Tough, well-written look at the harsh state of the nation in postwar Vietnam, written by a former AFP correspondent who worked in Hanoi in the mid-1990s.

The Smaller Dragon, by Joseph Buttinger (Praeger, 1958). A hard-to-find but eminently readable account of Vietnam's history through 1900.

The Tunnels of Cu Chi, by Tom Mangold and John Penycate (Berkeley, 1985). Explores the wartime stories from this 125-mile (200 km) network of Viet Cong tunnels west of Saigon.

Understanding Vietnam, by Neil L. Jamieson (University of California Press, 1993). Spotlights Vietnamese prose from the 1930s to sort out what U.S. policymakers failed to see or understand during the war.

Vietnam: A History, by Stanley Karnow (Penguin, 1983). Centers on the Vietnam War, with background on Vietnam's early history and French colonialism.

Wandering through Vietnamese Culture, by Huu Ngoc (Gioi Publishers, 2004). Available only in Vietnam, this cultural historian's musings on Vietnam's villages, landscapes, traditions, food, and family is beautifully written, unimpeachably authoritative, and indispensable for any traveler who wants to plumb the depths of this culture.

Where the Ashes Are, by Nguyen Qui Duc (Addison-Wesley, 1994). A poignant memoir by a man whose family suffered imprisonment, death, and exile, yet endured it all with courage and grace.

Hotels & Restaurants

In the early 1990s, Vietnam lacked even a single hotel as smart, clean, or efficient as a typical Holiday Inn in the U.S. But those days are past. Now, first-rate accommodations are available in all the major tourist hubs–Hanoi, Ho Chi Minh City, Hue, Hoi An, Nha Trang, Dalat, and Phan Thiet. While the restaurant scene is not as expansive, the dining in Hanoi and Ho Chi Minh City is superb.

Hotels

Vietnam Tourism rates its hotels on a five-star system to distinguish between grades of hotel. Unfortunately, too many of the hotels that won, say, three stars from Vietnam Tourism ten years ago have not reinvested in the property or kept pace with contemporary standards.

The best hotels in Hanoi and Ho Chi Minh City rival the best hotels anywhere. The rooms can be luxuriant, the staff elegant, the service a joy, and the character both deep and resonant. With the exception of the Metropole in Hanoi and the Palace in Dalat, however, most of Vietnam's historic hotels–the Continental, Grand, Majestic, Morin, and Rex–remain in the grip of state-run enterprises that don't have the expertise to provide a world-class hotel experience. Among the more impressive state-owned entities are the Ana Mandara and the Evason Hideaway, each run by professional hoteliers.

Beyond Ho Chi Minh City and Hanoi, the ranks of high-caliber hotels thin rapidly, though that's changing. Hue, for example, lacked a decent hotel as recently as early 2005. Now it boasts some of the best hotels in the country. It's a similar story in Sa Pa, Nha Trang, and Can Tho.

The resort hotel scene along the coast is a mixed bag. At places run by Six Senses, Novotel, and Anantara, there's a high degree of sophistication, but too many other resorts have been built by amateur hoteliers who failed to seek professional advice.

Hotels off the beaten path are often state-run, which usually means bland decor prevails, the restaurant often closes for weddings, and the karaoke lounge is still blaring at 11 p.m. In the hinterlands, refrain from booking a room in the biggest hotel. Instead, go in search of the newest hotels. They're usually owned by Vietnamese entrepreneurs who are hard working, friendly, accommodating, and anxious to make a dollar.

In terms of rates, most of the high-end hotels in Ho Chi Minh City and Hanoi start at about $200 per night, with only a handful of accommodations ranging higher.

A wide variety of charming hotels lie in the budget range, often charging less than $25 per night, though it may take some browsing to find one that meets your expectations. Again, a newer hotel usually signals an entrepreneur at work. Start there.

In recent years, many new mid-range places have opened, especially in Hanoi and Ho Chi Minh City, offering four- or five-star comforts at remarkably cheap rates ($25–$75). Do take a look at a room first to ensure that it has windows and is not next to a construction site.

Most hotels include a buffet breakfast in the standard rate. At high-end places, these breakfasts are worth getting up for. At budget places in the cities, you can expect something continental, while in the outskirts, they'll serve Vietnamese fare.

Hotels across all budget ranges provide some measure of in-room amenities–from high-end sponge wash pads to little plastic shampoo bottles in the budget rooms. Most rooms include small refrigerators and a selection of snacks.

Restaurants

Dining out is a real treat in Vietnam, especially in the major cities. For $20, a meal out in Hanoi will get you ambience, sumptuous cuisine, and friendly service. It's like Paris of the 1920s–cheap, exquisite, and guaranteed not to remain this good much longer.

Both Ho Chi Minh City and Hanoi boast an ample selection of restaurants and cuisines beyond the hotel lobbies, from high-end Vietnamese to Italian, French, Indian, and American. They fly in lamb from Colorado these days, and most of the beef comes from Australia.

Beyond Ho Chi Minh City and Hanoi, quality restaurants are harder to find than quality hotels. Places like Hue and Vung Tau remain bereft of options beyond the high-end hotels. You can still find wonderful food, but the ambience is often subpar.

Except at high-end restaurants, don't expect courses to arrive in traditional succession: appetizer, soup, salad, and entrée. It's more likely to come either all at once or as it's prepared. If you'd prefer the kitchen to stagger the dishes, go ahead and ask, but then cross your fingers (a gesture best done beneath the table, however, as it's an obscenity in Vietnam).

Except at high-end places, diners often choose their own chopsticks from a tabletop bin. Consider bringing your own utensils, as washing with piping hot water is not customary in Vietnam. Don't be surprised if you're charged for the wet napkin provided for cleanup. If you don't open it, you can ask staff to remove it from the check.

If you're forced to wing it for a restaurant choice, follow the universal rule of thumb and eat where the locals eat. Avoid places thronged with tourists. As the Vietnamese say, such places "cut your head off" with the price and serve subpar fare.

Organization & Abbreviations

Hotels and restaurants for each city or town are listed by price, then in alphabetical order.

Hotel restaurants are noted only if they are stand-out destinations; all luxury hotels will have in-house restaurants.

Many hotels and restaurants accept all major cards. Smaller ones may accept only some. Abbreviations used are:
AE (American Express),
DC (Diners Club),
MC (MasterCard),
V (Visa).

HANOI

Hotels

HILTON HANOI OPERA
$$$$$
1 LE THANH TONG
TEL 04/3933-0500
FAX 04/3933-0530
hanoi.hilton.com
Adjacent to the Opera House in Hanoi's most elegant neighborhood, this Hilton is challenging the Metropole as the city's leading high-end hotel. With spacious rooms, Wi-Fi connectivity in the lobby, and marble appointments in the bathrooms, the Opera may be the city's most comfortable perch.
269
All major cards

MELIA HOTEL
$$$$$
44B LY THUONG KIET
TEL 04/3934-3343
FAX 04/3934-3344
meliahanoi.com
This high-rise business hotel is sandwiched between Hoan Kiem Lake and the French Quarter. You may not need the rooftop heliport, but the third-floor outdoor swimming pool offers a great escape from the city. In-room amenities include pillowed bathtubs. A band plays in the lobby every night.
306 P
All major cards

SHERATON HANOI
$$$$$
K5 NGHI TAM
11 XUAN DIEU
TAY HO DISTRICT
TEL 04/3719-9000
FAX 04/3719-9001
sheraton.com/hanoi
Ten minutes from the city center, the Sheraton sprawls across its own peninsula on West Lake and abuts the city's most fashionable expat neighborhood. The rooms are spacious, and the upper floors feature long water views. Though the main body of the hotel is a world-class high-rise, a collection of terra-cotta-tiled Asian pavilions with flying eaves cluster about the hotel's ground floor, the swimming pool, and lush landscaped gardens.
299 P
All major cards

SOFITEL LEGEND METROPOLE HANOI
$$$$$
15 NGO QUYEN
TEL 04/3826-6919
FAX 04/3826-6920
sofitel-legend.com/hanoi
If you want to enter a living fantasy of indolence à la *Indochine,* look no further. The Metropole is a perfectly preserved outpost of colonial French elegance. The decor is period perfect, and the hotel's two restaurants—**Spices Garden** (see p. 248) and **Le Beaulieu**—are among the best in Hanoi. With the reserve of a grande dame, the Metropole lives up to its legendary status.
363 P
All major cards

QUEEN HOTEL
$$$
65 HANG BAC
OLD QUARTER
TEL 04/3826-0860
FAX 04/3826-0300
queentravel.vn
This small, friendly place right in the heart of the Old Quarter has rooms full of character, with lots of traditional touches (the owner is an architect). There's a delightful room for relaxing on the second floor, and the travel desk can help with travel arrangements. Don't miss the tiny, tranquil, rooftop garden.
10
All major cards

CHURCH BOUTIQUE HOTEL
$$–$$$
9 NHA THO
HOAN KIEM DISTRICT
TEL 04/3928-8118

PRICES

HOTELS

An indication of the cost of double room in the high season is given by $ signs.

$$$$$	Over $175
$$$$	$125–$175
$$$	$75–$125
$$	$25–$75
$	Under $25

RESTAURANTS

An indication of the cost of three-course meal without drinks is given by $ signs.

$$$$$	Over $20
$$$$	$15–$20
$$$	$9–$15
$$	$3–$9
$	Under $3

FAX 04/3828-5793
nhatho.churchhotel.com.vn
This newer accommodation is well aware of Western tastes. While small, the rooms are clean and nicely appointed, with wood floors, comfortable furniture, and nice lighting. The location is also superb, on fashionable Nha Tho.
20 All major cards

ESSENCE HANOI
$$–$$$
22 TA HIEN
HOAN KIEM DISTRICT
TEL 04/3935-2485
FAX 04/3935-2487
essencehanoihotel.com
Right in the heart of Hanoi's Old Quarter, this stylish mid-range place offers well-equipped, good-value rooms. Staff can help with travel arrangements, and the ground-floor eatery, the **Essence Restaurant** (see pp. 248–249), is one of the best spots in town for a meal.
30
All major cards

CLASSIC STREET
$$
41 HANG BE
HOAN KIEM DISTRICT
TEL 04/3825-2421
FAX 04/3934-5920
classicstreet-phoco hotel.com
This cozy, family-run place is ideally situated a few steps from both Hoan Kiem Lake and the Old Quarter. Fixtures and fittings are very tasteful, and rooms are bright, spacious, and comfy. The enthusiastic staff go out of their way to help guests enjoy their stay.
16 MC, V

NEW STAR HOTEL
$–$$
9 HANG THUNG
HOAN KIEM DISTRICT
TEL 04/3934-3608
FAX 04/3934-8502
newstarhotelhanoi.com
Located on a non-touristy street on the eastern fringe of the Old Quarter, this place represents excellent value, featuring good-sized rooms with balconies and bathrooms with tubs.
20 MC, V

Restaurants

BOBBY CHINN
$$$$$
77 XUAN DIEU
TAY HO DISTRICT
TEL 04/3719-2460
bobbychinn.com
TV celebrity cook Chinn is one of the darlings of the Hanoi culinary set, a Vietnamese whose gastronomic creations rival the best in the West. This is his signature restaurant, featuring two silk-lined dining rooms and a lounge with shisha pipes. The short menu is constantly changing, but includes dishes like blackened barramundi on braised banana blossoms.
50
All major cards

VINE WINE BOUTIQUE BAR & CAFÉ
$$$$$
1A XUAN DIEU
TEL 04/3719-8000
FAX 04/3719-8001
Don't be surprised if you find yourself ordering a bottle of wine at this intimate restaurant in Hanoi's West Lake District: 1,200 bottles grace the wall-mounted racks, imbuing the dining nooks with a nicely lit ambience. The menu is largely Western, with plenty of pasta and pizza dishes, though there's a Mexican menu as well. Fancy Mediterranean seafood ragout or an Angus wood-grilled steak? They're both available here, along with specialty burgers and dynamite desserts like Cuban Rum Tiramisu.
90 AE, MC, V

SOMETHING SPECIAL

GREEN TANGERINE
$$$$–$$$$$
48 HANG BE
TEL 04/3825-1286
FAX 04/3926-1797
Green Tangerine fuses French and Eastern fare in a shop that is itself a fusion of French colonial and Old Quarter "tube house" architecture. Both of the owner's French grandfathers married Vietnamese women during the colonial era, and the chef is French, too. Look for the ironwood stairway, framed 1928 blueprints of this one-time silk shop, and the poems in the Heavenly Well Courtyard—an exquisite setting for a menu that is refreshed every six months. The lamb and beef are flown in from New Zealand, the salmon from Norway. Try the crab remoulade as an appetizer and the scallops marinated in a tangy, orangey base.
80
All major cards

LY CLUB
$$$$–$$$$$
4 LE PHUNG HIEU
HOAN KIEM DISTRICT
TEL/FAX 04/3936-3069
lyclub.vn
Housed in a one-of-a-kind brick villa and surrounded by greenery, Ly Club has the hushed ambience of a gentleman's club, though diners are serenaded by piano music or traditional Vietnamese music in the evenings. The well-composed à la carte menu is strong on both Vietnamese and Western cuisine, with dishes like coconut heart and prawn salad, while the set menus are imaginative. This is an ideal choice for a special occasion.
44
All major cards

SPICES GARDEN
$$$$–$$$$$
SOFITEL LEGEND METROPOLE HANOI
15 NGO QUYEN
TEL 04/3826-6919, ext. 8208

At the landmark Metropole (see p. 246), Spices Garden dishes out some of Vietnam's finest cuisine, whether your appetite calls for traditional Vietnamese or nouvelle fusion. With a singular passion for Vietnamese soul food, master chef Nguyen Thanh Van is blazing new ground.

70 All major cards

PRESS CLUB
$$$$
59A LY THAI TO
TEL 04/3934-0888
FAX 04/3934-0899

You'll feel like a businessman at the end of a long day in old Indochina when you sit down to dinner at Press Club, on the third floor of a six-story downtown building. The menu is continental, the chef is renowned, the outdoor terrace is a grand place for a cocktail, the bar is deep, and the atmosphere lives up to its billing as a club. The Norwegian salmon is marinated and cured in a house recipe, then smoked with green tea. Austrian rack of lamb is drizzled with a lamb-balsamic reduction sauce. Be sure to leave room for the exquisite melted chocolate pudding with vanilla ice cream and raspberry sauce.

70 All major cards

WILD RICE
$$$–$$$$
6 NGO THI NHAM
TEL 04/3943-8896
FAX 04/3943-6299

The fledgling restaurant barons who opened Wild Rice a few years ago really stir up the creativity, delivering classic renditions of traditional Vietnamese favorites. The prawns in tamarind sauce are exceptional, as are the shrimp and banana spring rolls. Garbed in traditional *ao dai* dresses, waitresses make their rounds through the salon-style dining rooms of an old French villa.

120 All major cards

AU LAC HOUSE
$$$
13 TRAN HUNG DAO
TEL 04/3933-3533
FAX 04/3933-3522

Dine on the second-floor terrace of this monumental colonial French villa, which boasts a menu as Vietnamese as Au Lac, the legendary mother of Vietnam, herself. Tamarind and chili sauces are delightful on the crab and shrimp, while the crab spring rolls are generously stuffed. During the colonial era, the home belonged to a Vietnamese doctor.

150 All major cards

LA
$$$
25 LY QUOC SU
TEL 04/3928-8933

In addition to its cozy ambience, there's much to like about this small, intimate bistro. For a start, the uncluttered menu includes such diverse dishes as pork loin in mustard sauce and crab cakes with chili mayonnaise, with several tempting desserts, too. The decent wine list is adjusted seasonally, and prices are very competitive.

40 MC, V

MEDITERRANEO
$$$
23 NHA THO
TEL 04/3826-6288
FAX 04/3928-7690

Strategically located between St. Joseph's Cathedral and Hoan Kiem Lake, the dining area of this Italian trattoria spills onto a chic street of popular cafés and boutiques. The homemade mozzarella is delicious. Also try the roast beef, sliced thick and sandwiched between grilled eggplant, zucchini, and tomatoes. Don't leave without tasting the homemade chocolate ice cream, which holds its own with any ice cream anywhere.

60 All major cards

POTS 'N PANS
$$$
57 BHI THI XUAN
HAI BA TRUNG DISTRICT
TEL 04/3944-0204
potsnpans.vn

Occupying a stylishly refurbished, three-story property in the French Quarter, Pots 'n Pans is an excellent example of the imagination and ingenuity found so frequently in Hanoi kitchens. The staff here cut their culinary teeth at KOTO, a long established restaurant that provides training in hospitality industries for street kids. The menu features tempting items like crispy skin sea bass with prawn and ginger and sesame noodles, and there's a chef's table on the third floor.

120 All major cards

ESSENCE RESTAURANT
$$–$$$
ESSENCE HOTEL, 22 TA HIEN
HOAN KIEM DISTRICT
TEL 04/3935-2485
FAX 04/3935-2487
essencehanoihotel.com

Most hotels in Hanoi have restaurants that are passable, but this one is outstanding. Set behind the lobby on the ground floor of the Essence Hanoi hotel (see p. 247) in the heart of the Old Quarter, Essence Restaurant has a relaxed, intimate atmosphere and a menu to make diners drool. It includes many imaginative dishes such as sea bass in potato crust with

green beans and cream sauce. Staff is neither fawning nor inattentive, but hover in the background awaiting your call.
45
All major cards

HOA SUA
$$–$$$
34 CHAU LONG
BA DINH DISTRICT
TEL 04/3942-4448
Housed in a renovated French villa, this nonprofit restaurant feeds the soul as well as the stomach. It serves as a proving ground for orphans being trained for service in the country's hospitality industry. Try the tuna in wild mushroom sauce or the beef tenderloin in a blue cheese and black pepper sauce and finish with the signature chocolate mousse.
128
All major cards

NEW DAY
$–$$
72 MA MAY
HOAN KIEM DISTRICT
TEL 04/3828-0315
This is the perfect place for a cheap, tasty meal when you're not too worried about the ambience. They serve a fantastic range of Northern Vietnamese dishes, such as *bun cha* (rice noodle with grilled pork). And if the menu confuses you, you can always wander into the kitchen and take your pick from the ready-made dishes there.
60 Cash only

NGON
$–$$
18 PHAN BOI CHAU
TEL 04/3942-8162
Ngon means "delicious," and the aptness of this restaurant's name is immediately evident in the contented expressions on the faces of the throngs of diners who crowd in here each day. The formula is simple, and very effective: Provide a vast range of regional specialties, prepared to perfection, at a very reasonable price and in a welcoming ambience. Seating is in and around a large colonial house, and the clientele is mostly local, testifying to the authenticity of the dishes.
500 MC, V

BUN BO NAM BO
$
67 HANG DIEU
TEL 04/3923-0701
If you visit only one noodle shop, make it this classic spot in Hanoi's Old Quarter. By the end of lunch, the floor here is a tangle of banana leaves, napkins, and other detritus, but first and foremost all that trash is a testament to the popularity of this place. *Bun bo* is the specialty. The bowls are deep, and the shaved beef is lean and palatable. Each bowl of dry bun noodles is frosted with chopped peanuts, garlic, and fresh herbs.
120 Cash only

THE NORTH

CAT BA ISLAND

HOLIDAY VIEW
$$
ROAD 1/4
CAT HAI DISTRICT
TEL 031/3887-200
FAX 031/3887-208
holidayviewhotel-catba.com
Occupying a high-rise at the east end of Cat Ba town, the Holiday View is a clean and functional if somewhat unsophisticated mid-range option.
120 MC, V

HA LONG

SOMETHING SPECIAL

EMERAUDE CLASSIC CRUISES
$$$$$
46 LE THAI TO
TEL 04/3935-1888
FAX 04/3825-5342
emeraude-cruises.com
The *Emeraude*, a modified replica of a French paddle wheeler that cruised Ha Long Bay in the 1920s, is the best venue for enjoying the scenic wonders of Vietnam's most dazzling seascape. The 38 air-conditioned cabins are classically appointed. Decked with potted ferns and banana plants, the planked and canopied rooftop terrace inspires indolence. If you've dreamed of a nostalgic journey through colonial Indochina, this is it.
38
All major cards

HUONG HAI JUNK
$$$
22 BLOCK C, GARDEN VILLAS ZONE, CAI DAM, BAI CHAY, HALONG CITY
TEL 033/3511-1682
FAX 033/3840-108
huonghaijunks.com
A fleet of eight Huong Hai junks launches from the Ha Long wharf every afternoon at 12:45 and overnights in a vast arena of limestone karsts. Meals are served on board. Rooms are air-conditioned, and each comes with stunning water views.
54 on 8 boats
All major cards

HAIPHONG

HARBOUR VIEW
$$$$
12 TRAN PHU
TEL 031/3827-827
FAX 031/3827-828
harbourviewvietnam.com
A faithful re-creation of a grand colonial hotel, the Harbour View is as good as it gets in the busy port city of Haiphong. The hotel caters to business travelers, with in-room DSL ports and comfortable common areas. Rooms exude a warm, colonial glow with rich teak furnishings. An experienced

English hotelier holds the staff to high standards.
122 All major cards

GREEN MANGO
$$$
231, 1-4 STREET
TEL 031/3887-151
greenmango.vn
That fusion cuisine this good is available in Cat Ba is simply astonishing. The fresh seafood is artfully prepared by a chef who opened one of Hanoi's finest restaurants and is now on his own in an otherwise culinary backwater. With indirect lighting and a musically imaginative atmosphere, the ambience is city hip.
70 All major cards

SA PA

SOMETHING SPECIAL

TOPAS ECOLODGE
$$$$
24 MUONG HOA
CAU MAY
TEL 020/3872-404
FAX 020/3872-405
topasecolodge.com
Perched atop a 3,000-foot (900 m) mountain, the Topas Ecolodge is a frill of white-granite bungalows far removed from downtown Sa Pa. Each bungalow offers a breathtaking view of the Muong Hoa Valley and the Ta Van River, whose rapids and waterfalls are audible from each room's private veranda. Meals are served in a renovated Tay communal house with similarly spectacular views. The lodge dispatches guests to the valley's farthest reaches in the company of smart, friendly guides.
25 DC, MC, V

HOLIDAY SA PA
$$
16 MUANG HOA
TEL 020/3873-874
FAX 020/3872-788
holidaysapa.com
Offering valley views from nearly every room, this is a relative newcomer to Sa Pa's overaccommodating hotel scene. The spacious rooms feature working fireplaces and hardwood floors.
42 All major cards

VIET EMOTION
$$–$$$
27 CAU MAY
TEL 020/3872-559
Located near Sa Pa's market on the town's main street, this restaurant with attentive staff offers a good range of Western and Vietnamese dishes. In addition to breakfasts, sandwiches, and burgers, there are specials such as goose with orange sauce. They serve several cheeses, and tapas are also a specialty. There's also free Internet access.
75 MC, V

BAGUETTE & CHOCOLAT
$–$$
THAC BAC
TEL 020/3871-766
hoasuaschool.edu.vn
Graduates of the Hoa Sua school/restaurant (see p. 249) staff this restaurant and bakery. The cuisine is both Western and Vietnamese, and the restaurant's ovens turn out bread, cakes, and pastries daily. A large open hearth can take the chill off after a long trek.
35 All major cards

NATURE BAR & GRILL
$–$$
24 CAU MAY
TEL 091/2270-068
The perfect place to warm up on a chilly day; there's a huge brick fireplace and the house specialty are grills served on sizzling hot stone plates.
62 Cash only

PRICES

HOTELS

An indication of the cost of double room in the high season is given by $ signs.

$$$$$	Over $175
$$$$	$125–$175
$$$	$75–$125
$$	$25–$75
$	Under $25

RESTAURANTS

An indication of the cost of three-course meal without drinks is given by $ signs.

$$$$$	Over $20
$$$$	$15–$20
$$$	$9–$15
$$	$3–$9
$	Under $3

NORTH CENTRAL

DONG HOI

SUN SPA RESORT
$$–$$$
MY CANH, BAO NINH
QUANG BINH
TEL 052/3842-999
FAX 052/3842-555
sunsparesortvietnam.com
In the 370 miles (600 km) between Hue and Hanoi, there's no more pleasant accommodation than the Sun Spa Resort. The rooms are surprisingly sophisticated, with laptop portals, tasteful decor, and banks of windows. Facilities include a pool, spa, fitness center, and water sports such as parasailing and windsurfing.
234 All major cards

HIEU GIANG
$–$$
138 LE DUAN
TEL 053/3856-856
FAX 053/3856-859
Built in 2000, this small, friendly place is a decent

option for travelers seeking proximity to the DMZ. The rooms are plain but functional, with air-conditioning, satellite TV, and mini-bars.
27
Cash only

NAM DINH

VI HOANG
$–$$
153 NGUYEN DU
TEL 0350/3849-290
FAX 0350/3646-704
Run by Nam Dinh Tourism, this is the best hotel in town, in a spot that overlooks the town's central park and lake. While you wouldn't write home about the accommodations, the hotel crams all the basics into small, comfortable rooms.
90
Cash only

NINH BINH

THUY ANH HOTEL
$–$$
55A TRUONG HAN SIEU
TEL 030/3871-602
FAX 030/3871-602
thuyanhhotel.com
This hotel, owned by Mr. De, earns high praise for maintaining exceptional levels of cleanliness and staff attentiveness at budget rates. Rooms in the back wing are more comfortable and less noisy than streetside rooms. A rooftop bar catches the breeze at night.
37
All major cards

VINH

SAIGON KIM LIEN
$$–$$$
25 QUANG TRUNG
TEL 038/3838-899
saigonkimlien.com.vn
This state-run hotel is about as good as it gets in Vinh, though the decor is outdated. The hotel faces an East German–designed apartment complex.
77
All major cards

HUE & CENTRAL VIETNAM

DANANG

FUSION MAIA
$$$$$
TRUONG SA, KHUE MY WARD
TEL 0151/3967-999
FAX 0511/3967-888
maiadanang.fusion-resorts.com
Here's a neat idea—an all-inclusive spa resort where rates include two spa treatments a day. All rooms come with private pool and garden, and each guest is assigned a "fusionista"—a kind of hip butler—to advise on spa treatments and to ensure a smooth stay. The resort is right on the beach just south of Danang.
87
All major cards

HYATT REGENCY DANANG
$$$$$
TRUONG SA, HON HAI WARD
TEL 0511/3981-234
FAX 0511/3981-235
danang.regency.hyatt.com
Sprawling across a huge stretch of beach south of Danang and near the Marble Mountains, the Hyatt Regency is a super-modern resort that offers its guests every conceivable comfort, as well as several dining options, including the **Pool House, Green House,** and **Beach House.** Shuttle buses are on hand to run guests into town.
200
All major cards

APSARA
$$$
222 TRAN PHU
TEL 0511/3561-409
FAX 0511/3562-001
Apsara's decor was inspired by the nearby Cham Museum. Outdoor gardens include a faithful copy of Phan Rang's Cham towers, and mealtime performances feature Cham dancing. But the food is all Vietnamese, highlighted by Danang's best seafood dishes.
300 All major cards

WATERFRONT
$$–$$$
150-152 BACH DANG
TEL 0511/3843-373
waterfrontdanang.com
The upstairs terrace at Waterfront is one of the best people-watching spots in Danang, as it looks over the riverside promenade of Bach Dang. The menu includes a broad range of Vietnamese and Western dishes, and there are also imported beers and wines. They sometimes have live music and always sports on TV.
120
All major cards

BREAD OF LIFE
$–$$
4 DONG DA
TEL 0511/3565-185
breadoflifedanang.com
All staff at this delightful café are deaf, but that doesn't prevent them from turning out some delicious comfort food such as pancakes and bacon and eggs. The best spot for breakfast in Danang.
56
All major cards

HOI AN

NAM HAI
$$$$$
DIEN DUONG VILLAGE
TEL 0510/3940-000
FAX 0510/3940-999
ghmhotels.com
This luxurious place has stolen the crown as Hoi An's top resort, with a choice of one-bedroom villas or pool villas. Raised platforms and split levels give a marvelous sense of space, and sitting areas

enjoy fabulous views of the landscaped gardens and beach. Private pools are temperature controlled, and facilities include a spa, gym, and tennis and badminton courts.

100 All major cards

ANANTARA HOI AN RESORT

$$$–$$$$$

1 PHAM HONG THAI
TEL 0510/3914-555
FAX 0510/3914-515
hoi-an.anantara.com

A five-minute walk from Old Town, this riverside resort is one of the poshest places in Hoi An. The rooms are terraced, with an upper-level bedroom and lower-level seating area, fronted by a plushly furnished balcony. The large, inviting pool beside the river is complemented by a bar and a massage hut.

94 All major cards

HOI AN RIVERSIDE RESORT

$$$–$$$$$

175 CUA DAI
TEL 0510/3864-800
FAX 0510/3864-900
hoianriverresort.com

The Do River winds past this cluster of French-Vietnamese villas, set in a tropical garden several miles from Old Town and a half mile (1 km) from the beach. One of Hoi An's oldest resorts, it's a bit frayed around the edges, but the views are lovely. From river-view rooms and the restaurant, you can watch farmers working sweet-potato fields on the far bank.

63 All major cards

MANGO ROOMS

$$$

111 NGUYEN THAI HOC
TEL 0510/3910-839

This eclectic Old Town hot spot is an incubator for some of the most fun, creative, and delicious fusion dishes around. The fusion here, however, is not with the traditional Europe but with Latin America. Go for the "Exotic Dance" (shrimp wrapped in beef) or "La Cubana" (flame-broiled beef chunks with Cuban rum). The ambience is as irrepressibly hip and cheerful as Duc, the young owner-chef, who emigrated to the United States as a boy and returned to Vietnam in 2003.

105 MC, V

GOOD MORNING, VIETNAM

$$

102 NGUYEN THAI HOC
TEL 0510/3910-227

This Italian-run chain restaurant makes for a fine detour through Italian fare when you need a break from rice and noodles. The pizza is superb, and the dining area is cozy. Look for other locations in Saigon, Vung Tau, Mui Ne, and Nha Trang.

30 Cash only

HAI CAFÉ & RED BRIDGE COOKING SCHOOL

$$

98 NGUYEN THAI HOC
TEL 0510/3863-210

Old Town's Hai serves traditional Vietnamese fare, and its charismatic chefs will show you how to create some of the dishes—squid salad, spring rolls, grilled fish in banana leaves—in an hour-long class before dining. Hai's sister outfit is the Red Bridge Cooking School, which offers a half-day class and lunch but not dinner.

120 All major cards

HUE

SOMETHING SPECIAL

LA RESIDENCE

$$$$–$$$$$

5 LE LOI
TEL 054/3837-475
FAX 054/3837-476
la-residence-hue.com

This is one of the top three hotels in Vietnam. Anchored by a 1930 guesthouse built for the colonial administration and restored for a 2005 grand opening, the hotel flaunts art deco lines, fixtures, and decor. The pool overlooks a lush, wild garden on the Perfume River's south bank, as well as the flag tower bastion of the citadel. Furnishings are comfortable, consistent, and visually enticing. The business center has free Internet, and the lobby is wired for Wi-Fi. Its **Le Parfum** restaurant (see p. 253) is Hue's only fine-dining venue.

122 All major cards

IMPERIAL

$$$$

8 HUNG VUONG
TEL 054/3882-222
FAX 054/3882-244
imperial-hotel.com.vn

One of Hue's newest hotels, this 16-story building stares down at the rest of Hue from lofty heights, and its five-star rooms and facilities have not gone unnoticed by discerning travelers; it has attracted several dignitaries to its well-appointed rooms. It offers a full range of facilities such as spa, casino, and several restaurants and bars.

191 All major cards

CENTURY RIVERSIDE

$$$–$$$$$

49 LE LOI
TEL 054/3823-390
FAX 054/3823-394
centuryriversidehue.com

Once Hue's best hotel, this Soviet-inspired riverside hotel still touts its four-star rating from Vietnam Tourism, though that's simply the benefit of grandfathering. That said, all rooms have balconies, and the river views are grand, especially if you bunk in the right wing.

138 All major cards

SAIGON MORIN

$$$–$$$$$

30 LE LOI
TEL 054/3823-526
FAX 054/3825-155
morinhotel.com.vn

Opened in 1901 and spruced up during a renovation in 1995 to 1997, the Morin is Hue's grande dame of hospitality, perched along the south side of the river at one end of the city's old French trestle.

180 All major cards

LE PARFUM

$$$$

LA RESIDENCE, 5 LE LOI
TEL 054/3837-475
FAX 054/3837-476

At La Residence (see p. 252), Le Parfum is Hue's only elegant fine-dining venue. The dining room is trimmed in art deco fixtures, and it's big windows take in river views. The Western cuisine is superb. Try the tuna steaks, breaded pork cutlets, and salad with roasted eggplant and goat cheese.

146 All major cards

AN DINH VIEN

$$–$$$

7 PHAM HONG THAI
TEL 054/3824-076
FAX 054/3833-019

Groups making advance requests will be provided the silk robes and headdresses of a king, queen, and attendant mandarins for dinner. Court musicians lead your procession through the corridors to royal banquet rooms for a feast of royal fare. This is truly sumptuous dining. The presentations are fancifully arranged (e.g., radishes cut into peacocks, tomatoes sliced like lanterns) and the dishes excellent. Though it lacks the polish of a world-class venue, it's long on honesty and earnestness.

300 Cash only

TROPICAL GARDEN

$$–$$$

27 CHU VAN AN
TEL 054/3847-143

A troupe of traditional musicians plays for patrons every evening in this restaurant's indoor dining hall. Outside, diners sit under a thatched cabana and amid an intimate tropical garden. The food passes muster, with well-prepared beef, fish, and shrimp dishes, while the service is just adequate.

100 MC, V

HOT TUNA

$$

37 VO THI SAU
TEL 054/3616-464

With pine furnishings and red-checked tablecloths, the interior of this unassuming eatery is very appealing. The staff is very attentive, and the wide-ranging menu includes pasta, steaks, and burgers, as well as Hue specialties. Diners may access the Internet and use the pool table upstairs, both free of charge.

36 Cash only

MANDARIN CAFÉ

$$

24 TRAN CAO VAN
TEL 054/3821-281

For 15 years the Mandarin has been dishing out hearty fare to a mostly backpacker clientele. The affable owner, Mr. Cuu, is an excellent resource for travel info regarding central Vietnam.

60 Cash only

SOUTH-CENTRAL COAST

LONG HAI

ANOASIS BEACH RESORT

$$$–$$$$$

DOMAIN KY VAN
TEL 064/3868-228
FAX 064/3868-229
anoasisresort.com.vn

Cottage and family bungalows and villas drape the hillside of this 32-acre (13 ha) tropical getaway that overlooks a long beach. Decor in the bright, high-ceilinged bungalows features terra-cotta tiles and furnishings styled from green-painted wrought iron. The resort's general manager used to run a number of posh Sofitel properties in Vietnam, and this is his "retirement project."

46 All major cards

NHA TRANG

ANA MANDARA RESORT & SPA

$$$$$

TRAN PHU
TEL 058/3522-222
FAX 058/3525-828
sixsenses.com

Fronting Nha Trang's municipal beach, the Ana Mandara is renowned for exquisite service, its Six Senses Spa, beautifully appointed bungalows, and tropical gardens nourished with water from bamboo pipes. The resort's two pools and two restaurants overlook the sea and offshore islands.

74 All major cards

SUNRISE BEACH RESORT NHA TRANG

$$$$–$$$$$

12 TRAN PHU
TEL 058/3820-999
FAX 058/3822-866
sunrisenhatrang.com.vn

The Sunrise towers over the beachside boulevard in an elegant, neo–French colonial high-rise. Highlights include marble floors, spacious rooms with balconies and sea views, a tenth-floor lounge, and an ornate, round pool that resembles a Roman bath.
121 All major cards

YASAKA SAIGON NHATRANG
$$$–$$$$$
18 TRAN PHU
TEL 058/3820-090
FAX 058/3820-000
yasanhatrang.com
At this Vietnamese-Japanese venture, the narrow end fronts the ocean, but jutting alcoves in every room provide sea views. You'll find free Wi-Fi and a tour desk in the lobby, an on-site disco, and no less than seven rooms devoted to karaoke.
201 All major cards

NHA TRANG LODGE
$$$–$$$$
42 TRAN PHU
TEL 058/3521-500
FAX 058/3521-800
nhatranglodge.com
This solid mid-range option on beachfront Tran Phu boasts balconies and ocean vistas in every room. The blonde-wood furnishings are tasteful and comfortable. There's free Wi-Fi in the rooms, a decent pool, and two restaurants. The adjacent hotel casino stays open through early morning.
125 All major cards

LA SUISSE HOTEL
$$
34 TRAN QUANG KHAI
TEL 058/3524-353
FAX 058/3524-564
lasuissehotel.com
This place typifies what Nha Trang is famed for—its good value accommodations and restaurants (compared with the rest of the country). For $30 you get a big, bright room with air-conditioning, cable TV, and free Wi-Fi, plus friendly staff and a convenient location.
30 All major cards

PERFUME GRASS INN
$–$$
4A BIET THU
TEL 058/3524-286
FAX 058/3524-977
perfume-grass.com
Located on Nha Trang's "budget street," Perfume Grass is full of character, and all rooms are a bit different in terms of layout and furnishings. There aren't many facilities, but all you need is just a few steps away, including the beach.
14 Cash only

LOUISIANE BREWHOUSE
$$$–$$$$
29 TRAN PHU
TEL 058/3521-948
Much more than a restaurant, this rambling place right on the beach is more like an entertainment center, with its own swimming pool for guests' use and live music at night. Besides an extensive menu of Western and Vietnamese dishes, there's a pizza corner, a sushi corner, and delicious beer from the local microbrewery.
120 All major cards

NHA HANG YEN'S RESTAURANT
$$–$$$
3/2A TRAN QUANG KHAI
TEL 093/3766-205
Yen's serves up some of the yummiest grub in Nha Trang from a location just on the edge of the budget district: Great spring rolls, melt-in-the-mouth clay pot dishes, tangy shrimp and pomelo salad, and cheap beer to wash it all down.
44 Cash only

PRICES

HOTELS
An indication of the cost of double room in the high season is given by $ signs.

$$$$$	Over $175
$$$$	$125–$175
$$$	$75–$125
$$	$25–$75
$	Under $25

RESTAURANTS
An indication of the cost of three-course meal without drinks is given by $ signs.

$$$$$	Over $20
$$$$	$15–$20
$$$	$9–$15
$$	$3–$9
$	Under $3

SOMETHING SPECIAL

LAC CANH
$$
44 NGUYEN BINH KIEM
TEL 058/3821-391
A Nha Trang institution since before 1975, Lac Canh is a griller's delight. Here diners cook their own marinated slabs of tuna, chunks of spicy beef, and other meats on small, tableside, charcoal-stoked braziers. The menu otherwise roams the Vietnamese repertoire and packs a punch with its rocket shrimp spring rolls. Lac Canh is especially popular with the locals and is always crowded, both inside and outside in a shaded dining area.
100 Cash only

LA TAVERNA
$–$$
115 NGUYEN THIEN THUAT
TEL 058/3812-259
One of Nha Trang's longest-standing restaurants, La Taverna is the place to go for lovingly prepared Italian cuisine. The menu includes pages of homemade pasta dishes,

pizzas, and lots of seafood too. The ambience is like a typical Italian trattoria.

36 All major cards

LANTERNS

$–$$

34/6 NGUYEN THIEN THUAT

TEL 058/2471-674

This place has become hugely successful so there can be a bit of a wait at peak eating hours, but it's worth it. The set meals are excellent value, while the specialties of the house include hot pot and BBQ. They also serve pasta and burgers if you need a break from Vietnamese, and cooking classes are available too.

62 All major cards

NINH HOA

SIX SENSES HIDEAWAY & SPA

$$$$$

NINH VAN BAY

TEL 058/3524-268

sixsenses.com

You get your own butler at the Six Senses Hideaway, as well as your own pool and wine cellar —among the reasons this is the most expensive night's stay in the country. While the resort is state owned, the management is foreign, and the service is sophisticated. Inaccessible by land, the bungalows cling to the end of a rocky peninsula on land once managed by the military.

58

All major cards

PHAN THIET/MUI NE

PRINCESS D'ANNAM RESORT & SPA

$$$$$

KE GA BAY

TEL 062/3682-222

FAX 062/3682-333

princessannam.com

Spread over 45 acres (18 ha) on the booming coast south of Phan Thiet, the Princess d'Annam rivals Hoi An's Nam Hai (see pp. 251–252) for luxury and commitment to a stylistic ethic. Designed by a renowned Singaporean architect, the villas and furnishings evoke a cool, modernist sensibility. Nine pools inspire indolence, as does the 20,000-square-foot (1,850 sq m) spa. The private beach looks out on a hundred-year-old landmark lighthouse.

57

All major cards

COCO BEACH

$$$

58 NGUYEN DINH CHIEU

MUI NE BEACH

TEL 062/3847-111

FAX 062/3847-115

cocobeach.net

It's hard to find a more exquisitely manicured garden than the one at Coco Beach, and there's much to keep you within the confines of this high-walled compound. The varnished wood bungalows are cozy, nicely situated, and angled so everyone has a view of the sea from their verandas. One restaurant teeters over the strand, while the other spills tables and chairs onto a veranda with ocean views.

34

All major cards

HOTEL DU PARC PHAN THIET

$$$

1 TON DUC THANG

TEL 062/3822-393

FAX 062/3825-682

phanthietresorts.com

Formerly run by Novotel, this delightful resort is embraced by a Nick Faldo–designed golf course on three sides and by beachfront to the east. All rooms have a balcony and views of the ocean or golf course. Minutes from downtown Phan Thiet, the resort feels far removed. *Golf* magazine voted the ninth hole one of world's 500 best holes.

123

All major cards

SOMETHING SPECIAL

RUNG (FOREST)

$$$

67 NGUYEN DINH CHIEU

MUI NE BEACH

TEL 062/3847-589

FAX 062/3847-590

The same cultural eccentricities that inspired the Crazy House in Dalat and the Cao Dai Great Temple in Tay Ninh also spawned this quirky restaurant-in-a-forest on the Mui Ne strip. The food is beside the point here, where tree slices serve as tabletops, cement columns are wrapped in bark, and mechanized bamboo chimes serenade diners on a terrace garden. The strains of a *dan bau* fiddle accompany surprisingly good Vietnamese and Western cuisine.

150 All major cards

QUY NHON

AVANI QUY NHON

$$$–$$$$

GHENH RANG

BAI DAI BEACH

TEL 056/3840-132

FAX 056/3840-138

avanihotels.com/quynhon

This resort lies well off the blazed tourist trail on Bai Dai Beach, 10 miles (16 km) south of Quy Nhon. Offering stunning views, the rooms are big (a minimum 450 sq ft/ 42 sq m) with architectural echoes of the Cham culture.

63

All major cards

WHALE ISLAND

SOMETHING SPECIAL

WHALE ISLAND RESORT

$$$$

2 ME LINH, NHA TRANG

TEL 058/3513-871

FAX 058/3513-873
whaleislandresort.com
Twenty-eight quaint bamboo-and-thatch bungalows hug a short beach that overlooks a blue-water bay on otherwise deserted Hon Ong (Whale Island). The bungalows are purposely rustic, in keeping with the principles of responsible ecotourism. That said, electricity powers the lights, and there is hot water in the winter months. Diving and snorkeling are favorite pastimes, as are catamaran sailing, canoeing, birding, swimming, and hiking on a 2.5-mile (4 km) loop trail.
28 MC, V

CENTRAL HIGHLANDS

BUON MA THUOT

DAM SAN HOTEL
$$$
212–214 NGUYEN CONG TRU
TEL 0500/3851-234
FAX 0500/3852-309
Located about half a mile (1 km) from the center of town with views out back over lush hills, this hotel is Buon Ma Thuot's coziest place to stay. It may not be five-star, but the rooms have neat touches such as the use of local textiles in the decor. The staff is helpful, and there's a reliable tour operator on site as well.
60
All major cards

TAI
$$
91 NGUYEN KHUYEN
TEL 093/5315-757
This newish place in a re-developed area north of the town center is a boon for Western visitors, as restaurants with English menus are hard to find in Buon Ma Thuot. The menu covers a wide range of rice and noodle dishes, and prices are very reasonable.
80 All major cards

DALAT

SOMETHING SPECIAL

DALAT PALACE
$$$$–$$$$$
12 TRAN PHU
TEL 063/3825-444
FAX 063/3825-666
dalatresorts.com
With chandeliers in the lobby, in the chambers, and in the bathrooms, the Dalat Palace is one of Vietnam's most sumptuous hotels. Despite the hotel's art deco facade, the interior is opulent Victorian. The rooms' heavy draperies, brass bathroom fixtures, old-style floor fans, and oriental rugs on polished wood floors, complemented by the notes of a pianist drifting up from the salon, are the elements of a working time machine. Its **Le Rabelais** restaurant offers gourmet French cuisine in one of the city's most elegant venues.
43
All major cards

DU PARC HOTEL DALAT
$$–$$$
7 TRAN PHU
TEL 063/3825-777
FAX 063/3825-888
dalatresorts.com
Opened in 1932, the Du Parc is a polished, mid-range hotel and the best option in town after the opulent Dalat Palace. Daylight streams through the antique casement windows, showing off the polished wood floors. The stairway wraps around a classic open elevator shaft that houses an antique cabin of iron filigree.
140
All major cards

DREAMS
$–$$
151 & 164B PHAN DINH PHUNG
TEL 063/3833-748
dreamshoteldalat.com
This place really is something of a dream for budget-minded travelers, offering mid-range facilities at rock-bottom prices. Guests are also treated to a filling breakfast, and some bathrooms even have Jacuzzis or massage showers.
16 Cash only

CAFÉ DE LA POSTE
$$$
12 TRAN PHU
TEL 063/3825-444
Once a French colonial department store, this café now offers bistro dining downstairs, with massive burgers and other Western dishes, and fine Vietnamese dining upstairs. Aside from Le Rabelais at the Dalat Palace, this restaurant delivers the city's finest mealtime ambience.
90 All major cards

NAM SON
$$
54 KHU HOA BINH
TEL 063/3821-147
Centrally located Nam Son serves a broad menu of Vietnamese dishes anchored by shrimp, pork, chicken, beef, and fish served with locally grown vegetables. The plate-glass facade frames views of downtown and the central market.
60 Cash only

V CAFÉ
$$
1/1 BUI THI XUAN
TEL 063/3520-215
This cozy café run by an expat American has some great homemade pies, but also features pizzas as well as Asian and Mexican food. It can get quite lively in the evenings when live musicians entertain.
60 All major cards

LONG HOA
$
6, 3 THANG 2
TEL 063/3822-934
This menu cuts to the marrow of Vietnamese cuisine, with slight diversions for spaghetti and steaks. Specialties include hot pots, barbecued shrimp, and venison. Try the excellent homemade yogurt for dessert.
80 Cash only

NHAT LY
$
88 PHAN DINH PHUNG
TEL 063/3821-651
In Dalat's backpacker district, Nhat Ly offers fine dining at budget prices. Try the shrimp in tamarind sauce, or any of the pork or beef dishes in tomato sauce. Vegetarian fare is a hit.
100 Cash only

KON TUM

INDOCHINE HOTEL
$$
30 BACH DANG
TEL 060/3863-335
FAX 060/3862-762
indochinehotel.vn
Kon Tum's best hotel—albeit somewhat lacking in character—the Indochine takes full advantage of the lovely views across the river to hills in the south. The carpeted rooms are well equipped, and there's a restaurant on the top floor; a business center on the first floor offers Internet access.
63
All major cards

HO CHI MINH CITY

Hotels

CARAVELLE HOTEL
$$$$$
19 LAM SON SQUARE, DISTRICT 1
TEL 08/3823-4999
FAX 08/3824-3999
caravellehotel.com
Opened on Lam Son Square in 1959, the Caravelle is a Saigon classic and landmark unto itself (see p. 196). The ten original stories were refurbished in 1998 and complemented by a neighboring 24-story tower. The tenth-floor **Saigon Saigon** bar in the old wing remains the city's best perch for a drink.
335
All major cards

LEGEND HOTEL SAIGON
$$$$$
2A TON DUC THANG, DISTRICT 1
TEL 08/3823-3333
FAX 08/3823-2333
legendsaigon.com
Opened in 2001, the Legend caters to international guests with four on-site restaurants, serving Japanese, Chinese, and international cuisine. Some rooms overlook the river, and the hotel also has a pool. The vaulted stained-glass ceiling in the lobby recalls an Edwardian-era railway station.
282
All major cards

PARK HYATT SAIGON
$$$$$
2 LAM SON SQUARE, DISTRICT 1
TEL 08/3824-1234
FAX 08/3823-7569
saigon.park.hyatt.com
Boasting great views from its upper stories, this Hyatt does everything you'd expect of a high-end New York hotel, only better, with an earnest, highly trained staff. The finest in-room touch? A shower head that rains onto the bathroom's marbled floor. Were he still living, this is where Graham Greene would hang his hat.
176
All major cards

RENAISSANCE RIVERSIDE HOTEL SAIGON
$$$$$
8–15 TON DUC THANG
DISTRICT 1
TEL 08/3822-0033
FAX 08/3822-5666
renaissancehotels.com/sgnbr
Marriott's only hotel in Vietnam, the Renaissance rises 21 floors above the river, with sweeping views. A classic, glass-vaulted atrium lightens the corridors, and the spacious rooms feature colonial decor.
349
All major cards

SHERATON SAIGON
$$$$$
88 DONG KHOI, DISTRICT 1
TEL 08/3827-2828
FAX 08/3827-2929
sheraton.com/saigon
The Sheraton is its own world within a world. Inside are eight bars and restaurants, a spa, pool, tennis courts, and boutiques. The plush, business-ready rooms overlook the river and the city's top attractions.
472
All major cards

REX HOTEL
$$$$–$$$$$
141 NGUYEN HUE, DISTRICT 1
TEL 08/3829-2185
FAX 08/3829-6536
rexhotelvietnam.com
During the war, this building served as the U.S. Bachelor Officers' Quarters, while the ground floor hosted the legendary Five O'Clock Follies press briefings. After a recent makeover, it has been transformed into one of the city's top hotels. The rooftop terrace is worth the elevator ride up.
289
All major cards

SOFITEL PLAZA SAIGON
$$$$–$$$$$
17 LE DUAN, DISTRICT 1
TEL 08/3824-1555
FAX 08/3824-1666
accorhotels.com/asia
Among the best business hotels, the Sofitel sits on Le Duan, 150 yards (135 m)

from the U.S. Consulate. Rooms boast five-star amenities, while the poolside bar specializes in gin and vermouth. Its **L'Olivier** restaurant (see below) offers fabled French cuisine.

290 All major cards

PULLMAN SAIGON CENTRE
$$$$–$$$$$
148 TRAN HUNG DAO, DISTRICT 1
TEL 08/3838-8686
FAX 08/3838-9179
pullmanhotels.com

On the site formerly occupied by the Metropole Hotel, the sleek tower of Pullman Saigon, opened in 2013, now offers some of the most modern and comfortably equipped rooms in town. Even if you don't stay here, check out the views from the rooftop bar on the 30th floor.

306 All major cards

MAJESTIC SAIGON
$$$$
1 DONG KHOI, DISTRICT 1
TEL 08/829-5517
FAX 08/3822-9744
majesticsaigon.com.vn

The Majestic is one of the city's colonial grande dames. At the base of Dong Khoi, its art deco facade curves around the corner, while balconies jut from its river-view rooms. Look for the original stained-glass dome in the lobby. The rooms are comfortable with antique furnishings and marble fittings in the bathrooms.

176 All major cards

CONTINENTAL
$$–$$$
132–134 DONG KHOI, DISTRICT 1
TEL 08/3829-9201
FAX 08/3829-0936
continentalvietnam.com

The Continental has seen better days and is sustained by them. Still, it's a solid mid-range option, with spacious rooms. It's still possible to sit on the terrace in front and enjoy the scene in Lam Son Square.

86 All major cards

MADAM CUC
$$
127 CONG QUYNH
TEL 08/3836-8761
FAX 08/3836-0658
madamcuchotels.com

If you don't need all the buzzers and bells that come with an expensive, five-star hotel, consider this welcoming alternative. Rooms at Madam Cuc's are basic but clean and comfortable, and you'll be treated like a member of the family.

32 All major cards

SPRING HOTEL
$$
44–46 LE THANH TON
DISTRICT 1
TEL 08/3829-7362
FAX 08/3822-1383

When you factor in its price and central location, the Spring may be the best deal in town. Rooms come with satellite TV and comfortable beds with clean linens. Breakfast in the lobby features a set menu.

45 MC, V

Restaurants

AU MANOIR DE KHAI
$$$$$
251 DIEN BIEN PHU, DISTRICT 3
TEL 08/3930-3394

Set in a gorgeous colonial villa surrounded by a lush garden, this exclusive restaurant is operated by the owner of Khai Silk (see p. 263), a local fashion guru. Thick carpets and flowing drapes provide a plush ambience, the smartly dressed staff is super efficient, and the French cuisine is sublime. Try the grilled lamb tenderloin with mustard sauce, washed down with a wine from the extensive list.

32 All major cards

PRICES

HOTELS

An indication of the cost of double room in the high season is given by $ signs.

$$$$$	Over $175
$$$$	$125–$175
$$$	$75–$125
$$	$25–$75
$	Under $25

RESTAURANTS

An indication of the cost of three-course meal without drinks is given by $ signs.

$$$$$	Over $20
$$$$	$15–$20
$$$	$9–$15
$$	$3–$9
$	Under $3

L'OLIVIER
$$$$$
SOFITEL PLAZA SAIGON
17 LE DUAN, DISTRICT 1
TEL 08/3824-1555

Every twelve weeks, a marquee chef flies in from somewhere like France or Spain for a week-long tour de force in the kitchen of the Sofitel Plaza's French restaurant (see pp. 257–258). Between tours, the regular, Cambodian-born, French-reared chef explores French cuisine in this airy space overlooking South Vietnam's old embassy row. There are set lunches and dinner, too.

80 All major cards

MANDARINE
$$$$
11A NGO VAN NAM, DISTRICT 1
TEL 08/3822 9783
FAX 08/3825-6185

Dine on one of six levels in this refurbished home on a calm side street in the midst of downtown. The specialty here is duck, though the menu strays as far as bird's nest soup, shark fin soup, and sliced abalone. Musicians play Vietnamese tunes on Tuesdays and Thursdays and European classics other nights.

160 All major cards

ZAN Z BAR

$$$–$$$$$

19-21 DONG KHOI, DISTRICT 1

TEL 08/6291-3686

This super-hip restaurant on Dong Khoi makes an ideal pit stop while exploring the sights downtown. The classy ambience and slick service complement an imaginative menu with dishes like creamy vodka salmon fettuccine.

60 All major cards

CAFÉ CENTRAL AN DONG

$$$–$$$$

4TH FL., 18 AN DUONG VUONG

DISTRICT 5

TEL 08/3833-6688, ext. 2221

Located in An Dong Plaza, this spot is great for recharging after a tour of the temples in Cholon. Though there's a good à la carte selection here, the big draw is the buffet (both lunch and dinner), which presents diners with an amazing array of Vietnamese, Japanese, and Western dishes. Everything is prepared to perfection, so you're likely to refill your plate over and over.

230

All major cards

MAXIM'S NAM AN

$$$–$$$$

13/15/17 DONG KHOI

DISTRICT 1

TEL 08/3829-6676

FAX 08/3823-0644

Maxim's is a storied 1950s–60s nightclub, with a stage, dance floor, booths, and raised seating. But it's all dining now. The chic restaurant serves Vietnamese classics. Try the grilled red snapper and shrimp paste appetizer, cooked around a sugarcane core. A three-piece orchestra plays jazz and pop nightly.

200 MC, V

THE TEMPLE CLUB

$$$–$$$$

29–31 TON THAT THIEP

DISTRICT 1

TEL 08/3829-9244

FAX 08/3914-4271

During the colonial era, this spot served as a guesthouse for pilgrims to the still-active Hindu temple across the street. The brick walls, colonial fixtures, separate bar, and club room out back portend a great Saigon evening. The largely Vietnamese menu specializes in regional foods.

80 All major cards

VIETNAM HOUSE

$$$–$$$$

93–95 DONG KHOI, DISTRICT 1

TEL 08/3829-1623

For anyone unfamiliar with Vietnamese cuisine, this restaurant, set in a shuttered colonial building in the city center, provides the perfect introduction. Go for one of the well-thought-out set menus, which offer a range of different tastes and textures. A pianist entertains downstairs, while a traditional folk ensemble plays upstairs.

65 All major cards

SKEWERS

$$$

9A THAI VAN LUNG, DISTRICT 1

TEL/FAX 08/3822-4798

Skewers' menu roams the Mediterranean, from sea bass basted in Moroccan sauces to Greek gyros and Turkish baklava. The house specialty is anything skewered. Lamb chops imported from New Zealand are as plump and round as small steaks. Also try the goat cheese appetizer, nestled in a crumbly homemade pastry cup. Finish with the cinnamon-spiced apples and ice cream.

80 All major cards

BISTRO 48

$$–$$$

48 LE THI RIENG, DISTRICT 1

TEL/FAX 08/3833-2932

Tucked away in a side street near Ben Thanh market, this non-touristy place attracts an eager local crowd with its extensive menu of Western and Vietnamese dishes. Go for the fish with shallots and Chardonnay sauce or the soft-shell crab with lemon sauce.

44 All major cards

LA FENETRE SOLEIL

$$–$$$

1ST FLOOR, 44 LY TU TRONG

DISTRICT 1

TEL 08/3824-5994

This cool spot tucked away near the Ho Chi Minh City Museum typifies Saigon's café culture. With bare brick walls and mismatched furnishings, it's a great place to settle in with a sandwich and juice in the daytime. On Wednesday evenings they run salsa classes; on Thursdays live jazz is the entertainment.

50 DC, MC, V,

TANDOOR

$$–$$$

74/6 HAI BA TRUNG, DISTRICT 1

TEL 08/3930-4839

FAX 08/3930-4125

Indian cuisine is particularly well represented in Saigon, and this little gem near the city center is arguably the best Indian restaurant in town. As its name suggests, the specialty is tandoor—kabobs of chicken, mutton, or fish marinated then grilled in a traditional clay oven over charcoal. The set lunches are very good value.

52 MC, V

LITTLE SAIGON

$$

185/16 PHAM NGU LAO
DISTRICT 1
TEL 08/3836-0678
FAX 08/3836-7947

On a well-trodden alley in the backpacker district, Little Saigon is a nicely lit indoor-outdoor place that delivers all of the Vietnamese basics, as well as burgers, pizza, Hue cuisine, Japanese cuisine, vegetarian fare, clay pots, and hot pots.

46 All major cards

SOZO

$$

176 BUI VIEN, DISTRICT 1
TEL 090/9306-971

Established to help disadvantaged kids, this café offers a cool refuge from the hectic streets of the budget district. Head upstairs and enjoy a crispy baguette or a yummy curry while checking your email with the free Wi-Fi.

42 Cash only

SOMETHING SPECIAL

NHA HANG NGON

$–$$

160 PASTEUR, DISTRICT 1
TEL 08/3827-7131
FAX 08/3827-7127

It's standing room only for lunch and dinner at this modern Saigon classic, where street food is king and the ambience perfect. Here you'll find the best *bun bo Hue, bun thit nuong, banh xeo, che,* and *pho,* without having to sit on tiny stools or suck in exhaust fumes. The dining areas spill from a gutted French villa into courtyards and up stairways to balconied perches in adjoining annexes. Don't confuse it with the former location at 138 Nam Ky Khoi Nghia, where a copycat restaurant serves inferior fare.

700 All major cards

MEKONG DELTA

CAN THO

GOLF HOTEL

$$$–$$$$$

2 HAI BA TRUNG
TEL 0710/3812-210
FAX 0710/3812-282
vinagolf.vn

There's not a golf course within 50 miles (80 km) of this grass green tower, but it still rates as the best digs on Can Tho's main drag. The carpeted rooms are also painted grass green. Bathrooms are especially nice.

101 All major cards

KIM THO

$$–$$$

1A NGO GIA TU
TEL 0710/2227-979
FAX 0710/2221-299
kimtho.com

This smart, mid-range hotel offers stylish rooms with state-of-the-art fixtures and fittings, plus fantastic riverside views, at very competitive prices. Thick mattresses and plump pillows guarantee a good sleep, and a decent buffet breakfast is included in the price.

51 All major cards

NAM BO BOUTIQUE HOTEL

$$–$$$

1 NGO QUYEN
TEL 0710/3819-139

The owner of one of Can Tho's most popular restaurants has now opened a cute boutique hotel in the floors above the relocated restaurant, providing just seven suites with superb views of the riverfront. The roof terrace is ideal for breakfast or evening drinks.

7 All major cards

NAM BO

$$–$$$

1 NGO QUYEN
TEL 0710/3819-139

With views of the esplanade and the river, Nam Bo is the second best perch in town after Sao Hom. This tried-and-true place is popular with foreign diners, thanks largely to the relaxing ambience and attentive service. The menu spans Vietnamese, Western, pizza, and vegetarian, while the varied beer list includes Guinness.

72 All major cards

SAO HOM

$$–$$$

HAI BA TRUNG
TEL 0710/3815-616

Perched along the river in a restored French colonial market, Sao Hom boasts the best real estate of any restaurant in town. Its menu runs from East to West, including Mekong specialties and good pizza.

120 MC, V

MEKONG

$–$$

38 HAI BA TRUNG
TEL 0710/3821-646

Open since 1965, but for a five-year hiccup after 1975, the Mekong fronts the river on Hai Ba Trung. The friendly owners speak English, and their ample, affordable menu is almost wholly Vietnamese.

28 Cash only

CHAU DOC

VICTORIA CHAU DOC

$$$–$$$$$

1 LE LOI
TEL 076/3865-010
FAX 076/3865-020
victoriahotels-asia.com

One of five Victoria hotels in Vietnam, the Chau Doc looms large on the river. The floors are wood planked, and river-view rooms have balconies.

92 All major cards

TRUNG NGUYEN
$–$$
86 BACH DANG
TEL 076/3561-561
FAX 076/3868-674
Unlike other budget hotels in Chau Doc, Trung Nguyen powers up its generator for air-conditioning during power outages. While small, the tiled rooms are scrupulously clean, and the beds are great. The hotel also rents out bicycles and motorbikes.
15 All major cards

HA TIEN

DU HUNG
$
27 TRAN HAU
TEL 077/3951-555
FAX 077/3852-267
The friendly staff is eager to please at this smart mini-hotel. Rooms are tiled. Amenities include refrigerators and hot showers.
24 Cash only

HAI VAN
$
57 LAM SON
TEL 077/3852-872
There are no elegant dining choices in Ha Tien, but this place serves up consistently good Vietnamese and Chinese food, as well as a few Western dishes, in simple surroundings. It's a good place for Western breakfasts as well as a wide choice of Vietnamese dishes.
80 Cash only

MY THO

CHUONG DUONG
$–$$
10 30 THANG 4
TEL 073/3870-875
FAX 073/3874-250
This cheerfully bright place on the river is plagued by director's choice decor and musty rooms—but as good as it gets in My Tho. The rooms do boast river views, with balconies on the second floor.
27 Cash only

PHU QUOC

LA VERANDA
$$$$$
BAI TRUONG
TEL 077/3982-988
FAX 077/3982-998
laverandaresorts.com
This luxury boutique resort enjoys a great location right in the middle of Long Beach, and guests are pampered by the attentive staff. Rooms in the two-story, colonial-style building and private villas provide every comfort. There's an excellent spa and swimming pool, and the resort also features the island's top dining venue in the **Pepper Tree.**
70 All major cards

MANGO BAY
$$–$$$
ONG LANG BEACH
TEL 077/3981-693
mangobayphuquoc.com
This collection of tastefully appointed, thatched-roofed bungalows on the island's west side boasts great sunset views. Far from the developing strip on Long Beach, this isolated getaway is perfect for reading, lounging, or simply enjoying the peaceful surroundings. The wonderful on-site restaurant is perched on a terrace along the water, and decent snorkeling lies just offshore.
40 All major cards

RACH GIA

HONG NAM
$
BLOCK B1 LY THAI TO
TEL 077/3873-090
FAX 077/3873-424
In addition to being near the town market and plenty of decent places to eat, the Hong Nam's rooms come equipped with air-conditioning, refrigerators, desks, and phones. Some rooms have several beds.
28 Cash only

HAI AU
$$
2 NGUYEN TRUNG TRUC
TEL 077/3863-740
While this restaurant was obviously built as a reception hall for weddings and other functions, the terrace along the canal makes for pleasant, canopied dining. The menu is all Vietnamese and well executed. Try the grilled pork.
500 Cash only

VINH LONG

CUU LONG HOTEL
$–$$
1, 1 THANG 5
TEL 070/3823-656
FAX 070/3823-848
Vinh Long's best hotel falls short with polyester drapes and bedspreads, thin foam mattresses, and steel-framed doors of opaque glass, but its riverside setting is grand. The balconied rooms are equipped with air-conditioning, small refrigerators, and local TV.
24 MC, V

PHUONG THUY
$$
PHAN BOI CHAU
TEL 070/3824-786
Perched along the Mekong, this place offers great upriver views to My Thuan Bridge. The food's only so-so, but you can eat your fill of shrimp, fish, squid, frog, and other Vietnamese favorites.
80 Cash only

Shopping

The low cost of labor has turned Vietnam into a deliriously attractive shopping experience for buyers with First World spending power. Silks, tailored suits, and such handicrafts as ceramics, lacquerware, baskets, and wood carvings remain popular items throughout the country.

Most Vietnamese cities and towns orbit a market that caters to local needs, where merchants sell such staples as food, clothing, and household goods. Westerners generally visit these markets out of curiosity, though you're apt to find far better buys here than in shops geared to tourists.

Traditionally, most items for sale lack price tags, though that trend is changing, especially in upscale shops. On Saigon's Dong Khoi, the most popular shopping strip in the country, vendors commonly offer three prices—one to locals, another to foreigners, and still a third to Japanese, who are less likely to haggle.

While such name-brand companies as Nike and Ikea operate factories in Vietnam, most branded items you'll find for sale—Gucci, Coach, North Face—are knockoffs. Piracy remains a huge problem. In the Pham Ngu Lao District, pirated CDs sell for about 60 cents and DVDs for about a dollar, despite official prohibition.

Vietnamese artists and craftspeople also have a flair for mimicry. Painters copy with such skill that one of the country's leading hotels has seen fit to hang homegrown copies of European masterpieces. Tailors will try their hands at pictures of clothes torn from magazines, often with better results than if you're measured for clothing.

Don't expect bargains on electronics. And don't expect to return anything. Vietnamese merchants hew to the old-school rule of "you buy it, you own it," case closed.

Souvenirs & Gifts

Though street vendors will try to sell you Zippo lighters and dog tags and tell you they're precious war relics, don't believe a word of it—they're all fakes. Fortunately, Vietnam has a wealth of distinctive products that make excellent souvenirs and gifts. These include brightly colored lacquerware bowls and trays; intricately embroidered paintings and clothing; purses and shoulder bags made of hill-tribe patchwork textiles; sexy silk or satin *ao dai;* reproduction paintings and propaganda posters; unusual musical instruments and water puppets.

You won't have to look far to find them either. In tourist areas like the Old Quarter in Hanoi and the budget district in Saigon, the streets are lined with shops selling products that are geared toward foreigners looking for mementoes of their stay.

Antiques & Artifacts

Be careful not to buy anything too old. Vietnamese law prohibits travelers from exporting antiques. Even if you purchased a knockoff Cham sculpture or an intentionally distressed wood carving, be sure to carry a receipt. More than one hapless traveler has surrendered that old-looking opium pipe to airport customs officials.

54 Traditions, 30 Hang Bun, Hanoi, tel 04/3715-0194, 54traditions.com.vn

Le Cong Kieu, District 1, Ho Chi Minh City. An antique hunter's dream, this Saigon street offers a lot of old colonial decor—lamps, cameras, fans, picture frames, phones, tables, and trunks. If it's fake, it's a well-done fake. Also shop here for parallel sentences, imperial coins, and abacuses.

Nguyen Freres, 2 Dong Khoi, Ho Chi Minh City, tel 08/3823-9459

Arcades & Malls

Saigon Center, 65 Le Loi, District 1, Ho Chi Minh City, tel 08/3829-4888. Appliances, menswear, bedding, cafés, a supermarket, and a toy store.

Saigon Square, Le Loi & Nam Ky Khoi Nghia, District 1, Ho Chi Minh City. Expats shop at this arcade, which is a step up from the municipal market but a step down from the trendy, modern mall. Name-brand stuff, sold in shops that strive to look Western. A good place to stock up on casual clothes or a new pair of trainers.

Trang Tien Plaza, Trang Tien & Dinh Tien Hoang, Hoan Kiem District, Hanoi. This upscale venue has jewelry and cosmetics, high-end luggage, digital cameras and supplies, men's and women's fashions, a Sony electronics outlet, and bona fide wines and liquor. A 2013 makeover has left the place gleaming.

Books

Vietnam's English-language book selection is slim. Be sure to bring your own, or browse the used-book shops in the backpacker districts for the best selection of contemporary titles. Otherwise, try your luck at:

The Bookworm, 44 Chau Long, Hanoi, tel 04/3715-3711, bookwormhanoi.com. Quite simply Hanoi's best bookstore, run by a lover of the written word.

Fahasa Bookstore, 40 Nguyen Hue, District 1, Ho Chi Minh City, tel 08/3822-5796

Infostones Bookshop, 41 Trang Tien, Hanoi, tel 04/3826-2993. Centrally located near Hoan Kiem Lake. Several neighboring booksellers also offer English-language titles.

Phuong Nam, 2A Le Duan, Ho Chi Minh City, tel 08/3822-9650. Stocks imported books in English, French and Chinese.

Clothing

Vietnam's tailors are fast, cheap, and talented. Men can have suits made for less than $100 (but up to $200 or more for higher quality material). Women can have silk *ao dai* dresses made for much less. You can also buy interesting, off-the-rack designs at many places in Ho Chi Minh City and Hanoi.

A Dong Silk, 62 Tran Hung Dao, Hoi An, tel 0510/391-0579, adongsilk.com. Tried-and-tested tailor making men's and women's garments.

Khai Silk, 113 Hang Gai, Hanoi, tel 04/3825-4237. Khai was catering to Westerners as far back as 1992, long before the current rash of silk shops realized there was money to be made from foreign tourists.

Song, 75 Pasteur, District 1, Ho Chi Minh City, tel 08/3824-6986, asiasongdesign.com. Embroidered evening wear, sarongs, resort wear, and dresses by French designer Valerie Gregori McKenzie.

Department Store

Diamond Department Store, 34 Le Duan, District 1, Ho Chi Minh City, tel 08/3825-7750. The prices at Vietnam's first modern department store are fixed, and you can trust the brand names.

Food & Drink

Annam Gourmet Shop An Phu, 16–18 Hau Ba Trung, Ho Chi Minh City, tel 08/3822-9332. Sells such imported and specialty foods as flavored olive oils and vinegars, *nuoc mam* (fish sauce), pasta, teas, bitters, and lagers.

The Warehouse, 15/5 Le Thanh Ton, District 1, Ho Chi Minh City, tel 08/3825-8826, and 59 Hang Trong, Hanoi, tel 04/3928-7666, warehouse-asia.com. In a country where you can't always trust the authenticity of a bottle of wine, you can trust the merchandise here. Also sells accessories, books, and glassware.

Markets

Ben Thanh Market, Quach Thi Trang Square, District 6, Ho Chi Minh City. Vietnam's most famous market, as popular with locals as tourists. A good place for off-the-rack clothes, luggage, and street food.

Binh Tay Market, Thap Muoi, District 5, Ho Chi Minh City. This market in the heart of Cholon offers better buys than the more touristy Ben Thanh Market. This is the place to go for staples.

Dong Xuan Market, Old Quarter, Hanoi. Dating from the 1880s, the city's best known market is a lively place where it's as much fun to people-watch as browse.

Shopping Areas

Hanoi

Nha Tho. Home furnishings, clothing, coffee, and restaurants that cater to foreign travelers all line this little row between St. Joseph's Cathedral and Hoan Kiem Lake. Also check out **Au Trieu** *(a short walk north on Ly Quoc Su & then left)* for fashions that court Western tastes.

Old Quarter. This section of town comprises Vietnam's most fascinating market, a unique fusion of commercial and residential space. Streets are named after the products historically sold here, though the lines are somewhat blurred today. For example, you'll find silk on Hang Gai ("hemp street").

Ho Chi Minh City

Cholon, District 5. This is Chinatown. *Cho lon* means "big market," and you'll find two of the city's three best known markets here. One is Binh Tay (see Markets) and the other is **An Duong,** on An Duong Vuong, which is very popular with Taiwanese.

Dong Khoi, District 1. Vietnam's version of Fifth Avenue features upscale shops selling silk, jewelry, handicrafts, antiques, and home decor. Definitely worth the stroll, but expect to pay top dollar.

Le Thanh Ton, District 1. Embroidered fabrics, handbags, and furnishings in boutiques with the flair you find in Western malls.

Hue

Tran Hung Dao. You'll find Hue's storied **Dong Ba Market** along this street, as well as most of the city's boutiques.

Specialized Shopping

Vietnam's craft villages are major tourist attractions, especially those outside Hanoi, including **Bat Trang,** which turns out the country's best ceramics, and **Van Phuc,** a thousand-year-old silk village. Others include:

Danang. In nearby Lang Da ("stone village") at the base of the Marble Mountains, villagers churn out sculptures carved mostly in stone imported from Thanh Hoa, not local limestone and marble.

Hoi An. Hoi An's tailors have carved out a reputation for being fast, deft, and reliable. Buy your silk, get measured, and walk away with a custom suit or dress for incredibly little money.

Hue. Hue is renowned for its traditional conical hats, with embroidered motifs fashioned around the underside. You'll find the best selection on the ground floor of the central Dong Ba Market.

Phu Quoc. If you've a taste for nuoc mam, Phu Quoc Island and Phan Thiet are the wellsprings of this pungent condiment.

Sa Pa. You'll find ethnic embroidery and brocade at the tourist market beside Sa Pa's market, while hill-tribe minorities peddle handmade blankets and garments on the street and in their villages.

Entertainment

With the exception of water puppetry and chamber music *(ca tru),* it's difficult to find venues for Vietnam's traditional performing arts, such as *cheo* (folk opera), *cai luong* (classical theater), *nha nhac* (court music), and *quan ho* (folk singing). In Hanoi and Ho Chi Minh City, be on the alert for sporadic performances at the opera houses and theaters. Those drawn to nightlife will find a range of hot spots in Hanoi and Saigon.

Theater

Chamber Music

Ca tru, or chamber music, has enjoyed a revival of late and was recognized by UNESCO in 2009 as a World Intangible Cultural Heritage. Visitors to Hanoi can experience this haunting music at **28 Hang Buom** on Tuesdays, Thursdays, and Saturdays at 8 p.m.; tickets are $10. There are also sometimes performances at **87 Ma May** and at **Dinh Kim Ngan** *(42 Hang Bac).* Check catruthanglong.com for details.

Cinema

English-language cinema is in its infancy in Vietnam. Unless you succumb to the lure of curbside pirates selling illegally copied DVDs, your choices are slim. These two movie houses are your best bets:

Bobby Brewers, 45 Bui Vien, District 1, Ho Chi Minh City, tel 08/3920-4090, bobbybrewers .com

Hanoi Cinematheque, 22A Hai Ba Trung, Hanoi, tel 04/3936-2648

Opera

The French built three opulent opera houses in Vietnam in the early 20th century. They've all been restored, but there are no set performance schedules. Call or, better yet, stop by to check on upcoming shows.

Haiphong Opera House, Hoang Van Thu, Hong Bang District, Haiphong

Hanoi Opera House, 1 Trang Tien, Hanoi, tel 04/3993-0113

Municipal Theater, 7 Lam Son Square, District 1, Ho Chi Minh City, tel 08/3829-9976

Water Puppetry

Golden Dragon Water Puppet Theatre, 55B Nguyen Thi Minh Khai, District 1, Ho Chi Minh City, tel 08/3827-2653, goldendragon theatre.com. Enjoy 50 minutes of nonstop fun watching Vietnam's marvelous water puppets. Shows at 5 p.m., 6:30 p.m. and 7:45 p.m., tickets $7.50.

Thang Long Theatre, 57 Dinh Tien Hoang, Hanoi, tel 04/3825-5450, thanglongwaterpuppet.org. Just off the northeast shore of Hoan Kiem Lake, Thang Long's setting is ideal for the thousand-year-old art form of water puppetry. The music is great, and the theater is plush and air-conditioned. Buy tickets at least a day in advance for the best seats. The troupe also travels widely.

Nightlife

Hanoi

Bia hoi corner, corner of Ta Hien and Luong Ngoc Quyen in the Old Quarter, is where you'll find other visitors looking for nightlife in Hanoi, squatting on stools and quaffing glassfuls of dirt-cheap draft beer.

Cama ATK, 73A Mai Hac De, Hai Ba Trung District, tel 091/5631-120, cama-atk.com. One of Hanoi's coolest bars to hang out in, with frequent art and music events, plus a well-stocked bar.

Funky Buddha, 2 Ta Hien, tel 04/3292-7614. One of the city's newer lounge bars, attracting hip, young Vietnamese to shake their stuff on the dance floor.

Hanoi Rock Store, 61 Ma May, Old Quarter, tel 098/7132-586, linkhanoi.com. One of the newest bars to try its luck in the Old Quarter, this place describes itself as a "concert bar" and features live music, DJs, and regular themed parties.

Minh's Jazz Club, 3rd floor, 65 Quan Su, Hoan Kiem District, tel 04/3942-0400, minhjazzvietnam .com. The place for jazz in Hanoi. Club owner and saxophonist Quyen Van Minh is a legend on the rise.

Ho Chi Minh City

Allez Boo, 195 Pham Ngu Lao, District 1, tel 08/6291-5424. In the heart of the budget district, Allez Boo jams in backpackers for drinks, music, and cheap eats. Great spot for in-country tips.

Apocalypse Now, 2B–2C Thi Sach, District 1, tel 08/3825-6124. For more than 20 years, expats and hip locals have gathered nightly at Apocalypse Now to drink, dance, play pool, and otherwise cavort. The later it is, the better it gets.

Saigon Saigon, Caravelle Hotel, 10th Fl., 19 Lam Son Square, District 1, tel 08/3823-4999. The city's best perch for a drink, with views of historic Lam Son Square and the nearby Continental on up Le Loi toward the Ben Thanh Market. Sophisticated ambience and live music every evening.

Sax 'n Art, 28 Le Loi, District 1, tel 08/3822-8472. A good spot to catch some cool jazz from 9 p.m. each evening, but check if there's a cover charge before you sit.

Activities & Festivals

The active set can choose from cycling, mountain biking, diving and snorkeling, trekking, kayaking, golf, and tennis, while more than 200 major festivals are held in Vietnam throughout the year.

Active sports

Cycling & Mountain Biking

Scenic Highway 1 is a perfect cycling venue. Many tour companies offer packages that include support vehicles. Or, just take off on your own with supplies; you'll find lodgings within a day's ride all along the highway. Off-road biking is risky, given the amount of unexploded ordnance in the countryside, but **Phat Tire Ventures** *(109 Nguyen Van Troi, Dalat, tel 063/3829-422, cell 091/3843-8781, fax 063/3820-331, phattireventures.com)* offers safe routes.

Diving & Snorkeling

Diving and snorkeling sites line Vietnam's 2,135-mile (3,444 km) seaboard, especially off the south-central coast near Nha Trang and Con Dao Island. Check out the reefs off Hon Mun Island near Nha Trang via a tour boat or on a trip with **Rainbow Divers** *(90A Hung Vuong, Nha Trang, tel 090/8781-756, divevietnam.com).*

Golf

There are now 25 top-class golf courses in Vietnam, with more than 60 more on the way. The best courses are near Ho Chi Minh City, Hanoi, Danang, Phan Thiet, and Dalat. Most courses accept walk-ins, and rates vary from around $50–$60 on weekdays to more than $100 on weekends. Check out *golfasian.com/golf-courses/vietnam-golf-courses* for details of all courses.

Vietnam Golf Resorts, 6 Thai Van Lung, Ho Chi Minh City, District 1, tel 08/3520-2045, fax 08/3520-2046, vietnamgolfresorts.com

Kayaking

Paddlers should venture north to Ha Long Bay; a kayak grants entry to caves that bore through karst islets into stunning lagoons.

John Gray Sea Canoe, johngray-seacanoe.com/vietnam

Rock Climbing

The best places in Vietnam for organized rock climbing are Dalat and Ha Long Bay; contact **Phat Tire Ventures** (see Cycling & Mountain Biking) in Dalat or Asia Outdoors *(222, 1-4 Street, Cat Ba, tel 031/3688-450, asiaoutdoors.com.vn)* on Cat Ba Island. For other rock-climbing locations, check out *vietclimb.com.*

Swimming

Vietnam's best beaches fringe Phu Quoc Island in the clear waters of the Gulf of Thailand. Other fine strands line the Con Dao Islands and the south-central coast. Ha Long Bay is notable both for its scenery and buoyant salt water. Coastal waterfalls also offer great swimming holes.

Trekking

The top trekking destinations are Sa Pa, Dalat, Kon Tum, and Dak Lak, roughly in that order. Many tour companies (see p. 239) lead treks, and limited solo trekking is possible, especially around Sa Pa; the most challenging climb is up nearby 10,312-foot (3,143 m) Fan Si Pan, Vietnam's tallest peak.

Festivals

January/February

Keo Pagoda Festival. Duck catching and hurling contests are among the attractions at the Buddhist celebration held twice yearly (Jan./Feb. and Sept./Oct.) at this beautiful pagoda in north-central Vietnam, just east of Nam Dinh.

Perfume Pagoda Festival. From late January through the end of spring, thousands of Buddhist pilgrims worship at this scenic cluster of temples, shrines, and pagodas southwest of Hanoi.

Tet Nguyen Dan. Tet, which begins on the first day of the first lunar month (Jan. or Feb.), is the granddaddy of all holidays in Vietnam (see pp. 240–241).

March/April

Thay Pagoda Festival. This Buddhist festival on the seventh day of the third lunar month (March or April) commemorates Tu Dao Hanh, the father of water puppetry. The pagoda grounds just west of Hanoi host puppetry performances and the ceremonial bathing of Hanh's statue.

August/September

Kate Festival. The Cham people celebrate their New Year in late September (or early October) by commemorating their ancestors, heroes, and deities. The festival is especially vibrant at the Po Klong Garai temple, west of Phan Rang.

Keo Pagoda Festival (see January/February).

Mid-Autumn Festival. AKA the Moon Festival, or Children's Tet. Colorful lanterns, dragon dances, and candies abound.

Ongoing

Hoi An Full Moon Festival. On the 14th day of each lunar month, Hoi An residents turn off the streetlights, illuminate Old Town with colorful lanterns, and stroll the avenues free of vehicles.

INDEX

Bold page numbers indicate illustrations.
CAPS indicates thematic categories.

ILLUSTRATIONS CREDITS

Cover: Felix Hug/Corbis; Spine: hadynyah/iSockphoto. **Interior:** All photographs by Kris LeBoutillier except for the following: 14–15, ducvien/Shutterstock.com; 20, catshiles/iStockphoto.com; 31, Barbara A. Noe; 36, Nguyen Thi Kim; 41, © Dinh Dang Dinh/Another Vietnam; 44, Patrick Christain/Getty Images; 47, Bettmann/Corbis; 54, Courtesy European Art Gallery; 60, Chau Doan/OnAsia; 72, pcruciatti/Shutterstock.com; 76, Kimberley Coole/Lonely Planet Images/Getty Images; 83, Cristal Tran/Shutterstock; 84, Frédéric Soreau/Photononstop/Corbis; 94, Sapsiwai/Shutterstock; 100, Ron Emmons; 112, Hoang Tran Minh/iStockphoto.com; 121, AP Photo/Vietnam Pictorial/Trong Thanh; 126, Courtesy The Zoological Society for the Conservation of Species and Populations (ZGAP), Germany; 142, Sphinx Wang/Shutterstock.com; 186, William Manning/Corbis; 190, David Cherepuschak/Alamy; 193, Ko.Yo/Shutterstock; 219, ducvien/Shutterstock.com; 229, Alain DeJean/Sygma/Corbis; 234, Nguyen Duy Phuong/Shutterstock.

National Geographic
traveler
Vietnam

Published by the National Geographic Society
Gary E. Knell, *President and Chief Executive Officer*
John M. Fahey, *Chairman of the Board*
Declan Moore, *Executive Vice President; President, Publishing and Travel*
Melina Gerosa Bellows, *Executive Vice President; Chief Creative Officer, Books, Kids, and Family*
Lynn Cutter, *Executive Vice President, Travel*
Keith Bellows, *Senior Vice President and Editor in Chief, National Geographic Travel Media*

Prepared by the Book Division
Hector Sierra, *Senior Vice President and General Manager*
Janet Goldstein, *Senior Vice President and Editorial Director*
Jonathan Halling, *Creative Director*
Marianne R. Koszorus, *Design Director*
Barbara A. Noe, *Senior Editor, National Geographic Travel Books*
R. Gary Colbert, *Production Director*
Jennifer A. Thornton, *Director of Managing Editorial*
Susan S. Blair, *Director of Photography*
Meredith C. Wilcox, *Director, Administration and Rights Clearance*

Staff for This Book
Justin Kavanagh, *Project Editor*
Elisa Gibson, *Art Director*
Ruth Ann Thompson, *Designer*
Carl Mehler, *Director of Maps*
Mike McNey & Mapping Specialists, *Map Production*
Hannah Lauterback, *Contributor*
Marshall Kiker, *Associate Managing Editor*
Michael O'Connor, *Production Editor*
Galen Young, *Rights Clearance Specialist*
Katie Olsen, *Production Design Assistant*

Production Services
Phillip L. Schlosser, *Senior Vice President*
Chris Brown, *Vice President, NG Book Manufacturing*
Nicole Elliott, *Director of Production*
George Bounelis, *Senior Production Manager*
Rachel Faulise, *Manager*
Robert L. Barr, *Manager*

Artwork by Maltings Partnership, Derby, England (pp. 78–79 & 138–139)

The National Geographic Society is one of the world's largest nonprofit scientific and educational organizations. Founded in 1888 to "increase and diffuse geographic knowledge," the member-supported Society works to inspire people to care about the planet. Through its online community, members can get closer to explorers and photographers, connect with other members around the world, and help make a difference. National Geographic reflects the world through its magazines, television programs, films, music and radio, books, DVDs, maps, exhibitions, live events, school publishing programs, interactive media, and merchandise. *National Geographic* magazine, the Society's official journal, published in English and 38 local-language editions, is read by more than 60 million people each month. The National Geographic Channel reaches 440 million households in 171 countries in 38 languages. National Geographic Digital Media receives more than 25 million visitors a month. National Geographic has funded more than 10,000 scientific research, conservation, and exploration projects and supports an education program promoting geography literacy. For more information, visit www.nationalgeographic.com.

For more information, please call 1-800-NGS LINE (647-5463) or write to the following address:
National Geographic Society
1145 17th Street N.W.
Washington, D.C. 20036-4688 U.S.A.

For information about special discounts for bulk purchases, please contact National Geographic Books Special Sales: ngspecsales@ngs.org

For rights or permissions inquiries, please contact National Geographic Books Subsidiary Rights: ngbookrights@ngs.org

National Geographic Traveler: Vietnam
(Third edition)
ISBN: 978-1-4262-1363-2

Printed in Hong Kong
14/THK/1